Musial

Missouri Biography Series

William E. Foley, Editor

Musial

From STASH to STAN THE MAN

James N. Giglio

University of Missouri Press

Columbia and London

Copyright © 2001 by
The Curators of the University of Missouri
University of Missouri Press, Columbia, Missouri 65201
Printed and bound in the United States of America
All rights reserved
5 4 3 2   05 04 03 02 01

Library of Congress Cataloging-in-Publication Data

Giglio, James N., 1939–
    Musial : from Stash to Stan the Man / James N. Giglio.
        p.   cm.—(Missouri biography series)
    Includes bibliographical references (p.) and index.
    ISBN 0-8262-1336-7 (alk. paper)
    1. Musial, Stan, 1920– 2. Baseball players—United States—
Biography. 3. St. Louis Cardinals (Baseball team)—History.
I. Title. II. Series.

GV865.M8 G34 2001
796.357'092—dc21   2001023365
[B]

♾™ This paper meets the requirements of the
American National Standard for Permanence of Paper
for Printed Library Materials, Z39.48, 1984.

Jacket Designer: Kristie Lee
Text Designer: Vickie Kersey DuBois
Typesetter: BOOKCOMP, Inc.
Printer and binder: Thomson-Shore, Inc.
Typefaces: Helvetica, Palatino

Dedication

To members of the Knights

of the Kitchen Table, who

have managed to take my

money monthly for more

than twenty years—David

Castillon, Stan Fagerlin,

Don McInnis, Jim O'Brien,

Milt Rafferty, and Vern

Thielmann—winners all!

Contents

Preface

Anyone approaching Busch Stadium, the home of the St. Louis Cardinals, from the main entrance at Walnut and Broadway will immediately come upon the bronze statue of Stan "The Man" Musial, whose inscribed pedestal honors "baseball's perfect warrior, baseball's perfect knight." Even though the statue bears only a slight resemblance physically to the baseball player who spent his entire major-league career in St. Louis, from 1941 through 1963, it symbolizes one of the game's premier performers, a Hall of Famer who brought a unique style to the ball diamond.

The 6-foot, 175-pound Musial batted in a deep crouch, moving the bat and his hips in a hula-like wiggle, with his body twisted away from the plate in cobra-like fashion. He peered out over his right shoulder while holding the bat two feet from his body, positioning his feet close together, and standing back in the batter's box. As the ball approached, he uncoiled, and with the bat pulled back, he dipped his right knee, and then unleashed a vicious, level swing, after having shifted his weight onto his front foot and then elevating his back one. Brooklyn Dodgers coach Ted Lyons once suggested that Musial "looks like a kid peeking around the corner to see if the cops are coming."[1] In the outfield and on the basepaths, the Donora Greyhound, as the press called him in his earlier years, displayed gazelle-like speed in running down fly balls and going from first to third on a single.

Musial ended his playing career with a lifetime .331 batting average. His 3,630 hits (1,815 at home and 1,815 on the road), 1,949 runs scored, 1,951 runs batted in, and 725 doubles were National League career records at the time of his retirement. He also left behind several major-league records, most notably the most career total bases (6,134) and extra-base hits (1,377). Since 1963, Hank Aaron, Pete Rose, and a few others have surpassed Musial's record performances, but he remains today second in all-time total bases and extra-base hits, third in doubles, fourth in hits, and in the top ten in career slugging average, runs scored, runs batted in, games played, and at bats. Only sixteen others who reached the majors after 1900 have higher career batting averages. Incredibly, Musial averaged only thirty-three strikeouts per season, about one in every eighteen at

1. Bob Broeg, "The Mystery of Stan Musial," 52.

bats, in contrast to present-day hitters who routinely exceed one hundred strikeouts annually.

The Busch Stadium statue symbolizes more than a record-setting performer, for Musial gained a reputation for being a team player whose major consideration always was to win ball games even if it came at the expense of individual achievement. He hustled constantly and routinely played through painful injuries. Few superstars had earned as much approbation from peers for his humanity, which ran the gamut of individual acts of kindness, empathy, and just good-natured fun. On countless occasions Musial winked at the nonfraternization rule in game situations by congratulating rookies for their first career hits, praising others for personal milestones, or encouraging those battling lengthy slumps. Teammates and rivals alike greatly enjoyed Musial's playful demeanor, which masked a shyness and an incredible toughness. He also epitomized, arguably more so than any other superstar, the selfless knight who promoted community goodwill by signing autographs for hours in stadium parking lots, restaurants, and virtually anywhere else and by participating in various charitable activities, all of which occupied time that might have been spent in relaxation. Rarely, if at all, did he refuse to talk with the press. He responded with grace while exhibiting a self-deprecating wit as he often credited others for team victories.

Moreover, nobody ever charged him with betraying his wife, Lillian, or ignoring her and their four children. He seemed the antithesis of today's superstars, many of whom have not only succumbed to drugs, alcoholism, crime, or infidelity but also exhibited an unbelievable selfishness in spurning young autograph seekers, reporters, and charitable institutions.

My intent is to place Musial, a son of a Polish immigrant father and a second-generation American mother of Slovak parents, into the context of the times as I deal with the Great Depression, race, wartime and postwar America, life as a sports professional, baseball as a changing business, and urban life. I am concerned about how the times helped to shape Musial. I also seek to illuminate Musial as a personality, delving further into the images that are associated with him as a role model, especially his warmth and sensitivity, his devotion to family, and his sense of sportsmanship. I am interested, too, in probing for imperfections to confirm his humanity. In short, to what extent does Musial conform to the monument? As important, how did he approach the game of baseball and life? And how did one affect the other?

It has not always been easy to corroborate some of Musial's own and others' assertions about his personal life, let alone to uncover new material or provide penetrating insights. In 1964 Musial and his Boswell, Bob Broeg, the Baseball Hall of Fame sportswriter and editor of the *St. Louis Post-Dispatch* who made a career out of writing about Musial, collaborated in publishing *Stan Musial: "The Man's" Own Story*. It dealt with Musial's major-league career in excellent fashion, but it glossed over Musial's private life, especially relating to the Donora, Pennsylvania, years; gave scant attention to controversial issues; and provided little understanding of the varied aspects of Musial's personality. It also emerged prior to Musial's service as President Johnson's physical fitness director, his year as general manager of the Cardinals in 1967, and his expanding involvement in various entrepreneurial enterprises. Jerry Lansche's more recent *Stan the Man Musial* (1994) was too brief, inadequately researched, and too geared to the baseball buff to qualify as a full-fledged biography. Other sports journalists, especially those from St. Louis, have been no more revealing as they focused narrowly on Musial's baseball exploits. Many of them, including Broeg and Robert Burnes and Jack Herman of the *St. Louis Globe-Democrat*, wrote about Musial while moonlighting for the St. Louis–based *Sporting News*, the so-called bible of baseball. Founded by Al Spink in 1886, the weekly *Sporting News* particularly enjoyed a wide readership in the 1940s and 1950s under the staid direction of publisher J. Taylor Spink, who had close ties with the baseball power structure.

St. Louis sportswriters felt keenly the competition that existed with New York and other more dominant eastern urban markets over which sports teams and stars deserved national attention. They trumpeted Musial's exploits and his humanity in the face of an eastern media blitz on behalf of Joe DiMaggio, Ted Williams, Mickey Mantle, and Willie Mays. Occasionally, accomplished eastern writers such as Roger Kahn and Jack Sher in *Sport* and other magazines more thoughtfully focused on Musial, but their coverage was brief, too replete of analysis, and too narrowly concentrated to be of much use to a full understanding of Musial.

My objective was to supplement journalistic sources with in-depth discussions with Musial. Herein lies my greatest disappointment—and greatest surprise. Aside from a fifteen-minute telephone interview in December 1995, Musial refused to cooperate to the extent that he even advised friends and associates to remain silent. Obviously, I have had to come to terms with this apparent contradiction in Musial's personality.

Still, a number of Musial's Donora high school classmates and other early acquaintances have responded to lengthy on-site or telephone interviews, which proved invaluable to an understanding of Musial's parents, his early athletic experiences, and his emergence from the Great

Depression of the 1930s in a community that was hard hit. I gained much from my visits to that former mill town just south of Pittsburgh where even today a sign proclaiming Donora the Home of Champions graces the main highway into the borough. The reference encompasses not only Musial but also Arnold Galiffa, who starred as Army's quarterback in the late 1940s; Deacon Dan Towler, the running back for the 1951 National Football League champions, the Los Angeles Rams; Ken Griffey of the 1970s Cincinnati Reds; as well as several other sports heroes. The Donora years represent an important key to understanding Musial. Consequently, this book is almost as much about Donora as it is about St. Louis or even Musial.

I have also profited from interviews with Musial friends in St. Louis, including sportscaster Jack Buck, former Cardinal general manager Bing Devine, and Broeg, and from using the Musial collection at the *Sporting News* archives in that city. My regret is that the *Sporting News* refused to make available the extensive correspondence of J. Taylor Spink, which would have shed light on a number of Musial-related matters during the 1940s and 1950s.

Beyond St. Louis, I relied mostly on the Branch Rickey Papers in the Library of Congress, the Lyndon Johnson Papers in the Lyndon Baines Johnson Library, the Thomas Marshall Baseball Oral History Collection in the University of Kentucky Library, and especially the Musial collection at the National Baseball Library. More important, I also depended on the results of a questionnaire sent to some thirteen hundred former National Leaguers who competed with or against Musial. More than three hundred responded to open-ended questions about Musial's personality, accomplishments, and limitations; some wrote several pages of comments. The majority of respondents were ballplayers, usually pitchers, who performed for less than three years in the major leagues. Many of them remembered some particular kindness from Musial, which reinforced their beliefs in his humanity. Virtually no negative comment came from any of the players, which might or might not have been the case if more of the established stars had responded. In any case, I relied on the aforementioned respondents for additional information on such matters as the proposed National League player strike of 1947, a response to Brooklyn Dodgers Jackie Robinson's integration in the major leagues.

Stan Musial played at a time when major-league baseball dominated the attention of a sports-minded America. With the exception of World War II when military service drew most of the stars away, player performance was of high quality. These golden years produced some of the greatest players ever, most notably Williams, DiMaggio, Mantle, Bob Feller, Warren Spahn, Mays, and Aaron. Stability governed much of the period as the same sixteen major-league teams remained in the same cities from 1902 through 1953. Moreover, with the reserve clause binding players to their original teams until owners traded them, there was much less player movement. Stars especially remained with the same clubs throughout their entire careers, linking players to their communities.

Musial also performed in the midst of encroaching change, beginning with the racial integration of the major leagues in 1947. By Musial's retirement at the end of the 1963 season, every major-league ball club contained at least one black player. With the influx of blacks, the game reached a higher level with greater emphasis on speed, particularly on the base paths. By the mid-1950s ball clubs also began to move from their traditional homes, beginning with the Boston Braves' migration to Milwaukee in 1953 and the St. Louis Browns' shift to Baltimore in 1954. In 1958 the major leagues moved to the Pacific Coast when the Brooklyn Dodgers became the Los Angeles Dodgers and the New York Giants moved to San Francisco. This not only necessitated a change in travel from trains to airplanes but also eroded traditional loyalties and contributed to the increase in revenues as sellout crowds greeted the teams who played in those West Coast cities.

More than this, baseball dollars increased markedly as a result of lucrative contracts for television rights for World Series and All-Star games as well as for ordinary day-to-day contests. This resulted in higher profits for owners and, to a much lesser extent, the players. Even though the reserve clause held sway, the players managed to secure a pension plan that applied to those with at least five years of major-league service who had reached the age of fifty; they also formed a Players' Association that was destined to play a significant role in the changes of the 1970s and 1980s.

Moreover, Musial witnessed—and profited from—the expansion of major-league baseball in 1961–1962, when four new major-league teams emerged, diluting the talent pool, which enabled Musial to extend his career another two seasons. Even so, Musial's .330 average in 1962, at the age of forty-two, represents an unusual achievement in a remarkable career.

Throughout my study, I have sensed that there was more to Musial than what was contained in his autobiography and the journalistic accounts. In fact, he was a far more complex man—extremely proud, sensitive, and sometimes contradictory. The extent to which this has altered the symbolic monument is but one aspect of the book.

Acknowledgments

My fascination with major-league baseball began as a youngster in Akron, Ohio, when the Cleveland Indians, in dramatic fashion, won the 1948 World Series. Lou Boudreau, Bob Lemon, Bob Feller, Dale Mitchell, and Gene Beardon became my heroes, followed by Early Wynn, Mike Garcia, Rocky Colavito, Herb Score, and many more. The late '40s and '50s indeed represented a halcyon period for the Tribe. I recall how disappointed I was, however, to witness the Indians' defeat in the fourth and final game of the 1954 World Series at old Municipal Stadium. My interest in Stan Musial and the Cardinals in those years was casual, although I remember cherishing a classic rendering of Musial's unorthodox batting stance on the 1949 Bowman baseball card.

It never occurred to me to write a biography of a baseball player until eight years ago when William E. Foley, editor of the Missouri Biography Series, asked me to tackle Stan the Man. Foley understood that my research focused on the twentieth-century presidency, but he also knew of my interest in the national pastime. By then I had become aware of how other historians meaningfully integrated the study of sports figures into our national history. In that respect, I owe a debt to Jules Tygiel, Charles C. Alexander, William J. Baker, Susan E. Cayleff, and many others for their contributions.

Like baseball, writing a book requires a team effort. Repositories and libraries play a most significant role; consequently, I wish to thank Willa J. Garrett, Frances R. Wolff, Byron Stewart, and Lynn S. Cline of the Duane Meyer Library at Southwest Missouri State University (SMSU); William J. Marshall and Jeffrey S. Suchanek of the Special Collections and Archives division at the Margaret I. King Library of the University of Kentucky; archivist Stephen P. Gietschier of the *Sporting News*; the Manuscript Division staff at the Library of Congress; and the librarians at the National Baseball Library. Without their assistance this book could not have been written.

Equally as important are the hundreds of people who responded to my queries and requests for interviews, many of whom are former classmates, neighbors, and baseball associates of Musial's. It is impossible to thank them all by name except in the bibliography, but four of them deserve special mention: William V. Bottonari of Camp Hill, Pa.; Bob Broeg of St. Louis; Florentino Garcia of Donora, Pa.; and John William Leddon of

Lovettsville, Va. I wish to acknowledge, too, the contributions of Jim Kreuz of Lake Jackson, Texas, who allowed me the use of his taped interviews, and Ruth W. Miller of Donora, Pa., who furnished me with addresses and other information early in this project.

I am also deeply indebted to those who read various drafts of the manuscript: my estimable colleague Dominic J. Capeci, Jr., who brought the wisdom of the scholar to the task; Vernon Cashel of Springfield, Mo., a longtime St. Louis sports enthusiast, who viewed it from the perspective of the informed fan; Fran Giglio, who, with a casual interest in sports, presented a woman's dimension; and Clifford Whipple of Springfield, Mo., who provided the insights of the clinical psychologist. I also wish to thank the two evaluators for the University of Missouri Press. All, in their own way, contributed much to the study. This probably would have been a better book had I adopted more of their suggestions.

My thanks, too, to the State Historical Society of Missouri for two Richard S. Brownlee Fund grants and for permission to reprint verbatim material from my article, "Prelude to Greatness: Stanley Musial and the Springfield Cardinals of 1941," published in the *Missouri Historical Review*, July 1996. As always, I appreciate the support of SMSU, which provided me with a sabbatical leave and a teaching-load reduction. I wish to thank, too, the former head of the History Department at SMSU, Matt Mancini, for underwriting the mailing of my questionnaire to former major leaguers and my telephone interviews, the latter of which his successor, Marc Cooper, also agreed to support. My gratitude to Michael Boyle, a history graduate student at SMSU, for helping me with the bibliography and to Charles Hedrick, an SMSU Religious Studies professor, who graciously listened to my frustrations and problems relating to this study during our jogs.

Most important, I wish to thank my family for tolerating my obsession with the book: my wife, Fran, who has always supported me; my sons, Peter and Tony; my daughter-in-law, Erin; and even our cat, "Kitty." In their own special way, they all contributed to preserving what is left of my sanity.

James N. Giglio
October 19, 2000

Musial

Growing Up Poor in the "Home of Champions"

In surveying downtown Pittsburgh from one of its southside hills, one witnesses the confluence of two great rivers—the Allegheny and the Monongahela—to form the majestic Ohio. Today near the point where the rivers meet one can see Three Rivers Stadium, the home of the Pittsburgh Pirates. The view is breathtaking, especially when the ballpark is illuminated at dusk. By following the Monongahela eastward from its westerly sweep into Pittsburgh, one can discern a meandering course to the south, knifing deeply through rugged terrain. This is the Mon Valley, and it includes McKeesport, Clairton, Monongahela, Webster, Donora, Monessen, Charleroi, California, and numerous other towns toward the river's headwaters in the mountains of West Virginia. Numerous bridges traverse the river to accommodate the highway traffic that runs along its two sides. Stanley Frank Musial was born in the borough of Donora about twenty-eight miles south of Pittsburgh on November 21, 1920.[1]

In 1920, Pittsburgh, the nation's leading steel center, represented the hub of the industrial activity of western Pennsylvania. Around Pittsburgh existed more than 30 steel mills, 60 glass factories, and 350 coal mines. Clouds of smoke spewed from the local factories, scattering soot over the houses throughout the metropolis. Industrial noises—the clanging of metal on metal, the loud horns or whistles that designated shift changes, the chugging of steam locomotives, and the distinct sounds of river traffic—beat a constant refrain. More bulk tonnage—coal, steel, and gravel—traversed Pittsburgh's three rivers than passed through the Suez and Panama Canals combined.

By 1920, Donora of Washington County had emerged as an industrial hotbed—one of Pittsburgh's little sisters. The source of Donora's industrial might was the American Steel and Wire Company, a subsidiary of U.S. Steel. The Donora operation had emerged at the turn of the century along the high west bank of the Monongahela River, which undertakes a

---

1. Despite Musial's use of the middle name of Frank, according to Earl W. Halstead, president of Baseball Bluebook, Inc., his middle name is Francis. Halstead consulted Musial's birth records in Donora and Harrisburg, Pennsylvania. Earl W. Halstead to Chris Roewe, July 3, 1967, Stan Musial Collection, *Sporting News* archives, St. Louis.

huge horseshoe course around the town. The blast and the open hearth furnaces were located on the south side. Further northward along the barge-laden river were the rod mills and wire plant, and finally, five years before Stan's birth, came the Donora Zinc Works company in the north part of town. Rods and wire were manufactured from steel billets, and then after an acid bath to enable the zinc to adhere, the wire underwent galvanization at the zinc works plant. The zinc works soon became the largest and most efficient producer of zinc and sulfuric acid in the world; some seventy thousand tons of zinc came from there annually. Altogether, the American Steel and Wire Company's holdings encompassed a two-mile area along the river. Its chief products included barbed wire (Donora probably produced the most tonnage in the world), cable for suspension bridges, screws, nails, wire rope, electrical and music spring wire, and woven wire fences.

Such industry exacted a price. The residue from the smoke stacks created a perpetual cloud, dumping heavy metal dusts, along with carbon monoxide gas and sulfurous fumes, over the entire area. Since the wind usually blew eastward across the river, Donorans saw barren hills in the near eastern horizon; the only foliage to survive in Webster, a village to the east, was the milkweed plant. Donoran houses, meanwhile, turned a dingy gray. Youngsters rolling in the brown grass of South Donora found themselves covered with black soot, while northsiders exposed their skins to a yellowish residue. One former resident remembered the yellow-colored snow in winter. An acrid odor prevailed, another constant reminder of the mills.

The air pollution would finally reach crisis proportions in late October 1948 when weather conditions prevented the air from rising above the hills and cliffs around Donora. A heavy fog covered the landscape. By November 1, twenty had died and six hundred needed medical attention; thousands more were ill. For this Donorans received unwanted national exposure. Before and after the death-dealing smog, air pollution remained a health problem. A mill nurse remembered complaints of "zinc works jitters," including nausea and shakiness, from workers who resigned themselves to the fact "that smoke puts bread on our tables."[2]

Nearly all Donoran men labored in the mills. In 1920 more than 30

---

2. Lynne Page Snyder, " 'The Death-Dealing Smog over Donora, Pennsylvania': Industrial Air Pollution, Public Health Policy, and the Politics of Expertise, 1948–1949," 117–39; Script, "Historical Slides for Donora Diary—Beginnings," Donora Historical Society, furnished by Norma Ross Todd, Donora, Pennsylvania.

percent of the community's fourteen thousand residents were foreign-born. Most of the immigrant men walked down the steep hills with lunch pails to one of the factories. Donora's immigrant population was incredibly diverse, but most came from Eastern and Central Europe. Slovaks generally lived on the south side, attended St. Dominic's, one of six Roman Catholic churches, and found employment in the steel and wire factories. Italians usually occupied the central part of Donora around Third Street, belonged to St. Phillip parish, and worked alongside Slovaks and other ethnics. Most of the Poles were scattered along the north side, worshiped at St. Mary's Catholic Church, and also gravitated to the mills. "Spanishtown," in north Donora, was occupied by Spanish descendants and immigrants who had worked with zinc in Spain. They, of course, worked in the zinc works. Many other nationalities found a home in Donora, including Scots who were skilled lead burners. Around seventy-five Jewish families also resided in Donora during the 1920s. Many of them were merchants. They lived in every section of the community and worshiped in a small synagogue built in 1911. Unlike some of the other industrial communities, blue-collar workers, regardless of race and ethnicity, managed to get along inside and outside the factories of Donora.

In 1920 blacks represented 6 percent of the town's population. Like the immigrants, they were encouraged to migrate to Donora during World War I. Most of them had come from the South. They lived in the low-income areas: in the alleys near the center of town, on the north side, near the high school on Second Street, and in "Little Africa" on Waddell Avenue. Two churches—First Baptist Church and St. Paul Baptist Church—accommodated the black population. Blacks were employed in the mills out of a belief that they could handle the heat better.

Even though some blacks lived in white neighborhoods and their children attended Donora's only junior high and high school, they, like blacks in other northern communities, often felt the sting of racism. An active Ku Klux Klan burned crosses across the river. Blacks quickly determined that while some Donoran establishments welcomed their business, others did not. They were relegated to the balconies of local movie theaters, and they were not accepted at some of the downtown restaurants and other businesses. One of Musial's classmates, who worked in a drugstore, remembered serving a soft drink to a black friend. After he left the proprietor smashed the glass in the sink, warning that if it happened again, the employee could "get the hell out."[3] Less racism existed in the

3. Florentino Garcia telephone interview, January 9, 1997.

school system, however. Some of Musial's classmates developed close relationships with the five blacks in the 1939 high school graduating class. Stan and other white athletes competed with blacks from junior high school onward.

Further up the social strata were the mills' foremen and middle managers. They came from some of Donora's oldest families, many of whom were generations removed from their European roots. A number of them lived in Cement City, so called because the houses were concrete. Built in 1917 by the American Steel and Wire Company high on a hill in the southwestern part of town and varying in design, the one hundred homes presented an attractively planned development that included carefully positioned terraces, shrubbery, and shade trees, which lined the yellow-brick streets. Cement City offered a stark contrast to the drab, often dingy housing of the mill workers below. The industrial elite, meanwhile, lived in the Terrace area near the zinc works; Fischer Heights, about three miles outside of town; or in one of the neighboring communities. Almost always nonethnics and Masons, most of them transferred into Donora from other American Steel and Wire plants.

Stan Musial's father, Lukasz, first appeared in Donora in early 1910 following his emigration to the United States. Little is known about him as a young man other than what he provided in his naturalization papers. He was nineteen years old at the time of his arrival, 5 feet 7 inches tall and 150 pounds in weight, with blond hair and gray eyes. His estimation of height and weight are probably an exaggeration, since those who remember him insist that he was wiry and barely five feet tall. A Pole, he came from the village of Mojstava in the province of Galicia, at that time part of Austria-Hungary. Departing from Hamburg, Germany, on January 24 on the *President Grant*, he arrived at Ellis Island six days later. From New York he went immediately to Donora. Like so many Poles at the turn of the century, he came from a peasant background and probably intended to return with savings from industrial jobs. Lukasz was one of about 1.5 million Poles arriving in the United States between 1899 and 1913, the vast majority of whom were male, single, and Catholic.[4]

4. Lukasz Musial naturalization papers. As spelled, the village of Mojstava does not seem to exist today. Perhaps it was incorrectly recorded at the outset. Library of Congress Polish area specialist Ronald D. Bachman believes that the "t" in Mojstava was in fact a hard "l" and that the "oj" combination is a dialectal variation for "y" and that "av" and "ow" are interchangeable—hence Myslowa, which is in the Galician part of the Ukraine. Ronald D. Bachman to James N. Giglio, September 26, 1997, in possession of Giglio. Musial is incorrect in claiming that his father was born on a farm

Like nearly 90 percent of his Polish counterparts, Lukasz settled in an industrial area, seeking an unskilled laboring job. A cousin directed him to Donora; it may well have been Aggie Musial, who lived two doors down from Lukasz in 1920. According to the contemporary record, Lukasz held several different jobs during his first ten years in Donora—including "machine helper" and porter at the Public Hotel. Soon after his arrival he met Mary Lancos, the fourteen-year-old daughter of immigrants from Austria-Hungary. One of nine brothers and sisters, Mary, who was born in New York City, had first toiled as an eight-year-old housekeeper. She was big-boned, nearly six feet tall, and had untapped athletic ability. According to Stan Musial's recollection, she and Lukasz had met at a dance. At the time Lukasz knew no English, but Mary had learned enough Polish from working with Polish girls in the wire mill to communicate with him.[5]

They married on April 14, 1913, in Donora; he was nearly twenty-three years old, while she was sixteen. The marriage certificate listed her as twenty-one, an indication that she might not have obtained her parents' permission, a state requirement for anyone less than twenty-one years of age. Four daughters—Ida, Victoria, Helen, and Rose—followed over the next six years before the first son appeared on November 21, 1920. Lukasz, who had longed for a son, named him Stanislaus and called him by the Polish nickname of Stashu. That was soon shortened to Stash, and it has remained Stan's nickname among longtime friends. Pronounced with a soft "a," it sounded like "Stush." After he entered public school, teachers and adults in general addressed him as Stanley (or Stan), as did his mother. The family and locals pronounced the surname Mu-shill, not Mu-si-al. Two years after Stan came the birth of a brother, Ed, nicknamed "Honey" by a neighbor supposedly because he laughed a lot. Ed lacked the emerging confidence of his older brother. "I had an inferiority complex;

near Warsaw, a considerable distance from Galicia. Stan Musial, *Stan Musial: "The Man's" Own Story, as Told to Bob Broeg*, 6. In recent years he and Lil came to believe that his ancestors came from Przemsl in eastern Poland. *St. Louis Post-Dispatch*, January 24, 1999. For the Polish migration, see James Pula, *Polish Americans: An Ethnic Community*, 17–18.

5. For Lukasz Musial's early days in Donora, see his naturalization papers and data from the Fourteenth Census of the United States. For Mary Lancos, see Musial, *Stan Musial*, 5–6. Musial claims that her parents came from the eventual state of Czechoslovakia. The 1920 census merely lists Mary's parents as being from Austria-Hungary. The surname Lancos is probably Hungarian in origin. Many Slovaks adopted Hungarian names as the result of centuries of Hungarian domination in parts of the Slovakian region. Bachman to Giglio, September 26, 1997.

I was shy," he later said. This trait may have kept him from being a ballplayer of Stan's caliber, despite his considerable ability.

The two brothers were baptized at St. Mary's on Second Street, about eleven blocks from their home. Despite the Polish family practice of sending their children to Catholic schools, the Musial children attended Castner Elementary School in their neighborhood because St. Mary's lacked a parochial school. At Castner teachers insisted that Stash write with his right hand, which possibly contributed to his stammer when excited. At least for a while, Lukasz insisted that the children attend special Polish language classes, which St. Mary's probably sponsored. Although Lukasz became a naturalized citizen by 1920, he spoke broken English and read and wrote only in Polish. According to Ed Musial, he read a Polish-language newspaper.[6]

In recalling his youth, much of it during the Depression years of the 1930s, Stan Musial idyllically remembers a father who never earned more than four dollars a day and who usually took home eleven dollars every two weeks. He worked in the wire mill's shipping department, loading wire bales onto freight cars. Stan occasionally walked down the hill to greet him when he heard the five o'clock whistle. Invariably, "Pop," as he called him, held back an apple or a cookie from his lunch pail for Stash. To supplement the family's meager income, the mother and sisters did domestic work as well as tending to most of the chores at home. Stash assisted them and in high school pumped gas at night at a local Spur Gas filling station.

By the time he was seven years old his parents had moved the family from rental housing on Seventh Street in the central part of town to the maternal grandparents' home on 1139 Marelda Avenue near Thirteenth Street on the upper north side. The gray-colored, imitation brick shingle house was in an undeveloped area in the poorer part of Donora. It sat on a bed of coal, which the family mined for heating purposes. The gravel street fronting the house contained the distinct odor of raw sewage because of some deficiency in the sewer system. The box-like, two-story

6. Marriage License, Lukay [sic] Musial and Mary Lancoss [sic], April 14, 1913, Washington County, Pennsylvania, Marriage License no. 22400; Ed Musial telephone interview, April 10, 1994, conducted by Jim Kreuz, Lake Jackson, Texas; Ed Musial interview, August 6, 1996. Kreuz conducted several interviews in 1994 for his two short pieces on Musial in sports publications.

dwelling contained only two bedrooms, which Stan's parents, at least one grandparent, and six siblings somehow shared.[7]

With greater affection, Stan Musial recalls his mother's influence on his early life. She "manufactured" his first baseballs from assorted material sown together. She also stretched their meager earnings by purchasing potatoes, flour, sugar, and coffee in bulk. Following her directive, the children picked blackberries and elderberries for preserves. In an outdoor oven she baked ten loaves of bread at a time. "There was always something to eat," Musial later joked with only slight exaggeration, "cabbage soup, cabbage salad, steamed cabbage, and every other kind of cabbage. No more cabbage for me. I can't even look at it." Mary Musial was obviously an enormously energetic woman. William Bottonari remembered that she had "a spring in her step" as she walked by his family home on the Saturday preceding Palm Sunday with a basket of baked goods to be blessed at the church. She showed affection for her children, taught them to respect their elders, and sought to instill in them a strong work ethic and devotion to the church. If anyone did otherwise they were soundly disciplined. Everyone who knew the family has insisted that she was Stash's greatest influence at home.[8]

Life in Donora during the Great Depression was worse than Musial portrayed it. In fact by 1933 the Depression had cost Pennsylvania more than 5,000 manufacturing establishments; only New York suffered more. The state had lost some 270,000 manufacturing jobs and ranked next to New York in unemployment. No state had more people on relief. In Donora the unemployment percentage surely exceeded that of the state. One contemporary national account reported that in March 1932 only 277 workers out of a population of 13,900 still had their regular jobs.[9]

Sometime in early 1932 the American Steel and Wire operation had virtually shut down. This event somehow escaped the *Donora Herald-American*, a conservative Republican organ that parroted Secretary of the Treasury Andrew Mellon's contention that the Depression was a godsend to purge the American economy of its excesses. Donora's sole

7. The Edward L. Stokes family, who presently reside in the Musial house, provided information about it in an interview on May 21, 1997, as did William Bottonari, telephone interview, April 12, 1997.

8. Wally Carew, "He's a 'Cardinal' Too!" 10; Bottonari telephone interview, November 5, 1996.

9. Thomas H. Coode and John F. Bauman, *People, Poverty, and Politics: Pennsylvanians during the Great Depression*, 14–15; "No One Has Starved," 24.

newspaper repeatedly blamed the Depression on high taxes and excessive government spending in its clarion call for a balanced budget. At the same time it insensitively featured on its front pages a lavish fete for mill foremen at the zinc works, including "fat, luscious" oysters from the Rappahannock River in Virginia. One rare instance of its reporting local production came in August 1932 when the newspaper described the "red flames, showering sparks, and smoke" that emanated from five open-hearth furnaces, signifying that the mill had resumed part-time operation. Never did company-town control seem more in evidence. Indeed, the *Herald-American*'s copublisher, William Hamilton Watson, served as the chief burgess of Donora and did the bidding of the American Steel and Wire Company.[10]

Ordinary Donorans expressed their resentment during the 1932 elections, despite management warning workers that if the Democrats won, "Don't come to work." Ignoring the *Herald-American*'s endorsement of President Herbert Hoover, who managed to capture the traditional Republican state vote, Donorans overwhelmingly voted for Franklin Roosevelt, as did the rest of Washington County. In fact, in a remarkable turn of events, no Republican candidate for national, state, or local office received a plurality of votes in Donora. Election evening culminated in a torch light parade that ended in the center of the town with the singing of "Happy Days Are Here Again." For the remainder of the 1930s Democrats managed to carry virtually every race in Donora.[11]

The election rebellion only partly reflects how bleak the situation was for mill employees and their families in 1931 and 1932. At most, workers labored one day a week. Musial classmate John "Bill" Leddon recalled that his father did not work at all. "The grocery store carried us," he remembered. Out of worry, his mother never slept in bed. Eugene Norton, another classmate, remembered people "knocking on our door for food." Musial neighbor Joe Barbao temporarily lost his job at the zinc works and consequently worked nights protecting garden plots at Palmer Park from thieves.[12] The newspaper reported arrests of those who stole small amounts of coal. Out of desperation, other incidents of thievery occurred.

10. *Donora Herald-American*, December 24, 1931, July 2, 20, 1932, January 29, 1931, August 29, 1932.
11. Arnold Hirsch interview, May 22, 1997, and Ed Pado telephone interview, November 20, 1996; Bottonari interview, December 10, 1997.
12. John W. Leddon, Jr., telephone interview, December 5, 1996; Eugene Norton telephone interview, November 20, 1996; Ken Barbao telephone interview, June 19, 1997.

While merchants and the newspaper organized special promotions in the summer of 1931 that enabled children to attend a movie for a nickel and receive a free ice cream cone, no such activity in 1932 was disclosed. By then the *Herald-American* had suddenly stopped publishing the comic strips.

Until Roosevelt's New Deal, no real national relief effort assisted the unemployed in Donora or anywhere else. State relief activities in Pennsylvania were meager given the constitutional restrictions that prevented state indebtedness beyond $1 million. So the burden of relief fell upon the private and public organizations of Washington County and Donora. Initially, the Donora Central Board of Charities and the local chapter of the Red Cross did the most. The former provided groceries, shoes, coal, and funds for hospital care. The Red Cross distributed flour in bulk, cloth, garments, and seeds for vegetable gardens. Various locations around the city, including Palmer Park, became garden sites. Local grocers also extended accounts to enable people to eat, farmers relinquished fruit for a community canning project for the needy, and the American Steel and Wire Company performed a modicum of charity work. In June 1932 Father Joseph Ronconi, pastor of St. Phillip Neri Catholic Church, opened a soup kitchen. For months it enabled hundreds of schoolchildren daily to receive a nourishing lunch. But like most communities, Donora found it difficult to meet the needs of its people. By April 1931 the Board of Charities was running out of money, Father Ronconi had to shut down his kitchen periodically because of insufficient donations, and city officials had to reduce services because of lack of funds.

Donorans had to rely on themselves and do without. Eventually, New Deal relief agencies helped to combat unemployment. The *Herald-American* reported some WPA activity in Donora in the mid-1930s, but it characteristically placed greater emphasis on the importance of local charity and grossly underreported various New Deal area projects. In any case, by early 1937 the press disclosed an even greater boost in production at the American Steel and Wire Company, an indication the Depression was waning, at least until the recession of that fall. The local economy continued its resurgence in 1939 as the nation began to prepare for war.

During the economic crisis the Musial family verged on destitution. Early in the Depression Lukasz either was laid off or had his work week appreciably shortened. Like so many families, the Musials had to accept flour and other necessities from the Red Cross and charities. Lukasz's excessive drinking contributed to the difficulties. One contemporary remembered that "it caused a great deal of discord in the family," for "his desire to have that sedative . . . was overwhelming." Another Donoran described him as "the poorest guy in town."[13] Like others seeking escape, he stopped at beer gardens, became inebriated, and was sometimes robbed of his pay on the way home. All of this embarrassed his oldest son, causing friction between the two. Whatever Stash might have felt he kept to himself, as friends sensed a reluctance to talk about it. Lukasz's drinking put an even greater stress on Stash's mother, who had to work more, including cleaning one of Donora's movie theaters. Often this exhausted her. After Stash became a local sports figure, merchants such as clothier Sy Rosenberg furnished him with clothing and other necessities. This accentuated the needs of the sisters and Ed, who usually felt left out. Out of sorrow and desperation for her children, Mary Musial, remembered one acquaintance, began to "appropriate" things for them. Tragically, this led to kleptomania, the taking of items for no apparent need, undoubtedly sparked by the stresses of those troubled years. This became a mental disorder that the son eventually had to address through intermediaries once he moved to St. Louis.[14]

That Musial overcame so well the enormous hardships of his youth is extraordinary. His story represents one of the great success stories in American sport. Of course, Musial's natural athletic ability—his extraordinary eyesight, eye-hand coordination, and quickness of foot—had contributed. What athleticism he inherited from his parents is questionable, but in addition to her considerable energy and strength, Mary could run with authority, and despite his slight build, Lukasz was physically strong. As a child Stan increased his dexterity and muscular strength by participating in gymnastics at the Polish Falcons Lodge in downtown Donora. Stan's skinny body belied the powerful back and shoulder muscles built partly from that activity. Tumbling added to his agility, enabling him to somersault easily after making circus catches in the field.

More than this, Musial had enormous determination. As a little boy he came to understand where his abilities lay. Sports became an expression

13. Robert O'Lenic telephone interview, December 5, 1996; Edward Sukel interview, May 22, 1997.

14. Florentino Garcia telephone interview, June 11, July 9, 1997; Patricia Pizzica Cupper interview, May 23, 1997; Nancy Barbao Rumora telephone interview, November 3, 1997. Little has been published on kleptomania; one of the best studies is Susan L. McElroy, James I. Hudson, Harrison G. Pope, and Paul E. Keck, "Kleptomania: Clinical Characteristics and Associated Psychopathology," 93–108, which describes kleptomania as a common mental disorder that usually affects women and may be related to other forms of psychopathology. See also Susan L. McElroy, Paul E. Keck, Jr., and Katherine A. Phillips, "Kleptomania, Compulsive Buying, and Binge-Eating Disorder," 14–25.

of his self-worth. He loved to compete, and he fought to win at every turn. Ed Musial remembered that when they played as youngsters on different baseball teams, Stash hit a long drive to the outfield, which Ed deliberately kicked underneath the fence for a ground-rule double. When the inning ended, he jokingly told Stash how he had "held" him to a double; the next time Ed batted, Stash, who was pitching, purposely hit him between the shoulder blades. When Stash lost, he sometimes cried, Ed recalled. Most often he outshone the competition, which drove him even more to succeed. A quiet confidence emerged, a deep faith in himself, reinforced by strong religious conviction. He rarely missed Sunday Mass; that sort of devotion persuaded one of his high school teammates to return to the faith. Moreover, he remained humble, instinctively aware of how fickle and difficult life can be.[15]

A winsome appearance further explains his rise. His rosy cheeks, quiet demeanor, and handsome features added to his attractiveness as a youngster. Among friends he smiled more often and even giggled on occasion, without dominating any conversation. He was especially shy and deferential with adults. He learned to listen attentively to their advice and profited from their assistance. To many of them, Musial became a "special project" because of his family circumstances, his extraordinary athletic ability, and his appreciation, which caused benefactors to want to help even more. From childhood on, he attached himself to a number of surrogate fathers or mentors, beginning with neighbor Joe Barbao, and followed by outstanding educators at Donora High School, especially coaches Michael "Ki" Duda and James K. "Jimmie" Russell; local businessman Frank Pizzica; eventually baseball managers Dick Kerr and Ed Dyer; and St. Louis restaurateur Julius "Biggie" Garagnani.[16]

None loomed larger in Musial's childhood than Barbao, who helped him develop his talent as a ballplayer. Of primarily Spanish ancestry,

15. Ed Musial telephone interview, April 10, 1994, conducted by Kreuz; Garcia telephone interview, January 9, 1997.
16. A 1970s study from a Yale University research team, which examined successful middle-aged American males, suggested that every one of them had mentors. Usually eight to fifteen years older than the protégé, the mentor (almost always a male) combined the roles of surrogate parent and mature friend. Aside from the cultivator of the "dream," he could act as teacher to enhance the protégé's skills and intellectual development, as sponsor to facilitate advancement, and as host and guide. Above all, he usually served as a model whom the protégé could admire and emulate; in times of stress, he might provide counsel and moral support. In instances of material need he might also furnish food and clothing. Males with weak or tyrannical fathers were particularly attracted to mentors. Although mentoring could extend well beyond a protégé's adolescence, it rarely continued after the latter reached the age of forty.

Barbao worked at the zinc works and also pitched for and managed the company team. Barbao lived on Taylor Avenue, about a block away from the Musials. A pre-teenage Musial anxiously awaited the thirty-year-old Barbao's arrival from work so that he could be around him and his brother as they warmed up for a zinc works contest. Often Stash and his brother, in imitation, threw next to the Barbaos. There were many warm summer evenings when Stash talked with Barbao about major leaguers such as left-handed pitcher Lefty Grove of the Philadelphia Athletics, probably Stash's favorite player; Carl Hubbell, a New York Giants left-handed hurler; and third baseman Pie Traynor of the Pittsburgh Pirates, the team Stash dreamed of playing for. A special bond developed between the two. Stash could converse with Barbao in ways he found difficult to do with his father. It was Barbao who taught him how to throw a curve ball and how to handle himself on the diamond. Barbao made him bat boy for the zinc works team and eventually moved him into the lineup despite the grumbling of players because of Musial's age and his not being a dues-paying member of the Zinc Works Athletic Association. Barbao also eventually got Musial a job in the zinc works in the offseason once Stash had entered professional baseball.[17]

Stash's earliest baseball competition began with neighborhood young-sters his own age. They included Bob O'Lenic, a Polish American in spite of his name, who played high school baseball with Musial. Musial often went to O'Lenic's house for lunch and remained close to him into adulthood. Musial remembered that whenever they failed to have enough participants for a game, they used to hit bottle caps with a broomstick, which improved their eye-hand coordination. Otherwise, they played ball on a field, which they converted into a baseball diamond and eventually a tennis court, naming it Yama AC, an ethnic expression for flat land, according to O'Lenic. They "appropriated" the tennis net; "we were very honest except when we had to steal something," O'Lenic later joked.[18]

A mentoring relationship enabled a number of promising athletes to overcome their disadvantaged backgrounds. Jesse Owens, the track hero of the 1936 Olympics, was only one of many to receive that assistance. What made Musial's situation so unusual was the number of mentors he had from childhood to adulthood. Daniel J. Levinson with Charlotte N. Darrow, Edward B. Klein, Maria H. Levinson, and Braxton McKee, *The Seasons of a Man's Life*, 97–101, 149. See also William J. Baker, *Jesse Owens: An American Life* (New York: Free Press, 1986), 20–21.

17. Musial, *Stan Musial*, 10–14; Ken Barbao telephone interview, June 17, 1997; Joe Barbao, Jr., telephone interview, June 26, 1997.

18. *Los Angeles Times,* March 15, 1984, clipping in Stan Musial Collection, *Sporting News* archives; O'Lenic telephone interview, April 15, 1994, conducted by Kreuz.

Yama AC contained an upward incline in left field, which restricted the fielder, and a right field designated out of bounds because of the high grass and a downward slope. It was at Yama AC that the southpaw Musial learned to hit to left field.

Following elementary school, Musial expanded his circle of relationships considerably, because Donora had only one junior high. He attended classes with all the other Donoran youths of similar ages, bringing various nationalities and races together. This included Bill Leddon, of English-Welsh ancestry, from Cement City; blacks Grant Gray and Joseph "Buddy" Griffey, the future father and grandfather of major leaguers Ken Griffey and Ken Griffey, Jr., respectively; Ed Pado, a second-generation Slovakian American from the south side; and Eugene "Fats" Norton, a Polish American, from central Donora.

In 1936 Stash and other junior high youngsters competed in a summer baseball league, which they organized with various sections of Donora providing teams, eight of them in all. Local merchants furnished jerseys; the players conducted a raffle, which they rigged so that they could buy baseballs. The merchants, who bought most of the tickets, ignored the skulduggery. Designated players submitted the line scores of games to the *Herald-American*, which published the results the following day. The newspaper also reported summaries of the local "mushball" (softball) leagues, which included junior high entries, and basketball box scores of the various homerooms from the junior high and high school. Donora High School football coverage often dominated the front pages, and game attendance sometimes exceeded four thousand at the high school's Legion Field. This sort of response reflected the significance of sports to a community seeking escape from daily hardships. It also provided a way for the *Herald-American* to deflect the dismal local economic news and engage in boosterism.[19]

The fifteen-year-old Musial first appeared regularly in the Donora sports pages in early 1936 as a basketball player for St. Mary's in the rugged City League. He eschewed junior high school play to compete with older players, a decision that revealed his growing self-confidence and his maturity as a performer. A local columnist noted that he "is at an age when a youngster is all legs," but "he is a clever ball handler and a good shot. Provided he puts on a little weight and height his name should find

19. Information on the summer baseball league comes from Norton interview, May 22, 1997; Norton telephone interview, 1994, conducted by Kreuz; Pado telephone interview, November 20, 1996.

its way into the headlines within a year or two." He also played baseball
for the Heslep All-Stars, one of the summer league teams, which included
brother Ed and Bob O'Lenic. Stash played in the outfield and pitched.
His achievements caused the newspaper to contend that "the slender and
rather frail looking Musial" is "probably the outstanding player in the
local circuit." His play enabled Heslep to capture the mythical league title
that July. A disappointed Ed Pado of the Kenneth Cubs remembered that
"we thought nobody could beat us. We thought we were big shots, and we
got mad [after losing to Heslep] and almost got into a scuffle afterwards."
That summer Musial's name appeared in mushball box scores, and he
played elsewhere as well. O'Lenic and others called him "iron man"
because of his endless energy, the first of his many nicknames.[20]

By July Musial also had appeared in the uniform of the Donora Zinc
Works team managed by Joe Barbao. Americo Park, just north of the
zinc works, constituted the home field, characterized by a short left field
because of intruding trolley tracks. Again Musial learned how to take
advantage of short left fields. Playing against much older players in
the eight-team Industrial Mon Valley League that included entries from
neighboring Monessen and Belle Vernon, he at first entered the games
in the outfield as a late-inning substitute. Pinch-hitting on one occasion,
Musial remembered being so nervous that he swallowed his gum while
striking out. The 5-foot 4-inch 140 pounder made his pitching debut
against Monessen on August 4, striking out five in four innings. The
newspaper predicted stardom for Musial but cautioned that despite "his
world of stuff, he is too small for steady playing now."[21] Contrary to
Musial's recollection, contemporary evidence is lacking that he struck out
thirteen in six innings of relief in one game that year. (Two years later, on
April 14, 1938, he did fan seventeen against Monessen.) In this period he
also played American Legion ball, which further prepared him for high
school and professional baseball.

His accomplishments centered around basketball and baseball at Donora High School, a red-brick building that now serves as an elementary
school. At best he was an average student who, like most of his classmates,
took the nonacademic curriculum. As he himself admits, he did little
studying. Leddon remembered that Musial excelled in wood workshop;

20. *Donora Herald-American*, March 10, July 19, 22, 1935, July 16, 1936; Pado telephone interview, May 14, 1994, conducted by Kreuz. Musial first appeared on the sport
pages in July 1935 when he pitched a few games for the Waltower Tigers. O'Lenic
telephone interview, December 5, 1996.

21. *Donora Herald-American*, July 31, 1936.

Musial's shop teacher, according to Leddon, said that had Musial not gone into baseball he would have been the world's best left-handed carpenter. His senior yearbook revealed that he held no class offices nor participated in formal class activities other than sports. Although his yearbook picture suggests a seriousness that unquestionably existed, he was described as "friendly, full of fun, and neat." From all accounts, he shined on the dance floor. Few performed the polka as proficiently at the Polish Falcon Club, suggesting a sense of rhythm that served him well in sports. He also excelled in table tennis, an indication of superb eye-hand coordination.

Teachers were especially fond of him because he was so mannerly. One, in signing his yearbook, extended her best wishes "to the boy with the sunniest smile and [the] rosiest cheeks I've ever seen."[22] Another recalled his earnestness during a class discussion of John Steinbeck's *Grapes of Wrath*. When the subject of migrant workers came up, Musial volunteered that he "saw a group of women like that the other day . . . camped right on the edge of town and they dressed just like hoboes. They even wore pants."[23] The class erupted in laughter with the teacher remembering that Stash blushed for the remainder of the period. His most serious academic commitment came as a senior when he walked to the junior high school with two other classmates to take elementary algebra, a future requirement in the event he enrolled in college.

As did other students, Musial walked to school and to athletic and social activities. Few students had access to automobiles in that era. Moreover, their parents rarely drove their vehicles, even to work. Leddon's only use of the family car came in his senior year when he drove fellow students to a debate club skating party and when he attended the prom, which required a four-mile trip to pick up his date. Otherwise, he would have walked like other prom attenders. Leddon claimed that he could not recall a single athlete having access to an automobile while in school. Like 70 percent of Donora's families, Stash's parents, of course, owned no car.[24]

At Donora High Stash met his future wife, Lillian Labash, whose father, Sam, ran a family grocery store on South McKean Avenue near the downtown area. Of Russian heritage and one of eight siblings, the petite,

22. *Varsity Dragon*, Class of 1939 Yearbook, 56, 28. Musial's personal copy of the yearbook is housed in the St. Louis Cardinals Museum, Busch Stadium, St. Louis. Leddon, telephone interview, December 5, 1996; Pado telephone interview, May 14, 1994, conducted by Kreuz.

23. A. F. Miller, Jr., to Roger Kahn, November 1, 1957, in possession of Norma R. Todd, Donora, Pennsylvania. Todd is the former A. F. Miller.

24. John W. Leddon to James N. Giglio, November 16, 1997, in possession of Giglio.

attractive, brown-haired Lil, known as "Shrimp" to her classmates, was in her last year when fellow senior Dick Ercius introduced her in the fall of 1937 to Stash, then still a junior. Ercius at the time was dating one of Lil's sisters. Lil remembered that she and Stash soon shared a table at Herk's drugstore where they arranged a date. The following week he never spoke to her, causing her to wonder whether a weekend engagement still existed. But he appeared and gave her a "peck on the cheek" afterward. She later teased that she fell in love with Musial's legs while watching him play basketball.

The *Varsity Dragon,* the school newspaper, noted that fall that Stash was "keeping Lillian Labash company after school hours." He indeed often walked the mile or so down the hills to the Labash grocery store to see her. Lil later contended that Stash, not having much to eat at home, came to the store for sandwiches and milk. Little is known otherwise about their early relationship except that Lil affectionately mentioned him in the class will; her caring for him was occasionally expressed in the *Varsity Dragon.* That publication also mentioned the interest of at least one other young lady in Musial. Others have mentioned that female students found him appealing. Whether Stash resisted such temptations after meeting Lil is debatable. From the time of his marriage in the summer of 1940, however, no hint of infidelity has ever emerged.[25]

Musial experienced his first high school athletic competition as a sophomore in December 1936. His basketball coach, "Jimmie" Russell, a twenty-nine-year-old protégé of Knute Rockne, had come to the school from Notre Dame in 1931 to invigorate the football program. One week after Russell's arrival, Rockne died in an airplane crash. Dark complexioned, stocky, and animated, the five-foot seven-inch Russell eventually turned the Orange and Black Dragons into a powerhouse. Russell's football teams of the 1940s included such future college greats as Arnold Galiffa of Army and "Deacon" Dan Towler of Washington and Jefferson and the professional Los Angeles Rams. In Musial's time, Russell often started two blacks in the backfield, Buddy Griffey and Hank Murphy, whom the press and teammates labeled the "gold dust twins." Of the two the short, bull-legged Griffey was the more capable; a skilled left-footed punter and a sure tackler, his enormous speed accounted for several game-winning

25. *St. Louis Post-Dispatch Magazine,* December 14, 1994, 14; *Varsity Dragon,* November 12, 1937, February 11, 1938, in possession of Bottonari, Camp Hill, Pennsylvania; Bottonari telephone interview, August 12, 1997. Regarding Musial and other women, Musial confided to a classmate that there was someone else when he played minor league baseball at Williamson, West Virginia. Confidential source.

touchdowns his senior year, making him an All-Valley selection. An insight into Russell's character occurred when the coach brought Griffey and the rest of the team to a popular restaurant in downtown Donora following a game. When the owner refused to serve Griffey and Murphy because they were black, Russell said that if they did not eat there, no one on the team would. The restaurant proprietor then changed his mind. It was Russell, too, who threatened to dismiss linemen who failed to block enthusiastically when Griffey and Murphy played in the backfield together. Russell later turned down the coaching job at North Carolina State University because he did not want to coach in a racially segregated state. Considered the most inspirational academic teacher at Donora High, where he taught history, Russell, like Rockne, used the football field and the basketball court to instruct players to love their parents and attend church. Undoubtedly, Musial took his messages to heart.[26]

It is unlikely, however, that Russell elevated Musial's skills as a basketball player. As adept as Russell was in teaching football technique, he knew virtually nothing about the intricacies of basketball. Musial teammate "Fats" Norton claimed that "we knew more basketball than he did." On one occasion, according to Norton, Russell offered to purchase a dozen tennis shoes from a sales representative—a former University of Pittsburgh basketball player—provided that he showed Russell how to set up defenses. Even Norton conceded, however, that Russell was a "good handler of kids."[27]

Musial played sparingly his sophomore year. He failed to start until the postseason tournament in March. Afterward, he led the Donora Cubs, a junior class team, to the championship of the Waynesburg tournament where he topped his teammates with ten points in the final contest. That set the stage for Musial's final season as a high school basketball player in his junior year. By then he had approached nearly six feet in height and weighed about 145 pounds, size enough to play the forward position. He had perfected a running left-handed hook and outside set shot. He also drove to the basket well and was a skilled ball handler. No one worked harder. When formal practice ended and the gym lights were dimmed as players departed, Musial remained on the floor alone practicing the same shot or move over and over again. A former teammate, in recalling those winter evenings, concluded that he had been guided by the "example of

26. Joseph "Buddy" Griffey interview, May 24, 1997; James K. Russell obituary, *Pittsburgh Post-Gazette*, May 16, 1995, clipping in possession of Bottonari.
27. Norton interview, May 22, 1997.

a true champion."[28] In time Musial seemed to display a natural grace that made his moves appear effortless.

The 1938 Dragons became the best Donora basketball team of that generation. The team won the Section IV championship for the first time ever and advanced to the Western Pennsylvania Interscholastic League Championship, where it performed dramatically. Despite the town's football tradition, the hoopsters captured the allegiance of Donorans in what turned out to be a special season. The club included the six-foot, big-boned but misnamed "Fats" Norton who played forward; Dick Ercius, a six-foot three-inch, blond-haired football brawler who jumped center; outgoing Florentino "Flo" Garcia, a diminutive speedster at guard from Spanishtown, whose family recently had moved to Donora from McKeesport; and "coach" George Kosko, the floor general "midget" guard who loved to tell teammates what to do. The sixth man was the tall, wiry, and determined black, Grant "Jug" Gray. According to a younger brother, Gray had a temper and could be an intimidator on the basketball court.

Despite starting slowly against non-league competition, the quintet peaked against league foes, including Monongahela, Monessen, and Charleroi, which resulted in a 10–1 league mark by mid-February, giving Donora its first basketball championship ever. At most home games the team played before a packed house. Norton, Musial, and Ercius carried the team in scoring with Norton and Musial topping all scorers in the five sectional leagues of Washington County. In an era when winning basketball teams usually scored no more than 40 points a game, Norton averaged 11 and Musial 10 points per contest. For their overall play, the *Herald-American* selected them to the all-section team along with Ercius. Sports reporters often employed the adjectives "clever" and "sly" in describing Stash's play.

Just before the postseason tournament, Musial contracted a bad cold, which verged on pneumonia, causing the Russells to care for him in their home. According to one of his teammates, Stash had failed to get proper attention because the mother worked and the father was often inebriated. By tournament time Stash had almost fully recovered. The University of Pittsburgh hosted the annual event. The team attended an early afternoon movie near the university campus before going to the Schenley Hotel to eat and rest. The management there told the players that Grant Gray could not stay in one of the private rooms because of his skin color. This caused Flo Garcia to respond to teammates: Gray "was good enough to come to my

28. Leddon to Giglio, November 16, 1997.

house and eat with me; he was good enough to play ball with me. They can go to hell." Musial then asked, "What are you going to do, Flo?" The latter said, "I won't play." "Stash then said," according to Garcia, "I am with you"; Norton concurred, as did the other players.[29] Coach Russell, soon informed, backed his players. To avoid a potentially explosive situation, the facility relented. Even so, it installed a screen in the dining room to separate Gray from his teammates and the other guests. Musial surely recalled the Grant Gray affair some ten years later as he came to terms with Jackie Robinson and the integration of major-league baseball.

As it turned out, Gray played a key role defensively in the first tournament game against undefeated Washington High School. Of the 3,000 fans who attended, some 700 to 800 came from Donora. Musial contributed 10, Ercius 11, and Norton 12 points, the latter making three goals near the end of the game to ensure a 36–31 victory. With 1,000 locals watching, Donora's Cinderella season ended in the next game against powerful Har-Brack. Regardless, the Dragons made it interesting after falling behind 14 to 1 at the end of the first quarter. The stars were Ercius with 14 points, Musial with two interceptions for scores in the fourth quarter, and Garcia, whose basket tied the game in the final minutes to send it to overtime, only to lose 39–33.

The Har-Brack contest concluded Musial's varsity basketball career even though he had one year of high school remaining. His playing minor-league baseball that summer would cost him his eligibility. Musial continued to play basketball for various independent teams, including Charleroi Pharmacy in the Cannonsburg tournament, where he was named to the all-tourney team. Charleroi had been the Dragons' most bitter rival in 1938, the only team to beat them in Section IV competition. Yet their top players successfully courted Musial after the season ended. So unlike Norton and other teammates who played on home teams, Musial went elsewhere. A Charleroi sportswriter soon praised his "all around play that overshadowed everyone else in the tourney. Musial's friendly attitude plus his playing ability made him many friends," the writer concluded.[30] This would not be the last time that Musial would win over the opposition.

From his senior year on, Stash joined several other independent basketball teams sponsored by various Mon Valley merchants. None were more important than Frank Pizzica's Monongahela Garagemen, reputedly the

29. Garcia telephone interview, January 9, 1997; for Musial's cold, ibid. and Norton interview, May 22, 1997. Norton mentioned Russell's concern that Musial "might not get proper care at home."
30. *Donora Herald-American*, February 18, 1938.

finest team in the upper Mon Valley. Decked in green and yellow uniforms, the Garagemen contained seasoned players such as Jim Conte, who had once starred at Monongahela High School. Yet by early 1940 Musial, the youngest team member, became one of the Garagemen's two top stars and often its leading scorer. The *Herald-American* now referred to him as "the best basketball player ever to wear the traditional orange and black" of Donora High.[31]

Frank Americus Pizzica soon became one of Stash's closest friends and a surrogate father. One of thirteen children of Italian parents and the first sibling born in America, Pizzica owned a De Soto–Plymouth dealership in Monongahela in the 1930s; by 1948 his business sold Buicks. Always nattily dressed in coat and tie even in his own home, he had done extremely well in automobile sales. In time he owned an entire block on residential Marne Avenue, where he lived with his wife and two children. Pizzica was a sports enthusiast who probably met Stash when he played baseball with the zinc works team. An extremely generous man, Pizzica took a liking to Musial and wanted to help him. He provided him with clothing and otherwise assisted the Musial family. How much he paid Stan for playing for the Garagemen is unknown. It was Pizzica who goaded Stan to overcome his shyness with strangers. "Keep your head high, look 'em in the eye and give 'em a warm, firm handshake, not a dead fish," he advised. Later, when Musial played for the St. Louis Cardinals in Pittsburgh, Pizzica either entertained Musial and his friends there or had a new Buick with a full tank of gasoline waiting for him at the airport, which Musial drove to Monongahela and Donora. He and roommate Albert "Red" Schoendienst often came to Pizzica's home, where they were treated to Italian cuisine. By that time in his career, whenever he faced important decisions, Musial routinely checked with three or four individuals. Frank Pizzica was one of them.[32]

Close observers have often asserted that Stan Musial was a better basketball than a baseball performer. Ed Musial has made that claim. Clearly he eventually could have had a basketball scholarship at one of the major schools, perhaps at Villanova or the University of Pittsburgh, where Musial later suggested he was recruited. The local newspaper referred to a possible promising collegiate career, but scholarship offers were never reported, probably because Stash was entering only his junior year when

31. Ibid., February 22, 1940.

32. Musial, *Stan Musial*, 29; Cupper interview, May 23, 1997; Garcia telephone interview, June 11, 1997; Norton interview, May 22, 1997.

he signed a professional baseball contract. As good as Musial was on the basketball court, he dominated the baseball diamond even more in his one year of high school ball, which immediately followed the championship basketball season.

The 1938 Musial-led Donora baseball team was the school's first effort since 1923. A number of individuals contributed to its resurrection, but none more so than its first baseball coach, Michael "Ki" Duda. Known as Ki because of his childhood affection for Kaiser Wilhelm of Germany, Duda was the product of a large and impoverished family of Austrian ancestry. A 1927 graduate of Donora High School, he played football at St. Vincent College in western Pennsylvania, where he considered the priesthood until he fell in love with the attractive and vivacious Verna Fincik. He returned to Donora to work in the mill until he accepted a pay cut in 1934 to teach English at the junior high and coach at the high school. The muscular, dark-complexioned six footer rarely said very much; with his peers he usually listened and grinned. Duda was an overachiever; he took graduate courses in the evenings and summers at the University of Pittsburgh, eventually earning his doctorate and becoming district school superintendent and then president of California State College at California, Pennsylvania. As an assistant football coach at Donora, handling Russell's interior line, his philosophy remained simple: "You beat up on the other guy."[33] Duda did not like to lose.

Yet Duda had a warm, caring side. Having no sons, he became especially attached to the players on his teams. Buddy Griffey recalled how much he "loved" Ki Duda. Another former player called him a saint who took him and teammates to camp around Latrobe, Pennsylvania, and to ball games. Ed Musial called him "our second father," "the man I looked for." But Ed also remembered how tough he could be against wrongdoers. When Duda caught him smoking during baseball practice, Ed remembered that he "kicked my fanny all the way up the hill." But no one received Duda's attention more than Stan Musial. "Stan was his project," according to Norton; "he watched him like a guardian." Pado suggested he was like a father to Stan. Duda took Stash everywhere. From high school on, Stash usually did not make a move without consulting Duda.[34]

33. Leddon telephone interview, December 5, 1996. Other information on Duda comes from Sukel interview, May 22, 1997; *Varsity Dragon*, December 17, 1937; Musial, *Stan Musial*, 14.

34. Griffey interview, May 24, 1997; Ed Musial telephone interview, April 10, 1994, conducted by Kreuz; Norton interview, May 22, 1997; Pado telephone interview, May 14, 1994, conducted by Kreuz.

Because of Coach Duda's limited knowledge of baseball, he secured Charles "Chuck" Schmidt of Cement City to assist. No more than two or three years out of high school, Schmidt had starred in the baseball summer league as a shortstop and was considered a pro prospect. Those wearing the white uniforms with orange and black trim of Donora High included youngsters who had competed with Stash since the sixth grade, many of whom remained his friends for life: the blond-haired Eddie Pado, who caught Stash when he pitched and was an outstanding pitcher in his own right, hurling a no-hitter the following season; O'Lenic, a chatterbox who played shortstop with his glove almost off his hand; left-handed Buddy Griffey, an excellent center fielder adept at chasing down long fly balls and running the bases; brother Ed, who played the outfield and first base as a sophomore; the popular, good-looking "Fats" Norton, the 6-foot, 190-pounder at third base and the only senior on the team, who hit home runs whenever he occasionally connected; the light-haired "Billy" Leddon, "the Cement City kid," known for his erratic play and his doubles and triples; and Paul Hendrickson, a sandy-haired, left-handed curveball pitcher of Swedish ancestry, who always wore his hat crooked.[35]

Musial became the linchpin; he had already signed a contract with the St. Louis Cardinals as a pitcher, but remained eligible by not yet playing for pay. He was by far the most mature and accomplished performer on the team, hurling with a quick kick up and release. His assortment of pitches included a superb curveball, a spinless slowball that danced as it approached the plate, and an excellent fastball. When holding runners on base, Musial had the bill of his cap down so low that one could barely see his eyes. First baseman Leddon remembered how terrified he was because he never knew whether Musial was going to rifle it to him or to the plate. His devastating pickoff move began with his leg and upper body committing to the plate while throwing to first base, a procedure minor-league umpires would quickly disallow. As a hitter, he had the unique peek-a-boo stance that he would later demonstrate in the big leagues, except he did not crouch or coil nearly as much. Whenever he waited to bat or pitch he habitually twisted his neck as if to unloosen a kink, a mannerism that remained with him throughout his career.[36]

The 1938 Donora team tied for second in league competition with a 7–3 record (9–3 overall). Poor defensive play kept the Orange and Black

35. Much of what I learned about the baseball team comes from Leddon to Giglio, February 19, 1997, in possession of Giglio.

36. Leddon telephone interview, December 5, 1996; Jim Kreuz, "Musial Records Another Hit at High School Team Reunion," 121.

from capturing the Section VI title. In one of Musial's two losses, in which he limited the opposition to three hits, the team committed five errors. His second defeat was a two-hitter against Monessen in a game also decided by errors. Musial finished with a 4–2 record. His outstanding outings included the opening-day three-hitter against Monessen in which he struck out seventeen and a two-hitter against Monongahela. Musial's only bad performance came against the Charleroi Cougars on May 11 when he gave up five runs in the last inning of a 9–8 win. That shelling caused locals to question Musial's potential as a pitching prospect in professional baseball, which led to newspaper speculation that Musial's arm was hurting. A *Herald-American* sports columnist detected the smell of liniment around Musial and observed his reluctance to use a fastball that lacked its usual smoke. Musial had probably overworked his arm by relieving in most of the games he did not start. Whatever the problem, he finished the season with a victory over Monongahela.[37]

As outstanding as his pitching was, Musial proved to be an even more adept hitter. He led the section with a .455 average and contributed instrumentally to every Donora victory but one with his clutch hitting or his pitching. In only one game did he fail to hit. His most spectacular clout, a game-winning grand slam, came against Monongahela at Legion Field in April. The ball traveled 388 feet on the fly, rolling to the right field fence, 452 feet from home plate. By the time the fielder reached the ball, Musial had already scored. For his hitting efforts he made the all-section team as an outfielder. Pado, the Dragons' only other selection, was chosen as a pitcher despite winning one less game than Musial. In assessing the talent of the Donora High ball club, classmates envisioned three Dragons reaching the major leagues: Musial, Pado, and O'Lenic, whose .353 batting average was the second highest on the team.

As it turned out, only Musial, of course, made it to the big time. For some, World War II drastically altered their lives. Pado enlisted in the navy right after high school, participating in the 1944 invasion of Okinawa. Leddon ended up becoming a career army officer and saw combat duty in three major wars. O'Lenic spent four years in the army, including combat in the European theater with the Eighty-fifth Division.

The most tragic story involved Buddy Griffey, who followed Grant Gray to Kentucky State College on a football scholarship. He played sparingly because they thought "I was too small," Griffey remembered. He returned to Donora in 1939 to work in the mill. He soon married and

37. *Donora Herald-American*, May 11, 1938.

became the father of a girl and four boys, one of whom was Ken Griffey, a future member of the Cincinnati Reds teams that won World Series in 1975 and 1976. In 1952 Buddy abandoned his family for Cleveland, Ohio, where he was promised a better mill job. Griffey later explained that he had tried to bring his family to Cleveland, but his wife refused to come. In any case, the Griffey family momentarily went on welfare, and Mrs. Griffey, who would divorce Buddy, had to rely on domestic work. Community members helped out, especially by providing financial assistance to the children. Local journalist Ed Gray, no relation to Grant Gray, encouraged Kenny to participate in football and baseball. Gray, his first coach, remembered that the mother never missed a game from the time that Kenny, a model youngster, was ten years old. After making the Reds ball club, Ken Griffey often visited Donora but never his father in Cleveland. The estrangement isolated Buddy Griffey not only from Ken, but also from his grandson, Ken Griffey, Jr., of the Cincinnati Reds, who scarcely remembers him.[38]

Of Musial's 1938 teammates, Ed Musial alone embarked on a professional baseball career. As talented in some ways as his brother, he never fulfilled his promise, partly because of a four-year military stint in World War II (Stash would miss only one year of professional baseball due to the war). He found it difficult to live in his brother's shadow, causing him to think less of himself. Whatever the reasons, Ed lacked self-confidence, discipline, and drive. He began to drink excessively and became a notorious "skin" chaser throughout his minor-league career, which did not endear him to the ball clubs who signed him. During four years in the low minor leagues beginning in 1946, he played on nine different teams. His best effort came with Fayetteville of the Coastal Plain League, where he hit .334. In his last year of minor-league competition, he endured an 0 for 52 streak at the plate and still managed to hit .275. Only afterward did his life eventually become more settled following marriage and children. But even then, he lived a sometimes troubled existence in large part because of drinking and health problems.[39]

In contrast, Stash's first exposure to professional baseball had begun even before high school play. He signed a contract with the St. Louis Cardinals' Monessen ball club of the Class D Penn State League on September

38. Garcia telephone interview, January 9, 1997; Griffey interview, May 24, 1997; Ed Gray telephone interview, July 26, 1997.

39. The "skin" expression comes from Ed Musial interview, August 6, 1996; Garcia telephone interview, January 9, 1997; Cupper interview, May 23, 1997.

29, 1937, several months before the start of the aforementioned high school basketball and baseball season and about two months before his seventeenth birthday. Not until February 1938 was the signing made public. Andrew French, the business manager of the Monessen club, had seen Musial play in summer competition. He was impressed enough by Musial's pitching to ask him to appear at Monessen's Page Park for a tryout.

Player-manager Ollie Vanek, a squat, ruddy-faced, and soft-spoken man, conducted the workout. Vanek had been an outstanding hitter prior to sustaining a career-threatening injury. Now in his mid-twenties, he had a good understanding of what it took to be a successful ballplayer. He remembered Musial as looking like a grammar school kid with pink cheeks, clad in a T-shirt, cotton work pants, and canvas sneakers. "He had a pretty fair curve," according to Vanek; "I also liked the way he hit, but believe me, I had no idea that the skinny kid I saw that day would be the Stan Musial [of tomorrow]. He seemed to love to play ball, but he was very shy, almost the sort of kid you'd forget if you didn't look twice at the way he slugged the ball" and pitched.[40] After working out on a couple of occasions, Vanek and French visited Musial's home several times to obtain Lukasz's signature for the underage Musial. Vanek usually waited in the car during these visits.

Exactly what was said is uncertain. The only persons in the room were Stan's parents, French, and sometimes Vanek. Ed Musial came and went during the discussion. The mother did all of the talking for the family, according to Vanek, communicating with Lukasz in Polish. One thing is certain: Lukasz did not want his son playing professional baseball. He was adamant about that. From 1942 on Stash has consistently maintained that Lukasz advised him to accept a basketball scholarship so that he could obtain a college education and make something of himself. That story, first told by *St. Louis Post-Dispatch* sportswriter J. Roy Stockton in 1942 and then repeated many times by Musial and others, is embedded in the Musial lore. Even Vanek has often repeated it.[41]

However inspirational a tale it may be, it is most likely untrue. First of all, most Eastern European immigrant fathers wanted their sons employed in the factories as soon as possible to supplement the family income. Permitting Stash to complete high school was as much education as Lukasz

40. Jack Sher, "The Stan Musial Nobody Knows," 63–64.

41. Ibid., 64; Ollie Vanek interview, December 9, 1996. For the first appearance of the basketball scholarship story, see J. Roy Stockton, "Rookie of the Year," 29.

probably wanted him to have. Indeed, Stash was the only family member
to graduate from high school. Moreover, Stash had not yet really acquitted
himself as a basketball player; consequently, the scholarship argument
could not have been used at this time. Most important, even though
most of them are now dead, there remains the challenging testimony from
teachers, teammates, and others in the community who, talking with Stash
at that time, understood that Lukasz had no thoughts about his son going
to college.

The evidence first surfaced in 1957 when Roger Kahn, writing an article
on Musial for *Sport* magazine, employed a Donora journalist to obtain
background information on Musial. Norma Miller interviewed Duda,
Russell, and many others. She reported to Kahn that Stan's father "was
not anxious to have Stan sign up . . . thinking that Stan should go to work
instead of wasting his time playing ball. Dr. Duda went to Stan's aid
in convincing his father that a baseball career was not a mistake." Even
though Kahn elected to ignore this testimony in his article, others have
confirmed it, including a couple of Musial's classmates, one of whom
claimed that the father said, "go to the mill, get a job, make money and
forget about college." Flo Garcia thought that Lukasz was angry because
Stash would make only sixty-five dollars a month playing baseball. He
could make more than that in the mill, where he would be well treated
as a local sports hero. The initial low salary indeed became a sore point
in the years to come. Vanek remembered Musial's mother, after being
reintroduced to him years later at an affair in honor of Musial, angrily
saying, "Oh, you are the one who wouldn't give him more money."[42]

Conversely, the faculty at Donora High School at first sought to persuade Musial to pursue college because they thought that higher education would provide him with the greatest opportunity for future success.
They customarily did this with other student athletes, many of whom
secured athletic scholarships as Musial could have done. Some of them
also probably wanted Musial to finish out his athletic eligibility at Donora,
which was in jeopardy if he accepted payment from a professional ball
club. Football coach Russell even sought Musial to play in the backfield;
to Russell, he was a natural given his arm strength, his exceptional speed,
and his athleticism. In one of the few times Musial rejected advice from
his male elders, he elected to follow his heart. He probably knew, too,

42. Miller to Kahn, November 1, 1957; Norton interview, May 22, 1997; Garcia
telephone interview, January 9, 1997; Sukel interview, May 22, 1997; Gray telephone
interview, July 26, 1997. For Vanek's comment, Vanek interview, December 9, 1996.

that he would have a difficult time academically since he was avoiding the college preparatory courses and had little interest in school. Stash credited Miss Helen Kloz, the school librarian, for advising him to pursue his dream. If college was not part of it, she insisted, he should put it aside. Duda soon reasoned that he could always go to school while playing ball. In the end, Lukasz reluctantly relented, even though it took tears from Stash and Mary's pleading for it to happen. In the final scene, with French present, as described in Musial's own contrived story, Mary supposedly asked, "Lukasz, why did you come to America?" In broken English, he responded, "Because it's a free country, that's why." Yes, said Mary, "and in America a boy is free not to go to college, too." It was then, according to Musial, that his father signed.[43]

If Lukasz's opposition to the signing had nothing to do with a college education for his son, why did Stash repeatedly offer that explanation? One possible reason was his immense pride and sensitivity; he wanted everyone to think well of his family. His manufactured story provided a romantic backdrop to his rise. One could easily admire an immigrant father seeking for his son what he could not obtain for himself. Probably, too, Musial felt enormous guilt for defying his father, which caused the latter not to speak to Stan for "a few years." He wanted to make his father feel better about himself following Stan's subsequent success with the Redbirds. In any case, Musial came to confess regret for not obtaining a college education, and to a feeling of inferiority because of that deficiency. Consequently, his messages to young people always included the importance of higher education.[44]

All indications are that Stan soon had mixed feelings about playing in the Cardinals system. One reason for this was the harsh action that major-league baseball commissioner Judge Kenesaw Landis had taken against Cards general manager Branch Rickey in March 1938. Landis made free agents of seventy-four low-classification Cardinal farmhands because of Rickey's illegal ownership of more than one ball club in the same minor league. This did not directly affect Musial, but he undoubtedly heard criticism that the Cardinals represented an outlaw organization, one that probably would not treat him well. Musial's paltry signing figure did nothing to inspire confidence. By mid-April the local newspaper reported

43. For Musial's account, Musial, *Stan Musial*, 17–22. That anecdote originated in Stockton's 1942 article, "Rookie of the Year," 29. Stockton, who knew the value of a good story, could have embellished it. Bob Broeg interview, April 1, 2000.
44. Carew, "He's a 'Cardinal' Too!" 11; Musial, *Stan Musial*, 17.

that Musial had about made up his mind to pitch for the zinc works instead of a St. Louis farm team, probably also a momentary attempt to appease a father who remained critical of the signing decision.[45]

On May 11, however, another *Herald-American* press account indicated that Musial would play for the Cardinals after all and was scheduled to leave for a Georgia training camp on June 5 before assignment to the Albany, Georgia, farm team. For some reason, Musial failed to report and instead awaited the arrival of a Yankee scout for a tryout. A couple of days later, on June 9, it was rumored that he had inked a contract with Newark, a Yankee farm club. The columnist, in disbelief, reminded readers that he could not sign with another team until the Cards released him. It got worse the following day when the newspaper reported that he was working out with the Pittsburgh Pirates. Irv Weiss, a local businessman, had driven Musial to Forbes Field, then the ballpark for the Pirates, where he met childhood idol Pie Traynor, no longer an active player. A local reporter found a red-faced Musial on the field amid several young ladies who sought his autograph. He informed friends that he did not intend to abide by his Cardinal contract. Whether he sought a release is unknown. After several tryout sessions the Pirates apparently discussed a minor-league contract with Musial until the latter confessed that he had already signed with the Cardinals. At that point the Pirates lost interest. Besides, that organization had reservations about him anyway because of his supposed scrawniness.[46]

Musial's behavior in this period is inexplicable despite his apparent questioning of his Redbirds decision. His later defense that he had not recently heard from the Cards and consequently thought that they had forgotten him does not ring true because the *Herald-American* reported more than once that the Cardinals were arranging for his assignment. So, this episode may have involved a momentarily confused seventeen-year-old who listened this time to some bad advice from locals who either desired that he play for the nearby Pirates, wanted him to make more money, or had reservations about the Cardinals organization.

45. Donald Ray Andersen, "Branch Rickey and the St. Louis Cardinals System: The Growth of an Idea," 131; Musial, *Stan Musial*, 24; *Donora Herald-American*, April 20, 1938.

46. For Stan's wavering, see *Donora Herald-American*, May 11, June 10, 17, 1938. The columnist, Hal Lauerman, today is a retired public relations executive in Donora, who claims to remember nothing about Musial reassessing his contract with the Cardinals. Hal Lauerman interview, May 22, 1997. The scrawniness statement comes from Cupper interview, May 23, 1997.

Another possible consideration occurred in the midst of Musial's successful high school baseball season and on the eve of the tryout controversy. John Bunardzya, a Donora sportswriter who wanted the Pirates to sign Musial, took him to Pittsburgh for his first major-league game. The Giants defeated the Pirates that day, but Musial remembered beautiful Forbes Field, including tree-covered Schenley Park, which graced the area beyond the red-brick left-field wall. Going home from the game, he might have fantasized about the possibilities of playing for the beloved Pirates. After watching a few innings that day, he had told Bunardzya, "I think I can hit big league pitching," but he felt much less confident about his hurling ability.[47]

Soon after the Pirate tryouts, Musial agreed to report to the Cardinals' Williamson, West Virginia, Class D ball club of the Mountain State League as a pitcher instead of to neighboring Greensburg, Pennsylvania, of the Penn State Association, where he was slated to go. He requested an assignment further from Donora in the event he failed. At least he could do so without having local rooters witness it.

47. Musial, *Stan Musial*, 23–24.

Rickey's Farm

M usial's departure for Williamson closely preceded the resurgence of the St. Louis Cardinals, who were slowly retooling from the glory days of the Gashouse Gang in the mid-1930s. In 1938 the Cards would finish only sixth in the eight-team National League, but the following year they would come in second. Much of the credit belonged to Branch Rickey, the scholarly, colorful, and sagacious general manager who originated and managed the Cardinal farm system, which was producing stars such as Enos Slaughter and Johnny Mize. Rickey dictated that the organization yield annually at least eight players of major-league caliber. What the Cardinals could not use, Rickey sold to other ball clubs to offset organizational costs as well as to provide him with a percentage of the sale. By the end of the 1930s the farm system contained thirty-two teams, ranging from Rochester, Columbus, and Sacramento in Double A ball down to the twenty ball clubs at Class D level. The Cardinals owned fifteen of the teams and had working arrangements with the rest, including Williamson, which was municipally owned. With fourteen minor-league teams each, the New York Yankees and the St. Louis Browns came the closest to matching the Cardinals. Given the more than five hundred minor-league ballplayers in the Cardinal chain, Musial's chances of rising to the majors from Williamson, at the depths of the system, remained slim at best.[1]

Williamson, the county seat of Mingo County, hugged the West Virginia–Kentucky border about 240 miles southwest of Donora. Most of its ninety-four hundred inhabitants drew their income from the more than one hundred coal mines in the area. Coal was so dominant that one of Williamson's public buildings, the Coal House, had side walls constructed of that substance. The weekends brought hardworking, raucous mountaineers to town to frequent the saloons and let off steam. Aside from the bars, the movie theater, the pool parlor, and the baseball park, Williamson offered little else to do.

The Class D Williamson Colts of the Mountain State League competed against teams within a 110-mile radius of the town, ranging from Bluefield,

1. Donald Ray Andersen, "Branch Rickey and the St. Louis Cardinals System: The Growth of an Idea," 138–39, 161.

a railroad town, on the Virginia border to tiny Ashland, Kentucky, along the Ohio River. Traveling to the games involved navigating the hilly, curvy roads either in a bus or in cars owned by players. Because weekday games took place at night, that meant returning home in the early hours of the morning, since the club provided no overnight allowances except for games at Huntington, easily the league's most populous community at seventy-five thousand. Aside from practice, the players found little to occupy their days. Musial claimed he shot so much pool that he felt like Minnesota Fats.

From the moment of his departure from Donora, Musial became so homesick that he questioned his decision to play professional baseball. Being greeted at the Williamson bus station by E. S. Hamilton, the team's general manager, only partly assuaged his loneliness. Adjusting to professional baseball even at the Class D level added to the challenge and frustration, particularly since he joined the team a month after the baseball season had begun. The team's player-manager, the hawk-nosed, tobacco-chewing, and salty Nat Hickey, had been a professional basketball player for the Boston Celtics in the 1920s in addition to playing minor-league baseball. Hickey took a liking to the hardworking and quiet Musial.

In the weeks ahead Hickey showed considerable patience in handling the southpaw pitcher. In his first outing on July 1 against the Huntington Bengals, Musial allowed four hits and four runs in three innings. He was wild, and he committed several balks by relying on his pickoff move from high school. Obviously, he had much to learn about pitching. Hickey nevertheless continued to pitch Musial, who won his next game. For the remainder of the campaign Musial threw erratically, either winning with little difficulty or collapsing in the early innings as a starter or in late innings in relief. In one August contest he failed to survive the first inning. By early September he started some games in center field because of his occasional hitting as a pitcher.[2]

Despite its mediocre 58–60 third-place finish, Williamson qualified for the postseason President's Cup playoff. In the third game of a deadlocked series against Logan, Musial went nearly four innings before leaving the mound with the score at 5–5. He finished in center field, going hitless at the plate, in a losing effort, which ended the season. Overall, his pitching record mirrored the performance of the team. He had a 6–6 won-loss record and a 4.66 earned run average (ERA), walking a whopping 80

---

2. Musial, *Stan Musial*, 26–28. All statistical data came from the local newspapers of the minor league teams for which Musial played.

batters in 110 innings. In 62 at bats, he hit only .258, partly due to the dismal "candle lighting" that prevailed in Class D ball. Wid Matthew, Rickey's emissary, filed a charitable report on Musial with the home office, stating: "Arm good. Good fast ball, good curve. Poise. Good hitter. A real prospect."[3]

On September 8 Musial returned home for his high school senior year with the satisfaction that he had more than survived his first year of professional competition. He had even managed to save a little money from his monthly salary. Hickey recalled fondly that Musial had not only sent ten dollars a month home to his mother but also attended Mass regularly and had made novenas, a Roman Catholic prayer ritual lasting nine days. In Donora he now occupied much of his nonschool time with Lil, working in the Labash grocery store, playing basketball for the Pizzica Garagemen, and pitching for the zinc works team in the spring of 1939. He and Lil shared social time with young faculty families from the high school, especially the Dudas. Ki had written Musial encouraging letters during that trying first season in minor-league ball.[4]

Musial became so anxious to begin minor-league competition in 1939 that he asked Lil to stand in for him at his high school graduation. In June Musial received instructions to depart for Albany, Georgia, a Class D team in the Georgia-Florida League. At the last moment Albany optioned him to Williamson, which had a new ballpark and manager, Harrison Wickel, a soft-spoken shortstop, who inherited an improved team. Musial, feeling more certain of himself, shared an apartment at the Mountaineer Hotel with three teammates, including outfielder Walt Sessi, a fellow Mon Valley product, who would later hit a key home run for the St. Louis Cardinals in the 1946 pennant race.

Despite occasional wildness, Musial, wearing the new baseball shoes Ki Duda had given him, got off to a great start, winning his first three games and helping his own cause by getting key hits. By the end of June he also occasionally played in the outfield. Then the "Keystone Kid," as the local newspaper called him, faced a series of reversals that made him a part-time player until late in the season. In early July he walked twelve men against Ashland; this was followed by an 8–5 loss to Huntington where he walked ten and struck out twelve. In his next start in late July he walked five and threw three wild pitches in five innings. After that game he did not pitch regularly again until the end of August. The *Donora Herald-American*

3. Ibid., 28.
4. Jack Rawlings, ed., *The Sporting News Stan Musial Scrapbook from 1941 to 1963*, 43.

reported that he had suffered from a "nervous and run-down condition," which the Williamson paper more accurately labeled a sore arm. Musial had suffered occasional arm and shoulder problems since high school, aggravated by being thrown into a wall in a high-school basketball game. His late-season hitting, more than his pitching, contributed to the Colts winning the Mountain League championship.[5]

In the first round of the postseason playoffs against Huntington, Musial pitched two successive games, winning both, even though he gave up eleven walks in seven innings in the second outing. Against Bluefield in the postseason finals, Musial went five for six with two home runs and five runs batted in in the second game, easily his best hitting performance of the season. But neither he nor his teammates could sustain the good play in the final two games with Musial playing in the field, and Bluefield won the series.

Musial's regular-season statistics showed some improvement from 1938: he finished with a 9–3 record and a 4.30 earned run average. Yet he appeared in fewer games and averaged more than eight bases on balls per nine innings, only one less on average than he fanned. He tied for fourth best among Colt starters in wins. Manager Harrison Wickel filed the only known report on Musial to the Cardinals home office. It had come in mid-July at the height of Musial's pitching problems, and its exaggerated tone reflected the manager's impatience: "This boy is quite a problem. He is by far the wildest pitcher I have ever seen. He hasn't pitched a complete game here in ages and he must average at least 10 walks a game. He has fair stuff and at times he has a good fast ball and a pretty good curve. He will strike out just as many as he will walk, but I certainly can't depend on him, and most of the games he has won we have given him a dozen or more runs. . . . I recommend his release because I don't believe he will ever be able to find the plate." Despite the finality of the last statement, Wickel felt compelled to say more: "I don't think he has enough stuff to get by. I've noticed that when he does get the ball over, he is hit rather freely, and I am led to believe that his wildness is his effectiveness. The opposition never gets anything good to hit. The only place he can pitch is Class D, where the player strikes at almost anything a pitcher tosses up there. I am at a loss to say definitely what to do with him. He has the best of habits and is a fine boy."[6]

5. *Donora Herald-American*, August 24, 1939; *Williamson Daily News*, August 23, 1939.

6. Musial, *Musial*, 30.

Wickel said nothing about Musial's hitting, which resulted in a .352 average, fourth best on the team, an indication that he might make it on his batting ability. By September he often played in the outfield following an injury to one of the regulars. In short, while Musial showed progress from 1938, the results were mixed. Nevertheless, he was doing exactly what he wanted to do—and it showed. A sports editor for the *Williamson Daily News* asserted that he was "one of the best-liked ball players ever to hit Williamson." And he adjusted well enough to the community that he seemed content to stay. He wrote Duda, however, that his mother wanted him to come home. All of this suggests that his relationship with Lil might have momentarily waned.[7]

When Musial returned to Donora in September he found the town booming following a bituminous coal strike that spring. More than that, mounting war clouds in Europe, following Germany's invasion of Poland, along with Japan's continued aggression in China, led to war contracts at home as the United States began to increase her military might. At the same time the process of unionizing the mills, part of a nationwide phenomenon since the mid-1930s, had about run its course. The zinc works, the *Herald-American* reported, was almost 100 percent unionized by the spring of 1940. Production and wages had hit new levels for the 1930s; for Donorans the Depression had ended.[8]

Musial had plenty of opportunity to work after his homecoming, either in the Labash grocery store or in the mill. Joe Barbao probably placed him in the zinc works that fall, where he was employed during the off-season during the war years. Although most workers usually faced arduous and sometimes dangerous duties, management treated Musial well. He did no hard physical labor, and supervisors kept him from the smoke. He also continued to play basketball that winter for the Garagemen and Cy's Men's Store and drew closer to Lil. They might have even talked about marriage. Also, by 1939 Ed Musial had left home to work in a CCC camp.[9]

As spring approached the nineteen-year-old Musial eagerly anticipated the approaching baseball season. For the first time he would play a full season. The Albany ball club, which owned his contract and had optioned him to Williamson in 1939, now sold him to Asheville, North Carolina, of the Class B Piedmont League. Following spring training for Cardinal

7. *Donora Herald-American*, September 28, 1939; Stan Musial to Ki Duda, September 2, 1939, in possession of Veronica Duda.

8. *Donora Herald-American*, August 7, November 21, 1939, May 8, 1940.

9. Garcia telephone interview, July 9, 1997.

Class B and C clubs at Columbus, Georgia, Asheville optioned him to the Class D team in Daytona Beach, Florida. His salary rose from seventy to one hundred dollars a month, but the demotion proved a disappointment to Musial, who, believing he could pitch at B level, felt that he was given no chance of making the Asheville club.

Even so, despite the greater distance from Donora and Lil, Daytona Beach was a veritable paradise next to grimy Williamson. Known for its triple waterfront, along with its magnificent ocean beach of white sand, Daytona had become a major resort community. More than sixteen thousand inhabitants lived there, some in exotic houses of Italian Renaissance, Mediterranean, or Spanish colonial design, which were, of course, totally unlike anything in Donora. Huge live oak, magnolia, and bay trees, along with native palms, graced many of the residential streets. Oleander shrubs, with their long-lasting pink and white blossoms, also blanketed most of the neighborhoods. Daytona's underside included a sizable number of underpaid workers. Many of the community's blacks, who constituted 33 percent of the population, worked at the resort hotels as cooks, waiters, and bellboys. Otherwise, they served as domestics or occupied other menial jobs. This represented Musial's first exposure to a completely segregated society, which dictated separate drinking fountains and restrooms in public areas, including ballparks.

The Daytona Islanders competed in the Florida State League, an eight-team league that stretched across northeast Florida, including teams in DeLand, Sanford, Leesburg, Ocala, Orlando, Gainesville, and charming St. Augustine, the oldest permanent white settlement in the United States. As difficult as road games were by buses, Musial must have marveled at the flat, agriculturally rich terrain and the other novel scenes while making the circuit. Indeed, Musial, writing to the Dudas, acknowledged that he enjoyed playing in Florida.

Fortuitously, the manager of the Islanders was the unusually kind and capable Richard Kerr, small in stature but large in heart and integrity, who would have a great impact on Musial at a crucial time in his minor-league career. The forty-seven-year-old Kerr had pitched for the Chicago White Sox as a rookie in 1919. The left-hander from St. Louis not only won thirteen games for the pennant-winning Sox but also garnered two victories in the World Series even though eight teammates, including Shoeless Joe Jackson and Eddie Cicotte, had collaborated with gamblers to fix the series. Despite Kerr's heroics, which brought him national attention, and despite his twenty-one and nineteen wins in 1920 and 1921, respectively, the notoriously cheap Sox owner Charles Comiskey refused to elevate Kerr's salary in 1922. Kerr ended up holding out, leading to a lengthy suspension; by the time he returned in 1925 his skills had deteriorated.

Still, Kerr apparently held no bitterness toward organized baseball. He remained positive as a Class D manager and helped Musial with his pitching immediately upon his arrival. Musial later claimed that Kerr had taught him concentration, control, and how to use his legs for more leverage on the mound. Musial's curveball improved markedly under Kerr's tutelage. Knowing of Musial's hitting prowess at Williamson, which was confirmed in the batting cage in Daytona, Kerr soon worked Musial into the outfield. Given the fourteen-player rosters of D ball, one or two pitchers usually played regularly in the field. At Daytona Beach, Musial usually played right field, and right-handed thrower Jack Creel occupied center; whenever Creel pitched, Musial moved to center field. Creel remembered Musial as "always laughing and playing tricks on people. He kept everyone on their toes and alert. . . . Nobody wanted to be the butt of his jokes." In this way did he slowly learn to overcome some of his shyness. But, at the same time, Creel recognized his competitiveness. Since Creel could outsprint him, Musial challenged him to a foot race every few days. "He did not like to lose," Creel recalled. Kerr saw those same traits as he witnessed the amount of time Musial spent in the batting cage and elsewhere practicing. Kerr became more certain about Musial's character in spring training when the ballplayer came into the hotel lobby around seven in the morning. Immediately expecting the worst, Kerr asked, "Where you been? Roaming?" "No sir," Musial responded, "I'm coming from Mass."[10]

That response only reinforced Kerr's decision to take Lil and Musial into his home following Lil's arrival in Daytona Beach in May. By then Kerr and his wife, Cora, known affectionately as "Pep," understood Musial's financial difficulties, particularly the anticipated medical expenses. At the time Lil was six months pregnant. What prevented them from getting married in Donora sometime prior to spring training is unknown. Given the mores of Eastern European families of that era, their situation must have caused some hand-wringing in the two families. The Musials have understandably concealed this matter, probably initially to protect their young son, but also undoubtedly because it conflicted with their religiosity as well as Stan's role-model image.

10. Jack Creel to James N. Giglio, August 24, 1996, January 21, 1997, in possession of Giglio; Irv Goodman, *Stan, the Man, Musial,* 33.

They filed for a marriage license on May 23, 1940. They were married two days later at St. Paul's Roman Catholic Church in Daytona Beach, with Dick and Cora serving as witnesses. Lil wore a chiffon pastel pink dress with pastel blue accessories and a shoulder corsage of white oleanders. In early August she gave birth to Richard Stanley Musial, named, of course, after Dick Kerr. The team gave the Musials a baby carriage, and the fans provided a playpen and baby clothes. Cora Kerr also drove Lil to the home ball games, where they sat in the car to view the competition. The Musials never forgot the Kerrs' kindness; years later they provided them with the use of a house in Houston where Dick had labored as a construction company timekeeper since World War II. When Kerr died of cancer in May 1963 the Musials attended the funeral. More immediately, in 1940 when a teammate made a derogatory comment about Kerr, Musial, who rarely showed anger, had to be pulled off of him.[11]

Musial played his heart out for Kerr in 1940. His performance for the Islanders surpassed his previous efforts at Williamson. On the mound, he steadily grew sharper as the season progressed even though he never was Daytona's top pitcher as later reported; the staff ace was Creel, who won twenty-one games and later hurled briefly for the St. Louis Cardinals in 1945. Musial's major problem continued to be his wildness, which resulted in eight or nine walks in bad outings. Still, his 18–5 mark and 2.62 ERA (second to Creel) qualified him as the league's best southpaw pitcher. He hit and played the outfield superbly; his line drives, sprayed to all fields, won several key games as he batted .311 in 405 plate appearances.

Musial's overall play contributed to the Islanders' resurgence beginning in late June, when the team found itself fourteen games out of first place. In July the Islanders prevailed in thirteen consecutive games, Creel won ten straight, Musial began a lengthy hitting streak, and Kerr brought the club together by getting rid of a troublesome player. On August 9, on Dickie Kerr night, the team had reached the top of the standings by beating

11. For the Musials' wedding, see *Donora Herald-American*, June 6, 1940; for Richard Musial's birth, *Donora Herald-American*, August 14, 1940. See also Application for Marriage License, May 22, 1940, Volusia County, Florida, book N, 160, and Marriage License, May 25, 1940, Volusia County, C. J. no. 5074, copies of which were obtained from the circuit court, Deland, Florida. In his autobiography and in earlier interviews, Musial claimed that he and Lil were secretly married on his birthday in 1939. Musial, *Musial*, 31. Contrary to myth, the Musials did not give the Kerrs title to a house; it remained in the Musials' name from 1958 to 1964 until sold by them. Harris County Tax Office records, copies in possession of Giglio. For Musial's anger, see *St. Louis Post-Dispatch*, May 7, 1963, clipping in Musial Collection, National Baseball Library, Cooperstown, New York.

the first-place Sanford Seminoles as Musial captured his sixteenth victory. On that glorious evening the fans presented Kerr with a one-hundred-dollar war bond and Musial with baby gifts.

Two days later, on August 11, the euphoria abruptly ended in the second game of a doubleheader against Orlando. With Creel on the mound and Musial in center field, the batter hit a sinking low liner to left center, which a diving Musial attempted to snare. His somersault technique, which he had mastered as a youngster, betrayed him when his spikes caught the ground, causing his left shoulder to hit the turf hard. He felt immediate pain, and a knot soon emerged on the shoulder. Following X rays, which seemed to confirm that he had suffered a bad bruise, Musial underwent heat treatments. He missed one start before coming back to pitch against Ocala, winning 4–3, but he felt shoulder soreness and was not able to throw hard. The next day he made a brief appearance in the All-Star game in center field despite his selection as a pitcher. His last mound appearance came in the Shaughnessy playoffs against underdog Orlando; Musial gave up six walks and seven hits in four innings. Although he hit well against Orlando, the Islanders lost the series when Creel suffered a disappointing 2–1 loss in the final game, in which Musial tripled and scored the team's only run.[12]

The Musials remained in Daytona Beach after the season, and Stan worked in the sporting goods department of a Montgomery Ward store for twenty-five dollars a week. His major concern remained his left shoulder, which still bothered him. Surely he must have pondered the dim prospects of having to leave professional baseball and return to Donora to seek factory work. His father had already run into one of his high school friends in the Donora downtown area, saying "I told you he made a mistake." In this period Musial nevertheless received considerable support from Donorans such as Ki Duda, who often wrote to him. None spoke with more authority than Kerr, who reminded Musial that he hit more confidently than he pitched. Kerr offered encouragement that he could make it as a position player. How close was Musial to quitting in 1940? According to Musial, it never entered his mind. He and Lil were surviving on the one-hundred-dollar monthly minor-league salary. He told one reporter, he

12. Creel confirmed the particulars of the injury as Musial remembered them in his autobiography. Creel to Giglio, January 5, 1997, in possession of Giglio. Creel always believed that it was "a combination of the injury and [Musial's] control problems" that ended Musial's pitching career. For local coverage of Musial's fall, see the *Daytona Beach Morning Journal*, August 13, 1941.

later recalled, that he would play even in a mythical E league if necessary to stay in the game that he loved so much.[13]

Not knowing the extent of his injury, the Cardinals elevated Musial to the Columbus Red Birds Double A club, which purchased his contract. According to the existing rules, if Musial had not been promoted he could have been drafted from the Cardinal farm system by another major-league team. Consequently, Musial would attend spring training with the class AA and A players in Hollywood, Florida. There the professorial-appearing, bespectacled Burt Shotton, the skipper of the Columbus Red-birds, who later managed the Brooklyn Dodgers to two National League pennants, quickly determined that Musial failed to throw the ball hard and accurately enough to make it as a pitcher. But Musial's hitting impressed him. In one practice game, with Rickey in attendance, Musial slammed several line drives, causing Rickey to comment, "By Judas Priest! That man's not a pitcher. He's an outfielder." But outfielders must do more than hit. Musial had most of the necessary skills to play in the field, but could he regain his arm strength? Shotton recommended that he be sent down and tried as an outfielder.[14]

What followed represented one of Musial's two most frustrating periods in professional baseball. At first the Cardinals mistakenly sent him to Albany, Georgia, where Class D rookie and second-year players trained, before ordering him to Columbus, Georgia, the Class B and C camp. Musial became one of several ballplayers awaiting assignment or possible release. The latter remained a real possibility because the Cardinals customarily lost patience with ballplayers who failed to show significant progress in the lower minor leagues. And Musial at this point was "damaged goods." Understanding the situation, Musial felt the pressure. In one squad game, Jack Creel, who roomed with him, struck him out. Creel remembered that "he was very cool to me for a couple of days" until Creel made light of the incident.[15]

On another occasion, Clay Hopper, the manager of the Columbus, Georgia, club, needing left-handed pitching, used Musial in relief against the barnstorming St. Louis Cardinals despite Musial's pleas that he no longer pitched. He found himself facing the Cards after they had scored six runs in the first inning. Even though he retired the side with no further

13. Garcia telephone interview, January 9, 1997; Musial, *Musial*, 36.
14. Arthur Daley, "Mr. Musial Marches On," 83; Musial, *Musial*, 37–38.
15. Ollie Vanek telephone interview, December 31, 1997; Creel to Giglio, August 24, 1997.

damage, he yielded colossal home runs to Terry Moore and Mize in the second inning. He then pitched three scoreless innings, causing Hopper to throw him against the Phillies a few days later. In that relief outing he surrendered four hits, six walks, two wild pitches, and seven runs. Only at this point did the Cardinal brass at Columbus realize the correctness of Shotton's appraisal.[16]

Fortunately for Musial, he ran into a familiar face at Columbus. Player-manager Ollie Vanek, largely responsible for Musial's 1937 signing, was putting his new ball club—the Springfield, Missouri, Cardinals of the Class C Western Association—through its paces. Musial walked up to him, saying, "Mr. Vanek, can I speak to you [for] a minute?" "Sure kid. What's on your mind?" Vanek replied. As Vanek recalled the remainder of the conversation, Musial continued, "Do you remember me?" Vanek: "I know you from somewhere. I just can't place where, though." Musial: "Stan Musial from Donora." "I remember you now," Vanek replied. "You've grown up some. What class you playing in?" "Class D," Musial said, "Last year with Daytona." "Oh sure," replied Vanek, "I heard something about you." At this point, Musial, with tears in his eyes, asked, "Will you give me a chance on your ball club?" Vanek said he could work out with the team.

Yet Musial, given his arm problems, did not impress any of the Cardinals' B-level minor-league managers. Vanek remembered Rickey's presence at that meeting as the rosters for Class C players were being filled. Vanek recalled that he was one of two managers who volunteered to take Musial. Rickey gave him the nod. Vanek intended, he later said, to play Musial at first base. Conversely, Rickey remembered Vanek wailing when the former suggested Musial to him, "Please, Mr. Rickey, don't let me take him. I need good arms in the outfield with my pitchers." Given Rickey's propensity for taking credit for every organizational success, Vanek's account seems closer to the truth. Musial himself failed to clarify the contradictory stories. While his autobiography favored Vanek's testimony, he had earlier said that "I always tried . . . to impress [Mr. Rickey] after he had pleaded with Springfield to take me on trial." Vanek later denied the very plausible assertion that he had extracted a promise from Rickey that he would receive a replacement as soon as a healthy pitcher or outfielder became available. Contemporary evidence aside, he would have been derelict had he not sought such an arrangement. No one had expected that Musial would blossom into such an exceptional player during his

16. Musial, *Musial*, 38.

Springfield stay, which catapulted him to the major leagues by the end of the 1941 season.[17]

Vanek's team rolled into Springfield's Frisco Station on April 27 amid a crowd of 150 backers. The Queen City of the Ozarks, in the southwest corner of the state, was Missouri's fourth-largest metropolis with a population of sixty-three thousand. The Frisco and Missouri Pacific Railroads employed about one-fifth of the city's workers. Others labored in the furniture factories and planing mills and for a wagon manufacturer, drawing on the oak, hickory, pine, and walnut timber brought in from nearby rural areas. Dairy and poultry farms abounded, whose bounty Springfield converted into butter, cheese, dressed poultry, and dried eggs. The city's flour and feed mills and its bakeries absorbed the region's grain. On the debit side, the city lacked major industries other than the railroads, which were hard hit by the Great Depression. By 1940 laborers were leaving Springfield for defense jobs elsewhere. Consequently, the economic situation made it difficult to support minor-league baseball.

The arriving Springfield team was a superbly conditioned unit, soon to be reduced to the league maximum of fifteen ballplayers. Vanek praised two of his outfielders, Musial, who had hit well in spring training, and Roy Broome, the reticent left fielder. The right-handed Broome was not only a good hitter but also had a gun for an arm. Vanek planned to start Musial in right field, after briefly considering him for first base until realizing that first sacker Harold "Buck" Bush was too slow for the outfield. Vanek thought he could best protect Musial's arm by assigning him the short right-field area. Vanek positioned himself in center field. In 1940 he had hit .324 for Springfield after taking over the ball club late in the season. At twenty-eight he remained a proven performer and a patient, intense, and capable manager, well liked by his players.

The club's other strength rested in its pitching. Ralph Scheef, a lean 6-feet 1-inch right-hander, proved to be the best-looking pitcher in camp. Following his 14–6 record at Worthington in 1940 and his spring performance, the Cardinals rated him a top prospect. The lanky, red-haired "Lefty" Lloyd Hopkins, who had a 15–11 record for the 1940 Springfield

17. Vanek interview, December 9, 1996. Vanek told Jack Sher essentially the same story in 1949. Sher, "The Stan Musial Nobody Knows," 65. Vanek telephone interview, November 28, 1996; undated and untitled report on Musial, Stan Musial folder, Speeches and Writing File, Box 128, Branch Rickey Papers, Library of Congress, Washington, D.C.; Musial, *Musial*, 40; Arthur Mann, *Branch Rickey: American in Action,* 210. The replacement story was first told by J. Roy Stockton, "The Unusual Mr. Musial," 21; Vanek denied it in the December 9, 1996, interview.

team, was known for his pinpoint control and wicked curveball. The third starter, Sylvester "Blix" Donnelly, who possessed an exceptional curveball and fastball and would later be a St. Louis Cardinals World Series hero in 1944, had shown considerable promise with a 19–4 record at Daytona Beach one year prior to Musial's arrival in 1940. But illness and poor conditioning had caused him to fall to 7–13 at Springfield in 1940. Knuckleballer Al Papai, another future major leaguer, rounded out the staff.

The best of the remaining players included Dale Hackett, a rangy shortstop who had hit over .300 for Worthington in the Class D Western League the preceding season; Harold Olt, the third baseman and a last-minute acquisition who had batted over .300 for Cambridge in the Eastern Shore D league the preceding season; John Dantonio, soon to be labeled the league's best catcher, a future major leaguer, and Musial's closest friend on the ball club; and the muscular first baseman, Bush, who had hit for power in previous seasons. Also very much a part of the ball club was a fifteen-year-old South Side Catholic High School phenom catcher from St. Louis, whom Rickey concealed in Springfield from opposing major league scouts: Joe Garagiola, the future St. Louis Cardinal catcher and sports broadcaster. The prank-filled and jovial Garagiola assisted the groundskeeper, washed socks, caught batting practice, and shined shoes for the team.

In 1941 eight clubs, including the Cardinals, made up the Western Association. Joplin (Missouri), Topeka (Kansas), and Muskogee (Oklahoma) figured to be the league's best, followed by Fort Smith (Arkansas), Salina (Kansas), Hutchinson (Kansas), and St. Joseph (Missouri), whose franchise moved to Carthage (Missouri) in midseason. Opponents expected little from the Springfield team following its poor 1940 performance. The name Musial meant nothing to the opposition.

The 1941 Cardinals played their home games at White City Park on Springfield's north side at the corner of Division and Boonville. The park contained wooden grandstands on both sides of the infield. Aside from special promotions, which could boost the crowd to more than twenty-five hundred, the attendance stood in the two hundred to one thousand range. Even on the best of nights, very few of the city's blacks (3 percent of Springfield's population) attended games of the lily-white Western Association.

Even though the well-watered grass infield was excellent, the overall poor quality of the White City grounds made outfielding difficult. The inadequate lighting for night games, a common problem of minor-league baseball, contributed to fielding and hitting lapses. The park also had an unusual squared layout in which the left-field foul line extended to 365 feet, angling to 460 feet in center field, where the fence came to a point before it cut sharply inward to the right-field line only 300 feet from home plate. The short right field invited a number of home run balls, which sometimes smacked into the trollies going up and down Boonville Avenue.[18]

Vanek spent each morning working on Musial's fielding. He was the only player on the club who asked Vanek for extra fielding practice. Musial initially had difficulty judging liners hit directly at him. He usually broke inward too quickly, only to see a rising ball sail over his head. He also sought to compensate for his weak arm by charging ground balls too fast on the bumpy field. According to a former teammate, Musial began the season with the "worst arm on the team," which he soon rectified by throwing long in practice. Vanek also taught him a stretching exercise for his arm, which had restored Vanek's own limb to 85 percent strength. Vanek, an excellent hitting instructor, offered Musial only one suggestion to improve his batting. He noticed that Musial, when ready to hit, cocked his head so that his eyes were not level to the ground, causing him to uppercut the ball. Vanek instructed him to keep his head level and his eyes parallel to the turf.[19]

The heavy, baggy flannel uniforms Musial and his teammates wore displayed the two familiar Redbirds on the shirt front, hand-me-downs from the Cardinal organization. They provided little comfort on hot summer days, especially when leftover cleaning fluid caused a burning sensation

18. Max Raper, who pitched for the 1942 Springfield Cardinals, commented on the field conditions. Max Raper interview, September 20, 1995. Frank Mancuso, catcher for the 1941 Carthage team and the St. Louis Browns during the mid-1940s, referred to the inadequate lighting. Frank Mancuso telephone interview, November 14, 1995. The field dimensions, excluding the right-field line, which was mentioned as 300 feet in the contemporary press, are based on the best guesstimate. The author accepts team secretary Mary Jean Ferguson's and former Springfield Cardinal Mickey Owen's testimony for left field, although others remember it as ranging from 330 to 375 feet to the foul pole. Owen remembers center field as being 480 feet at its deepest point, while Raper and Jack Hasten claimed it was 460 feet. Mary Jean Ferguson telephone interview, November 5, 1995; Mickey Owen interview, August 25, 1995; Jack Hasten telephone interview, November 3, 1995.

19. Musial, *Musial*, 40; Pappi Walterman telephone interview, November 8, 1995. Duff McCoy, who worked out with the Springfield Cardinals that spring before moving to a Class D team, played catch with Musial and remembered that he could barely throw a ball. Duff McCoy telephone interview, November 12, 1995; Stan Musial telephone interview, December 6, 1995; Vanek interview, December 9, 1996.

on the arms and legs of ballplayers. The team switched from white to gray flannel for road games.

For that first game on April 30, some eighteen hundred shivering fans turned out to watch the Cardinals defeat the Joplin Miners, a New York Yankees farm team, 13–1. Batting cleanup, Musial went one for four and threw out a runner at second base, an indication that his arm was strengthening. Broome emerged as the batting star, however, with four hits, including three triples and four runs batted in, as pitcher Lefty Hopkins recorded the win. The next evening the Cardinals, behind Scheef, blew a five-run first-inning lead by committing five errors and giving up fifteen hits in a 15–7 loss. Despite his hitless performance, Musial scored a run and made two exceptional catches in right field.

On May 2, the following day, the Cardinals chartered a bus to Joplin for a two-game series, which fell victim to rain. The only entertainment provided on the bus was Musial's harmonica playing, which had begun to occupy his leisure time. Returning to Springfield, the team opened an eight-day home stand against Joplin with a Sunday afternoon game on May 4. The game marked the 1941 debut of Donnelly, whose sweeping curve struck out eight Miners in an 11–1 laugher; Musial hit a homer to the flagpole in right field. It was Musial's only hit in five at bats, and he carried a .154 average into a three-game series with the St. Joseph Ponies, a St. Louis Browns farm team. The Cardinals swept the series as Musial won the first game with two homers, including a 350-footer to right field, hitting the roof of a house across Boonville Avenue. He nearly hit a third home run, backing the right fielder to the fence. Musial's hitting overcame a fielding lapse that resulted in a St. Joseph run. Hopkins, who went to 2–0, became the recipient of the 4–3 victory. Musial continued his hot hitting in the final two games of the series, smashing three singles, a double, a triple, and a home run in nine plate appearances. He also contributed a circus catch in the outfield and some stirring baserunning. In the final series game, Rickey was in the stands to witness Musial raising his average to .350.[20]

The Cardinals continued their winning ways in a four-game set against the Salina Millers in White City Park, beginning on May 9. Salina, another league doormat, failed to capture a game as the Cardinals extended their streak to eight victories, thus moving into first place in the Western Association. In the first contest, Musial hit his fourth homer in as many games. He also crashed into the right-field fence to haul down a liner.

20. The harmonica story comes from Walterman telephone interview, November 8, 1995.

Because of his .375 batting average, Vanek moved him into the third spot of the batting order ahead of Broome. In recognition of Musial's stardom, the Sunday *News and Leader* featured him on the front page of the sports section. The caption, beneath a photograph of a slender Musial poised to hit, referred to the "Pennsylvania grocery clerk."[21]

The Cardinals' torrid pace resumed in a three-game set in St. Joseph, a historic river community north of Kansas City. The Redbirds extended their win streak to twelve games as Papai and Hopkins gained victories. The real story lay with the hitting as the team scored forty-three runs with Broome, Vanek, and Musial leading the way. Musial's nine hits in those three games boosted his average to .417, while Broome hovered around the .400 mark, and Vanek was close to .350. The win streak reached thirteen in a road victory against Topeka, with Musial raising his average to .431 after going three for five, and Donnelly winning his fourth game. Despite Musial's two hits, the Cardinals' only road setback came the next day when Topeka rallied for two runs in the ninth. A five-game series against Salina completed the road trip with the Redbirds beginning another winning streak behind the pitching of Hopkins, Papai, Donnelly, and others. The Pennsylvania grocery clerk continued his hot hitting, going ten for twenty-three and extending his hitting streak to ten games.

Following a rainout, the Cardinals resumed play at home on May 25 against the sixth-place Hutchinson Pirates in a four-game set. After capturing the opener for their sixth straight, the Cardinals split a doubleheader and lost the final game, the first time that the team had lost two consecutive games in 1941. They also lost Vanek to an injury for the next two weeks. Despite the losses, Donnelly and Hopkins each won their sixth straight, making them the top pitchers in the Western Association. Musial also remained among the league leaders, his average reaching .440. On May 28, with Hopkins leading the way, the Cardinals continued their homestand against the Topeka Owls with a 6–2 victory despite the ending of Musial's hitting streak at fourteen games. He more than made up for that the next evening when he hit three home runs and a single and drove in six runs in an 11–7 victory. One homer, almost in dead center, probably was the longest shot ever in White City Park. The following afternoon, Musial went two for six in a doubleheader split against Topeka marked by Donnelly's first loss of the season.

The Cardinals' exceptional play carried over into June as they garnered three out of four in Hutchinson, Kansas, where Hopkins and Donnelly

21. *Springfield News and Leader,* May 11, 1941.

won. The league's new hitting leader, Musial, kept up his slugging pace, and Vanek returned to the lineup. The one loss, part of a doubleheader, was an ugly affair. Because of an overtaxed pitching staff, Vanek called upon Musial in relief. He gave up six runs and five hits in the third inning without retiring a batter. Still, by June 3 the Cardinals had won twenty-seven of thirty-three and led Joplin by four and one-half games.

The team soon ran off ten straight wins over Hutchinson, the Fort Smith Giants, and the Muskogee Reds. The determining factor remained good hitting as most of the Redbird pitchers surrendered many runs. The most reliable hurler, Donnelly, won both ends of a doubleheader against Muskogee. He pitched a four-hitter in the seven-inning opener and relieved for the win in the nightcap. By June 13, Musial had hit in eight consecutive games and his average was around the .435 mark, with thirteen homers. Others also contributed at the plate, including Vanek, who raised his average to .410. On June 16, the *Leader and Press* reported that the Springfield Redbirds were the nation's only professional team with a winning rate of 80 percent.

Despite a loss to Muskogee on June 16, the Cardinals remained hot for the remainder of June. The only disturbing note came in a club announcement that Hopkins and Papai had taken selective service exams, an indication that war loomed on the horizon. Hopkins, who had been classified 1B because of defective teeth, now passed the exam with "flying colors." That concern soon abated, however, as Donnelly shut out Carthage on June 21, in a two-hitter in which he fanned thirteen without issuing a walk. On the following day, twelve hundred spectators witnessed Hopkins winning his thirteenth straight in a doubleheader sweep of Carthage in which Musial continued to hit.

By June 24, the Cardinals had increased their lead to ten and one-half games over Joplin. They had reached the crest of their 1941 ascendancy. Musial's league-leading average was hovering around .425, followed by Vanek at .377 and Broome at .314. Donnelly and Hopkins enjoyed the distinction of being the Western Association's top pitchers. Springfield fans would soon honor Musial and the two pitchers on fan appreciation night in early July.

Local coverage of Musial's and the Cardinals' success competed with the startling international news, making 1941 a bittersweet year, particularly for those of draft age. Nothing loomed larger than the war abroad, with Japanese aggression continuing in China and Indochina. Banner headlines in the two Springfield newspapers had also recorded the fall of Greece to the Nazis in April, the British evacuation of Cyprus in early

June, the German bombing of London that spring and summer, and Hitler's invasion of Russia on June 22. Newspaper accounts contained menacing battle maps that depicted Axis penetrations in the Middle East, the Mediterranean, and on the eastern front. It would be only a few months before Japan would decimate the U.S. Pacific fleet at Pearl Harbor, resulting in a declaration of war against Japan, Germany, and Italy and the military induction of millions of Americans, including fans and ballplayers alike.

The extraordinary major-league baseball season of 1941 at least in part offset the dismal international news. Nothing brought greater attention than New York Yankee Joe DiMaggio's record-setting fifty-six-game hitting streak, which caused Americans everywhere to ask, "Did he get one yesterday?" Another compelling baseball personality that summer resembled a telephone pole in build. He was a brash, awkward twenty-two-year-old whom sportswriters called "The Splendid Splinter" and ballplayers referred to as "The Kid." Nevertheless, Ted Williams of the Boston Red Sox set the American League on fire as his batting average remained above .400 throughout the summer, closing with a .406 average, the last major-league player to hit over .400. In the All-Star game in July he hit a three-run homer in the last of the ninth with two outs to carry the American League to victory. Later that summer baseball fans relished an electrifying National League pennant race between the Brooklyn Dodgers and the St. Louis Cardinals that extended into the final week of the season. Springfieldians, who bore an almost pathological attachment to the Redbirds, divided their attention between the high-flying local team and the St. Louis ball club. The one note of sadness came in the death of Yankee great Lou Gehrig at his home in the Bronx on June 2, following a lengthy and courageous battle with amyotrophic lateral sclerosis. The *Leader and Press* carried a touching photograph of former Yankee star Babe Ruth standing by the open casket of the "Iron Horse."[22]

Springfield had its own heroes who played on the local Cardinals ball club. The vast majority of the players came from rural or blue-collar urban backgrounds nationwide; their educational experience had ended in high school. Dedicated to the game, they were willing to make sacrifices in their quest to reach the major leagues. They mixed well with the working-class community of north Springfield. The players rented apartments and

22. For national baseball events during the summer of 1941, see Robert W. Creamer, *Baseball in '41: A Celebration of the Best Baseball Season Ever—In the Year America Went to War; Springfield Leader and Press,* June 4, 1991.

rooming houses near the ballpark and immediately caught the attention of northsiders for their well-mannered and friendly demeanor. They seemed to enjoy interacting with youngsters in the neighborhood. Five or six players lived in Susie Wicker's home at 1443 North Robberson, where she fed them well for less than ten dollars a week for room and board. Satisfied with Springfield, Musial told a local sports reporter that he would like to remain in the city for the entire year if he could secure a job.[23]

No ballplayer emerged as more of a favorite than Stanley Musial (as Springfield newspapers usually called him). In part, fans were fascinated with his exceptional hitting, resulting in line drives that pounded the Coca-Cola or 7-Up signs in right field; with his fielding, which included somersaults and other acrobatics on the outfield grass; and with his daring baserunning, characterized by his savvy delays between bases before advancing on ground balls. More than his play, old-timers recall the continual smile on his face. Generally quiet, he nevertheless amused bystanders when he did speak with "that funny [Pennsylvanian] accent." A Cardinal batboy remembered his always saying, "Give me a bat with a hit in it." Musial only had two bats at the time. If a questionable strike was called on him, recalled one umpire, he did not even look back because he knew he could hit the next pitch. What stands out was his unassuming personality, the trait most remembered about him. One Springfieldian met him at a downtown establishment where Musial was looking at baseball bats. Surprised that Musial appeared slight for such a powerful hitter, the youngster said, "You don't really look that big." Smiling, Musial responded, "I've really been lucky here," a response he came to use more and more. Another local reminisced about Musial frequenting a pool hall in the downtown Holland Building, where he and other ballplayers hung out to obtain major-league scores from the ticker tape. Again, he usually smiled at people and was friendly.[24]

Most locals remember Musial as a family man. A contemporary recalls that Musial borrowed forty dollars for bus fare so that Lil and their infant

23. Walterman telephone interview, November 8, 20, 1995; Robert Peace interview, October 11, 1995; Mary Louise Bryant to James N. Giglio, August 25, 1995, in possession of Giglio; *Springfield Leader and Press*, July 20, 1941; *Springfield Daily News*, July 4, 1941. Joe Garagiola, who lived at Mrs. Wicker's in 1942, referred to her as his "most valuable person in Springfield." Joe Garagiola telephone interview, November 22, 1995.

24. Mildred M. Lurvey to James N. Giglio, August 3, 1995, in possession of Giglio; Jack Mumford interview, August 16, 1995; Dale Freeman interview, July 31, 1995; Jack Peace interview, October 10, 1995; Bill Wilkerson telephone interview, November 2, 1995; Hasten telephone interview, November 3, 1995; Bill McQueary interview, August 2, 1995; Gene Lohmeyer interview, August 25, 1995; Abbott Williams interview, August 25, 1995.

son could join him. Prior to their arrival, he lived in the home of Loree Acton at 220 Scott Street, a couple of blocks from the ballpark. Afterward, the Musials shared an upstairs apartment with the Dantonios in the nearby residence of Arnett and Atlanta Shields at 969 North Benton Avenue. Stan and Lil could often be seen walking Dickie in a stroller around the neighborhood. Lil rarely missed a Springfield game. Sometimes, a thirteen-year-old usher carried the Musial toddler around the grandstands.[25]

Eyewitnesses are evenly divided over whether they envisioned Musial as a potential major-league player. One labeled him "a star among a bunch of dead lights"; another thought him a future major leaguer. Many remembered conversations at the games about his unorthodox batting stance that would supposedly keep him from the big leagues, an opinion shared by some scouts at the time. The infield play of shortstop Dale Hackett made him a more likely prospect to another observer. Regardless, the Springfield newspapers reported no gossip about Musial's possible elevation in the first months of the season.[26]

By then Hopkins's thirteen-game winning streak had ended in a 2–1 loss to Topeka on June 26 despite Musial's homer and single. The latter's play invited Jon Kennedy's *Leader and Press* cartoon of the "modest guy" Musial, which asserted that a "rival clubowner had offered the [St. Louis] Cardinals a blank check for him." (Cardinal owner Sam Breadon later claimed the New York Giants offered the Cardinals forty thousand dollars for Musial during this period.)[27] Thereafter, the Springfield team rebounded by winning three, including a doubleheader, in Carthage. Musial went four for nine, including his eighteenth and nineteenth homers, while Hopkins and Donnelly each won their fourteenth games against the cellar ball club. Vanek, however, soon expressed concern about his overworked mound corps as the Cards won one of a three-game series against first-division Muskogee at White City Park. One thousand fans saw the Reds win the opener 4–3 on June 30; the loss proved especially difficult because

25. McCoy telephone interview, November 12, 1995; Jack Peace interview, October 10, 1995; Williams interview, August 25, 1995; Dean "Bud" Stone telephone interview, February 12, 1996. The frustration of interviewing eyewitnesses fifty years after the fact reached its highest level when trying to locate Musial's Springfield residence; the author considered five different sites before settling on Scott Street and Benton Avenue.

26. Mumford interview, August 16, 1995; Williams interview, August 25, 1995; Hasten telephone interview, November 3, 1995; McQueary interview, August 2, 1995; Freeman interview, July 31, 1995; Gene Wickliffe interview, August 18, 1995.

27. *Springfield News and Leader*, June 29, 1941; Sher, "The Stan Musial Nobody Knows," 66.

Musial, Hopkins, and Donnelly were being honored for their stellar play in 1941. Despite making two great catches, Musial failed to hit in five at bats (his emerging slump, partly caused by being pitched inside, would take his average below .400 by the next week). The other honoree, Donnelly, was ejected from the bench.

The team's problems mounted in early July because of nagging injuries to Dantonio and Donnelly, hitting slumps by Musial and Broome, and less effective pitching from Hopkins. Too, the generally poor attendance at White City Park was disconcerting despite the thirty-five hundred spectators who were dazzled by a fireworks show on July 4. Both Springfield newspapers expressed a concern about the sparse crowds. Club president Al Eckert acknowledged that the approximately twenty thousand fans who had attended by mid-July represented only a slight increase over 1940. The financial loss thus far for the parent St. Louis organization, according to Eckert, was $5,064. Consequently, players worried that the Cardinals would pull out of Springfield in 1942, as Rickey had suggested they would, if the situation did not improve. As a result, the local chamber of commerce appointed a committee to promote interest in "a fine ball club" that generally drew better on the road.[28]

Problems aside, the Redbirds managed to best the Joplin Miners in two of three games in early July. On July 3, Donnelly, despite an injured wrist, blanked them 2–0 in a four-hitter and lowered his ERA to 1.53 while Musial hit a home run. The July 4 doubleheader featured the temporary return to form of Hopkins (now 15–2), who won the afternoon game, while Musial went two for seven for the two games. The next day, however, the Cardinals were forced to pitch first baseman Archie Templeton, who was quickly routed. In relief, Musial gave up six runs, twelve hits, six walks, and two wild pitches in two and two-thirds innings of a 22–10 shellacking. Never again would Musial seriously pitch in a professional baseball game.[29]

The pitching difficulties were critical, especially with several double-headers approaching on an extended road trip. Even worse, Hopkins and Papai had been classified 1A by their Illinois draft board. Upon the team's

28. *Springfield Daily News,* July 5, 1941; *Springfield Leader and Press,* July 1–3, 4, 1941. For the sparse crowds, see the John Snow column in the *Leader and Press,* July 1, 1941, and the Marvin Eisenberg column in the *Daily News,* July 11, 1941.

29. *Springfield News and Leader,* July 6, 1941. The one exception to Musial pitching professionally came on the last day of the 1952 season when, as a publicity stunt, St. Louis Cardinals manager Eddie Stanky pitched him against Frank Baumholtz of the Chicago Cubs, who reached on an error.

arrival in Joplin on Sunday, July 13, Papai announced he would report for military induction later that week. An anxious Eckert began to press Cardinal officials for pitching assistance, knowing that Hopkins also faced induction in the near future. Team spirit could not have been good for that Sunday doubleheader, even though Musial was three for six in two games, raising his average to .370. Lackluster hitting nonetheless cost the Cardinals both contests. Papai fell victim 5–1, and Scheef's eight-game streak ended 3–0. Again Donnelly saved the day by winning the final, raising his record to 18–1. The Cardinals returned to Springfield with a six and one-half game lead to face lower-division Hutchinson and Salina.

On July 16, Papai, pitching his last game for the Cardinals, won the opener against Hutchinson. He ended the season with a 7–6 mark. That game also convincingly ended Musial's batting slump: he had a double and two singles in four at bats. The Cardinals continued to feast on Hutchinson pitching the next evening with Scheef coasting to a 14–3 win and Musial hitting his twenty-fourth homer.

The Cardinals continued to rebound against Salina on July 19. Donnelly won his nineteenth, striking out twelve for his thirteenth straight win, equaling Hopkins's early season mark. As Rickey watched, Musial hit his twenty-fifth home run and a single, raising his batting average to .388. The previous day Rickey had called Vanek, asking if Musial could hit AA ball pitching; Vanek answered yes and added that Musial's throwing arm constituted only a slight weakness. Rickey said that he would come down to see for himself. That evening as Vanek and Musial moved to the outfield, the manager said, "Goodby, Stan." "What do you mean, goodby?" Musial inquired. "Just goodby," Vanek smiled. During the course of the inning, Vanek recalled that Musial "kept glancing over at him, looking puzzled and worried."[30]

More than five thousand spectators, the season's largest crowd, attended that game to celebrate Frisco night. The overflow sat in front of the outfield fence separated by a rope from the field of play. The next evening became the swan song for Hopkins, who then returned to Illinois for induction. His 9–1 victory against Salina ended his Springfield season with a 17–4 record. Musial hit his twenty-sixth homer in Hopkins's finale, a shot off the deep left-field fence. The pitcher was Eddie Lopat, a future New York Yankee great.

As it turned out, the Sunday double bill against Salina also represented Musial's final games in Springfield. He went one for seven in the split

30. Sher, "The Stan Musial Nobody Knows," 66; Vanek interview, December 9, 1996.

and went fishing the next day, an open date, with the Dantonios and Donnelly on the White River south of Springfield. A reporter located him and announced that the Cardinal organization was elevating him to the Rochester Red Wings of the International League, a playoff contender seeking assistance. That evening Musial told the press, "I really didn't expect anything like this. I do hate to leave Springfield but naturally I'm glad to go to Double A." That same evening he visited Vanek twice for advice on how to make the adjustment, the last time at midnight because he could not sleep.[31]

Musial's final statistics for the Springfield Cardinals included a .379 batting average, 94 RBIs, 100 runs scored, 132 hits, 27 doubles, 10 triples, 26 homers, and 15 stolen bases. He led the Western Association in batting average, homers, RBIs, and total bases. He topped his own team in every batting category but triples (Olt had 12). The most surprising statistic was Musial's 26 home runs. Never before had he displayed such power. Undoubtedly the short right-field fence, which Vanek thought shorter than the stated 300 feet, encouraged Musial to pull the ball more. Playing regularly in the field and perhaps profiting from Vanek's batting tips, Musial had also become a much better hitter. Moreover, he had proved that he could perform successfully in the outfield with an arm that grew stronger as the season progressed. Musial left so quickly that Springfieldians could not give him a proper farewell.[32]

The conventional wisdom is that Musial's departure contributed to the Springfield Cardinals' eventual collapse. It ignores, however, that Musial's replacement, Henry Redmond, came from Decatur in the Class B Three I League to hit .381 for the Springfield Redbirds with eight homers in forty-nine games. Hopkins's departure in the face of an already taxed pitching staff probably hurt more, as did the Joplin Miners' resurgence. They won thirty of forty-one games in August while the Springfield team won nineteen and lost seventeen. During this period, Joplin lost no key ballplayers to the draft. Also, Springfield replacement pitchers contributed little during the final month. Only Donnelly remained his consistent self as he started and relieved ball games down the stretch. On July 29, he won both ends of a doubleheader to go to 22–2. He set a new league single-season strikeout record of 304 in finishing the

31. Musial, *Musial*, 42; *Springfield Leader and Press*, July 22, 1941; Vanek interview, December 9, 1996.

32. Regarding his newly found power, Musial attributed it to daily play and the short right-field fence. Musial telephone interview, December 6, 1995.

year with a 28–6 mark, the league's only twenty-game winner. Even Donnelly's arm occasionally balked in key late season games, however. As a result the Cards lost the Western Association pennant on the last day of the season.

That collapse foreshadowed the misfortunes of several teammates who for one reason or another found promising careers impeded. Donnelly and Scheef, for example, suffered from arm problems, even though Donnelly eventually played in the major leagues from 1944 through 1950. Despite pitching brilliantly for the St. Louis Cardinals in the 1944 World Series, Donnelly never won more than eight games in any major-league season. The lack of a quality fastball contributed to Hopkins's subsequent failure. More perplexing, Redmond, Musial's promising replacement, who followed him to Rochester where he hit .326 in fifteen games, found his skills eroded after four years of military service. Scores of players suffered from that circumstance. As a result, Musial came to understand even more the tenuousness of life and how fate, as well as ability, can determine success or failure. For his own accomplishments, he remained thankful and humbled. His one known letter to Vanek from Rochester indicated that he was "getting the breaks and things are clicking swell for me." While missing the Springfield Cardinals, he did "enjoy missing . . . those long bus rides to and from Salina."[33]

Musial arrived in Rochester along with the more touted Erv Dusak, a slugging right-handed hitter from the Three I League. Rochester, the third-largest city in New York, stretched along both banks of the Genesee River and bordered the southern shore of Lake Ontario. Like Pittsburgh it had a heavy industrial base, specializing in photographic products, optical goods, dental equipment, railway signal apparatus, shoes, and clothing. The city's sizable immigrant population included Italians, Germans, Canadians, English, Poles, and Irish. Red Wing Stadium lay just north of the immediate downtown area on Norton Street. Called the Taj Mahal of the minor leagues when it opened in 1929, the steel and concrete stadium, paid for by the St. Louis Cardinals, could seat about nineteen thousand.

Former Donora High School assistant baseball coach Chuck Schmidt, now living in Rochester, met Musial at the train station. Schmidt would attend every game Musial played in Rochester. According to longtime

---

33. According to Vanek, Redmond's laziness also contributed to his problems. Vanek telephone interview, December 31, 1997; *Springfield Daily News*, August 15, 1941.

stadium employee Harold "Tiny" Zwetsch, "[Musial] showed up at the bullpen carrying his clothes in a paper bag."[34]

At the time the Red Wings, barely in fourth place in the standings, were fighting for a spot in the postseason playoffs. Managed by Tony Kaufmann, a former National Leaguer, the team needed additional hitting at the outfield positions. Musial and Dusak played immediately, the former in right field, hitting second in the batting order, and the latter in center field. In that first game at Syracuse on July 23, Musial went one for five and Dusak had three hits. The next evening Musial homered over the right-field wall. Still, his hits came sparingly in the first few games while Dusak was on fire, hitting .533 by July 27. Kaufmann, however, liked what he saw of Musial, who impressed him with his confidence at the plate.[35]

The best was yet to come. In his debut at Rochester Red Wing Stadium on July 29, Musial hit a homer, double, and two singles as the Red Wings defeated Baltimore 7–2. Musial elevated his average to .436 by the beginning of August before cooling down to .309 at mid-month. A couple of games stand out in this period: Against the league-leading Newark Bears, the New York Yankees farm team, Kaufmann asked Musial to fake a bunt to Bears third baseman Hank Majeski, a future major leaguer known to charge hard in bunting situations. Instead of bunting, Musial followed Kaufmann's instructions perfectly by punching the ball over the charging Majeski's head. Twice in the same game he performed this difficult maneuver for two-base hits, causing an amazed Kaufmann to ask whether he had done this previously. Without looking up, Musial replied, "Naw—it's easy."[36] In another game in that series, with Branch Rickey in attendance, Musial had four hits. In that Newark series Musial ended up with eleven hits.

Prior to another August contest against Montreal, Musial met Babe Ruth, the former New York Yankee slugger, who came to the Rochester stadium for a pregame hitting exhibition. The forty-six-year-old lumbering Bambino, sadly out of shape, swung futilely at a number of pitches from Kaufmann before smashing one out of the ballpark. Musial remembered the thrill of observing Ruth, the one major leaguer Musial's father knew by name. After the exhibition Ruth came to the bench to watch the Red

34. Chuck Schmidt telephone interview, December 31, 1994, conducted by Jim Kreuz; Jim Mandelaro and Scott Pitoniak, *Silver Seasons: The Story of the Rochester Red Wings*, 71.

35. *Rochester Democrat and Chronicle*, July 26, 1941.

36. Ibid., September 23, 1941.

Wings contest, only to disappoint Musial, who saw him consume a pint of whiskey that he had concealed in his pocket. Still, Musial struggled to impress Ruth with his own power, but managed only a single.[37]

By mid-August, despite the hitting of Musial and Dusak, the top batter on the Rochester club was left-handed hitter Jimmy Ripple, a former major leaguer who had hit .300 several times with the New York Giants and the Brooklyn Dodgers. The *Rochester Democrat and Chronicle* reported that the pennant-contending St. Louis Cardinals planned on calling Ripple up to replace Enos Slaughter, one of two injured outfielders. But Ripple broke his finger on August 21 and would not return until September. By then, Musial was on another hitting tear, and had supplanted the injured Dusak in center field. Despite tapering off by season's end, Musial finished the regular campaign with a three-for-five game against the Buffalo Bisons. In 54 games for Rochester, he hit .326 with 72 hits and three home runs in 221 at bats. Only Ripple, hitting over .400 prior to his injury, finished higher at .378; Dusak, meanwhile, came in third with a .305 average.[38]

The injury-plagued Red Wings, by virtue of a fourth-place finish, qual- ified for the International League playoffs. Their first-round opponent, the pennant-winning Newark Bears, eliminated them in six games. The Rochester club undoubtedly felt the loss of their star pitcher, future major leaguer Max Surkont, recovering from an appendicitis attack. "Steamer" Musial, as the local newspaper now referred to him for his quickness, contributed to the Red Wings' two victories by going two for five in one game and hitting a triple to right-center in the second win. In the fifth game, even though going hitless in five at bats, he electrified the crowd by jumping three feet in the air against the right-field wall to rob Newark of a home run.[39]

Immediately following the playoffs, Musial told his friend Schmidt, "I'll see you next spring. I'm never going to make that Cardinal outfield." (The Cardinals were starting an imposing trio: Slaughter, Terry Moore, and Johnny Hopp.) That night Musial took the night train to Pittsburgh, where he met Lil, who had recently returned to Donora with Dickie, and her sister Helen. Upon returning to Donora, Musial attended Mass on Sunday morning and then went to bed until Lil awakened him with a telegram that asked him to report to the St. Louis Cardinals for the final twelve games of the season. This took Musial completely by surprise. But the Cardinals

37. Musial, *Musial*, 43.
38. *Rochester Democrat and Chronicle*, August 17, 1941.
39. Ibid., September 12–14, 1941.

had taken note of his performance at Rochester. Undoubtedly, Kaufmann's glowing report to the front office describing Musial's improvised hitting against Majeski and Newark played a part. His overall assessment of Musial made the Rochester newspaper: "The kid is an iceberg. If you tapped him you'd have to get ice water out of his veins. Yankee Stadium or a cow pasture—all parks are just another place to play ball to him."[40] Dusak and George (Whitey) Kurowski, an outstanding third baseman who hit .284 for Rochester, were also called up for St. Louis' final drive, along with Walt Sessi, Musial's former Williamson teammate, from Houston.

Musial arrived in St. Louis on September 17. He secured a room at the Melbourne Hotel across from St. Louis University. Ollie Vanek, one of his few visitors, remembered calling on him there. Musial then went to Sportsman's Park where he soon walked out alone to center field "just to look over the place." He must have pondered in amazement his incredible rise from near extinction that spring to a pennant-contending major-league ball club seven months later. In typical fashion, he must have said to himself, "I'm so lucky!" After making $150 per month for Springfield and $300 at Rochester, he had signed for $400 a month, prorated for the final two weeks of the season, with Rickey, who had purchased his contract from the Columbus club. This also would constitute Musial's salary figure for the 1942 season. At this point Musial was not thinking much about money, however.[41]

At the time of Musial's arrival, St. Louis trailed the Brooklyn Dodgers by two games in a seesaw pennant race between two resurgent teams that had overcome the domination of the pennant-winning Cincinnati Reds of 1939–1940. The Dodgers, managed by Leo Durocher, the abrasive, feisty former Cardinals Gashouse Gang shortstop, featured the power hitting of Dolph Camilli and Joe Medwick and the superb pitching of Kirby Higbe and Whit Wyatt, the league's two most productive hurlers. The Cardinals' strengths were defense, exceptional team speed, and tremendous mound depth with six pitchers winning ten or more games. Managed by the patient, player-oriented Billy Southworth, who had learned much from

40. Schmidt telephone interview, December 31, 1994, conducted by Kreuz; *Rochester Democrat and Chronicle*, September 23, 1941.
41. Vanek interview, December 9, 1996; *Rochester Democrat and Chronicle*, September 17, 1941. Only Musial's Springfield salary is in dispute. Mary Jean Ferguson, the team secretary who wrote the checks, insisted that Musial made $125 per month, while Musial claims he received $150 per month. I used the latter figure, assuming that the payee should know better. Ferguson telephone interview, November 5, 1995; Musial, *Musial*, 48.

his previous managerial failure in 1929, the Redbirds, with injuries to key players Moore, Slaughter, Walker Cooper, Mort Cooper, and Johnny Mize, faced an almost insurmountable task. They almost defied the odds largely because of the incredible performance of Stan Musial, who kept the Cardinals in the race to the end. In twelve games, he hit .426, with 20 hits in 47 at bats, and performed outstandingly in the field and on the bases.

Musial debuted in the second game of a doubleheader on his first day with the club. Wearing number six because that available uniform fit him best, Musial replaced Estel Crabtree, Slaughter's backup, in right field. In his twenty-three years with the Cards, Musial would play all three outfield positions as well as first base, but he never wore any other uniform number; upon his retirement, the Cardinal organization also retired his jersey.

In that first game Musial faced Boston Braves journeyman right-hander Jim Tobin, the first knuckleballer he had ever challenged. Boston manager Casey Stengel, the future New York Yankee Hall of Fame skipper, remembered Musial's swing as more awkward back then and that he stood further away from the plate; consequently, he thought Musial susceptible to slow pitches. Badly overstriding against the fluttering knuckler, Musial indeed popped up weakly to the third baseman. The next at bat, however, with two outs and two men on base, Musial cut down on his swing and stayed back as he drove the knuckler to right-center for a two-run double. He finished with two hits in a Cardinal victory that reduced the Dodgers' lead to one game. The next day he had one hit in a losing effort, but he went three for three, including a double, against the Cubs in his third game. With the Dodgers losing two in a row, the Cardinals were within a few percentage points of first place with nine games remaining.

Despite Musial's hitting, some Cardinal veterans did not easily accept the rookie. After one or two swings in the batting cage, Musial heard Walker Cooper growl, "Get your ass out of there."[42] Moreover, in the final home stand, Southworth started right-handed power hitter Erv Dusak instead of Musial because the Chicago Cubs went with lefty Johnny Schmitz. Rickey, too, in general favored Dusak because of his supposed greater potential. He ended up going hitless in a game that the Redbirds lost in the ninth inning, while the Dodgers swept a twin-bill against the Philadelphia Phillies.

The Sunday doubleheader against the Cubs represented the apex of Musial's late-season surge. In the first game he played superbly in left

42. Dave Anderson, *Pennant Races: Baseball at Its Best,* 144.

field, making two great catches and throwing out a runner at the plate. He also had four consecutive hits, including two doubles, and stole a base. His defining moment came after his single in the ninth inning with the score at 5–5. With Musial on second base, Coaker Triplett topped a Ken Raffenberger forkball in front of the plate. Catcher Clyde McCullough threw to first base too late in a close play. As an argument developed between first baseman Babe Dahlgren and the umpire while McCullough stood by, hands on hips, ready to protest, Musial, without breaking stride, rounded third base and scored on a hit of some fifteen feet. Because of such daring, Musial soon became known in the press as the "Donora Greyhound," while Southworth exclaimed to one of his coaches, "That kid was born to play baseball."[43] In the nightcap Musial continued his splendid play with two hits as the Cards won 7–0, cutting the Dodgers' lead to one game.

That Sunday evening the Cardinals left St. Louis by train for their final road trip. By then Musial's teammates had become more accepting of the rookie as they kidded and congratulated him. Sitting next to Terry Moore in the Pullman car, Musial, too, began to open up, recounting how much of a confused rush the year had been. He mentioned the stressful spring and the home runs Moore and Mize had hit off of him in Columbus. Moore, in disbelief, laughed that Musial was that inept kid southpaw, calling over to Mize, "Hey, John, you won't believe this! Musial is the left-hander who threw us those long home-run balls . . . this spring."[44] By now veterans such as Mize were wondering why Rickey had not elevated Musial earlier.

In the Redbirds' five contests in Pittsburgh and Chicago, the team played well enough to capture three games, but the Dodgers performed even better by sweeping the Boston Braves, winning the National League pennant by two and a half games. The Cards finished the season with ninety-seven victories, usually enough to finish at the top. Musial continued to hit, clubbing his first major-league home run against Rip Sewell in the second game of the Pirates series. The next day he went two for four and ended up scoring the Cardinals' final run in the season's closer in Chicago. Most gratifying to him, he was able to bring Lukasz into the Pirates' Forbes Field clubhouse following the Sunday doubleheader and introduced him to Southworth and the coaches. He had reconciled with his father, who stood in awe of his son's success and remained proud of

43. Stockton, "The Unusual Mr. Musial," 96; Rob Rains, *The St. Louis Cardinals: The 100th Anniversary History*, 91.
44. Musial, *Musial*, 50.

him in the last years of an increasingly troubled and illness-plagued life. Lukasz would soon accompany Musial to spring training, where he shyly conversed with Cardinal officials.[45]

The Pittsburgh series also provided Donorans with the opportunity to proclaim Stan Musial Day on Tuesday, September 23, the first of other celebrations to come. With school canceled, a large number of students joined other well-wishers from the Mon Valley at Forbes Field to honor the first Donoran to make the big leagues since Bob Coulson played for the Cincinnati Reds in 1908. Musial received a traveling bag and money.

One other honor awaited Musial after returning home to Donora that fall. The Donora Zinc Works Athletic Association saluted Musial with a banquet in which Joe Barbao presented him with a wristwatch and a trophy. The association invited the Pittsburgh Pirates Hall of Famer Honus Wagner to attend. This seemed fitting because the Flying Dutchman, a native of western Pennsylvania, exemplified traits evident in the young Musial: modesty, a quiet demeanor, and a work ethic second to none. Wagner had also set the standard for career hitting records in the National League, most of which Musial would eventually break. A Musial friend approached Wagner at the banquet, offering him one hundred dollars if he would instruct Musial on hitting. "I took Stan aside," Wagner recalled, "and whispered to him to continue to bat the way he did that last month and never change. It was an easy hundred dollars," Wagner laughed.[46]

One final baseball game remained for Musial in 1941. On October 5, at Sportsman's Park, the Kansas City Monarchs of the Negro League played the Bob Feller All-Stars, a squad of big leaguers organized by Feller, the Cleveland Indians' pitching sensation. Feller's team included Cardinal catcher Walker Cooper, outfielder–first baseman Johnny Hopp, and Musial, while the Monarchs featured the legendary Leroy "Satchel" Paige, the Negro League's finest pitcher. The game represented one of several barnstorming exhibitions played between Negro League and major-league squads during the off-season in the 1930s and 1940s. At the time Sportsman's Park relegated blacks to the bleachers and the right-field pavilion, making it the only major-league park to practice segregation. Only after considerable deliberation did management agree to open the grandstand to blacks for this one game, attended by twenty thousand black and white fans. In one of Paige's least successful outings, the Feller

45. Sher, "The Stan Musial Nobody Knows," 67.
46. Arthur D. Hittner, *Honus Wagner: The Life of Baseball's "Flying Dutchman,"* 253–54.

All-Stars prevailed, with Stan Musial hammering a Paige fastball over the right-field pavilion roof.[47]

Musial had an unbelievable season. He had led three leagues in hitting average even though he had failed to get enough official at bats to qualify for a batting title in any one of them. Collectively, he had played in 153 games; collected 224 hits, including 41 doubles, 14 triples, and 30 home runs; drove in 122 runs; scored 151 runs; and batted .364. Only in 1948 would he reach comparable statistics solely at the major-league level. Clearly, 1941 was a turnaround year, his most crucial one professionally. Facing oblivion in the spring, he had reached stardom. What remained unclear was whether he could sustain that effort over an entire major-league season and whether he could handle the limelight and the pressure of major-league competition over an extended period.

47. Mark Ribowsky, *Don't Look Back: Satchel Paige in the Shadows of Baseball*, 203.

Rookie Supreme

A s Stan Musial began his rookie year of 1942, he had greater opportunity to explore the city that would eventually become his home. A former trading post, St. Louis had a rich tradition that evolved from French settlers prior to President Thomas Jefferson's Louisiana Purchase of 1803. Located about ten miles south of the convergence of the Mississippi and the Missouri Rivers along the crescent bend of the former, the city had long ago turned its back on the Mississippi. To be sure, barges and other vessels continued to carry commerce down the river in the twentieth century, but railroads and trucking had surpassed water transportation. The Romanesque Union Station in the downtown area housed the largest railroad terminal in the nation in the early 1940s. Five railroad bridges spanned the river to points eastward.

Like most urban communities, St. Louis had suffered economically and had lost population as a result of the Great Depression. But by 1940 the nation's eighth-largest city and Missouri's biggest (816,048 population) continued as one of the principal grain markets in the country and remained America's shoe capital, the home of the Brown Shoe Company and the International Shoe Company, despite the loss of several shoe firms to rural communities as a consequence of cost-reduction measures. The river city also housed several huge breweries, including Anheuser-Busch, Falstaff, and Carling, leading to the flippant comment that St. Louis was "first in booze, first in shoes, and last in the American League" (in reference to the St. Louis Browns). It remained the world's largest raw fur market and a world leader in the production of stoves and ranges, sugar-mill machinery, brick, and terra cotta. In 1940 less than 8 percent of the city workers had employment in any one industry.

The onset of World War II would create an industrial boom in St. Louis that extended into the postwar period. Thanks to nearly $570 million in government contracts, aircraft production—led by Curtis-Wright, the St. Louis Aircraft Corporation, and McDonnell Aircraft Corporation—contributed mightily to the local economy, as did federal allocations for ordnance-related products manufactured by Emerson Electric, Olin Industries, General Motors, and many other companies. Because of the wartime demand for public transportation, the St. Louis Car Company saw its streetcar sales soar. Wartime industry attracted more people to the community, especially blacks from the Deep South.

In the 1940s the wharf area also received a face lift as old buildings—mostly vacated warehouses and factories—were removed preparatory to the creation of a forty-block riverfront plaza, a memorial to Jefferson's Louisiana Purchase. Another generation would pass before that idea inspired a 630-foot, stainless steel arch, symbolizing St. Louis as the Gateway of the West; a modern baseball stadium; and several convention hotels.

Like other major cities, St. Louis contained a diverse ethnic population. The north side, mostly Democratic in politics, contained a sizable segment of working-class Irish Catholics, while south St. Louis housed a large concentration of Germans, mostly Republicans, who lived in virtually identical two-storied frame and brick houses. Czech, Bohemian, and Hispanic groups shared the southside area, with a large concentration of Italians in the southwest sector in a locale called "the Hill," known for its well-groomed bungalows, neighborhood restaurants, and major leaguers Yogi Berra of the New York Yankees and Joe Garagiola of the Cardinals. St. Louis also contained a sizable black community, which increased from 11.4 percent of the population in 1940 to 30 percent in 1960. Many of them lived in tenements immediately beyond the downtown business district.

Superficially, in the 1940s St. Louis seemed similar to any other metropolis with a major-league team. Its southernness made it different, however, for it belonged to a state that sanctioned segregation until the 1950s. Consequently, its racism overshadowed that of northern urban communities. Blacks attended separate public and parochial schools and were denied entry into St. Louis University and Washington University until well into the 1940s. The more exclusive restaurants were off-limits, as were the major hotels, including the Chase, which denied Jackie Robinson and other black major leaguers accommodations until 1954. Moreover, Sportsman's Park, the home of the Cardinals and the St. Louis Browns, remained segregated until May 4, 1944, when the two ball clubs finally announced that blacks could purchase tickets in the grandstand.[1]

The ballpark, a fixture in northwest St. Louis since 1866, was most easily reached from the flat inner city by heading north on Grand Boulevard, which bordered the right-field pavilion. Dodier Avenue ran along the first-base foul line, Spring Avenue paralleled the third-base stripe,

1. Richard S. Kirkendall, *A History of Missouri, Volume V: 1919 to 1953*, 328–32; Jules Tygiel, *Baseball's Great Experiment: Jackie Robinson and His Legacy*, 312.

and Sullivan Avenue bounded left field. Because of inadequate parking, most fans relied on streetcars, which lined up along Grand awaiting the game's ending. Two-family flats housing blue-collar workers dominated the congested area, along with assorted commercial properties, including a YMCA across Grand Boulevard. About three blocks from the ballpark north on Grand, Fairgrounds Park, one of the city's largest playgrounds, containing ball diamonds, tennis courts, and a swimming pool, soon closed to avoid integration. The adjacent Fairgrounds Hotel, in easy walking distance of the ballpark, became the home for many Cardinals and Browns ballplayers, including Stan Musial.

The facade of Sportsman's Park was nondescript, lacking the architectural grandeur of Philadelphia's Shibe Park or the distinctiveness of Pittsburgh's Forbes Field. The St. Louis facility had undergone several reconstructions into the 1920s, including the double decking of the grandstands and the covering of both single-decked stands running down the two foul lines. Bleachers occupied the entire outfield with the right-field segment shaded by a roofed pavilion. The seating capacity remained at thirty-four thousand throughout Musial's career there. The field dimensions favored left-handed hitters as the distance from home plate to the right-field foul pole was only 310 feet, to dead center 422 feet, and down the left-field line a whopping 351 feet. To prevent powerful opponents from hitting "cheap" home runs over the right-field wall, the stadium's owner, the anemic St. Louis Browns, erected a 33-foot screen that extended to right center at the 370 mark. From that point on the 11-foot wall provided the only barrier. The screen remained until the 1955 season when it was removed for one season. Of course, hits into it became playable balls usually resulting in doubles, many of them soon Musial's.

As was the case in most major-league ballparks of the Musial era, the outfield walls or fences were festooned with a wide array of advertisements to include Wheaties breakfast cereal, Lifebuoy Soap, various haberdasheries, GEM razors and blades, and Longines watches. The uniqueness of Sportsman's Park's ads related to the number of beer promotions, pronouncing: "Falstaff Beer, Choicest Product of the Brewer's Art"; "Here's How! Get Hyde Park Beer"; "Drink Alpen Brau"; and "Griesedieck Bros. Light Lager Beer." Not until August A. Busch, Jr., purchased the ballpark in 1953 would Budweiser ads grace the stadium. Undoubtedly, the heat and humidity of the St. Louis summer, which often drove temperatures above the hundred-degree mark, contributed to the thirst for beer. The hot weather made it particularly difficult to play on the sunbaked field, a disadvantage to opponents unaccustomed to the energy-sapping conditions.

By June grass no longer covered the infield between home plate and the pitcher's mound, while the outfield sod suffered from a mange-like condition.

The concession area beneath the grandstands represented another unique feature of Sportsman's Park. The numerous booths resembled a county fairground's midway. The concession operation ranked as the third-largest ballpark business in the country, with its most popular item the "Century of Progress Hot Dog," composed of veal, pork, and beef, wrapped in Persian or Australian sheepskin, and soaked in pineapple juice.[2]

Sportsman's Park had served as the Cardinals' home ever since Redbird owner Sam Breadon leased it from the Browns in 1921 for only thirty-five thousand dollars per year plus half the annual cleanup costs, an arrangement lasting for more than thirty years. A native Irish New Yorker, known to the St. Louis press as "Singing Sam" for his balladeering, the self-made Breadon went from being a seventy-five-dollars-a-month mechanic, to a successful automobile dealer, to the principal owner of the Cardinals by 1920. His symbiotic relationship with Branch Rickey, the vice president and general manager, made the Cardinals one of the most successful franchises in the major leagues. Mindful of his earlier poverty and of the Cardinals' modest crowds, the gray-haired, distinguished-looking Breadon sought to keep overhead low, an objective that Rickey shared. Breadon was so tight in fact that detractors would accuse him of having the plugs of the office electric clocks pulled at night. The Cardinal reputation for low player salaries was well deserved. Moreover, because of the enormous production of the farm system, Rickey could afford to unload excess minor-league talent and established players who had supposedly reached their peak in order to sustain the Cardinals financially and accommodate Breadon's and Rickey's lofty salaries. Player sales in 1940 had amounted to $368,000 when only 332,000 fans went through the turnstiles.[3]

The Breadon-Rickey partnership was coming to a close, however, by 1942. Despite the successful second-place finish in 1941, during which the Cardinals attracted 646,000 fans, their best draw since 1928, Breadon

    2. Lawrence S. Ritter, *Lost Ballparks: A Celebration of Baseball's Legendary Fields*, 187–95; William B. Mead, *Even the Browns*, x; Robert L. Tiemann, "Through the Years at Sportsman's Park."
    3. J. Roy Stockton, "Singing Sam, the Cut-Rate Man"; Bob Broeg, *Bob Broeg's Redbirds: A Century of Cardinals' Baseball*, 3; Andersen, "Branch Rickey and the St. Louis Cardinals System," 137–39.

refused to extend Rickey's contract beyond the 1942 season. Breadon had increasingly clashed with the strong-willed Rickey and had decided that probable U.S. entry into World War II boded ill for professional baseball, making Rickey's eighty-thousand-dollar salary unacceptable. Rickey would move to the Brooklyn Dodgers as general manager in 1943, where he eventually overcame the Cardinals' domination through a strong farm system and the integration of black ballplayers into the Dodger organization in the postwar era.[4]

By 1942, Rickey's Cardinal farm system had reached its apex. Virtually the entire ball club had emerged from the Cardinal plantation. The players were a collection of determined youngsters from low-income families, many of them from Dixie. Blessed with speed and exceptional athletic ability, they came to be known as the St. Louis Swifties. Team captain Terry Moore, one of the oldest members, had not reached thirty years of age on opening day. The pear-shaped Enos Slaughter, who hit .311 in 1941, remained a regular in right field, with Musial slated for left. Probably no outfield had as much speed, covered the gaps, and backed up one another as well as this one did.

Among the other former farm standouts were stocky third baseman George "Whitey" Kurowski, who excelled despite a shortened right arm because of osteomyelitis as a child; the tall, lanky Marty "Slats" Marion, who, in spite of a serious childhood leg injury, covered his shortstop position so effortlessly and with so much range that one sportswriter described him as "movin' easy as a bank of fog"; and second-year catcher Walker Cooper, a powerful and tough competitor who would rank as one of the National League's top backstops for a decade. Big Johnny Mize no longer patrolled at first base, however, even though he had hit 43 home runs and batted .314 in 1940 and .317 in 1941. Breadon shipped the "Big Cat" to the New York Giants for fifty thousand dollars and three journeymen players after tiring of Mize's bickering at contract time. Musial, describing him as "one of the finest hitters I ever saw," would later call the future Hall of Famer's departure a "mistake" that cost the team future pennants; no longer would the club have that added left-handed power to attack the short right field in Sportsman's Park.[5] In replacement the Cardinals platooned rookie Ray Sanders and Johnny Hopp at first base

4. Frederick G. Lieb, *The St. Louis Cardinals: The Story of a Great Baseball Club*, 203.

5. "Musial Says Dumb Deals Cost Cards 4 Pennants," undisclosed 1964 newspaper clipping in Musial Collection, National Baseball Library, Cooperstown, New York. See also Anthony J. Connor, ed., *Baseball for the Love of It: Hall of Famers Tell It Like It Was*, 181–82.

in 1942, both of whom had disappointing seasons for the next two years. At second base manager Southworth finally settled on Jimmy Brown after regular Frank Crespi failed to produce.

One of the team's key strengths remained its pitching staff, the pride and joy of the farm system. Anchoring the mound corps were six pitchers who had won 10 or more games in 1941, led by Ernie White, who had 17 victories in his rookie season; veteran Lon Warneke, another 17-game winner; Mort Cooper, Walker's older brother and one of the era's premier right-handers; Howie Krist; and Max Lanier. Three outstanding rookie hurlers also made significant contributions in 1942: John Beazley; twenty-one-year-old left-hander Howie Pollet, promoted from the AA Houston club after a 20–3 season with a 1.06 ERA; and Murry Dickson. The farm system abounded with several other pitchers ready for elevation to the major leagues.

In labeling the 1942 Cardinals the greatest team he ever played on, Musial recalled that defense, team speed, pitching, and spirit constituted its strengths: "We felt like we were unbeatable. We played together, and we spent a lot of time together. We had a great spirit on that team." He called Terry Moore "a great team leader, . . . a great competitor, and master center fielder," who "could chew out anyone he didn't think was giving 100 percent." Slaughter he thought the "greatest hustler of all time." Cooper could hit, catch, and run; with "Coop," according to Musial, "you didn't have to worry about squabbles with anybody else because if there was action, big Coop was in it." He remembered the determination and courage of Whitey Kurowski, who, following pitcher knockdowns, "invariably teed off on the next pitch." He thought Marion, with his range and "very accurate arm," one of the best defensive shortstops ever. In assessing the pitchers, he remembered Mort Cooper's good fastball and forkball and his amazing control and Lanier's ability to pitch well against contending ball clubs. He described Pollet as an artist with a moving fastball and a great change and slow curve. The handsome Beazley, Musial recalled, had "confidence, courage, control, a good fastball and good curve—everything to be great."[6]

At first, Musial must have wondered whether there would even be a 1942 season following the Japanese attack on Pearl Harbor on December 7, 1941, and the U.S. declaration of war soon afterward. The war threatened to suspend baseball activity as World War I had done on September 2,

6. Jerry Lansche, *Stan "The Man" Musial: Born to Be a Ballplayer,* 39; Stan Musial, Jack Buck, and Bob Broeg, *We Saw Stars,* 27–55.

1918. Some major leaguers, such as Hank Greenberg of the Detroit Tigers and Bob Feller of the Cleveland Indians, had already been inducted into military service.

In his "green light" letter to baseball commissioner Kenesaw Mountain Landis on January 16, 1942, President Roosevelt, however, conveyed a "personal opinion" that "it would be best for the country to keep baseball going" because of its recreational value. At the same time, Roosevelt continued, players of military age were expected to enter the services. Even though the game may have to rely on overaged players, thus lowering the quality of team performance, Roosevelt felt confident that this would not "dampen" the popularity of the sport.[7]

As it turned out, World War II had minimal impact on professional baseball in 1942. Although the Philadelphia Phillies surrendered nine roster players to the military, most major-league ball clubs lost considerably fewer. The Cardinals relinquished only reserve outfielder Walter Sessi and Johnny Grodzicki, their most promising rookie pitcher, who finished with an incredible 31–6 record for the Columbus Redbirds in 1941. Grodzicki, a paratrooper, would suffer a shrapnel wound in his right thigh just before V-E Day, considerably lessening his effectiveness in the postwar period. He was one of several major leaguers to return home impaired. The military's use of the railroads ultimately led to civilian travel restrictions, but railroad travel remained unrestricted for the major leagues in 1942. Minor-league baseball continued to function without alteration, too, at least until 1943 when the manpower drain crippled it, causing lower-classification leagues to disband. Even the Cardinal system would suffer appreciably.

In several ways the major leagues responded patriotically to the war effort of 1942. The Star Spangled Banner now became a regular ritual before every game. Ball clubs urged players to defer 10 percent of their salaries for the purchase of war bonds, which many of them did. Baseball moguls also agreed to a second All-Star game to benefit the servicemen's athletic fund. Too, they contributed the gate receipts of selected exhibition and regular-season games for servicemen's relief agencies. All of this represented only the beginning of what was to follow.

Musial's most immediate concern in the spring of 1942 was to make the Cardinals' club. During spring training, where countless reporters expected much of the boy wonder, Musial fell into a hitting slump during

---

7. For Roosevelt's message, see Richard Goldstein, *Spartan Seasons: How Baseball Survived the Second World War*, 19–20.

the Grapefruit League season, a perennial problem for him in Florida, which he later attributed to the distraction of a backdrop of waving palm trees and high blue skies. Also, at least one National League manager had questioned Southworth's judgment in playing Musial in left field because of the difficulty of a left-hander throwing across his body to second base on balls hit down the left-field line. Indeed, that sort of throw aggravated Musial's sore arm, which hurt for the entire 1942 season. If it had not been for his late-season heroics in 1941, Musial probably would have been sent back to AA ball that spring for more seasoning.[8]

Instead, the white-haired Southworth, exhibiting patience with young players, sat Musial down for a couple of exhibition games before reinserting him against right-handed hurlers, whom he bashed. Soon he stayed in against left-handed pitching too. On the trip to St. Louis afterward, Southworth told Musial, "Don't worry Stan, you're my left fielder. You can do it."[9] One day prior to the season opener, Rickey tore up Musial's old contract, raising his salary from four hundred to seven hundred dollars a month. This enabled Musial to bring Lil and Dickie to St. Louis, where the family found an apartment in the Lindell Tower on the city's west side. The following year they moved to the Fairgrounds Hotel. Musial now had all the incentives he needed. Against the St. Louis Browns in the perennial closing two-game series of the exhibition season, he connected for four hits.

On opening day Musial continued his hot hitting against the Chicago Cubs, singling and tripling off of right-hander Claude Passeau in a loss charged to pitcher Mort Cooper. The next afternoon Musial homered and singled twice. Then the Cards embarked on their first road trip, which began with a series in Pittsburgh.

Road games meant leisure travel by train until the 1950s. The National League had been composed of the same eight teams since 1901, a remarkable period of stability, with the St. Louis Cardinals the most western and southern club; the Chicago Cubs, Cincinnati Reds, and Pittsburgh Pirates in the Midwest; and the Philadelphia Phillies, New York Giants, Brooklyn Dodgers, and Boston Braves on the East Coast. Only the New

---

8. Musial, *Musial*, 53; "Lefty in Left? Sure Says Southworth," *Sporting News*, March 12, 1942; Danny Litwhiler to James N. Giglio, September 2, 1996, in possession of Giglio. Unless otherwise indicated, coverage of the 1942 contests, as well as subsequent season games, comes from either Musial, *Musial* or Lansche, *Stan "The Man."* Whenever factual differences occurred between the two, the author used the *St. Louis Post-Dispatch* to resolve the conflict.
    9. Musial, *Musial*, 54.

York Yankees of the American League and the Dodgers used airplanes prior to the 1950s, the former to reach St. Louis. Train travel created a bonding effect because of the amount of time ballplayers spent together, especially on overnights. Cardinal reserve catcher Del Wilber described a typical scenario where, following a Sunday day game in St. Louis, usually a doubleheader, the team would depart that evening on the New York Central. Once the team crossed the river, proceeding eastward, the players would "head back to the dining car and get something to eat. Then first thing you know you'd be in Indianapolis and you'd wake up the next morning and be in Albany, New York; then down the Hudson River to New York City."[10]

Train travel provided plenty of opportunity for card playing, mostly bridge; for instituting practical jokes, usually at a rookie's expense; or for talking baseball. The Cardinals usually arranged for two separate private Pullman cars. Regulars received lower sleeping berths and reserves upper ones in the sleeper. Whitey Kurowski remembered: "We used to always sit in the compartment of our sleeper, and we'd talk about that day's game . . . what happened that day . . . whether we won or lost . . . what we did . . . who we were gonna face tomorrow, or next week. Though we joked with each other and stayed loose, we were strictly baseball." Southworth summoned individual players to his compartment, sometimes with Moore or other veterans present, to go over opposition hitters and pitchers or review mistakes committed in recent games. On one occasion, Card rookie Bud Blattner related that Southworth instructed him on hitting.[11]

Perhaps the most enjoyable aspect of train travel was the dining car, where scrambled country eggs, big slices of ham, and "steaming pots of coffee" greeted players at breakfast and thick lamb chops and other quality meats—as good as those at the Waldorf—awaited them at dinner. Stewards then brought miniature bottles of alcoholic beverages for after-dining relaxation. Afterward, players might view the countryside from their compartments; they could tell what sort of crop year it was by the height of the corn or wheat. For some, it became a great way to experience Americana from its topography to its people, who witnessed their arrival at various train stations along the way.

10. Lansche, *Stan "The Man,"* 20. See also Harold Rosenthal, *The 10 Best Years of Baseball: An Informal History of the Fifties,* 87–95, which contains a chapter on train travel.

11. David Craft and Tom Owens, *Redbirds Revisited: Great Memories and Stories from St. Louis Cardinals,* 114–15; Harry Walker oral history transcript, A. B. Chandler Oral History Project, 27; Mark Kram, "Do You Hear That Whistle Down the Line?" 112.

Rail travel also had its negative side. The compartments in the sleepers contained much less space than hotel rooms, making it more difficult to sleep. Musial later claimed that he could never sleep well on trains. Moreover, because of the summer heat, the windows remained open at night, which exposed players to soot. To combat that problem, they slept with wet towels over their faces until Dr. Harrison Weaver, the Cardinals trainer, invented a filter apparatus for the nose.[12]

Often players arrived at their destination early in the morning, then had to secure their own bags, find a cab, and check in at the hotel. Without air-conditioning, ballplayers often found the heat unbearable as they tried to eat and sleep before an afternoon game. At the ballpark, according to Billy Herman of the Dodgers, it could be 110 degrees on the field. In the clubhouse afterward, it sometimes reached 120 degrees: "You take your shower, but there's no way you can dry off. The sweat keeps running off of you. You go out to the street and try to find a cab back to the hotel and go up to your room and you lose your breath, it's so hot in there. But the dining room isn't much better, so you order room service and stay right there and eat. Then you go to bed and try to sleep, but you can't, you're sweating so much. So you get up and pull the sheet off the bed and soak it with cold water and go back and roll up in a wet sheet. But it dries out after an hour or two, and you have to get up and soak it again." Duke Snider of the Dodgers recalled sleeping with the hotel window open, inviting the city dirt to enter and blacken the pillows. He singled out the Schenley Hotel in Pittsburgh as being the worst for that problem. Only the Cincinnati Netherland Plaza offered air-conditioning, limited to the lobby.[13]

But Musial never seemed to mind the inconveniences of the game. He had experienced much worse in his upbringing. Besides, it was part of the sport he loved. In 1942 he shared a room on the road with Ray Sanders, a typical rookie arrangement. He would have other roomies in the next couple of years, some unsuitable because of their affinity for alcohol or the night life. Musial enjoyed a beer or two and soon smoked cigars or cigarettes, the latter following his endorsement of Chesterfields—but he did everything in moderation. He loved to sleep late and enjoy a leisurely breakfast before going to the ballpark. In the evenings he relished meals at the dining rooms of the major hotels—whether it be the Kenmore Hotel in Boston or the Bellevue Stratford in Philadelphia. After dinner the movie

12. Kram, "Do You Hear That Whistle?" 112.
13. Lansche, *Stan "The Man,"* 20–21.

theater or musical entertainment beckoned, but he returned to the hotel soon afterward.[14]

Musial most altered his road-trip routine when the ball club played in Pittsburgh. He usually tried to spend time with family in Donora on those occasions. In that first venture in April he played at Pittsburgh's Forbes Field, and with his parents watching, Musial left the first game for a pinch-hitter as lefty Ken Heintzelman shut out the Cardinals. This was not the last time in 1942 that Southworth lifted Musial against left-handed pitching in favor of Coaker Triplett, who occasionally platooned with Musial in left field. Musial's performances against southpaws improved as the season progressed, and Southworth consequently began to play Musial regularly. Still, even though he eventually hit left-handers as effectively as righties, some lefties—especially Heintzelman and Ken Raffenberger and Johnny Vander Meer of the Reds—continued to give Musial fits. The first two tantalized him with their slow pitches, while Vander Meer threw smoke that moved up and in.[15]

In the early weeks of the season the Cardinals had difficulty hitting any pitcher. They were shut out in five of their first twenty-four games, and the team's winning percentage was only around .500. Musial's hitting remained inconsistent and his throwing arm weak. Only after the weather warmed did the arm strengthen. He also occasionally tumbled chasing fly balls in the outfield, a problem that continued until the next season when Card trainer Doc Weaver discovered that the baseball shoes Musial purchased when joining the club were too small. Musial was reluctant to discard them until Weaver took him in a cab to a sporting goods store in New York and bought him a new pair of shoes.[16]

Not until the league-leading Brooklyn Dodgers came to Sportsman's Park in mid-May did the Cardinals play improved ball. Those contests came closer to war than to ball games, because the two teams hated each other. Part of the animosity stemmed from an incident after the Cardinals had traded hitting standout Joe "Duckie" Medwick to the Dodgers on June 12, 1940. Six days later Cardinal pitcher Bob Bowman beaned Medwick at Ebbets Field following a heated argument with Medwick and Dodger manager Leo Durocher a few hours earlier at the Hotel New Yorker. The beaning had caused such a disturbance that Bowman had to be escorted from the field. After several days in the hospital Medwick

14. Irv Goodman, *Stan, the Man, Musial*, 10–11.
15. Musial, *Musial*, 55; Musial, Buck, and Broeg, *We Saw Stars*, 26, 51, 57.
16. Goodman, *Stan, the Man*, 42–43.

returned, but he never regained his former level of play. Even though no evidence exists that Bowman intentionally hit Medwick, the Dodgers thought otherwise. And with the aggressive, acerbic Durocher at the helm, Dodger pitchers, heeding their manager's admonition to "stick it in his ear," routinely threw at batters to intimidate them, especially against St. Louis.[17]

In the midst of considerable turmoil, including Medwick's stepping on Sanders's ankle at first base, the Cardinals swept the three-game series, with Musial contributing five hits. Mort Cooper's 1–0 shutout against Dodger ace Whit Wyatt served as another highlight against a team that usually brought out the best in the Cardinals.

Both teams continued to win regularly in June despite Musial's ankle injury on Memorial Day in Chicago, resulting from the snagging of his spikes on home plate as he tried to score from first on a short double. The injury kept him out of the lineup for a week; afterward he fell into a mild slump that caused his average to drop to .298. After winning seven straight, which put them four and a half games from the top, the Cardinals once again faced the first-place Dodgers in a five-game series at Ebbets Field in mid-June. Musial had a homer and a triple in the only Cardinal victory, raising his average to .315. With the Cardinals now seven and a half games behind the Dodgers, the Associated Press wrote them off as a serious pennant contender. At the All-Star break the Redbirds dropped yet another game behind. Even though Musial failed to join five teammates on the National League All-Star team, at least one Associated Press writer thought that he had been overlooked in the selection process.

It appeared that Sam Breadon had conceded the season when he sold reliable Lon Warneke, the "Arkansas hummingbird," to the Cubs for the waiver price at the All-Star break. Critics suggested that he unloaded the thirty-three-year-old Warneke, with a 6–4 record, because of his club-high fifteen-thousand-dollar salary, causing Breadon to bristle that he wanted to give highly regarded youngsters such as Beazley more work. As it turned out, the move represented the successful application of Rickey's philosophy, since Warneke's best days seemed to be behind him. Moreover, Beazley, whom one sportswriter in spring training called "another Dizzy Dean" because of his cockiness, control, and good stuff, soon emerged as one of the Cards' two aces. Immediately following Warneke's departure, Beazley pitched his first shutout in securing his ninth victory of the season.

17. Creamer, *Baseball in '41*, 74–76.

Several key series stood out as the Cardinals slowly began to make a move. The first involved back-to-back doubleheaders against the Dodgers in St. Louis on July 18 and 19, when both clubs suffered injuries to key players. In the first game on the second day, winning Cardinals pitcher Cooper strained a ligament in his arm, which was expected to sideline him for a week to ten days. The gutsy Cooper had suffered from chronic arm trouble as it was, having to chew aspirin during games to dull the pain. The second mishap, suffered by Dodger center fielder Pete Reiser in the nightcap, had much greater implications. A St. Louis native whom Commissioner Landis declared a free agent after the Cards had signed him, he soon became a Durocher favorite. Durocher put Reiser in center field in 1941, and the twenty-one-year-old won the National League batting title with a .343 average. Coming into St. Louis in July, he was pacing the league at .350. But on the nineteenth, with the score tied in the eleventh inning, Slaughter hit a long drive to the center-field wall, which a sprinting Reiser momentarily caught as his head banged into the concrete. "It was like a hand grenade had gone off inside my head," Reiser later recalled. By the time he got the ball to the infield Slaughter had scored the winning run. Because the Dodgers needed him, Reiser came back too quickly from his concussion. The dizziness and double vision persisted, causing his average to drop nearly fifty points by the end of the season. Described later by Durocher as probably the greatest all-around ballplayer he ever saw, Willie Mays included, Reiser would never regain his early form.[18]

The Cardinals captured one other game in that four-game series. In the Redbird win on the eighteenth, Musial singled in the go-ahead runs in a 7–4 victory. That key blow also fractured the finger of Dodger ace reliever Hugh Casey, disabling him for three weeks. On that same day, as antagonism mounted, Dodger right hander Les Webber, a pitcher of "limited ability," to use Musial's description, threw two consecutive knockdown pitches at the Cardinal left fielder, causing him to head toward Webber before being restrained by Redbird coaches. After the first knockdown, Musial had told Dodger catcher Mickey Owen, "Doesn't that damn fool know he can't hit me?"[19] Musial never again went after a pitcher. Later attributing his action to the impulsiveness of youth, he subsequently responded to deckings by concentrating even more on getting a base hit. Knockdowns, he later commented, were part of the game.

18. Lansche, Stan "The Man," 33; Creamer, Baseball in '41, 205–8.
19. Mickey Owen interview, August 25, 1995; Musial, Musial, 57.

And never more so than for the remainder of the season, for they affected the National League race. The Durocher Dodgers, the greatest perpetrators of such intimidation, caused the opposition to play harder against them. In Chicago in August, Cubs pitcher Hi Bithorn, after hearing Durocher yelling repeatedly "stick it in his ear" to his pitcher, went into his windup before throwing into the Dodger dugout in an attempt to nail Durocher. Soon afterward in Boston, Dodger ace Wyatt lost to the Braves for the first time in a knockdown frenzy that caused Braves manager Casey Stengel to say, "If I had a ball club as good as Durocher's, I wouldn't throw at a ball club as bad as mine. We're going to battle those guys all the harder from now on, and I've talked to Frisch, Wilson, and other managers who feel the same."[20]

Wyatt's loss on August 8 came three days after the Dodgers had reached their season's peak, a ten-game lead with a 71–29 record. Meanwhile, the Cardinals had turned the corner against Pittsburgh that same day. They tied the score in the ninth when Musial tripled and faked a steal home, causing the Pirate pitcher to balk. After the tying run, the game ended in a deadlock because of darkness after sixteen innings. Soon afterward, good pitching and team speed contributed to an eight-game winning streak. That swiftness became evident on the base paths as Cardinal baserunners threatened to take extra bases on virtually every hit. "My guys get jittery," Stengel explained, causing his fielders to make mistakes. In the field, the Cardinal outfielders used their exceptional speed to good advantage.

At home for a twenty-two-game stand in mid-August, the team never seemed more relaxed. They fell into the habit of playing zany music before and after games with trainer Doc Weaver's mandolin leading the way. Their victory song became Spike Jones's silly "Pass the Biscuits, Mirandy." All of this occurred in the midst of considerable jocularity.

Musial had now become a respected member of the ball club. He had shown his toughness in challenging Webber and exhibited competiveness and skill in every aspect of the game. At the plate he was one of the Cardinals' most consistent hitters. Standing deep in the batting box in his uniquely coiled, semi-crouched fashion, he often stroked balls to left field for base hits. Although swiping only six bases in 1942, he became a terror in taking the extra base or in flustering the pitcher by threatening to steal. Teammates soon called him Stash, after hearing Donorans addressing him that way, or Coal Miner because of his western Pennsylvania background. Marty Marion remembered him in front of his locker, quietly working on

20. Musial, *Musial*, 59.

his bats, scraping and filing the handles. He also had a habit of banging coat hangers on a chair to music, which put him in a rhythmic mood to hit. "He was a shy kid," according to Marion, but one who joined in the fun.[21]

Musial hit well into August, raising his average to .319 by the twenty-fourth. Boosted also by the pitching of Cooper and Beazley, the Cardinals continued their hot streak. The superstitious Cooper, who had been stuck at thirteen wins in 1942 and who had never won more than thirteen games previously in the majors, decided to change his uniform number from thirteen to fourteen against Cincinnati. He pitched a two-hitter against the Reds, wearing Gus Mancuso's uniform. Four days later he wore his brother's number fifteen jersey and then squeezed into Ken O'Dea's number sixteen against the Dodgers on the twenty-fifth. The latter win came after Brooklyn had taken a 1–0 lead in the thirteenth inning. It also reduced the Dodger lead to five and a half games. In that same series Beazley won his sixteenth in yet another extra-inning game.

In early September the Cards embarked on their final road trip with only thirty games remaining. Musial got the team off to a good start against the Reds with an RBI triple, breaking a 2–2 tie, enabling Beazley to raise his record to 18–5. The next day Musial exhibited his speed by scoring from first base on a single to deadlock the score. In the ninth Johnny Hopp stretched a single into a double and then scored on Kurowski's single. The Cards also captured the final series game with Cooper winning his sixth in a row, while wearing Harry Gumbert's number nineteen jersey. The Cardinals were now only two and a half games behind the Dodgers.

On September 11 the Redbirds traveled to Ebbets Field for the final two games with the Dodgers. The tension, according to Musial, had reduced the Cardinals' clubhouse to silence. Cooper, seeking his twentieth win, wearing Coaker Triplett's jersey, found himself in a scoreless duel with Wyatt for five innings before Slaughter drove in the first run in the sixth. The Cards managed a 3–0 victory; it was the sixth time Cooper subdued the Dodgers that year. The next afternoon lefty Max Lanier, always tough against Brooklyn, won 2–1. Kurowski delivered the key blow, a homer down the left-field line, against Max Macon. The Cards had tied the Dodgers in the standings, in winning twenty-nine of their previous thirty-four games.

St. Louis clearly had momentum as the team left for Philadelphia on Saturday morning. As players disembarked at the old Broad Street station, however, an incident threatened to erase their good fortune. Beazley

21. Marty Marion interview, December 10, 1996.

refused to permit a redcap to carry his bag, and, after being cursed in return, the hot-tempered pitcher threw his suitcase at the baggage porter. The porter then drew a knife, which caused Beazley to raise an arm in self-defense, resulting in a deep slash on his right thumb. With blood dripping everywhere, Beazley went after the assailant, but fortunately he was unable to apprehend him, which might have led to further injuries.[22]

Almost miraculously, Beazley pitched effectively the next day even in losing the first game of a doubleheader split. Meanwhile, the Dodgers lost their twin bill against Cincinnati. The next two victories over the Phillies resulted in large measure from Musial's clutch hitting: a lead-run double in a 6–3 win and then a two-run double in a fourteen-inning victory for rookie Dickson.

The momentum mounted in Boston on the sixteenth when Musial drove in two runs and scored another on the same day the Cardinals' front office placed World Series tickets on sale. The following day the team overcame a four-run deficit in the ninth inning when Southworth used Triplett as a pinch-hitter for Musial, who was hitting .314 at the time. Triplett singled against the left-handed Willard Donovan to win the game. Everything came up aces for Southworth and the team as they returned home with a two-game lead following Cooper's 1–0 victory over Warneke and the Cubs.

The Cards remained on fire at home by first sweeping a two-game series against Pittsburgh. With the Redbirds trailing by a run against Rip Sewell in the fifth inning of the second game, Musial hit a bases-loaded home run over the right-field pavilion. The Cards had won their 102nd game, a team record. The next afternoon Musial continued his hitting tear with three hits, two RBIs, and a run scored against Cincinnati, followed by another three-hit performance on the twenty-fourth as Cooper picked up his twenty-second win, again matching his jersey number.

At this point a Cardinal victory or a Dodger defeat would ensure a Redbird pennant, something team leader Moore refused to discuss. In a career full of second-place disappointments, he most remembered the Cubs' twenty-one-game winning streak to overhaul the Cards in 1935. He wanted the team to bear down in the remaining three games. Following a rainout the Cards season came down to a final doubleheader against the Cubs, with the team holding a game and a half lead over the equally hot Dodgers, who would end the season by winning ten of their last twelve games.

22. Musial, *Musial*, 62; Lansche, *Stan "The Man,"* 37.

The Cardinals swept the doubleheader, with often-injured Ernie White and Beazley securing the wins, the latter his twenty-first. Beazley and Cooper became the National League's only twenty-game winners in 1942. The team, winning forty-three of its last fifty-one games, ended up with a 106–48 record, two games ahead of the Dodgers. No National League team had won more since the Pittsburgh Pirates' 110 wins in 1909. J. Roy Stockton, the nationally known sportswriter for the *St. Louis Post-Dispatch*, who covered the Cards in the halcyon years between 1926 and 1946, rated the 1931 and 1942 teams the best of nine pennant winners. According to conventional wisdom, the 1942 addition's only limitation came in its seemingly modest offensive production. Slaughter (.318) and Musial (.315) finished second and third, respectively, in the league in batting average, but Slaughter's meager 13 homers led the team while Musial was second with 10. While Slaughter drove in a respectable 98 runs, Musial followed with only 72. The team strength offensively came in its overall balance. With few outstanding individual performers, the Cardinals nevertheless led the league in batting average (.268), RBIs (682), runs (755), triples (69), doubles (282), hits (1,454), and slugging percentage (.379), and finished second in stolen bases (71). It finished sixth in homers (60), however.

Even though the National League awarded no Rookie of the Year title until 1947, the unofficial designation arguably should go to Musial, with Beazley his major competition. Consistent in his hitting the entire year, he especially produced in clutch situations in the crucial final weeks. In his first major exposure to national print media, Musial became the subject of Stockton's article, "Rookie of the Year," published in the *Saturday Evening Post* in September, in which he claimed that Musial could run like a deer and hit like Ty Cobb.[23]

That same month Musial and the Cardinals were decided World Series underdogs against the powerful New York Yankees, who had won eight World Series in eight attempts since 1927 and had lost only four series games out of their last thirty-six contests. Even though Babe Ruth, Lou Gehrig, and other Yankee greats had long passed from the scene, the Bronx Bombers had plenty of power in the likes of Joe DiMaggio, Charlie "King Kong" Keller, and Joe Gordon, each of whom had driven in more than 100 runs and had hit more home runs than any Cardinal did in 1942. The Yankee pitching staff, anchored by Ernie Bonham (21–5), Spud Chandler (16–5), Hank Borowy (15–4), and Red Ruffing (14–

---

23. J. Roy Stockton, "Rookie of the Year," 29, 36.

7), led the American League with a 2.91 ERA. Under the direction of manager Joe McCarthy, the Yanks had coasted to the pennant with a nine-game cushion.

The series opened in Sportsman's Park on September 30 with 34,769 in attendance. With crafty veteran Ruffing in control against starter Cooper, the Yankees extended their lead to 4–0 in the eighth with Moore's two-out single that inning the only blemish. Aided by reliever Lanier's two errors, the visitors scored three more runs in the ninth before the Cards showed life in the bottom half of the inning. After Musial fouled out, the Cardinals rallied as Marty Marion's triple drove in the first two St. Louis runners of the game. With two outs, McCarthy then replaced Ruffing with Chandler after two more base hits. Two additional safeties followed before Musial, representing the winning run, came up with two runners on base. Usually a good low-ball hitter, he tried to hit Chandler's low offering over the right-field pavilion roof, but instead grounded sharply to the first baseman. Musial had made two of the Cardinal outs that inning in a 7–4 loss. Yet, despite being angered at his own performance, Musial took heart at the late-inning rally, believing more than ever that the Yankees were beatable.

The next afternoon the Cardinals threw their rookie sensation Beazley against right-hander Bonham, whose 2.27 ERA paced the team. Beazley continued his dream season by carrying a 3–0 lead into the eighth before the Yankees tied the score. Slaughter's double in the bottom half of the inning and Musial's RBI single, his first series hit, gave the team a one-run cushion going into the ninth inning. The key play came in the visitors' final at bat when, with no outs, pinch-runner Tuck Stainback raced to third on Buddy Hassett's line-drive single to right, which Slaughter fielded quickly near the line and then threw to Kurowski's ankles at third base, barely getting Stainback. Afterward, the Yankees went quietly.

The series now moved to "The House That Ruth Built," Yankee Stadium, in the Bronx. While the Cardinals were accustomed to playing in New York, nobody anticipated a three-game Cardinal sweep. Consequently, the Musials' decision for Stan to go without Lil made sense despite Breadon's one-hundred-dollar travel allowance for wives. Putting Lil up for three nights in a New York hotel would impose a strain on the family's meager finances. So, Lil traveled on the special train with the team as far as Pittsburgh and then planned to return for the windup in St. Louis. Other Cardinal wives followed similar strategies in avoiding the New York trip.

The opening-day crowd of 69,123 established a World Series record. Musial admitted to feeling numb on this historic occasion, and not only because he was a twenty-one-year-old only one season removed from

Class C ball. The three-tiered stadium created an enormous obstacle for left fielders because of the haze of cigarette smoke and the shadows created by the October sun, which blanketed left field, making it difficult to see batted balls. Both starting pitchers, Chandler and Ernie White, pitched outstandingly. The ace of the 1941 season, the injury-plagued White had managed only a 7–5 record in 1942. Yet the blond left-hander pitched the game of his life in outdueling Chandler, 2–0, the first time the Yankees were shut out in the World Series since the Cardinals' Jesse Haines had accomplished it in 1926. Three defensive gems proved the difference in game three. In the sixth, with two outs and a man on first, DiMaggio hit a liner to left-center, an almost certain triple after Musial fell as he headed for the ball. But Moore, running at full speed to his right, dove over Musial to make a backhanded catch. In the following inning Musial went back to the left-field corner to grab Gordon's drive heading for the lower stands. The next batter, Keller, forced a leaping Slaughter to climb the right-field wall to prevent another home run.

On Sunday, October 4, game four drew another record crowd of 69,902 to witness a slugfest in which Borowy failed to survive the Cardinals' six-run onslaught in the fourth inning. Musial contributed two hits as he opened the inning by bunting to the left side and then doubled to right to drive in the sixth run, thereby tying a World Series record for the most hits in an inning. But Cooper ran into trouble in the sixth when Keller's three-run homer contributed to a six-run rally that tied the game at six. The Cards remained unfazed. Led by longtime trainer Doc Weaver, the bench jockeys, who included reserves and diminutive equipment manager Butch Yatkeman, helped keep team spirits high with all sorts of cheers and hexes. The Redbirds rallied with two runs in the seventh and one in the ninth as Lanier pitched three scoreless innings in relief to record the win.

By now the Yankees had become frustrated and testy. As lineups for game five were exchanged at home plate, Yankee coach Art Fletcher, representing manager McCarthy, told the umpires that the Yankees wanted "that little guy" out of the Cardinal dugout. Team captain Moore, who stood in for manager Southworth, responded, "You don't mean little Butch. Why, he's in the dugout for all our games." Home plate umpire Bill Summers almost apologetically told Moore that he had no choice but to relegate Yatkeman to the clubhouse where he would have to listen to the game on the radio. After responding, "That's all right, Bill," Moore turned to Fletcher and said, "This is just one more reason why there's going to be no tomorrow in this World Series."[24]

24. Musial, *Musial*, 70.

That afternoon the Cardinals went with their ace, Beazley, who matched Ruffing in a 2–2 tie to the ninth inning, when Walker Cooper led off with a single. Kurowski, whom Ruffing had struck out three times in game one and held in check in game five, then drove a ball into the left-field stands near the foul pole for a 4–2 lead. In the bottom half of the inning the Yankees had two runners on with no outs. But after Jerry Priddy missed a bunt attempt, Cooper threw down to second base, catching a napping Gordon. Following the pickoff, the Yankees went down meekly, enabling Beazley to win his second World Series contest.

Kurowski, the other series hero, became the center of the clubhouse celebration. Nothing could have been sweeter. He not only had overcome the childhood loss of part of the ulna bone in his right forearm but also lost a brother in a mining accident in 1937 and his father from a heart attack that spring. Journalists now sang the Cardinals' praises, comparing their upset to the miracle Boston Braves victory of 1914 over Connie Mack's heavily favored Philadelphia Athletics. *Time* magazine called them the "kids." "Their outfielders," according to *Time*, "make octopus catches, pick off runners with the cool precision of anti-aircraft guns. Their runners beat out any bunt, are shamefaced if they can't make third from first on an outfield single."[25] Although no account singled out Musial's World Series play, *Time* certainly had him in mind in the aforementioned story. He had made a contribution in three out of the five games, although he hit only .222 overall, with four hits, including a double, which placed him near the bottom of the Cardinal regulars.

From New York, in the interest of economy, Musial decided to go directly to Donora with his parents, who had attended the final three games. He wired Lil in St. Louis to meet him in Donora. At New York's Pennsylvania Station, Musial said final good-byes to teammates who were heading back to St. Louis. Marion remembered him "crying like a baby, shaking hands with everyone."[26] Musial soon received a World Series check for $6,192.50 for one week's work, which easily surpassed his season salary of $4,250. He could now purchase clothes for himself and Lil, assist his parents, and buy war bonds. To cap a marvelous season, Donora proclaimed October 14 Stan Musial Day with a banquet highlighting the celebration. The pall of the war never left his consciousness, however; he wondered how many of his teammates would return in 1943 to defend their World Series title.

25. "The Kids," *Time* (October 12, 1942): 77–79.
26. Marion interview, December 10, 1996.

Pennants and Wartime

F rom 1943 through V-J Day in 1945, the war demanded many more sacrifices from major-league baseball, especially from the players. Among the top players who entered the armed forces in the spring of 1943 were Red Sox slugger Ted Williams and teammates Dom DiMaggio and Johnny Pesky; the Yankee Clipper, Joe DiMaggio; Brooklyn's Pee Wee Reese and Pete Reiser; and the Giants' first baseman Johnny Mize. In 1943 alone more than two hundred major leaguers found themselves in military uniform. The number of departures for each of the next two seasons easily exceeded the 1943 figure.

With the induction of Terry Moore and Enos Slaughter, the Cardinals lost two-thirds of their outfield in 1943. Pitching aces Johnny Beazley and Howie Pollet also departed, along with key subs Frank "Creepy" Crespi and Erv Dusak. Despite the inductions, which would cut much more deeply into the Cardinal roster in 1944, the franchise managed to flourish because of the depth of its farm system and because key players such as Whitey Kurowski, Marty Marion, and Johnny Hopp had chronic injuries that excluded them from induction.

Most important, the Cardinals still had Stan Musial, who performed even more superbly in the next two seasons as he learned to avoid bad pitches and hit with two strikes. While he showed more power in 1943 and 1944, Musial, primarily a line-drive hitter, continued to punch hits to left field on outside pitches and beat out slow rollers to the infield. He relied on only one person—coach Clyde "Buzzy" Wares—for hitting advice. Wares observed whether he was overstriding, standing too erect, or turning his head before making contact. If Musial had two or three bad days, he would go to Buzzy for assistance.[1]

Musial profited from the depleted talent pool, especially since he no longer had to bat against the likes of the Dodgers' Hugh Casey and the Reds' Johnny Vander Meer by 1944. In place of military-bound regulars, ball clubs relied on players who were either too young or old to be drafted or who had failed the induction physical. Joe Nuxhall of the Reds debuted as a fifteen-year-old pitcher in 1944, forty-year-old Gashouse Gang spark plug Pepper Martin returned to the Cards that same year as an outfielder,

---

1. Connor, ed., *Baseball for the Love of It*, 158.

and one-armed speedster Pete Gray performed for the St. Louis Browns of the American League. Most of these players drifted into the minors or retired after the war.

Musial avoided induction in 1943 and 1944 apparently because the Donora draft board had enough available young men to exempt him for being married with a son born before Pearl Harbor. Assuming financial responsibility for his parents also helped. Lukasz's deteriorating health, caused by a stroke, had forced him to retire in 1943 while in his early fifties. To stay in the good graces of the draft board, as well as to supplement his income, Musial also continued to work at the zinc works—a war-related industry—in the off-season. No evidence exists that Musial sought special consideration from the draft board. Had he come from an area containing fewer draft-age males, he could have been inducted as early as 1943.

Musial continued to call Donora home for the duration of the war. In St. Louis he maintained an apartment in the Hotel Fairgrounds large enough to accommodate Lil and Dickie. But his wife and son often returned to Donora, where the Musials also leased an apartment. Stan's and Lil's socializing evolved around a few friends in St. Louis, including the Marions, the Harry Walkers, the Pollets, and the Danny Litwhilers. Lil thought the Litwhilers were rich because they owned a car. The Musials also became especially close to St. Louis natives Sue and Ed Carson, a businessman, who met Stan in his rookie season. Rabid baseball fans, the Carsons shared dinners and conversations with the Musials into the postwar era. Both families had small children and modest tastes. Of course, during the off-season Stan and Lil spent their entire time close to their Pennsylvania families.

For a while in early 1943 it appeared that the Musials would remain in Donora as the baseball season began. Musial decided to reject the contract of Sam Breadon, which provided only for a $1,000 raise to $5,500. As much as he enjoyed playing baseball, his sense of self-worth conflicted with Breadon's offer. Relying on the assistance of Monongahela auto dealer Frank Pizzica, he drafted a letter asking for $10,000. He claimed that since Moore and Slaughter entered the service he would have to play "even harder." Later candidly calling the letter a mistake, Musial realized that it allowed Breadon to reply forcibly: "You will have no more to do this year than you did last year. I thought you were the kind of ball player that gave all you had in every game. Of course, we expect the same in 1943, if you sign a contract with us." After Musial countered with an offer of $7,500, Breadon replied that "no one in our organization has been advanced faster than you have been. We have had great outfielders on our ball club, including . . . Moore and Slaughter, and none of them in their second year received a contract for as much as $5,500."

Musial's response that higher taxes and inflation made such comparisons with Depression-era salaries unfair made no impact on Breadon. Breadon recommended that Musial come to St. Louis to discuss it further, and if he decided to sit out the 1943 season, the ball club would pay his round-trip expenses. Musial wisely decided to stay put, causing Breadon to send farm director Ed Dyer to Donora with a $6,250 offer. With Pizzica out of town, Musial, anxious to play ball, signed.[2] Afterward, he felt little warmth toward the aloof skin-flint Breadon. Like his teammates, he remained convinced that Cardinal ballplayers were underpaid in comparison with their National League counterparts. He also momentarily bore a privately concealed animus toward the reserve clause, which he thought gave owners like Breadon too much control. Whatever his feelings, Musial kept smiling and remained the consummate team player. Throughout his playing career he successfully avoided controversy and quietly did his job.

Meanwhile, Breadon continued to make money during the war. His overall payroll had shrunk because of the loss of regulars to military service. Also, to control wartime inflation, the federal government had imposed restrictions on the raising of salaries, which Breadon used to his advantage. Like other owners he chided ballplayers that they should be satisfied with their current pay at a time when big-leaguers were making twenty-one dollars a month while in the service. And even though attendance had generally sagged in 1942 and 1943, the Cardinals suffered only slight reductions because of their place in the standings. As a consequence, with a gain of $410,587, Breadon's Cardinals led the National League in profits during the war era.[3] Overall, only four clubs operated in the red during that period.

The frustrating conditions of wartime baseball offset whatever monetary gains existed for the owners. Beginning in 1943 spring training could no longer be held in the South because of the necessity to curtail nonessential train travel. This meant that clubs had to get in shape close to home—often in the rain and the snow. Sometimes this required working out in field houses and gymnasiums. Cairo, Illinois, became the Cardinals' training site, while the St. Louis Browns of the American League occupied

2. Musial, *Musial*, 74–75.
3. Goldstein, *Spartan Seasons*, 151–52.

nearby Cape Girardeau, Missouri. Other Midwest teams trained in various parts of Indiana.

Coming a week late, Musial flew into St. Louis and then was driven
to Cairo. Like other Cardinals he came with long underwear and winter
clothes, which Doc Weaver instructed them to bring. Luckily, he came
ready to play after having worked out with Pittsburgh Pirate outfielder
Jim Russell at Donora High School. The Cairo ballpark, Cotter Field, was at
best primitive; moreover, train travel restrictions prevented the team from
playing anyone other than an army team based in Memphis. Conditions
improved little in the next two years. In 1944 the team became afflicted
with the flu, while in 1945 Cotter Field was submerged under four feet of
water, causing the team to return to St. Louis to train in Sportsman's Park.[4]

Travel problems continued to affect major-league baseball during the
regular season. No longer were Pullman berths always available, and in
some cases players had to sit on their luggage because of the unavailability
of seats. Instead of steaks being served in the dining car, they faced a choice
of omelettes or various fish concoctions, also the fare in hotel restaurants.

By 1943 the war had also altered the liveliness of the baseball. Because of
the great demand for rubber in the production of war-related goods, A. G.
Spalding and Brothers, manufacturer of major-league baseballs, produced
the balata ball, which replaced the high-grade cork center and the rubber
inner-casing ball. Balata, made from the milky juices of tropical trees, now
covered a ground cork center, contributing to baseballs being 25 percent
less lively than the '42 variety.

Consequently, the 1943 season began with a number of 1–0 scores,
including the Cardinals' defeat to Cincinnati at Crosley Field in eleven
innings. Despite a Musial triple the next day, which Musial claimed
sounded like a "nickel rocket," the Redbirds lost another 1–0 game to
the Reds, again in extra innings. In the third contest, Musial scored on a
passed ball while attempting a steal of home as the Cardinals won 2–1.[5]
Consecutive shutouts followed as Pollet defeated the Reds 1–0 and Mort
Cooper beat the Cubs 4–0. No homer was hit until Joe Gordon's blast in
the Yankees' eleventh game.

The low-scoring contests concerned both the Spalding officials and the
league presidents. The former promised a more lively ball by combining
better materials with balata, which the American League adopted on May
9. On that day alone American Leaguers crushed six home runs, only three

4. Ibid., 116–17.
5. Musial, *Musial*, 77.

less than they had hit in the previous seventy-two games. National League president Ford Frick, meanwhile, had authorized the use of leftover balls from the '42 season even before the adoption of the modified new ball. By 1944 balata had given way to synthetic rubber, ending forever the wartime controversy over the quality of the baseball.

In those first weeks of the 1943 season, Musial hit .323, with five doubles and three triples among his twenty-one hits. Probably better than anyone else, he learned to adjust to the dead ball by hitting line drives "where they ain't." He was becoming the quiet leader of a team that was head and shoulders above the rest of the league. Joining Musial in the outfield was Harry "the Hat" Walker, a rookie backup with a .314 batting average in 1942, who now played center field. Danny Litwhiler, a fellow Pennsylvanian who became a lifelong friend of Musial, replaced Stash in left field. Litwhiler came to the Cards in a trade with the Philadelphia Phillies in exchange for outfielders Coaker Triplett, Buster Adams, and Dain Clay. Musial moved to right field, where he felt more natural throwing to the infield, enabling his arm to strengthen. The infield remained intact with the exception of rookie Lou Klein, who capably took over for the slumping Jimmy Brown at second base.

The heart of the Cardinals' strength continued to be its pitching staff. Cooper, the veteran mainstay, tied for the National League in victories with 21; Pollet won eight games before his induction in July; lefty Max Lanier contributed 15 victories; Murry Dickson went 8–2 as a spot starter; and Harry Gumbert quietly contributed 10 victories as a starter. Additionally, manager Billy Southworth received considerable support from three rookies: Alpha Brazle, a southpaw pitcher with a good sinker ball whom teammates called "Boots and Saddles" because of his western background; right-hander George "Red" Munger, known for his superb pickoff move; and left-hander Harry "the Cat" Brecheen, recognized for his exceptional control, screwball, and fielding ability. Although all three won between eight and nine games as spot starters and relievers in 1943, Brecheen alone eventually achieved stardom. Musial labeled him a good clutch pitcher, one who had an inspirational impact on the ball club. All in all, Cardinal pitchers led the league in several categories, including ERA and strikeouts.

Led by Cooper, who threw back-to-back one-hitters, and the hitting of Musial, who went on a twenty-two-game batting streak, the Cardinals took over first place in early July. They remained barely ahead of the second-place Dodgers until Cardinal pitching dominated in the second week of July. Beginning with Cooper's 7–0 blanking of Boston, the pitching staff hurled thirty-one consecutive scoreless innings. In that period Pollet pitched his third consecutive shutout just before receiving instructions to report to active duty in the U.S. Army Air Force on July 15. Two days earlier Musial had made the first of his twenty-five appearances in the annual All-Star game. In his initial at bat he contributed a sacrifice fly off of the Washington Senators' Dutch Leonard; his one hit, a double, came at the expense of Detroit Tiger lefty Hal Newhouser. Nonetheless, the American League won for the eighth time in the last eleven outings. The National League starter, Mort Cooper, suffered the loss after giving up four runs in two and one-third innings.

Afterward, the Cardinals went on a road trip, which saw them win sixteen out of twenty-five games followed by an 18–4 home stand that produced eleven straight victories. After the Phillies ended the streak on July 26, the second-place Dodgers came into town, nine games behind the Redbirds. The Cardinals swept the Dodgers in four games, leaving St. Louis with a 66–32 record, thirteen games ahead of the new runner-up Pittsburgh Pirates. For all practical purposes, the pennant race had ended.

On September 18 the Cardinals clinched the National League pennant after a doubleheader sweep of the Chicago Cubs. They ended up eighteen games in front of the Cincinnati Reds and twenty-six and a half games ahead of third-place Brooklyn, with a 105–49 record, one game less than they had won in 1942. Aside from a brilliant pitching staff, the key to the Cardinals' play remained Musial, who led the league for much of the season in capturing the batting title with a .357 average, the first of seven that he would win. He finished twenty-seven points ahead of runner-up Billy Herman of the Dodgers. He led the league in hits (220), doubles (48), triples (20), on-base percentage (.425), total bases (347), and slugging average (.562). He finished second in runs scored (108) and tied for the team lead in homers (13) and stolen bases (9). He played in every game (155) despite a twisted ankle late in the season, causing him to pinch-hit in one game. He also finished ahead of Walker Cooper for the National League Most Valuable Player award, the first of three for him. Fittingly, the Sporting News featured the twenty-two-year-old in two articles in 1943. One described his popularity with the fans, for whom he always made himself available for autographs.[6]

Even though the Yankees had no one to match Musial's statistics, they were a power-hitting club that led the American League in several hitting categories, including home runs. Outfielder Charlie Keller set the team

6. *Sporting News,* August 19, November 4, 1943.

standard with thirty-one homers. Moreover, the Yankees mound corps, paced by Spurgeon "Spud" Chandler (20–4), was nearly the equal of the Cardinals as it led the American League with a 2.83 ERA. Even though the Bronx Bombers had won seven fewer games than the Cards, they still finished thirteen and a half games ahead of runner-up Washington.

Wartime travel restrictions necessitated that the first three games of the World Series be played at Yankee Stadium, the remainder in Sportsman's Park. With 68,676 fans in attendance, on October 5, Southworth elected to start lefty Lanier instead of his ace Cooper, who had performed poorly against American League competition. In the sixth inning with the score tied at two, the game was decided when Lanier uncorked a wild pitch, enabling Frank Crosetti to score from third base. Yankee ace Chandler made the lead hold up in a 4–2 win in which Musial managed only a single, one of seven Redbird hits. The Cardinals' only victory came in the second game with Cooper on the hill against Ernie Bonham. His performance became even more dramatic because of the sudden death of his fifty-nine-year-old father the night before. Pitching as much with his heart as with his arm, Cooper held the Yankees to one run until the ninth before winning 4–3. The Cardinal hitting star was shortstop Marion, who gave the team the lead in the third inning with a homer to left. Musial also contributed by scoring from second base on a short single. Afterward, the mood remained somber, however, as Mort Cooper and his wife returned to Missouri to make funeral arrangements while brother Walker remained behind for the third game, a 6–2 loss in a Brazle–Hank Borowy matchup before a Series-record crowd of 69,990. Brazle actually held a 2–1 lead until the eighth, when two errors and a triple gave the Yankees a four-run lead.

Game four began in St. Louis on October 10. Providing moral support were Lieutenant Beazley and privates Moore, Pollet, and Jimmy Brown, home on leave. Southworth started fifteen-game-winner Lanier, who had pitched well enough to win in game one. He had a decided advantage over lefty Marius Russo, a journeyman with a 5–10 record. Manager Joe McCarthy had gambled to give the thirty-five-year-old Chandler another day's rest. Lanier went seven innings before leaving for a pinch-hitter. With the score tied at one, Brecheen surrendered the go-ahead run in the eighth on a sacrifice fly. Musial ended up with two hits but so did Russo, whose double proved more decisive. Russo's 2–1 complete-game victory left Southworth so frustrated that he uncharacteristically dismissed reporters by responding: "Ask your questions in a hurry and get the hell out of here."

The fifth and final game proved as disappointing. Replacing Walker and Litwhiler in the outfield with Hopp and Debs Garms, who would hit a combined 0 for 8, Southworth started Cooper against Chandler. Cooper fanned the first five batters and shut out the Yankees until the eighth inning when he threw a fastball across the middle of the plate to catcher Bill Dickey, who slammed it onto the roof of the right-field pavilion with two outs and a man on base. Those were the only runs of the game as Chandler scattered ten hits. For the first time, Musial went hitless as he walked, struck out twice, and grounded out. Overall, he batted .278 with five singles in eighteen appearances, one more hit than he made in the 1942 series, but it was a disappointment to Musial nonetheless. Despite the frustration of postseason play, the ball club gave owner Breadon a black marble desk set with the players' signatures on the bottom. It bore the inscription, "Presented to Sam Breadon as a token of good will and loyalty and with our congratulations on your success. With our hopes for many such years to follow. From your 1943 Cardinals." The presentation reduced the usually hard-boiled Breadon to tears.

A second consecutive World Series check undoubtedly sparked the players' generosity. The losers' share amounted to $4,321.99, which equaled about two-thirds of Musial's salary for 1943, a princely bonus for a twenty-two-year-old who had experienced hard times. Musial also received a three-year contract totaling $36,000, $4,000 less than what he requested. It provided for $10,000, $12,500, and $13,500, respectively, over a three-year period. Following the signing he headed to Donora where community members honored him on October 17 in an affair attended by Congressman Grant E. Furlong and Honus Wagner. Musial suggested that he would rather face the toughest pitcher in the National League than make a speech, but his sincere and friendly comments were well received.

After working in the zinc works into December, Musial agreed to join a USO tour with teammate Litwhiler, Borowy of the Yankees, Dixie Walker of the Dodgers, and Manager Frankie Frisch of the Pirates. It proved difficult getting ballplayers to participate, but Musial welcomed the chance to do something for the war effort. The group visited various military installations in Alaska and the Aleutian Islands to talk about baseball and show a film highlight of the 1943 World Series. The tour proved rigorous; four times a day they met with servicemen, afterward returning to their huts so hoarse that they could scarcely talk. On Christmas they found themselves stranded on a mountaintop near Dutch Harbor in the Aleutians where a boat waited for them. With no vehicles available, they ended up walking down the mountain in a blizzard against the wind.

The voyage in the Bering Sea, Litwhiler remembered, was so stormy that they all became sick. By early January, because of unforeseen difficulties, Walker and Frisch had returned home. The remaining three continued the tour, often visiting lonely outposts manned by a handful of soldiers.[7]

Following his return to Donora, Musial awaited the coming of the 1944 baseball season minus departing center fielder Walker, second baseman Klein, and pitchers Brazle, White, Dickson, and Howie Krist, followed by right-hander George Munger three months into the season. Additionally, despite varied infirmities, Walker Cooper and Litwhiler had been accepted for induction in 1944. On April 22 Musial's draft board also requested that he take a pre-induction physical in his hometown. He received permission to take it at Jefferson Barracks just south of St. Louis. Upon hearing from his draft board, he told the press, "Well, I have just written my wife a letter. Now I'll just add a little postscript to it." One month later Musial learned that he might be inducted at the end of May, which turned out not to be the case.[8]

The war had obviously made life more uncertain even though by 1943 some optimism had emerged following the Russian counteroffensive against the Nazis on Europe's eastern front and the American and British successes in North Africa and Italy. That optimism and hope resonated in the extremely popular musical *Oklahoma!* which opened on Broadway that spring. In June the Allied invasion of northern France enabled Americans to sense that the tide had turned against the Axis powers. Although no one thought that the war would end soon, more and more Americans anticipated eventual victory.

Nevertheless, the further depletion of the Cardinal ball club for the 1944 campaign caused Breadon to contend that "I've got a far better club in the army than I can put on the ball field," leading the Dodgers' Branch Rickey to retort, "I wish I had Sam Breadon's replacements."[9] Indeed, the Cardinals remained in a class by themselves. In addition to regulars who continued to play in 1944, including Sanders, Marion, Kurowski, Musial, Litwhiler, and Cooper among the position players, and pitchers Mort Cooper, Lanier, Brecheen, and Munger (for part of the season), the Cardinal management could depend on the capable Hopp, who replaced Walker in the outfield, and Emil Verban, who played 146 games at second

7. Goldstein, *Spartan Seasons*, 80–82; Musial, *Musial*, 79–80; Stan Musial to Chuck and Betty Schmidt, January 10, 1944, in possession of Chuck Schmidt.

8. Lansche, *Stan "The Man,"* 60–61; Bill Borst, *The Best of Seasons: The 1944 St. Louis Cardinals and St. Louis Browns*, 52, 79.

9. Lansche, *Stan "The Man,"* 59.

base for the departing Klein. Hopp, hitting .336, fell only eleven percentage points short of Musial's club-leading average. Also, Ted Wilks, a twenty-eight-year-old rookie up from Columbus to replace Munger (11–3) in early July, finished with a 17–4 mark, four shutouts, and a 2.64 ERA, second best on the club. He complemented well the stellar pitching of Cooper (22–7 and 2.46 ERA), who for the third consecutive year led the National League in victories; Lanier (17–12); and Brecheen (16–5). The club dominated the league in virtually every pitching category, including ERA (2.67).

The Redbirds also paced the league in batting average, even though Musial's .347 fell short of Dixie Walker's .357 for Brooklyn. Musial remained on top for hits (197), tied with Phil Cavaretta of the Cubs; doubles (51); and slugging average (.548). He finished second in runs scored (112) and was among the leaders in triples (14) and RBIs (94). He had clearly emerged as the National League's most dominant hitter. The league Most Valuable Player award, however, went to Marion, who won it primarily for his defensive play. Marion epitomized the superior defensive play of the team. Their scant 112 errors set a club record, as did their .982 fielding mark. Four Cardinals (Marion, Sanders, Kurowski, and Hopp) led their National League counterparts in fielding percentage.

The Cardinals had no difficulties in capturing a third consecutive pennant in 1944. In the season's opener in Pittsburgh, Musial drove in the first run of the campaign in the sixth and in the eighth singled again, stole second, and came home on Kurowski's hit for a 2–0 victory, a two-hitter for Pollet. The Cardinals never looked back. By the end of April the team was 9–2 and Musial led the league with a .447 average. Against the Reds on June 10, Cooper took a 13–0 lead into the ninth when Reds manager Joe McKechnie brought in pitcher Joe Nuxhall, at fifteen years, ten months, and eleven days, the youngest player to have ever played major-league ball in the twentieth century. In two-thirds of an inning, Nuxhall proceeded to walk five batters and give up two hits before heading for the showers. The first safety against him came off of Musial's bat, a line single to right field, his third hit for the day. Nuxhall later recalled that "he just dug in and stood up there. I'm throwing fastballs all over the place, . . . and he stood up there like I was a needle threader. And when I finally got that first pitch in there, wham!"[10]

Another rookie, shortstop Eddie Basinski of the Dodgers, a fellow Pole, also remembered Musial that summer. Mired near the bottom of the standings late in the season, Durocher's ball club still played like

10. Ibid., 61.

a contender against the Cards. Basinski recalled how much attention Durocher gave to Musial in the pre-game meetings, describing him as "a spray hitter with power. He can reach any fence, yet a true line drive hitter for high percentage." Durocher claimed that he had a way to stop Musial. "He grabbed a bat," Basinski continued, "and imitated Musial's unusual stance at the plate. [Durocher] noticed when Musial waited on a pitcher's delivery, he would relieve the tension in his coiled stance by releasing his left hand off the bat and swing the bat forward with his right hand in a complete circle and return it to his original position. Durocher commanded [his pitcher] to go into his stretch when Musial was up, regardless of men on base or not. He . . . ordered him to quick pitch Musial as soon as Musial released his left hand off his bat." That day Musial hit four doubles; the next afternoon at batting practice Basinski told Musial the clubhouse story. Musial just smiled and thanked Basinski without saying anything to anyone. "I became a fan of Musial's from that day on," Basinski concluded.[11]

Pitcher Bob Barthelson of the New York Giants remembered a game at the Polo Grounds in 1944 in which twenty-one-game winner Bill Voiselle was pitching. In his first at bat Musial hit a line drive to left field, followed by other liners to right and center field, and then a home run to right. "The greatest piece of hitting I [have] ever seen," Barthelson later claimed.[12]

Litwhiler, one of Musial's greatest admirers, recollected a 1944 contest in Philadelphia's Shibe Park in which the wind was blowing from left field. "Well, nobody will hit any into the left field seats today," Litwhiler remarked. "I will," Musial insisted. "If you do I'll kiss your butt on home plate," Litwhiler challenged. After Musial parked one into the left-field stands around the fifth inning, he turned to Litwhiler in the dugout and said, "Danny, do you want to do it now or after the game?"[13]

Musial did not always have the last laugh, however. In a story Stan himself told, Ron Northey of the Phillies hit a fly ball to Musial in center field. He lost it in the sun and then ducked at the last instant as it hit him on the head. Pepper Martin, playing right field, retrieved the ball and after throwing it in, said, "Are you all right?" An embarrassed Musial responded, "Yeah, I'm all right." Martin, deep in laughter, then said, "I hope you don't mind then because that was really funny."[14]

11. Eddie Basinski to James N. Giglio, September 5, 1996, in possession of Giglio. That same season Southworth got Musial to eliminate the circular motion with the bat.
12. Bob Barthelson to Giglio, August 29, 1996, ibid.
13. Danny Litwhiler to Giglio, September 2, 1996, ibid.
14. Ford "Moon" Mullen to Giglio, August 26, 1996, ibid.; Musial, *Musial*, 280.

By Independence Day Musial and the high-flying Cardinals had stretched their lead to ten and a half games, the greatest advantage a Cardinal team ever had by July 4. Musial obtained his one hundredth hit three days later and played in the All-Star game at Forbes Field on the eleventh. Playing center and right field, he had one single in four at bats, driving in a run in the National League's first victory since 1940. The Cardinals continued to roll, sweeping a four-game series with the Dodgers in mid-August. On August 16, in a 5–0 victory over the Giants, they won their eightieth game, the earliest day a major-league club had reached that milestone. By then Musial had fallen into a batting slump, which brought his average down to .348, eight points behind Walker.

His bid to capture a second batting title grew more difficult after he collided with Garms as they raced into right center after a fly ball hit by Cubs catcher Dewey Williams. Garms suffered cuts above his right eye and across the bridge of his nose and bruises on his arms and legs. Musial left the field on a stretcher, complaining of pain in his right leg and ankle. He was taken to St. Johns Hospital for X rays, where it was determined nothing was broken. His assorted injuries kept him out of the lineup for nine games, however, preventing him from reaching the two-hundred-hit mark. Upon his return he found it impossible to catch Walker for the batting title.

The Cardinals lost eight of nine in Musial's absence and fifteen out of their last twenty games, which prevented them from surpassing their 1943 record. Still, they finished fourteen and a half games ahead of second-place Pittsburgh. On the final day of the season, in a doubleheader against the Giants, Musial rallied by going six for nine, readying him for World Series play.

The American League pennant winner was none other than the St. Louis Browns. The undisputed underdog, the Brownies barely managed to win the league championship on the last day of the season, their only title ever. They captured the pennant by winning only eighty-nine games for a scant .579 winning percentage, the lowest for a league champ since 1928. They represented a collection of misfits and "4-Fers" (physically unfit for military service), who became the darlings of St. Louis because of their loser past, causing Lil Musial mistakenly to label St. Louis a "Brownie town." In 1943 they had actually outdrawn the Cardinals 508,644 to 501,265 because of the absence of a pennant race in the National League. Still, in 1944 only Browns shortstop Vern Stephens, who had 109 RBIs, led the American League in any hitting category. The Brownies had only one regular batting .300—outfielder Mike Kreevich at .309. The pitching staff, headed by Nelson Potter's 19–7 mark, excelled in no mound category.

Playing one another created some problems for the St. Louis teams. Manager Luke Sewell of the Browns and Southworth had jointly leased accommodations at the Lindell Towers since one was always on the road while the other played at home. Now that they were both homeward bound, one of them had to vacate. Fortunately, residents of another apartment invited Southworth to use theirs.

Favored by a two-to-one margin, the Cardinals' greatest danger remained overconfidence. This was particularly so in game one, October 4, when the Browns went with Denny Galehouse (9–10), their fifth-best starter. With Cooper pitching for the Cardinals, this smacked of a mismatch. Yet, after permitting only two hits, Cooper lost by a 2–1 score following a George McQuinn two-run homer in the fourth. The Cardinals might have lost the error-filled second game, too, had they not received superb relief work from Blix Donnelly, Musial's former Springfield Cardinals teammate. With the score tied at two, Donnelly entered in the eighth after Kreevich led off with a double against starter Lanier. Donnelly struck out the side, and then in the eleventh, with no outs, he quickly fielded a bunt to catch McQuinn going to third base. In the home half the Cardinals won when pinch-hitter Ken O'Dea singled Ray Sanders home from second base.

The Browns came back to win the third game after driving Ted Wilks to the showers in a four-run third inning. Seventeen-game winner Jack Kramer went all the way in a 6–2 contest. After three games Musial had managed only three singles in twelve at bats, with no runs scored and no RBIs. Obviously, the Browns had proved to be a better team than anyone expected.

Game four represented the turnaround game for Musial and the Cardinals. The Browns started Sig Jakucki (13–9), a hard-drinking former serviceman and minor leaguer who returned to professional baseball in 1944, boldly predicting that he would win twelve to fifteen games. Jakucki had won the pennant-clinching game against the Yankees on the last day of the season. Against the Cardinals, he performed less successfully. In the first inning Musial blasted a two-run homer high over the right-field pavilion roof, his only home run in World Series competition. Musial also contributed a double, single, and walk in five plate appearances, his best effort in fourteen World Series games. Brecheen scattered nine hits in a 5–1 win.

Cardinal supremacy continued in game five as the Redbirds won before a capacity crowd of 36,568 on Sunday. Galehouse surrendered home runs to Sanders and Litwhiler in a 2–0 win for Cooper, who fanned twelve to Galehouse's ten. The combined twenty-two strikeouts set a World Series single-game record. The record number of strikeouts (92) for the six-game series probably resulted from the distraction of white-shirt fans in the center-field bleachers, making it difficult for batters to see the ball. "It was lucky some one did not get killed," Musial later commented.[15] Musial committed the Cardinals' only error in the series when he misplayed Red Hayworth's single in right field.

The anticlimactic final game on Monday resulted in a 3–1 victory for Lanier, who was aided by Brownie errors and the relief pitching of Wilks. In his autobiography Musial rightly focused on the defensive play of Marty Marion as the top reason for the Cardinals' World Series success. While the human vacuum sweeper played errorless ball at shortstop, Marion's Brownie counterpart, power-hitting "Junior" Stephens, had three miscues, including a crucial one in game five. Musial finished with a respectable .304 average, third best on the team after Verban and Walker Cooper. In what proved to be a pitcher-dominated series in which the combined ERA was less than 2.00, Musial had one of four home runs hit by the two teams. In only the fourth game did his play contribute significantly, however.

Largely because of the limited seating capacity, only 206,708 fans witnessed the 1944 fall classic. As a result the winner's share came to $4,626, the smallest take since 1933. Nevertheless, that raised the Cardinals' three-year postseason amount to $15,141, a substantial sum considering what most ballplayers made annually.

Upon Musial's return to Donora, Lil gave birth to their second child, daughter Geraldine, and six weeks later, on January 23, 1945, Musial entered the navy. Pete Reiser of the Dodgers had tried to persuade Musial to join the army following Musial's induction physical. Reiser had entered the infantry in 1943 and was stationed at Fort Riley, Kansas, where Harry Walker and Al Brazle joined him.[16] The base commander's strong interest in baseball led to the development of a squad that matched up with the best of the service teams. At one time or another it included Murry Dickson, Ken Heintzelman of the Reds, Rex Barney of the Dodgers, and Joe Garagiola from the Cardinal farm system. That team played a lot of

15. Borst, *The Best of Seasons*, 249.
16. Stan Musial oral history transcript, Albert B. Chandler Oral History Project, University of Kentucky Library, 2–3.

games against other army installations, and it almost always won, Reiser advised Musial.

Musial elected instead to join the navy, which ended up delaying his induction, enabling him to complete the 1944 season. Moreover, it kept him out of combat. As it turned out, Walker, Brazle, and Heintzelman were transferred to the Sixty-fifth Division at Camp Shelby, Mississippi. They went overseas together and participated in the Battle of the Bulge in the winter of 1944–1945. Private First Class Walker recalled being involved in some of the worst fighting of World War II. On one occasion, while on patrol, he used his .45 revolver to shoot three German guards after one aimed a gun at his face. The following day his patrol ran into a German unit crossing a bridge. Walker, who was on point, opened up with his .50-caliber machine gun, shooting some of them and capturing the rest. For his military valor Walker received the Bronze Star and for getting hit with artillery shrapnel, the Purple Heart. He remembered those days with pain and sadness: "We saw people slaughtered like animals."[17]

Only a small minority of major leaguers who served in World War II shared Walker's combat experience. Others seriously wounded in combat included pitchers Lou Brissie of the Philadelphia Athletics and John Grodzicki of the Cards. Some came out of the ordeal emotionally disturbed. And yet others suffered disabilities while in training or in some other service-related activity. But the vast majority of major leaguers stayed out of harm's way. Indeed, most played baseball for various service teams to satisfy the egos of post commanders as well as to entertain service personnel, the latter a noble endeavor considering the boredom of military life amid the bleak locations of many installations.

Much of Musial's fourteen months in the navy involved playing baseball. For that he remained grateful and considered himself lucky, a word he often used. Typical of many Americans who confronted the two greatest crises of the twentieth century—the Great Depression and World War II—Musial experienced considerable uncertainty as to what life held for his generation. Seeing the harshness and unfairness of life, he concluded that one had little control over his own fate. Like many of his contemporaries he believed that one's talents and fate were God-determined.[18] In light

17. Walker oral history transcript, 40; Goldstein, *Spartan Seasons*, 252–53.
18. Joe DiMaggio also experienced the same feelings. See Rudolf K. Hearle, Jr., "The Athlete as 'Moral' Leader: Heroes, Success Themes and Basic Cultural Values in Selected Baseball Autobiographies, 1900–1970," 395–96.

of others' misfortunes Musial recognized how fortunate he was to have overcome his own tribulations. That kept a ready smile on his face for much of his playing career.

But as far as the war was concerned, in one important way Musial did contribute to his own destiny. While a few major leaguers enlisted early in the war and even requested combat duty, Musial, like most of his peers, followed his self-interest as best he could. An obvious exception, star pitcher Bob Feller of the Cleveland Indians, who had a III-C draft status because of his father's terminal cancer, enlisted in the navy anyway. "I thought it was the thing to do to be in the war and help win it," he later commented.[19] After six months of duty, he gave up a cushy physical fitness assignment to volunteer for gunnery school. He then joined the USS *Alabama* as chief of an anti-aircraft gun crew that saw considerable combat in the South Pacific.

Musial began his basic training in January 1945 at Bainbridge, Maryland, where he was photographed having his hair removed by a barber. When someone informed the barber who Musial was, the embarrassed man commented, "Why didn't you tell me who you were? I wouldn't have cut it so short." Musial responded meekly, "Thanks, but now I know how a guy feels when he's going to the electric chair." Musial played four or five baseball games at Bainbridge before being transferred to Shoemaker, California, which he described as a "hole." He continued to play baseball, on one occasion competing against Pepper Martin's team in San Francisco before being assigned to Special Services and shipped to Hawaii. At this point he anticipated remaining in the navy until the end of 1946, a reasonable expectation at the time despite the impending collapse of Germany.[20] The island-hopping campaign in the Pacific had brought American forces closer to Japan, but the Japanese remained a formidable foe. Taking the small island of Iwo Jima in March 1945 cost more than sixty-eight hundred American lives. It was expected that an invasion of mainland Japan would be costly given the fanatical nature of the Japanese military.

In Hawaii, Musial was assigned to a ship repair unit at Pearl Harbor, where he ferried personnel from battle-damaged ships to shore and back. He heard gruesome stories from crewmen about how the damages had occurred. He realized even more how lucky he was to have been spared

19. William Marshall, *Baseball's Pivotal Era: 1945–1951*, 340.
20. Musial, *Musial*, 83; Musial to Ki and Verna Duda, May 1, 1945, in Verna Duda's possession.

that experience. He was participating in an eight-team league in which most of the players were big-leaguers. He played three or four afternoon games a week before a packed house of ten thousand sailors. On October 18 he performed in the navy's little world series, with twenty-six thousand in attendance. An officer soon relieved him of his launch activity in the mornings when Musial complained that "after bouncing around in that launch for three hours . . . , God, my legs were like rubber. So I told him, 'Sir, I'm either going to play baseball on a regular basis or run the launch, because I can't be doing what I'm doing and do a good job playing baseball.' "[21] The officer quickly transferred him to a special athletic unit where he functioned as a physical education instructor.

In the fall of 1945 Musial's father once again became seriously ill in Donora. He was not expected to live. Through the intercession of the Red Cross, Musial received emergency leave orders to return to the States. After an "agonizing trip" home, he found Lukasz recovering from pneumonia. A published photograph remains of Musial on leave in his sailor suit, giving his pajama-wearing, bedridden father medication.

Following the emergency leave, Musial served the remainder of his time at the Philadelphia Navy Yard. His initial assignment involved the dismantling of a British destroyer. One day before he was scheduled to work, he walked over to the job site where he saw workers with blowtorches already performing. "I realized," he later admitted, "that a greenpea like me could wind up maiming myself or someone else." He reported to the athletic officer: "Sir, I'm a ship repairman who never has repaired a ship. For my sake and the Navy's can't you please have my orders changed?"[22] To his relief they were. Two months later Musial was discharged in March at Bainbridge, Maryland.

Musial managed to catch a train to Philadelphia as he began his trek home. With all public transportation slowed by the masses of discharged servicemen, he faced a wait of several days before he would be able to find a bus to the Pittsburgh area. So, he elected instead to hitchhike home on the Pennsylvania Turnpike in his service bell-bottoms, along with another former sailor. "Two old guys" on their way to Pittsburgh picked them up. As it turned out, the two men were members of the state legislature in Harrisburg. They were driving so slowly that Musial whispered to his companion that at that speed they would never get home. Soon after being asked who they were, the driver accelerated to eighty miles an hour and

21. Frederick W. Turner, *When the Boys Came Back: Baseball and 1946*, xiv.
22. Musial, *Musial*, 84–85.

drove Musial to his doorstep in Donora.[23] He had returned in time to spend a week with his family before the start of spring training for the 1946 season.

Unlike many major leaguers who served in World War II, Stan Musial suffered little hardship from the experience. True, he lost monetarily from the one-year hiatus, and it involved separation from family at a time when he was needed at home. But his tour of duty was short and personally productive. He was able to compete with the finest ballplayers of his time. And the only injuries he suffered were a twisted knee and a chipped bone in his hand, both of which occurred from playing baseball. Unlike some major leaguers who returned home emotionally scarred, physically impaired, or rusty after serving for three or four years far removed from athletic competition, he came back physically and mentally stronger than ever. He had learned to pull the ball more in the service in an effort to produce home runs for cheering servicemen. He now batted more from a crouch to reduce the strike zone while generating more power in his swing.[24]

The service experience also made him a bit more outgoing as he more willingly engaged others with his penchant for harmonica playing and parlor tricks, one of which included a fake thumb. More important, unlike most former servicemen—including some major leaguers—who had to struggle with economic uncertainty in the immediate postwar period, Musial had a guaranteed position waiting for him in the outfield of the St. Louis Cardinals. The future appeared exceedingly bright for Stanley Musial. He had earned that stature by his play in the early 1940s.

23. Turner, *When the Boys Came Back*, xiii; Musial, *Musial*, 85.
24. Terry Moore, for one, noticed the change in Musial's stance. Sher, "The Stan Musial Nobody Knows," 61.

Stan Musial's Donora High School
Yearbook photo, 1939.

Lillian Labash's Donora High School
Yearbook photo, 1938.

The basketball team from Donora that competed in the Polish Roman Catholic Basketball Tournament in Buffalo, New York, in March 1939. Musial is in the back row, far right; Richard Ercius is in the back row, second from the right. Courtesy of Jim Kreuz

The 1938 Donora High School basketball team, from the school's 1938 Yearbook. Included in the front row are Bill Leddon (third from left), Flo Garcia (fourth from left) George Kosko (fifth from left) and Musial (second from right). In the back row are Ki Duda (at far left), Richard Ercius (sixth from left), Grant Gray (seventh from left), and Jimmie Russell (far right).

The 1938 Donora High School baseball team, from the school's 1938 Yearbook. Front row, left to right: Ki Duda, Buddy Griffey, Bob O'Lenic, Paul Hendrickson, Oslowsky, Galiffa, Eugene Norton, Bill Leddon, Mr. Hayes. Back row: manager Fowler, manager Chuck Schmidt, Ed Pado, Stan Musial, Dzik, Paship, Piskor, Ed Musial, Lelik, manager Miller, manager Thompson.

Springfield Cardinals sluggers, 1941: Musial, Ollie Vanek, Roy Broome. Courtesy of the *Springfield News-Leader*

Musial, in his 1942 rookie season.
Courtesy of the National
Baseball Hall of Fame Library,
Cooperstown, New York

The Donora Greyhound, 1942.
Courtesy of the National
Baseball Hall of Fame Library,
Cooperstown, New York

One of Musial's many autograph signings, 1943.
Courtesy of the Sporting News Archives

Musial and his father, Lukasz, in the New Yorker Hotel on the eve of the 1943 World Series. Courtesy of AP/World

The great Cardinal outfield of the early 1940s: Enos Slaughter, Terry Moore, and Stan Musial. Courtesy of the Sporting News Archives

Musial, in the U.S. Navy in 1945.
Courtesy of the Sporting News Archives

Stan, Lil, son Dickie (age six), and daughter Geraldine (two), Donora, November 22, 1946. Courtesy of AP/World

Musial and longtime roommate Red Schoendienst. Courtesy of the National
Baseball Hall of Fame Library, Cooperstown, New York

Erv Dusak, Harry Walker, and Stan Musial embarking from Union Station, 1947. Courtesy of the St. Louis Mercantile Library

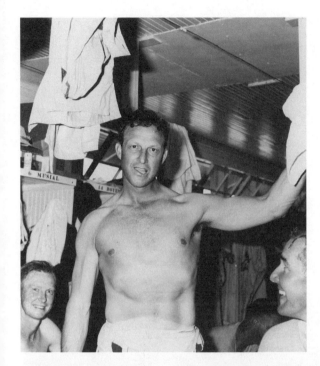

Stan Musial celebrating
a Cardinal victory.
Courtesy of the National
Baseball Hall of Fame
Library, Cooperstown,
New York

Musial and Cardinal owner Fred Saigh at contract signing time.
Courtesy of the Sporting News Archives

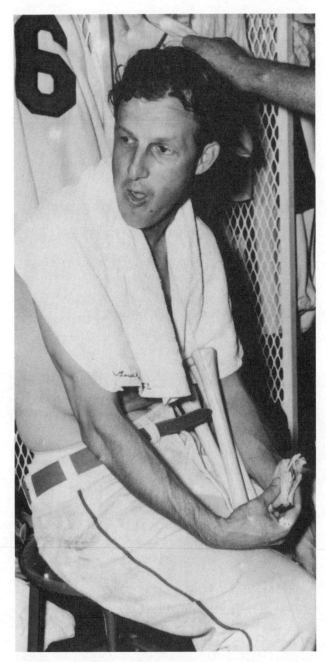

Musial, eating a sandwich between games of the famous
doubleheader of May 2, 1954, when he hit five home runs.
Courtesy of the St. Louis Mercantile Library

Musial struck by a
beanball thrown by
Brooklyn Dodgers
pitcher Johnny Podres,
September 23, 1956.
Courtesy of the
St. Louis Mercantile
Library

Musial honored at the Chase Hotel in St. Louis. From left: Ki Duda, Dick Kerr, Lil
and Stan, Ted Kluszewski of the Cincinnati Redlegs, Mary Musial, National League
umpire Al Barlick, and National League president Warren Giles.
Courtesy of the St. Louis Mercantile Library

Musial and his mother, Mary, following Stan Musial Night in Pittsburgh, May 24, 1958. Courtesy of AP/World

Musial and Julius "Biggie" Garagnani at their restaurant, August 1950. Courtesy of the Sporting News Archives

Musial, getting in shape for the 1960 season. Courtesy of the National Baseball Hall of Fame Library, Cooperstown, New York

Stan Musial, George Altman, and Curt Flood, early 1960s. Courtesy of the National Baseball Hall of Fame Library, Cooperstown, New York

President John F. Kennedy and Stan, Lil, and Janet Musial in the Oval Office, July 11, 1962. Courtesy of the John Fitzgerald Kennedy Library

Bob Broeg of the *St. Louis Post-Dispatch* and "Banj," 1963.
Courtesy of Bob Broeg

Musial saying good-bye following his final game, September 29, 1963.
Courtesy of the Sporting News Archives

President Lyndon B. Johnson and Stan, Lil, Janet, and Geraldine Musial at the
Physical Fitness Adviser swearing-in ceremony, February 26, 1964.
Courtesy of the Lyndon Baines Johnson Library

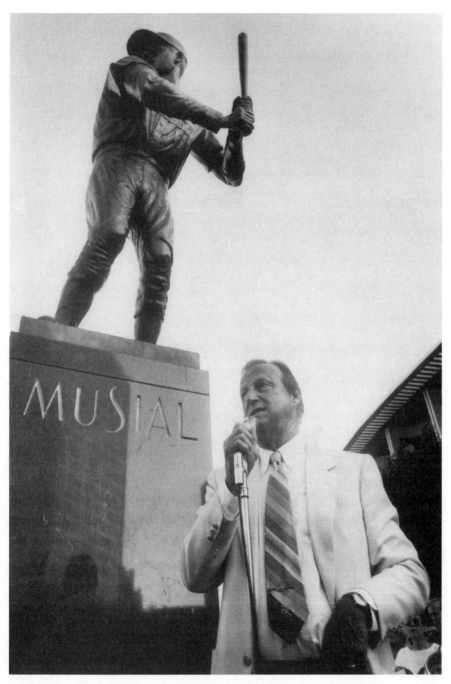

Stan Musial at the rededication ceremony after the Musial Statue at Busch Stadium was refurbished, July 17, 1986. Courtesy of the St. Louis Mercantile Library

Musial statuette, 1999. Courtesy of Harry C. Weber, sculptor

Return to Glory

T he Academy Award–winning film of 1946, *The Best Years of Our Lives*, poignantly captured the mood of immediate postwar America by focusing on the return of three servicemen—a dashing young air force officer, a sailor who lost his arms below the elbow, and a middle-aged sergeant who was once a middle-class banker. On the one hand, they, as well as the rest of America, felt the exhilaration, optimism, and hope that quickly followed the destruction of Axis tyranny as the United States emerged as the leading power in the world. And as the only principal power to escape the physical destruction of the war, the United States, through its vibrant economy, had already committed itself to prosperity and consumer abundance at home and economic reconstruction abroad. For its twelve million returning GIs especially, the American Century seemed at hand.

On the other hand, the war's aftermath soon ushered in disturbing changes that were not always easily accepted or understood. In place of Franklin Roosevelt, President Harry Truman of Missouri seemed less equipped to handle the perplexities of reconversion from a wartime to a peacetime economy. Strikes plagued the American workplace, with unions pushing for substantial increases in wages in compensation for the escalating cost of living and wartime sacrifices, including inadequate pay raises. While management chose to fight the unions on virtually every issue, the Truman White House found itself often alienating both management and labor in seeking to mediate the massive strikes. The Truman administration's flawed efforts to extend price and wage controls into the postwar era to combat crippling inflation also aroused considerable antagonism. Too, Truman's reform commitments, including full employment, the construction of some fifteen million new low-income housing units, federal aid to education, and civil rights, floundered in Congress. By the fall midterm election of 1946, Republicans had coined the slogan, "To err is Truman."

Unexpected changes also developed abroad. Instead of a "One World" environment in which nations would work harmoniously through the new United Nations organization, differences over postwar security soon created a Cold War in which the Soviet Union arguably threatened to engulf much of Central and Eastern Europe. Americans soon heard that the

United States must contain communism abroad, and Truman proclaimed the Truman Doctrine and the Marshall Plan, effectively ending American isolationism for the Cold War era. The communist menace created such anxiety at home that Americans became obsessed with the threat of subversion in our schools, scientific foundations, government, and elsewhere. All of this caused Americans to turn suspiciously on each other, with unscrupulous politicians exploiting fears and anxieties for their own political gain. At the height of the Red Scare in the early 1950s public pressure caused the Cincinnati Reds to change their nickname to Redlegs.

The Best Years of Our Lives explores yet another mood of the era, which reveals the irony in its title. For officer Fred, who came home to an unfaithful wife and a dead-end job; Homer, plagued by the worry that his childhood sweetheart would pity him for his disability; or banker Al, who found it difficult to resume insensitive banking practices without the fortification of alcohol, the postwar period hardly represented the "best years of our lives." The unfulfillment—if not the fraud—of American postwar promises not only affected the three protagonists in the celebrated film but also touched other returning servicemen and Americans in general. The various moods in the film—optimism, high expectations, uncertainty, even disillusionment—mirrored not only American society in general but the game of baseball as well, which, after all, represented a microcosm of American life.

The flood of returning ballplayers from the service added to the excitement of spring training in 1946. It intensified competition, too, as wartime players competed with players returning from the military for spots on team rosters. Realistically, it was expected that most of the wartime replacement players would be unable to compete with former regulars, but at the same time, owners anticipated that the returnees would not regain their pre-military form until weeks after the season began. As a consequence, the new commissioner of baseball, Albert "Happy" Chandler, permitted teams to expand their rosters by five players during this transitional period.

On paper, the St. Louis Cardinals remained the strongest team in the National League. Indeed, in 1945 the second-place Redbirds had narrowly missed a fourth straight pennant, without Musial, as Kurowski, Marion, Hopp, and Brecheen had good years. Additionally, Charles "Red" Barrett, who came to the Cards from the Boston Braves for Mort Cooper, led the league with twenty-one wins. The trade had little long-range significance, however, as Barrett failed to measure up to postwar competition and Cooper's arm problems ended his effectiveness.

One new Cardinal performer of 1945 continued to make a splash in the postwar era: Albert "Red" Schoendienst, who soon became Musial's closest friend on the team. Schoendienst was a freckle-faced redhead, so skinny and youthful in appearance that ballpark employees mistook him for the bat boy. The twenty-two-year-old nevertheless hit .278 and led the league with twenty-six stolen bases while wearing Musial's number six. Schoendienst had played left field in his rookie season, but he soon found his niche at second base.

Similar backgrounds and shared values brought Schoendienst and Musial together. Both came from financially strapped families, although Schoendienst was German Catholic rather than Polish. Both had emerged from small towns, Schoendienst from Germantown, Illinois. Both had overcome physical adversity, with Schoendienst suffering from hampered vision as the result of a hammered nail that ricocheted into his eye in a CCC camp during the 1930s. Both men loved the outdoors, and Schoendienst soon introduced Musial to quail hunting while Stash hooked him on golf. They were low-key, reticent personalities who enjoyed leisurely dinners and lengthy bull sessions about baseball. They also attended Sunday Mass together on the road. Musial soon would not only room with Red on road trips but also live near his teammate in southwest St. Louis. They even shared family activities together. Red's Mary O'Reilly mirrored Lil's devotion to her husband's career and her children.

Years later, during the 1956 season, when the Cards traded Schoendienst to the New York Giants, Musial first heard about it as he boarded a train out of St. Louis. He remembered that moment as the "saddest day of my career."[1] He ended up slamming the door to his train berth, refusing to open it for hours.

Musial also thought highly of Edwin "Eddie" Dyer, hired as manager in 1946 to replace Billy Southworth, whom the Boston Braves attracted with a better offer. The no-nonsense, polished, college-educated Dyer had seen considerable service in the Cardinal organization, most recently as director of the Redbirds AA-level farm clubs, before going into the oil business in Houston in 1944. Dyer had managed several Cards in the minor leagues; he was particularly close to Pollet, whom he employed in the off-season. He had long earned the respect of baseball insiders and proved more than the equal of Southworth.

Other newcomers included rookies Dick Sisler, the first baseman and son of Hall of Famer George Sisler, and catcher Joe Garagiola, the factotum

---

1. Red Schoendienst with Rob Rains, *Red: A Baseball Life*, vii.

of the Springfield Cardinals in 1941. Because of unreasonably high expectations for Sisler and Garagiola, Breadon made two foolish sales that had long-range implications for the Cardinals. He sent Johnny Hopp, who would bat .333 in 1946, to the Braves. Aside from his hitting, Hopp's value lay in his versatility as a first baseman and outfielder. In light of Sisler's disappointing 1946 performance, Hopp's departure became more crucial.

The greatest Cardinal loss remained Walker Cooper, however, who went to the New York Giants in January 1946 for $175,000. The right-handed Cooper, the best catcher in the National League, had excellent seasons with the Giants and the Cincinnati Reds in the late 1940s. Both Musial and Slaughter rightly contended that the loss of Cooper cost the Redbirds several pennants, for neither Garagiola, Ken O'Dea, or Del Rice came close to equaling Cooper's offensive production or matching his leadership on the field. Cooper's departure cost the Cardinals not only a long-ball threat but also balance at the plate, enabling opponents to challenge Musial's and Slaughter's left-handed power with southpaw pitching.[2]

Breadon used Cooper's dislike of Dyer, who had managed him in the minors, as a pretext for selling him despite Dyer's plea that he would work things out. Money remained the main motive; Breadon, tired of Cooper's constant haggling over salary, also wanted to ensure that he came out financially ahead in 1946 in the face of higher salaries. Dyer later contended that Branch Rickey would have never sold "Cooper's contract for cash only."[3] To make matters worse, Breadon also marketed Danny Litwhiler and Ray Sanders. As it turned out, 1946 became a banner year financially for Breadon and the other owners as fans flocked to the ballparks in record numbers. The increasing number of night games only added to the attendance figures, which sent the Cardinals over the million mark for the first time, shattering their 1928 standard by more than three hundred thousand.

Dyer also had to deal with returnees whose skills had evaporated in the military. For them the best years of their lives were behind them—at least as ballplayers. The promise of Johnny Grodzicki had ended because of combat-inflicted injuries. Infielder "Creepy" Crespi's major-league career vanished after he broke a leg playing ball in the service and rebroke it

2. For Musial's and Slaughter's assessments of the Cooper sale, see Connor, ed., *Baseball for the Love of It*, 181–82, and Enos Slaughter with Kevin Reid, *Country Hardball: The Autobiography of Enos "Country" Slaughter*, 81.

3. Eddie Dyer to Arthur Mann, August 22, 1956, Box 1, General Correspondence, Arthur Mann Papers, Library of Congress.

in a wheelchair race at a convalescent military hospital. The war also destroyed the promising careers of pitchers Johnny Beazley and Howard Krist. Beazley, the hero of the 1942 campaign, had been forced into a service game without warming up properly. Garagiola later claimed that his once overpowering curveball could now be caught with a Kleenex. Krist came back with combat injuries suffered in France in 1944. After going a combined 24–8 in the 1942–1943 seasons, he failed to win a game after his return. Other veterans made greater contributions, but their skills had obviously eroded. For some, like Harry Walker, the problem was only temporary. Following Walker's .237 batting average in 1946, Breadon traded him to the Phillies in early 1947, the year he won the batting title with a .363 average. For thirty-four-year-old Terry Moore, who lost three years to Uncle Sam, nagging leg problems and advancing age prevented him from regaining fully his former form. In 1946 injuries kept him out of more than sixty Cardinal games, although he remained an inspiring leader. Other Cardinal players such as Slaughter, Pollet, Brazle, and Musial showed little effect from military service, however. For them, especially Musial, 1946 seemed to bring nothing but fulfillment.

Musial came to camp at St. Petersburg healthy and trim at his customary 175 pounds, buoyed by the family addition of daughter Geraldine (Gerry). He had little difficulty readjusting to civilian life and major-league ball. Too, Breadon had consented to waive the second year of his contract because of military service, which meant that Musial was now earning $13,500 instead of $12,500. Yet 1946 brought some frustrations as well. In spring training he slipped during practice on the sandy soil at Waterfront Park, made more treacherous after soldiers used the park as a drill field during the war. Musial's strained ligaments in his left knee remained an occasional nuisance for the rest of his career.

Moreover, because of Sisler's mediocre performance, Dyer asked Musial to go from left field to the infield by June. The move, supposedly temporary until Sisler turned things around, lasted for thirteen years, with Musial alternating between first base and the outfield. Even though Musial's early infield experience as a pitcher helped him make the adjustment, first base required a lot of practice and total concentration on every pitch. It never was his favorite place to play. Publicly, however, Musial professed to enjoy the move and soon developed into an outstanding performer there. But his departure from the outfield created a void as a result of Moore's injuries and Walker's problems at the plate.

Musial's veiled frustrations went deeper, mirroring a discontent many other ballplayers felt at the outset of the season, one that had roots deep in the history of the game. Because of the reserve clause that bound players to particular teams until retirement or an owner-related action, owners in effect held total control over players' careers. Lacking bargaining power, ballplayers faced exploitation, from not only low salaries but also the absence of a retirement program, a minimum wage that provided marginal players with an adequate income, and compensation for player expenses during spring training. Musial and other Cardinals felt especially mistreated because Breadon had refused to pay star performers more than fifteen thousand dollars and had continued Rickey's premise that "a hungry player was a better ballplayer." But the problem went well beyond Breadon as major leaguers returned to unsatisfactory prewar contracts. As sacrificing GIs, they expected better; they were also imbued by high expectations—the promise of a better life in the postwar era, which soon conflicted with the grim reality of rising prices. Moreover, the recent gains of organized labor emanating from the 1930s resulted in federal legislation providing for an hourly minimum wage, the government guarantee of collective bargaining, and the right of veterans to their prewar jobs, all of which had a profound impact on ballplayers. Many understood that such advances came as a result of organizational activity and confrontation. How far they were willing to go to effect change was another matter, however.[4]

Like most players, Musial adopted a cautious approach. Neither he nor other Cardinals provided much support to Robert Murphy, a Harvard-educated lawyer who had worked for the National Labor Relations Board. After talking with a number of players, Murphy had concluded that they had no bargaining power with their employers. As a result, in early 1946 he organized the American Baseball Guild, which sought a minimum salary of sixty-five hundred dollars, the arbitration of contract disputes, and compensation to players of one-half of the money in their sale to another club. Murphy avoided a frontal challenge to the reserve clause, but his proposed reforms could involve striking to gain collective-bargaining rights. Postwar reaction against unionism, reflected in the passage of the Taft-Hartley Act, made this approach more risky; the national climate had grown more conservative in the face of a rabid anticommunism

---

4. The best account of the problems ballplayers faced is in Lee E. Lowenfish and Tony Lupien, *The Imperfect Diamond: The Story of Baseball's Reserve System and the Men Who Fought to Change It*. "Max Lanier" interview in Donald Honig, *Baseball When the Grass Was Real: Baseball from the Twenties to the Forties Told by the Men Who Played It*, 209. For players' attitudes about organizing, see, for example, Turner, *When the Boys Came Back*, 54–56.

that sought to protect American institutions from "radical" impulses. No institution seemed more inviolable than baseball, the national pastime.

Most major leaguers, many of whom came from southern mill towns, found striking unacceptable. Many others felt vulnerable to owner retaliation. Murphy in fact suffered a setback in June when he narrowly failed to obtain a favorable strike vote from the Pittsburgh Pirates despite their association with a union-dominated community. It seemed clear that while ballplayers such as Musial wanted some sort of player organization, they did not want a union to represent them. It was equally clear that Murphy had frightened the owners into addressing player grievances.[5]

The Mexican League fracas of 1946 also put fear into the moguls. Millionaire Jorge Pasquel, president of the league and an importer-exporter along with his five brothers, used his wealth to entice underpaid major leaguers to play south of the border. He promised the moon, including major league–like facilities and long-term contracts and bonuses in an eight-team league. Alarmed major-league owners quickly warned their players that joining an outlaw league constituted a violation of the reserve clause, subjecting them to suspension. Commissioner Chandler announced that jumpers would be banned from organized baseball for up to five years.[6]

Among those who defected were marginal major leaguers such as Danny Gardella of the Giants and Louis Olmo of the Dodgers. By March 1946, however, the Pasquels began to sign quality players, most notably catcher Mickey Owen of the Dodgers and Vern Stephens of the St. Louis Browns. The Cardinals were particularly vulnerable because of their lower salaries and their popularity in Mexico. By May Max Lanier, Lou Klein, and Freddie Martin had signed contracts. Martin, who had pitched brilliantly in Class AA ball in 1941 before spending four years in the service, had been underused in early 1946, while Klein had lost his starting position to Schoendienst at second base. Lanier was by far the Cards' greatest loss, one that could have been averted. He felt unappreciated after winning seventeen games in 1944 and pitching well in the World Series. Upon Lanier's return from the service in early 1946, Breadon refused to increase his 1944 salary of ten thousand dollars. Following a brief holdout, Lanier received a paltry $500 raise. He began the 1946 season with six consecutive victories, all of them complete games. Pasquel's final offer

5. For Murphy's activities, see Lowenfish and Lupien, *The Imperfect Diamond*, 139–53. For Musial's views, see Musial oral history transcript, 36–38.

6. The best coverage of the Mexican League fracas is in Turner, *When the Boys Came Back*, 60–65, 125–35, and Marshall, *Baseball's Pivotal Era*, 45–63.

of a $25,000 bonus to sign and $20,000 annually for five years seemed especially attractive after Lanier felt pain in his pitching elbow in his last two starts, a problem he kept to himself.

Following the signing of Lanier, the Pasquels moved more aggressively to acquire other Cardinals, including Moore, Slaughter, and Kurowski. No Cardinal invited more attention than Musial because of his stardom and his agonizing vacillation. The inducement ultimately included offers reputedly ranging from $130,000 to $175,000 for five years, half of which was to be paid immediately. This came at a time when Musial's $13,500 salary compared poorly with Williams's $40,000 or Hal Newhouser's $45,000.

Musial has consistently claimed that he never seriously considered the Mexican offer. In September 1946, three months after he decided to remain with the Cardinals, he even wrapped himself in Old Glory as he told J. G. Taylor Spink of the *Sporting News*, "Sure, they stuck that dough under my nose and I suppose I could have written my own ticket. But please get this. It may sound like waving the flag and hollering 'Hooray for Uncle Sam.' But this is from the ticker. My dad came over from Poland. He worked in a steel mill. . . . he worked hard. But he never kicked. This was his dream, the good old USA." Musial suggested to Spink that his decision to stay had also been influenced by Slaughter's and Moore's decisions not to go to Mexico. In an oral history for the University of Kentucky in 1978, Musial said that while the money was a great temptation, he never gave the Pasquels' invitation a "serious thought." In his 1964 autobiography he reiterated in a slightly qualified fashion: "I don't think I ever seriously considered going, but [Jorge] Pasquel was determined. His offer kept going up."[7]

Yet assertions that Musial seriously entertained the Mexican offers came from the contemporary press and from Owen, who contacted Musial on behalf of the Pasquel brothers. Ray Gillespie of the *St. Louis Star Times*, another agent for the Pasquels, also talked to Musial. The most often reported aspect of the story involves the visit of Owen and Alfonso Pasquel to Musial's Fairgrounds Hotel apartment on June 6 to convince a wavering Musial to finalize an apparent verbal agreement. According to a contemporary newspaper account, Pasquel made three separate offers to Musial during his short stay. Owen was also there to affirm that the

7. *Sporting News*, September 25, 1946, 4; Musial oral history transcript, 26; Musial, *Musial*, 90.

Pasquels had honored every one of their promises to him and that life in Mexico was grand.

To begin the meeting, Owen asked Musial whether he had spoken to the Mexicans. When Musial replied that he had not, Owen then asked whether he knew Roy Henshaw, a former major league pitcher working for the Pasquels. Musial admitted, "Yeah, I know Henshaw"; he also conceded that he had talked to Henshaw about playing in Mexico after Owen related that Henshaw had told him that he had contacted Musial in Chicago sometime in May where Musial made a verbal commitment to play for the Pasquels. The arrangement called for Musial to receive a twenty-five-thousand-dollar bonus and a five-year contract of twenty-five thousand dollars annually, tax free. On May 26 the public address announcer at the Puebla-Veracruz game indicated that Musial would join the Mexican League and be in Mexico momentarily. Instead, Musial visited with a concerned Breadon and Dyer on June 2, four days before the Fairgrounds Hotel meeting, telling them that he would remain a Cardinal.[8]

Not knowing of Musial's apparent change of heart, Jorge Pasquel asked his brother Alphonso and Owen to drive to St. Louis to finalize the deal. In that June 6 encounter at the Fairgrounds Hotel, Pasquel presented Musial with five ten-thousand-dollar checks, a bonus, Musial recalled, with a five-year contract in the offing. Owen remembered that he "thought Musial was going to swallow [his] cigar when [he saw] all that money on the table. It would be peanuts to him now, but then it looked like more money than they had in Donora, Pennsylvania. He wouldn't say much. He just kinda held back and looked at it, bit on his cigar some more, and blew smoke all over the place."[9]

Because of Musial's hesitation, Owen felt that he had already signed a new contract with the Cardinals, a matter that Musial refused to discuss. By this time the local papers were abuzz about the possibility of Musial leaving. The *Sporting News* included in its feature story of June 19 a photograph of Pasquel and Owen dining in a St. Louis restaurant while awaiting Musial's response. During this period panicky reports circulated that Musial was seen packing, supposedly for Mexico, which the *Sporting*

---

8. Mickey Owen oral history, Albert B. Chandler Oral History Project, University of Kentucky Library, tape no. 3; Marshall, *Baseball's Pivotal Era*, 57; *St. Louis Post-Dispatch*, June 7, May 26, 1946; for Breadon's public statement on Musial's vow to stay, see ibid., June 6, 1946. On May 31, Musial, in a brief telephone interview just before checking out of a Pittsburgh hotel, evasively commented that "I don't think I will go, but I haven't told [the Pasquels] yes or no." *St. Louis Star Times*, May 31, 1946.

9. Owen oral history, tape no. 3; Marshall, *Baseball's Pivotal Era*, 57.

News and local newspapers soon dispelled by reporting that the Musials were moving into a furnished bungalow on Mardel Avenue in southwest St. Louis.[10]

In mid-June Musial finally issued a statement to the press that the Pasquels had made an offer "that was hard to turn down. All that money makes a fellow do a lot of thinking before he says no," he explained. When a reporter asked if he might change his mind, Musial coyly responded, "I'm still young. I should be able to make a lot of money for a long time here in the United States. Let's consider this Mexican thing a closed matter for the present. Let's say no more." In the weeks ahead the Pasquels told Musial that he could "write his own ticket."[11]

The question remains as to not only why Musial decided to remain in St. Louis, but why he seemed so willing to bolt. After all, other stars such as Ted Williams and Joe DiMaggio never gave the Pasquels' approaches much thought. Their much higher salaries surely were a major consideration for not doing so. But for a while it seemed to matter little to Musial that he remained under contract with the Cards through 1946. Once before, in 1938, he had attempted to put aside a Cardinal minor-league contract after the Pirates had indicated an interest in him. Feeling mistreated, he had few qualms about fighting for the best arrangement for himself even if it meant discarding a contract. His affable demeanor concealed a tough core shaped by the hardships and embarrassments he and his family had to endure. Living in Donora during the depths of the Depression had schooled him to grab whatever he could. Every indication exists, too, that because of a financial obligation to his parents, he needed more money. Genuinely grateful for his good fortune, he understood, though, that one also had to make his own luck.

What kept him in St. Louis? Perhaps, Lil had something to do with it; Owen claimed that she did not want to leave the country. Perhaps, the quick return of Vern Stephens to the Browns on June 5 suggested that conditions were less than satisfactory in Mexico. The St. Louis newspapers, too, reported incidents involving Jorge Pasquel's unprofessional behavior at Mexican League games. What role Breadon might have played in the final decision is less clear. Little indication exists that he promised Musial anything at this time. His providing Musial with five thousand

10. Marshall, *Baseball's Pivotal Era*, 57; *Sporting News*, June 19, 1946, 2.

11. *Sporting News*, June 19, 1946, 2. Bob Broeg's column in the *Post-Dispatch* claimed that "Musial was almost incoherent when it came to explanations to live up to his Cardinal contract and promises repeated . . . to President Sam Breadon and Manager Eddie Dyer that he would stick with the Redbirds." *St. Louis Post-Dispatch*, June 7, 1946.

dollars late in the season for staying seems paltry next to the Mexican offer. If Musial intended to use Pasquel as leverage for a substantial salary adjustment, it had clearly failed. By early June, however, Breadon was so convinced that Musial—and others—might leave that he flew to Mexico City to visit with Jorge Pasquel, which earned a five-thousand-dollar fine from Chandler for weakening the commissioner's position against an outlaw league. Chandler had already announced his five-year ban on the eighteen jumpers. Reinstatement afterward, he announced, would not be automatic. Such retribution surely must have given Musial pause. Was Pasquel's money really worth it?[12]

Manager Dyer asked that same question when Musial sought him out. Musial felt very close to the mentoring Dyer, and in the end he heeded his advice. According to Dyer, who spoke to New York journalist Frank Graham about the matter in 1948, Musial had told a frantic Breadon that he was going to Mexico. Breadon asked Dyer to talk with him about it before the game that evening. Lacking an office in the clubhouse, Dyer talked to Musial privately in the equipment room. Dyer began by saying, "I know how you feel about this offer . . . I'd like to get that kind of money, too. But there are other things we must think about. You have a contract with the ball club, haven't you? He said, 'yes' and I said: Stan, signing a contract is just giving your word, that's all. An honorable man doesn't go back on his word. You wouldn't want your children to think their father isn't an honorable man, would you? Musial then said he would not go to Mexico." That defining moment probably occurred just before Musial's meeting with Alfonso Pasquel and Owen. By that time, Owen remembered, "something was gnawing at him." And that may well have been the conversation Musial had with Dyer. Owen said it best some thirty years afterward: "It was the greatest thing that happened to him that he didn't go."[13]

Not only would Musial have surrendered his best statistical years had he left, but also he would not have been reinstated until after June 1949 when players such as Lanier, Klein, and Sal Maglie returned, the former two to the Cards and the latter to the Giants. Moreover, he would

12. Owen oral history, tape no. 3; *St. Louis Post-Dispatch,* June 3, 1946; Musial, *Musial,* 91; Stockton, "Singing Sam, the Cut-Rate Man," 138.
13. Owen oral history, tape no. 3; Frank Graham, *Graham's Corner,* undated clipping in Musial Collection, *Sporting News* archives. For Musial's closeness to Dyer, see Musial oral history transcript, 27. Earlier, Musial had talked to Frank Pizzica about the Mexican offer; Schoendienst claimed Pizzica gave Musial "good advice." Red Schoendienst telephone interview, February 4, 1997.

have found playing conditions intolerable in most of the Mexican parks. Lanier remembered one in which goats grazed in the outfield prior to the games and another where train tracks ran across the outfield, requiring the suspension of play when trains came through. Drinking water had to be boiled, and housing was usually inadequate. Much of the travel occurred on old buses that had to negotiate dangerous mountain roads, shades of Williamson and Class D ball. After a year and a half, the Pasquel brothers began to cut salaries, causing most of the former major leaguers to return home, where they were treated as lepers until their reinstatements. Most important, Musial would have missed out on the elevation of player salaries that occurred after the 1946 season.[14]

Nevertheless, the challenge of Murphy's Guild and the Mexican League had frightened the moguls of the major leagues into making concessions to the players by removing some of the dissatisfaction. Three player representatives from the two leagues, including Marion of the Cards, participated in the deliberations, which led to a minimum salary of five thousand dollars; twenty-five dollars per week for spring training expenses, known as "Murphy money" to the players; and the announcement of a pension plan. The latter idea, another sop to forestall unionization, had first resulted from discussions between Marion and trainer Doc Weaver of the Cardinals.

Marion, an emerging team leader on player-grievance issues, and Weaver had worked out a pension plan during a rainout day in New York that would provide benefits to any major leaguer with five years' service upon reaching the age of forty-five. The plan required matching contributions from players and owners involving revenues coming from the All-Star game, the broadcasting of the World Series, and from eight midseason interleague exhibition games. Later, television revenue would be included. The owners bought into the plan after some modifications. They also agreed to extend the players' ten-day severance clause to thirty days and to not cut salaries more than 25 percent in contract renewals. But players failed to obtain an agreement for the arbitration of disputes and voting rights on the joint committee dominated by the owners. Moreover, following the defeat of Murphy's Guild, owners imposed a restrictive clause in the players' contract, making it more difficult for players to challenge the reserve clause. Branch Rickey even charged that opposition

14. For Lanier's account of conditions in Mexico, see his oral history transcript, Albert B. Chandler Oral History Project, and "Lanier" interview in Honig, *Baseball When the Grass Was Real*, 219.

to the latter came from those with "avowed Communistic tendencies." The establishment also sought to extend the season beyond 154 games as a way to finance the concessions. So, problems between players and management had scarcely ended.[15]

In fact, in some ways they were only beginning as some ballplayers, banned as a result of Mexican League play, had already filed suit against the owners for engaging in a punitive monopoly. Matters relating to the pension plan, arbitration, raising the minimum wage, and player participation in decision making also festered into the 1950s. Only later did Musial become more involved as a player representative for his club. In 1946, while supporting the pension plan and the other related proposals, Musial opposed Murphy's Guild even though he favored some form of players' organization. Letting others speak for him, his major mark came with his bat in what turned out to be the most exciting Cardinal season in the post–World War II era.

Musial proved that he was an emerging superstar by his performance against veteran stars returning from the war. Never had his play proved so crucial in so many games, especially in the early part of the season with Kurowski not performing well, Marion hurt, Moore hobbling in center field, and the departure of three Cardinals to the Mexican League.

The campaign began with a 6–4 loss against Pittsburgh on a cold, rainy afternoon in Sportsman's Park. Dyer went with sentimental favorite Johnny Beazley, whose dead arm failed to take him beyond the fourth inning. Kurowski's error later in the game led to two unearned runs, which cost the Cardinals the contest. Musial momentarily stirred the crowd by beginning his postwar career with a single. For the next couple of weeks the Cardinals made it to the top of the standings before record-setting crowds that often grew impatient when the team did not always win. During a doubleheader loss to the Reds in early May, angry fans booed Dyer whenever he exited the dugout. Even the popular Musial became a target. The new mood, managers and players agreed, permeated both leagues. Part of it reflected the anger, resentment, and impatience of former GIs who found adjustment to civilian life difficult. One former serviceman asked, "Would you start cheering everybody the moment you got out?"[16]

---

15. For Marion's involvement in the pension plan, see Marty Marion oral history transcript, Albert B. Chandler Oral History Project, 18–20; Musial, *Musial*, 99–100; and Turner, *When the Boys Came Back*, 194–96. For an overall assessment of players' gains, see Lowenfish and Lupien, *The Imperfect Diamond*, 148–52. The Rickey quotation comes from Lowenfish and Lupien, 165.

16. Quotation in Turner, *When the Boys Came Back*, 117.

By the time the Cardinals began their eastern road trip in mid-May they found themselves two games behind the surprising Dodgers. The promise of the preseason had soon evaporated because of the innumerable injuries—war-related or not. Dyer was clearly worried. At this juncture he faced the prospect of losing his most talented veterans to the Mexicans. Because of talk of player strikes and unionism as well, baseball had entered a period of unrest, "bordering on revolution," as Musial later described it.[17]

The opening road series involved the resurgent Dodgers of whom much less was expected. The wily, combative Durocher brought out the fire in his players, however, as he superbly integrated returning veterans such as Kirby Higbe and Pete Reiser with rookies Carl Furillo and Gene Hermanski and wartime stars such as Dixie Walker, Eddie Stanky, and Augie Galan into a winning unit. The Cardinal-Dodger rivalry now reached a new level of intensity, especially at cozy Ebbets Field, an old brick facade in the Flatbush section of Brooklyn. Fans there sat so close to the field that historian Doris Kearns Goodwin remembered that "we could hear what the ballplayers said to one another."[18] Limited to thirty-two thousand in seating capacity, the noisy crowd retained a near pathological identity with "de Bums," creating havoc for visiting clubs. The emotions heightened whenever the Cards came to town. The only team west of the Mississippi, they "seemed almost like frontiersmen in flannels," according to baseball writer Don Honig, a team to be respected and feared. Moore of the Redbirds recalled the fan abuse: They would throw "firecrackers, bottles, anything they had handy." After the game, as Cardinal players left the ballpark for the subway, fans tried to remove their hats and tie clasps and squirted ink at them from fountain pens. Jeff Cross, a utility Cardinal infielder, remembered Dodger fans as "crazy, nutty people."[19]

The games themselves, more akin to war than to sporting events, frightened umpires who worked them. According to Moore, they would always tell the players before the first game, " 'Boys let's have a good series.' Then sure enough, all hell would break loose." Musial acknowledged that he "was so charged up before the [Dodger games], man, I could go out there and climb six fences and I wasn't the only one. Our whole team was up." The ritual included constant needling from both sides, led by Durocher, sometimes humorously. Marion recalled Durocher pointing to the lean Musial at first, Schoendienst at second, and Marion at shortstop,

---

17. Musial, *Musial*, 88.
18. Doris Kearns Goodwin, *Wait Till Next Year: A Memoir*, 48.
19. Turner, *When the Boys Came Back*, 122.

shouting, "You couldn't get a pint of blood out of the whole bunch." As he had done in the early '40s, Durocher also frequently shouted to his pitchers to "hit him in the head" as a way to intimidate the batters. Following a knockdown, according to Musial, the players would get back up, thinking nothing of it. They would merely await the retaliation of their own pitchers. "We had some tough guys," he acknowledged.[20]

The Cardinals temporarily moved into first place by a few percentage points after Lanier went eleven innings for the win in the first game of the series. The second game featured a confrontation between Slaughter and Dodger pitcher Les Webber, whose pitches came perilously close to Slaughter at the plate. Slaughter then bunted down the first-base line, and as Webber came over to field the ball, Slaughter deliberately crashed into him. As the two went at one another both benches cleared. Dyer muscled his way between Slaughter and Webber to end the confrontation. When Slaughter went to right field, fans greeted him with boos, which suddenly turned silent after he made a shoestring catch of Galan's low liner. He followed this with another marvelous catch near the scoreboard, then threw to first to double up Furillo. Slaughter's defensive play had preserved Pollet's 1–0 shutout. Even though Musial's hitting did not figure in the two victories, he, too, made a clutch catch and left Brooklyn hitting .388, a percentage point below Dixie Walker's league-leading average.

Afterward, the Cardinals continued on their road trip to Boston and then Philadelphia, where "the weather was usually a little cooler, the lobster was good, and the pitching staff was weak," as Musial assessed it. The team could do no better than split with the Braves, with Beazley again getting hit hard. After winning a doubleheader in Philadelphia under difficult circumstances because of a train strike delaying their arrival, they returned to New York for a doubleheader with the Giants. There the bottom fell out as Lanier, Klein, and Martin left for Mexico. Schoendienst probably became the first to know when he found roommate Lanier's luggage gone, along with a note on the bureau, "So long, Red, keep hitting those line drives. I'll see you next winter, and we'll go hunting."[21] Nothing hurt the team more.

Then things kept getting worse. Following the Giants series, the ball club found it impossible to use the trains to reach Cincinnati for a night game because of a massive rail strike, coverage of which blanketed the

20. Ibid.; Connor, ed., *Baseball for the Love of It*, 142; Marion oral history transcript, 50; Musial oral history transcript, 46.

21. Turner, *When the Boys Came Back*, 124, 125.

front pages of every newspaper in the country. Nineteen players ended up flying to Ohio, where thunderstorms forced them down in Dayton, about fifty miles from Cincinnati. They then piled into cabs for the drive to Crosley Field. In the cab in which Musial, Slaughter, and Buster Adams were riding, the hood latch broke, causing the cab driver to lie across the hood to keep it down while Musial drove to the park with his head out of the side window so that he could see the road. Breadon wondered what else could go wrong as he faced the prospect of losing Musial and others to Mexico. During the disaster of late May and early June the Cards began to lose ground to the Dodgers, falling seven games behind at the July All-Star break. Even though the Dodgers had their own problems with injuries, the Cards seemed to be in the midst of a major collapse.

Several considerations turned the season around. One involved the inspiring locker-room speech of Kurowski, who finished with .301 average following a bitter holdout. Kurowski confessed to having been tempted by Mexican money, but he felt honor bound, he said, to play for the Cards because he was under contract, and he vowed to do anything to win the pennant. Other players also stepped forward, including Pollet, who told Dyer after Lanier's departure that he could start every four days and pitch a game in relief between starts. Pollet indeed became the workhorse of the Cardinal staff, hurling 266 innings and compiling a 21–10 record and an ERA of 2.10, league-leading figures. Dickson (15–6) also had an outstanding season, and Brecheen and Brazle finished strongly. Among the position players Slaughter also had a tremendous year, playing in every game, driving in a league-leading 130 runs, and hitting .300. In the end, however, no one carried the club more than Musial.

Following his decision to remain a Card, he moved to first base, where he became a more than dependable performer. His clutch hitting stood out in the weeks ahead.[22] In one of his streaks in June, covering twenty-two games, he averaged .410. As a result, the Cards started to win again. After winning five out of seven at the beginning of a fifteen-game road trip, they blew into Brooklyn only one and a half games behind the Dodgers. Even though the home team won two out of the three, Musial went eight for twelve, one of several phenomenal series he would have in hitter-friendly Ebbets Field where the distance to the power alley in right field was only about 315 feet and 297 feet down the right-field line. The concrete right-field wall, nineteen feet tall with a screen sixteen feet high above

22. Excellent coverage of his clutch hitting can be found in Donald Drees, "Iceman Musial," 17–22.

it, became an inviting target for Musial as his drives either sailed over the screen onto Bedford Avenue or more frequently slammed against the wall or screen for doubles. On one occasion that summer sportswriter Bob Broeg of the *St. Louis Post-Dispatch*, seated in the press box, thought he had heard fans chanting, "Here comes that man" whenever Musial came to the plate. When he asked traveling secretary Leo Ward about it at dinner, Ward explained that they were shouting, "Here comes the man." Broeg would soon publish the anecdote in his newspaper column, providing Stan the Man with his most defining signature, one that Musial himself fully embraced.[23]

Musial's success against the powerful Dodgers had more to do with his competitiveness than to the closeness of the fences at Ebbets Field. For in a crucial four-game series in St. Louis in mid-July, Musial dominated the Redbirds' sweep, beginning with the Sunday doubleheader on July 14 before a capacity crowd. In the first game he walked in the first inning and eventually stole home. With the score at three-all in the eighth, he singled to start a two-run rally, resulting in a 5–3 win. In the nightcap Musial's triple led to the tying run in breaking up southpaw Vic Lombardi's shutout. In the twelfth Stan the Man's homer won the game, 2–1. The following afternoon, again before a packed house, Musial produced two singles, a triple, and a two-run homer in a 10–4 victory. Only in the final game did another Redbird surpass his efforts at the plate as pinch-hitter Erv Dusak homered in the ninth with two aboard for a 5–4 win, for which he was to be called "Four Sack" Dusak. The elated Cardinals found themselves only one-half game out of first place. And Musial ended up with nine hits in eighteen at bats, an amazing performance coming as it did in such a key series. Musial's explanation for his consistently superior performance against the Dodgers involved Branch Rickey, whom Musial always tried to impress for giving him his start with the Cardinals.[24]

Musial's success in 1946 against the New York teams, especially Brooklyn, contributed to the sports world's greater awareness and appreciation of this talented performer. The New York writers generated considerable media attention, and they now began to write more about him, often comparing him to Ted Williams of the Boston Red Sox. In the next couple of years such well-known New York sportswriters as Arthur Daly, Roger Kahn, and Jack Sher devoted magazine pieces to him in such publications

23. Musial, *Musial*, 93. Musial's friends claim that he responds on the telephone as "Stan the Man."
24. Mann, *Branch Rickey*, 210.

as *Sport*. Despite the considerable coverage that Musial also got from the St. Louis–based *Sporting News*, he still failed to receive as much attention as East Coast stars. In time Musial gained greater recognition for his play in the annual All-Star games, but not in 1946, when Ted Williams had four hits, two of them homers, in his home ballpark while the American League crushed the National Leaguers, 12–0, in the most lopsided All-Star victory ever. Playing left field, Musial failed to get a hit in two at bats.

Afterward, the close pennant race carried into August and September between the two front-runners, with Musial continuing to hit. In a four-game run in August he went on a fifteen-out-of-nineteen streak. In one contest in Boston he had five consecutive hits, the last of which won the game. Against Brooklyn later that month, Musial homered in a 3–2 defeat, then had four hits the next day in a 14–8 win. He finally surpassed Hopp and Dixie Walker in batting average with a .374 mark on August 15.

By early September the Cards had surged to a lead of two and a half games after winning thirteen out of eighteen at home. During that period Musial raised his batting average to .380. In the next couple of weeks both teams continued to play well even though Musial slumped a bit. By the final week the Cards still held a slim lead, preserved by Brecheen's 1–0 shutout of the Cubs on September 23 and Musial's dramatic home run the next day against the Reds with two outs in the ninth to tie the game, which Dusak won in the tenth by homering. On the final day of the season, the Cardinals missed a golden opportunity, however, squandering Musial's two-run homer when George Munger fell victim to a five-run sixth inning. For the first time ever in the history of the major leagues, two clubs ended the season tied for the lead. They would take their 96–58 records into a postseason playoff, one game at one park and possibly two at the other in the best-of-three series. Durocher won the toss and elected to begin in St. Louis. He had already lost fourteen out of twenty-two games with the Cards that year. He needed an opening win in St. Louis to apply the pressure.

The playoffs began at Sportsman's Park on Tuesday, October 1, in front of 26,012 fans on a very hot day. In a surprise move, Durocher, the consummate gambler, went with a rookie who had won only three games that season. But twenty-year-old Ralph Branca had pitched a brilliant 5–0 shutout against the Cards in his last effort. Durocher banked on him coming through once again. Branca faced wily southpaw Howie Pollet, the most consistent of the Cardinal pitchers. Pollet had the ability to throw strikes in pressure situations and rarely beat himself. Even though clearly the Cardinal ace in 1946, he was hurting. In an August game against the

Giants, an overworked Pollet had relieved without properly warming up. He felt a sharp pain in his arm, which became chronic. His back and shoulder also bothered him, adding to his vulnerability. But he pitched well enough to win as he defeated Branca, 4–2. Musial was called out in the first inning on a questionable third strike, which caused a rare stare at the umpire, but he then tripled off the wall in right center in the seventh and scored to give the Redbirds a 4–2 lead. He also walked in the third and scored. The real hitting hero, however, was twenty-year-old catcher Joe Garagiola, who had three hits and drove in two runs.

The next day the Redbirds took the train to New York, and Murry Dickson opened the series at Ebbets Field on Thursday. A fourteen-game winner, Dickson had a wide assortment of pitches, which he threw from various angles. He and his teammates jumped on Dodger left-hander Joe Hatton, also a fourteen-game winner, early with doubles by Musial and Moore and triples by Dusak, Slaughter, and Dickson. Entering the ninth with an 8–1 lead, Dickson made it interesting by giving up three runs, and, with the bases loaded and one out, Brecheen struck out the next two batters to preserve the victory. For Musial it was especially memorable; in his four full seasons with the Cardinals, he had contributed mightily to four pennants.

Moreover, he had his finest season as he led the league in hitting with a .365 average, thirty-two percentage points higher than the runner-up, Johnny Hopp. He also topped the league in hits (228), official at bats (624), runs scored (124), doubles (50), triples (20), slugging average (.587), and total bases (366). Additionally, he hit 16 homers and drove in 102 runs. He also made the successful transition to first base, with a respectable fielding average of .990. Baseball writers overwhelmingly selected him once again as the National League's Most Valuable Player; he received twenty-two of the twenty-four first-place votes, with the other two going to Slaughter. In February 1947 at the New York baseball writers' dinner, he would receive the Sid Mercer award as the top major-league player of the year. Unlike in 1943 or 1944, Musial's accomplishments had come against the best the National League had to offer, added proof that he had emerged as the league's premier hitter.

The Cards also continued their dominance of the National League in several hitting categories, including batting average (.265), RBIs (665), and runs scored (712). In pitching, despite the monumental loss of Lanier, they led the league in ERA (3.01) and shutouts (18), with starters Pollet, Dickson, Brecheen, and Brazle carrying most of the load. Out of the bullpen, dependable Ted Wilks finished with an 8–0 record.

The Cards, however, figured to fall before the powerful Boston Red Sox, who finished twelve games ahead of runner-up Detroit. On paper their offense dwarfed that of St. Louis. They were led by American League MVP Ted Williams, who hit .342 with 38 home runs, 123 RBIs, and a whopping 156 walks. Boston featured two other .300 hitters, Johnny Pesky (.335), who led the league in hits (208), and Dom DiMaggio (.316), the bespectacled younger brother of the Yankee Clipper. Their potent pitching staff contained two twenty-game winners, David "Boo" Ferris (25–6) and Tex Hughson (20–11), along with Mickey Harris (17–9) and Joe Dobson (13–7). Sports analysts anticipated that the Musial-Williams matchup represented an important key in the series.

The first game opened at Sportsman's Park on October 6, a bright, sunny day that cast deep shadows across home plate, which affected the hitters' ability to see the ball coming from the sunlit mound. The game developed into a pitching duel between Pollet and Hughson, with the Red Sox taking a 1–0 lead until the sixth, when Musial's two-out double tied the score. Two innings later DiMaggio lost Garagiola's high fly in the sun, allowing the tie-breaking run. The gutsy Pollet carried the 2–1 lead into the tenth inning when, with two outs, long-ball-hitting Rudy York, correctly anticipating a change-up, homered to left for a 3–2 Boston victory. Musial recalled that he had never seen Dyer lower than after that first game. Both Musial and Williams finished with one hit. Williams felt particularly frustrated because of a sore elbow and the Cardinals' employment of a Boudreau-like shift (named after the Cleveland Indians manager), which left Marion on the left side of the infield, with third baseman Kurowski moving to the right side of second base. Whereas Musial would have hit ball after ball to left field to demolish the shift, Williams elected to challenge it.

The next day, before a packed house, screwball specialist Brecheen went against ace Boston lefty Mickey Harris. Cardinal backup catcher Del Rice improbably became the hitting star with two hits, along with Brecheen, who drove in the first run. Brecheen scattered four singles in pitching a 3–0 shutout in which both Musial and Williams failed to hit safely. On one third-strike screwball, Williams swung with such ferocity that his bat flew into the Cardinals' dugout.

Musial performed better in game three, played in Boston's Fenway Park on October 9 on a cool, sunny afternoon with most spectators in coats and hats. He walked and stole second on Boo Ferris in the first inning before being picked off of second base. Years later Ferris asked Musial what he was thinking about that so distracted him. Musial laughed, responding, "I have no idea."[25] In the ninth, he also tripled with two outs, but to no avail. Ferris scattered six hits in pitching a 4–0 shutout. The key blow came in the first inning off the bat of York, a three-run shot over the left center-field wall. Williams played no major part in the win; frustrated by the shift, he elected to bunt on the third-base side, his only hit of the game. The next day the *Boston Globe* infuriated Williams with its sarcastic headline, "Williams Bunts."

In game four, to rest Pollet and Brecheen, Dyer gambled on Munger, who became the beneficiary of twenty hits off of Hughson and others, including Musial's two-run double and four hits apiece by Slaughter, Kurowski, and Garagiola as the Cardinals won, 12–5. The Red Sox regained the series lead in game five when a spent Pollet failed to get out of the first inning. Williams drove in his first series run in that frame with a single to right. Brazle, in relief, failed to shut down the Red Sox attack, while Boston's Joe Dobson pitched a four-hitter for the 6–3 win. In the fourth inning his slider hit Slaughter on the elbow, causing the Cardinals outfielder to leave after the swelling prevented him from flexing his arm.

The series shifted to Sportsman's Park for game six on Sunday, October 13. Although advised not to play by team physician Robert Hyland, Slaughter risked possible amputation of his arm by insisting on being in the lineup. He ended up getting the last of the Cardinals' five hits in a brilliant pitching effort by Brecheen, who, despite an aching arm, went all the way in a 4–1 win. "The Cat" gave up a walk and a single to Williams, but he forced York to hit into two double plays by keeping his screwball low and away.

The seventh and final game deserves all the acclaim it has received as one of the all-time World Series classics.[26] It had both heroics and drama. It had to compete, though, with the newspaper headlines of the pending dramatic execution of the eighteen convicted Nazi war criminals, including Hermann Goering and Joachim von Ribbentrop, who had been on trial all summer at Nuremberg.

The final contest transcended Musial following his wasted first-inning double, his sole hit in the game. The Cards took the lead in the fifth behind Dickson, who contributed a run-scoring two-base hit off of Ferris. In the eighth, however, the Red Sox had the tying runs on second and third with no outs before Dyer replaced Dickson with Brecheen. Weak and feverish

---

25. Turner, *When the Boys Came Back,* 237n.
26. For the best coverage of the final game, see ibid., 241–55.

from the flu and with his pitching arm hurting more than ever, Brecheen retired the side, but not before DiMaggio's double tied the score. Thinking about stretching it into a triple, DiMaggio had accelerated between first and second base, thereby pulling a hamstring, which forced him from the game.

In the Cardinals' half of the eighth, Boston replaced DiMaggio, "The Little Professor," with Leon Culberson in center field, and Bob Klinger relieved Dobson on the mound. Klinger promptly gave up a single to Slaughter. But Kurowski's sacrifice bunt attempt failed, and Rice flied out to Williams in left. With two outs, Harry Walker, who had enjoyed an outstanding series with a team-leading .412 average, hit the ball into left center, while Slaughter legged it to second on a steal attempt. Culberson came over quickly to field the ball but casually threw it to Pesky, the shortstop, who went out to short left center for the relay. By that time Walker was within a few strides of second base. (Hence the game's official scorer gave Walker a double instead of a single, igniting a controversy as to whether Walker should have been credited with a single or a double.)

Meanwhile, Slaughter continued his mad dash around the bases. Apparently neither Culberson nor Pesky thought Slaughter intended to score on the play. As "Country" rounded third, the off-balance Pesky momentarily held the ball, then threw home. By that time Slaughter had slid across the plate while catcher Roy Partee moved forward to catch the ball, a photographic scene reprinted countless times. Pesky has been unfairly crucified for not hurrying the relay home, which negates Culberson's role. (DiMaggio, a strong-armed, aggressive outfielder, later said that "Slaughter would never have scored if I'd been in center field.") It also minimizes the daring and determination of Slaughter, who had ignored third-base coach Mike Gonzalez's signal to stop at third because he had said to himself as he rounded second, "God dang, boy! You can score on this."

The dramatics continued in the top of the ninth as Brecheen gave up singles to the first two batters. Manager Joe Cronin then ordered Pinky Higgins to sacrifice bunt, enabling the runners to advance. But faulty execution permitted third baseman Kurowski to make a play at second instead of first. Following Partee's foul out to Musial at first, McBride then hit a screwball off the end of the bat that moved crazily toward second base. Schoendienst charged the ball and, as it rolled up his arm, finally gained control of it and tossed it to Marion at second base for the out just as Higgins began his ferocious slide. The Cardinals had won the World Series—its sixth championship.

The win, a team effort, included such unlikely heroes as Walker and Garagiola as well as Slaughter, Kurowski, and Brecheen, who was credited with three wins and an ERA of 0.45 in twenty innings pitched. Even though Musial had carried the team at the plate throughout the regular season, his performance during the World Series proved disappointing. He hit .222, including four doubles and a triple among his six hits, and he drove in four runs. He consoled himself that he had outperformed Williams, who finished with a .200 average, four singles and one RBI. The individual winning share amounted to only $3,742.34, partly because of the limited seating capacities of the two ballparks and also because the broadcasting money—$175,000—went into the players' pension fund.

The 1946 World Series would turn out to be Musial's last appearance in postseason play. Who would have thought that possible, considering that the twenty-six-year-old had already played in four championship series? For Musial and the ball club, if not for others, 1946 could be considered one of "the best years of our lives" despite all of the aforementioned tribulations and problems. For the next seventeen years, however, Musial and the Cardinals would futilely seek a return to glory. No season would seem more trying to Musial than the one in 1947.

A Troubling Year

O
n the night preceding the 1946 playoffs with the Dodgers, friends of Joe Garagiola threw a party for him and the Cardinals at Ruggeri's, a renowned Italian restaurant on the Hill near Garagiola's home. Sportswriter Bob Broeg remembered the dinner as also being a salute to Sam Breadon, the crusty club president. The gaiety of the evening suddenly soured after the dean of St. Louis sportswriters, J. Roy Stockton, responded to the toastmaster's request to speak. Stockton, who had a reputation for candidness especially after a couple of drinks, commented to Breadon, "Sam, you've always liked to slice the baloney thin, but this year, you may have sliced it a little too thin." Stockton, of course, was alluding to the quality players Breadon had sold, including Walker Cooper and Johnny Hopp. He suggested that if a few of them had been retained, it would not have been much of a race. Following the momentary silence, a reaction set in. According to Broeg, "Breadon was pissed"; so were Cards broadcaster Dizzy Dean and others.[1] Harry Caray, the demonstrative young broadcaster, spoke in Breadon's defense when he argued that, because of his private generosity, Breadon was hardly a cheapskate. Considerable applause followed Caray's testimonial. He soon emerged as the Redbirds' featured broadcaster on fifty-thousand-watt KMOX, which carried the Card games throughout the Midwest and much of the South.

Yet, despite the inappropriateness of his comments at a social gathering, Stockton correctly anticipated the problems the Cards would face for the upcoming 1947 season. Cooper's presence alone would have probably guaranteed the Cardinals the pennant that year; he hit .305, clubbed 35 home runs, and drove in 122 runs for the Giants in 1947. Nobody on the Cardinals came near those figures. Moreover, the catching staff became a major disappointment. The loss of World Series hero Harry Walker, who was traded to Philadelphia for Ron Northey, also proved significant, for Walker won the batting title in 1947 with a .363 average. The once vaunted Cardinal farm system also had stopped producing as many quality players as it had under Rickey's auspices. The one possible exception—pitcher Jim Hearn (12–7)—failed to make up for Cardinal ace Howie Pollet's inability

---

1. Turner, *When the Boys Came Back*, 214–15.

to recover from his back and shoulder ailments of 1946 as he sank to a 9–11 season.

Stan Musial also became a major consideration in the Cardinals' performance for 1947. He began the year by rejecting a proposed contract, embarking on his last holdout as a major leaguer. Based on his 1946 performance, Musial sought $35,000, a reasonable amount in comparison to Hank Greenberg's $85,000, Bob Feller's $72,000, Joe DiMaggio's $43,750, and Ted Williams's $75,000. Breadon offered $21,000, which he insisted represented a pay boost of $7,500. Musial claimed that the increase was only $2,500 since the $5,000 upgrade in the summer of 1946 had raised his salary to $18,500, for which, Musial said, he had to sign a new contract and pay taxes. Perhaps in response to Breadon arguing that dissatisfied Cardinals should also consider the customary World Series checks as part of their earnings, Musial, according to Feller, claimed at the Dapper Dan Dinner in Pittsburgh that winter that he would rather join Feller's barnstorming tour than play in another World Series because it provided three times more money.[2]

More certain than he was in 1943, Musial rejected Breadon's offer even though he agreed to meet with him again in February at the New York baseball writers' dinner. That afternoon Musial turned down Breadon's twenty-seven-thousand-dollar bid, which prevented the owner from announcing Musial's signing at the banquet. When spring training began, Musial became an official holdout; he took Lil and the children with him to St. Petersburg, where they awaited a breakthrough while staying at the Bainbridge Hotel. One evening Breadon came into the crowded hotel dining room. Musial, there with his family, asked him to join them. After a pleasant dinner together, Musial requested the checks, including Breadon's, but Breadon refused to let Musial pay; nor did he pick up Musial's tab. Although calling him in his autobiography a straight-shooter who paid his own way, Stan remained at best ambivalent about "Singing Sam."[3]

The impasse ended after Eddie Dyer asked Musial for a compromise position following a lengthy conversation with him. After Musial indicated thirty-one thousand dollars, Dyer reported that figure to Breadon, who finally agreed. The settlement made Musial the highest-paid Cardinal player ever, although Rogers Hornsby and Frankie Frisch had commanded more as player-managers. Despite probable informal advice from

2. Marshall, *Baseball's Pivotal Era*, 343.
3. Musial, *Musial*, 102.

longtime friends such as Frank Pizzica, Musial, who knew the value of a dollar, seemed to rely mostly on his own judgment. No evidence exists that newly acquired agent Fred Corcoran, who also represented a number of golfers and Ted Williams, played any part in the negotiations. Corcoran secured endorsements for Musial, as well as personal appearances, some of which Musial did without remuneration. Corcoran, when asked why he had not done more for his client, later said that Musial "never moved people the way Williams did."[4]

Musial also faced unexpected health problems. He came to spring training underweight and lacked power in his swing, causing him to overstride. After complaining about abdominal pain that winter, he had visited a Donoran physician, who recommended the removal of an infected appendix. Musial's aversion to surgery caused him to ignore that advice while keeping the problem from the ball club.[5] By opening day his health had been further affected. It showed in his performance. Against Ewell Blackwell, the gangling pitching ace of the Cincinnati Reds, he went hitless in four at bats. Although homering the next day against Eddie Erautt, Musial's slide had begun. So, too, had the team's; following a four-game split, the Cardinals soon lost nine straight, putting them in the National League cellar. By May 2 Musial was hitting only .174 after a disastrous .146 average for April.

Since the Musial-led Cardinals had been the overwhelming favorites to repeat as pennant winners, their dismal performance commanded considerable attention in the press. In the last week of April New York sportswriters, covering the Kentucky Derby in Lexington, decided to telephone the New Yorker hotel one evening to interview Dyer, whose ball club would play the Giants the next day. Unable to reach Dyer at around two in the morning, they presumptuously requested Musial's room. A writer asked Musial what was wrong with the club. After Musial suggested that he talk to Dyer, the writer then responded, "You haven't been so good yourself lately." Musial faintly said he had a pain in his belly: He was "lying on the floor," he went on, because he felt "better that way." He also mentioned that the doctor thought he had appendicitis. After hearing this, the writer supposedly said, "I'm sorry, Stan, I'm sorry I disturbed you. . . . The hell with the ball club. Take it easy, Stan, good night and God bless you."[6] Soon afterward, Musial was taken to a hospital.

4. Fred Corcoran with Bud Harvey, *Unplayable Lies*, 148.
5. Musial's brother said that Stan was afraid of doctors. Ed Musial interview, August 6, 1996.
6. Frank Graham, "The Cardinals' No. 6," 75.

During this trying period Kyle Crichton, a writer for *Collier's* magazine, felt rebuffed in his effort to arrange an interview with an ailing Musial and consequently wrote a rare critical piece on him, accusing Musial of "expanso Largesso cerebello" (a swelled head). Always overly sensitive about how he was perceived, Musial undoubtedly felt he had been mistreated. Manager Dyer described it as "the worst thing I've ever seen written about anyone."[7] St. Louis sportswriters later publicly expressed their own ire at Crichton. Musial eventually responded by becoming even more accommodating to the press.

In early May a New York physician recommended that Musial undergo emergency surgery. Dyer, after conferring with Breadon and team physician Robert Hyland on the telephone, flew a sedated Musial to St. Louis on May 9, accompanied by reserve catcher Del Wilber. Musial immediately entered St. John's Hospital, where Hyland confirmed the appendicitis and diagnosed tonsillitis as well. He recommended the freezing of Musial's appendix because surgery would sideline him for nearly a month. Following the conclusion of the 1947 season Musial would have both his appendix and tonsils removed.

Meanwhile, he slowly regained strength, thanks to Hyland's treatments, Lil's cooking, and five days' rest before returning to the lineup. Breadon helped by agreeing to keep vacant two thousand seats in center field, enabling Musial and others to see the ball better while at bat. Musial had blamed his poor hitting at Sportsman's Park during the World Series and on Sundays to a packed house. As a result, Musial slowly regained his batting prowess, enabling the Cards to begin their slow climb out of the basement.

The final reason for the Cardinals' decline involved Branch Rickey, who had rejuvenated the Dodger farm system with quality prospects, including players from the Negro Leagues. Jackie Robinson, the first of the black players to make it to the majors, became the spark plug of the Dodgers' 1947 pennant-winning team, and he was soon followed by Roy Campanella, Don Newcombe, and several others, guaranteeing Dodger domination into the mid-1950s. As a result, the Dodgers had become, to use Musial's word, a "dynasty." Over that same period the Cardinals made only feeble efforts to snare top Negro League players. Not until 1954 did the club purchase the contract of a black player, Tom Alston of

---

7. Kyle Crichton, "Ace in the Hole," 14; Bob Broeg, "Cards Crack Back at Writer of Musial Blast in Magazine," *Sporting News* (September 17, 1947), in Rawlings, *Musial Scrapbook*, 58.

the Pacific Coast League, who could not hit major-league pitching. The Cards would have to await the arrival of Bill White in 1960 for a quality black position player.

The changing nature of American society during the war years made Rickey's bold experiment possible. The migration of blacks northward for industrial jobs had strengthened them politically as well as economically. Their vote in northern communities influenced how political leaders would respond to race-related issues. The threatened black march on Washington, D.C., in 1941 had already caused the federal government to create a temporary Federal Employment Practice Commission to end the discriminatory practices of companies holding federal contracts, an approach liberals sought to extend into the postwar era. Moreover, since much of the U.S. wartime propaganda had been directed against the Nazis for their Aryan-race beliefs, black leaders such as Adam Clayton Powell, Jr., rightly argued the hypocrisy of discriminatory practices at home, which denied blacks the right to vote and attend integrated schools in the South, compete fairly for jobs and housing nationwide, or serve in integrated military units. Organized baseball, of course, totally excluded blacks. As a consequence, Powell and other black leaders had adopted the double "V" symbol, signifying victory against fascism overseas and Jim Crowism at home. The return of black servicemen from the front also reinforced the move toward greater racial equality. If blacks were good enough to fight, they certainly deserved integration into American society, civil rights leaders argued. President Truman's racial beliefs—at least relating to political and economic matters—were much affected by the World War II experience. Racial liberals were even more expansive in their views. The 1944 death of baseball commissioner Kenesaw Mountain Landis, a reactionary on organized baseball integration, further accommodated Rickey's actions.

Even though the somewhat pious Rickey had some sensitivity to racial matters, his motivations seemed much more complex. A brilliant elocutionist and workaholic who had graduated near the top of his law school class at the University of Michigan, the cigar-chomping, bespectacled sixty-five-year-old craved challenges and innovations. More than this, he wanted to win. He knew that tapping the greatest untapped talent pool in existence would enable him to overtake the Cards as well as attract a sizable number of blacks in New York to Dodger games.[8]

8. The best account on Rickey and the integration of the Dodgers is in Jules Tygiel, *Baseball's Great Experiment: Jackie Robinson and His Legacy* (New York: Oxford

Rickey's choice of Robinson as the first black to break the color barrier involved considerations beyond playing ability. Some would argue that Robinson may not have been the top Negro League player, but he had other attributes, including his shunning of alcohol and tobacco, his university training at UCLA, his experience competing in integrated athletics, his service as an officer in World War II when he bucked segregated practices, and his engagement to Rachel Isum, a college sweetheart, who impressed Rickey. Rickey saw in Robinson stability, maturity, and courage, all of which would be required to combat the certain opposition from racist owners, fans, and players alike. Because of the strong public support for Robinson at the time of his signing on October 23, 1945, club owners avoided expressing opposition as he progressed from the Montreal farm team to the Dodger roster in the spring of 1947.

Once the 1947 season began with Robinson playing first base, general manager Herb Pennock of the Philadelphia Phillies brazenly demanded, however, that Rickey keep Robinson from the road trip to Philadelphia. Robinson also received countless death threats through the mail. Some fans in Philadelphia, Cincinnati, and St. Louis were particularly militant in shouting racial epithets or booing Robinson. Often the enthusiastic cheering of blacks, who now flocked to the ballparks in great numbers, succeeded in drowning out the abuse. In St. Louis record crowds, including many blacks, attended the Cardinals-Dodgers series that spring. One black newspaper, the *St. Louis Argus,* gratuitously admonished blacks "to act like human beings" at the ballpark, "not like a tribe of cannibals."[9]

The greatest challenge Robinson faced came from opposing players, some of whom were blatant racists or afraid that integration might cost them their jobs. Indeed, Robinson encountered strong opposition from his own teammates, especially from the Dixie contingent. The Dodgers probably led the National League in the number of southerners on their roster. Some of them, steered by the popular Dixie Walker, the "people's cherce," initially refused to play with Robinson and asked to be traded. Only after Kentuckian Pee Wee Reese befriended him and he had proved himself on the field did most of the club rally behind Robinson, especially when he faced relentless racist abuse from opposing dugouts. No one carried it to greater extremes than Alabaman Ben Chapman, the manager of the Phillies. He encouraged his club to bombard Robinson with racial

---

University Press, expanded edition, 1997). See also Arnold Rampersad, *Jackie Robinson: A Biography.*

   9. *St. Louis Argus,* April 25, 1947.

venom arguably unequaled in the annals of the game. Chapman justified
this by insisting that taunting was common practice against rookies. More
than verbal invective, Robinson encountered beanings at the plate and
spikings in the field.[10]

Much talk centered on a player strike against Robinson that spring.
The reported ringleader, Walker, had contacts on other teams, including
brother Harry on the Cardinals prior to his trade to the Phillies. A conspir-
acy of silence and denial has persisted among the surviving participants,
most of whom refuse to admit to any anti-Robinson activity. They have
faced the embarrassment of being on the wrong side of history. No club
has met greater criticism for its role in a proposed strike than the St. Louis
Cardinals.[11]

The focus on the Cardinals seems unfair given the opposition to Robinson on other clubs, including his own. Outfielder Al Gionfriddo, who
began the season with Pittsburgh, insisted fifty years later that "every team
had voted on whether to play the Dodgers." Gionfriddo also confirmed a
planned strike on opening day with Dixie Walker as organizer. The Pirates,
according to Gionfriddo, decided to adopt a wait-and-see approach since
there was some question as to whether Robinson would make the Dodger
club.[12] Evidence exists that the Cubs voted to strike on opening day. Two
surviving Cubbies, pitcher Hank Wyse and catcher Dewey Williams, participated in the vote and understood that other teams were balloting too.
What prevented the strike from occurring is uncertain. Williams claimed
that before the game the team awaited a call from Walker, which never
came. Wyse insisted that a telegram came from the league office that said
that "anybody that [sic] didn't play would be barred for life." Williams
remembered team members felt that if "a colored player" must play they
wanted it to be Campanella, who was "a lot nicer." Robinson, he said, "was
too brash—another [Ed] Stanky" of the Dodgers. Consequently, according

10. Tygiel, *Baseball's Great Experiment*, 170–73, 182–85.
11. The best coverage of the proposed Cardinal player strike is in ibid., especially
185–88, and Roger Kahn, *The Era: 1947–1957: When the Yankees, the Giants, and the
Dodgers Ruled the World*, 53–62. I contacted fifty-two surviving players from the 1947
season (those who responded to my original Musial questionnaire), and twenty-nine
answered my query. The majority claimed that they had no recollection of strike
talk on the Cardinals or on any other team. One Cardinal player said that if he did
remember such an event, he would not comment on it. Ken Burkhart to James N.
Giglio, November 6, 1996, in possession of Giglio. A Pirate player, echoing a few
others, suggested that the "Cardinals did have a problem with [Robinson]." Wally
Westlake to Giglio, November 13, 1996, in possession of Giglio.
12. Albert Gionfriddo telephone interview, March 31, 1997.

to Wyse, Cub starting pitchers had standing instructions to deck Robinson: "Paul Erickson knocked him down four times before [Erickson] came up to hit. . . . We put in another pitcher so they couldn't get back at him," Wyse explained.[13]

The Cardinals' hostility toward Robinson easily matched that of the Dodgers and a few other clubs. Next to the Dodgers, the Redbirds had more players from the Deep South than any other team in the league, including Marty Marion of South Carolina, Terry Moore of Alabama, Enos Slaughter of North Carolina, Harry Walker of Mississippi, Howie Pollet of Louisiana, and Ken Burkhart of Tennessee—the first three the reputed ringleaders. Some, though tough and competitive to the core, were perfectly capable of treating Robinson humanely. This was particularly so of Marion, whom Robinson said "was always nice to me." Robinson remembered one game in which he slid into Marion at second base. Marion picked him up "anxiously" and asked if he were hurt.[14] Even so, most southerners were victims of their culture and responded predictably on issues relating to integration.

Racism, however, ranged far beyond Dixie; in the North it prevented Robinson from staying with teammates in the Ben Franklin Hotel in Philadelphia, misnamed as "the City of Brotherly Love." It had a stronger hold in the Midwest and the upper South. In the St. Louis press, sportswriters expressed, at best, little empathy toward Robinson. The St. Louis–based *Sporting News* had earlier opposed the integration of baseball. The virtual war the Cardinals waged with the Dodgers throughout the 1940s compounded the problem. Not only black, Robinson happened to be Dodger black as well.

Musial had little to say in his autobiography about Robinson. He mentioned elsewhere that he had watched Robinson play on an "all-colored team" after the 1946 season while barnstorming with Bob Feller's squad. Robinson made little impression on him as a ballplayer because of his short, choppy swing and his lack of grace in the field. Upon hearing of Robinson's promotion to the Dodgers, Musial remembered

---

13. Henry Wyse telephone interview, November 26, 1996; Dewey Williams telephone interview, November 20, 1996. See David Falkner, *Great Time Coming: The Life of Jackie Robinson from Baseball to Birmingham,* 166, for his interview with Wyse. Wyse suggested that I contact other Cubs, including Phil Cavarretta, who refused to talk about it, and Lennie Merullo, who altered his original written statement, by admitting that "a strike vote might have been taken." Lennie Merullo telephone interview, November 28, 1996.

14. Jackie Robinson, "A Kentucky Colonel Kept Me in Baseball," 87.

that the atmosphere seemed unready for a "colored" player, an expression often used at that time. Musial later told sportswriter Roger Kahn of the *New York Herald Tribune* that he heard talk among the Cardinals about Robinson: "It was rough and racial." But he never admitted that it went beyond that. In his autobiography, he said only that a strike vote had never occurred.[15]

Other Cardinal players deny any discussion of a strike. Slaughter later implausibly wrote that "we hadn't said one word to each other about the Robinson incident." Red Schoendienst also later claimed that "nobody ever said anything to me about [a strike]," while Marion failed to recall discussion of a strike in the clubhouse. Supposedly the only Cardinal who took the strike talk seriously was Dick Sisler, who told historian Jules Tygiel in the 1970s that "very definitely there was something going on . . . whereby they said they weren't going to play." Sisler contended that the strike planning came from older players.[16]

On May 9, Stanley Woodward, the distinguished sports editor of the *New York Herald Tribune*, first broke the news of a threatened Cardinals player strike against the Dodgers. Woodward received that information from Cecil Rutherford Rennie, a *Herald Tribune* sportswriter, who had heard the story from a concerned Dr. Hyland, the Cardinals' team physician, over a few drinks in early May. Rennie immediately telephoned Woodward, explaining that he could not write the piece because of his relationship with Hyland. Woodward, after checking some of the sources, decided to write it himself.[17]

According to Woodward, Cardinal players, after talking with other National Leaguers that spring, had discussed striking against the Dodgers in Brooklyn on the opening game of the series on May 6. Since the Cardinals would also play the Dodgers in St. Louis on May 20, some thought that a more opportune date to respond. Either way, this action, it was hoped, would set off a general strike involving other National League clubs for the purpose of terminating Robinson's stay.

Breadon, who got wind of the scheme from Hyland, flew to New York. While there he conferred with his players; what he heard disturbed him enough to act. Recognizing that a racial conflict would devalue a

15. Musial oral history transcript, 50–51; Kahn, *The Era*, 56; Musial, *Musial*, 104.
16. Slaughter, *Country Hardball*, 112, 108; Schoendienst, *Red*, 87; Red Schoendienst telephone interview, February 4, 1997; Marion oral history transcript, 51; Tygiel, *Baseball's Great Experiment*, 187; Dick Sisler interview, August 1, 1980, in Jules Tygiel Collection, National Baseball Library.
17. Kahn, *The Era*, 57–58.

franchise he secretly contemplated selling, he went to the New York office of National League president Ford Frick, who through Breadon left the Cardinals with the following message: "If you [strike], you will be suspended from the league. You will find that the friends you think you have in the press box will not support you. You will be outcasts. I do not care if half the league strikes. Those who do it will encounter quick retribution. All will be suspended and I don't care if it wrecks the National League for five years. This is the United States of America and one citizen has as much right to play as another. . . . You will find if you go through with your intention that you have been guilty of complete madness." Never had the wishy-washy Frick acted so forcefully. In a follow-up, Woodward acknowledged that he may have had some of the particulars incorrect, but he stood behind the story. Viewing his exposé as public service, he wagered that "it can now be honestly doubted that the boys from the Hookworm Belt would have the nerve to foist their quaint sectional folklore on the rest of the country."[18] Woodward's story probably stiffened the backbone of club owners, who now leaned on their players to keep playing. For his efforts Woodward received the E. P. Dutton Award for the best sports reporting for 1947.

To the Cardinals and their supporters, Woodward's revelation represented nothing more than "barnyard journalism"—a phrase Broeg later employed. Broeg contended that while a few players were upset, the Cardinals' opposition to Robinson was no different from other teams, and it did not lead to a strike vote. Breadon's trip to New York, he insisted, came because of the poor performance of the ball club, accentuated, Breadon thought, by the Robinson matter. An overreacting Breadon asked Moore and Marion in New York their opinion of manager Dyer and whether they intended to strike. Despite supposed reassurances, he still went to Frick's office, concerned about a possible boycott, Broeg admitted. It was then that Frick warned Breadon of the obvious consequences of the strike. A couple of days later, Breadon telephoned Frick from St. Louis; he called the affair "a tempest in a teapot," nothing more than a few players "letting off a little steam."[19] Later in 1947 Stockton acknowledged the anti-Robinson

18. *New York Herald Tribune*, May 9, 10, 1947. For the Cardinals' strike denial, see *St. Louis Post-Dispatch*, May 9, 1947. For Frick's guarded recollections, see Ford C. Frick, *Games, Asterisks, and People: Memoirs of a Lucky Fan*, 97–98. See also Kahn, *The Era*, 58–59, and Red Smith oral history transcript, Albert B. Chandler Oral History Project, 70–73, both of whom challenged various aspects of Frick's muted remembrances.

19. Kahn, *The Era*, 341; Bob Broeg, *Bob Broeg: Memories of a Hall of Fame Sportswriter*, 166–67.

feeling on the Cards, especially among the southerners. They "muttered in little circles" but reason prevailed, Stockton wrote. He, too, believed that Woodward had exaggerated the incident. Woodward's "foul up," according to St. Louis sportswriters, unfairly singled out the Cardinals as a racist club as well as harmed the careers of several ballplayers. Commenting years later on Woodward and the story, Slaughter contended that "that son of a bitch kept me out of the Hall of Fame for twenty years."[20]

The clash between the St. Louis and New York press over the Robinson issue prevailed into the 1990s, with award-winning journalists Broeg and Kahn firing the major salvos. Kahn remained critical of how the Cardinals had handled the Robinson matter. His major gripe centered on Broeg, who lacked "sensitivity to racial matters" and who he said attacked Woodward, the "greatest sports editor of the century," because Woodward had "scooped" him. Kahn contended that if "Musial were to talk at length about the Woodward scoop he'd be in the uncomfortable position of publicly correcting his Boswell. Dr. Johnson could do that. Stan Musial can't."[21]

In the mid-1990s Musial found himself uncomfortably seated between Broeg and Kahn at a dinner meeting in St. Louis to promote Kahn's book, *The Era: 1947–1957*. The two privately went after one another. While Kahn claimed that racism existed on the 1947 Cardinals, as it did everywhere in America, Broeg, whose signature bow-tie portrait had graced *Post-Dispatch* columns for nearly forty years, responded, "Roger, you're Jewish and you know about conclusion jumping, and you know what you guys have gone through, and yet you automatically want to go black and white when there were a lot of shades of gray." As the two went back and forth, they turned to Musial for affirmation. He seemed oblivious to it all, while cutting up his steak, before kicking Kahn's leg underneath the table to end the discussion.[22]

Musial publicly played down the Cardinals-Robinson controversy. At a Long Island University conference in 1997 honoring the fiftieth anniversary of Robinson's inaugural major-league season, he went beyond his

20. J. Roy Stockton, "My Case for the Cardinals," 13; Broeg, *Memories*, 167; Kahn, *The Era*, 341.
21. Roger Kahn to Giglio, December 6, 1996, in possession of Giglio.
22. Steven Gietschier, archivist of the *Sporting News*, was in attendance. Steven Gietschier interview, September 17, 1996; Roger Kahn telephone interview, December 12, 1996. For Broeg's statement, see James A. Vlasich, "Bob Broeg," in *Twentieth-Century American Sportswriters: Dictionary of Literary Biography 171*, edited by Richard Orodenker (Detroit: Gale Research, 1996): 27.

earlier measured denial that a strike vote occurred by insisting that the Cardinals never even talked about a boycott against Robinson's Dodgers.[23] Broeg aside, he undoubtedly had no desire to embarrass former teammates, particularly Slaughter, by revealing confidences.

Musial said more to Kahn in private about his views on race, probably because of Kahn's probing and Musial's respect for the New York writer, the author of *The Boys of Summer* (1973), a fascinating semi-autobiographical account of the Brooklyn Dodgers of the 1950s. Despite the racist feelings of the time, Musial affirmed that he "had no trouble with integration." He reminded Kahn that he "had played with a black kid in high school." (Musial actually played with two—Buddy Griffey and Grant Gray.) He also "knew that integration was overdue." Inexplicably, he claimed that his parents came to America for economic opportunity—seeking, like Jackie Robinson, the American Dream. (Musial's mother was born in New York.) He neglected to mention that he and his high school basketball teammates had opposed the exclusion of Grant Gray from the Pittsburgh hotel on the eve of the playoffs. It had been Flo Garcia, however—not Musial—who became outspoken on that matter. "I didn't know how to make speeches," Musial confessed in referring to the Robinson question. "Saying it to older players, that was beyond me. Besides," he continued, "I thought the racial talk was just hot air."[24] Musial's passive support for Robinson seems much in character.

There exists, however, an unsubstantiated, unlikely assertion, first published in the St. Louis press soon after the Cardinals' squabble over Robinson, that remains part of the lore. It concerns a supposed clash between Musial and Slaughter over Robinson and the proposed strike on the eve of the Brooklyn road series in early May. In the midst of heated discussion Slaughter—at times an angry, confrontational personality—allegedly hit Musial in the midsection, aggravating his appendicitis and forcing him to seek treatment. No one has admitted to witnessing that incident. Moreover, Slaughter and Musial vehemently denied it. In his autobiography Musial dismissed it by suggesting that Broeg had seen him naked and unmarked in the hotel room prior to an examination for appendicitis by the hotel physician. But a blow to the stomach would not necessarily have left a mark. Musial's and Slaughter's denials prove nothing one way

23. *Springfield News-Leader*, April 5, 1997; *New York Times*, April 5, 1997.
24. Kahn, *The Era*, 56–57; Musial also mentioned to sportswriter Maury Allen that his parents were both immigrants. Maury Allen, *Jackie Robinson: A Life Remembered*, 141.

or another. Any Musial admission would have reaffirmed Slaughter's alleged racism and jeopardized an otherwise harmonious relationship—one that became closer in time. The only other "evidence" is hearsay, coming from a longtime St. Louis historian, who had been told of the scuffle by someone close to the team.[25]

One thing is certain: Musial had expressed his support for Robinson in other ways. The best-known instance came in a game against the Dodgers at Ebbets Field on August 20, 1947, when Slaughter spiked Robinson at first base after Slaughter had come close to doing so earlier in the contest. Two days before, Joe Medwick of the Cards had spiked Robinson on the left foot, producing a bloody gash. Slaughter claimed improbably that he "never deliberately spiked anyone in my life."[26] He blamed Robinson for the incident because the inexperienced first sacker had placed his foot hurriedly in the middle of the bag in a play in which Slaughter was actually out by more than ten feet. "The basepaths belong to the runner," Slaughter intoned, "and I don't believe I have to apologize for not making an exception . . . for anyone." Besides, Slaughter asserted, Robinson's injury did not prevent him from staying in the game.[27] Others have defended Slaughter as a hustling player who did no more than play aggressive baseball.

Robinson and the Dodgers viewed Slaughter in a different way. Burt Shotton, the usually mild-mannered manager who had replaced Durocher for the 1947 campaign and again in 1948 at midseason, became so enraged at Slaughter for an attempt to spike Robinson in 1949 that he told a reporter, "Slaughter's a dirty player, and he always has been."[28] In the 1947 incident, Dodger pitcher Rex Barney saw Slaughter jump in Robinson's direction. Right fielder Carl Furillo remembered that Robinson had his foot on the edge of the bag, but Slaughter still got him just below the calf—by all appearances a deliberate intent to do bodily harm. The attack seemed so blatant to second baseman Eddie Stanky that he commented that "I've lost all my respect for [Slaughter]." Ralph Branca, working on a no-hitter, also saw it as deliberate. He went over to Robinson to say, "Don't worry Jackie, I'll get that son of a bitch for you." Robinson retorted, "No, Ralph, just get him out."[29]

25. Confidential interview, November 13, 1996.
26. *Sporting News*, August 27, 1947, 4.
27. Slaughter, *Country Hardball*, 111.
28. David Gough, *Burt Shotton, Dodgers Manager: A Baseball Biography*, 103.
29. Peter Golenbock, *Bums: An Oral History of the Brooklyn Dodgers*, 163–64; *Sporting News*, August 27, 1947, 4. Lester Rodney of the *Daily Worker* had a good view from

Robinson, who singled in the next inning, told Musial at first base that "I don't care what happens, but when I get to second base, I'm gonna kill somebody. I'm gonna knock [the second baseman] into centerfield. I don't care what kind of play it is, he's going down." Musial supposedly whispered, "I don't blame you. You have every right to do so." On another occasion in St. Louis, after several attempted spikings, an exasperated Robinson threatened to cut Musial only because he was at first base. If this bothered Musial, he never said so. Years later Robinson publicly apologized for what he had said. "It was a dumb thing for me to say," he acknowledged, for "Musial always treated me with courtesy."[30]

Durocher also marked Musial for retaliation after Cardinal pitchers threw at Robinson. Rarely did Musial complain; the exception came in early 1948 after a ball hit his bat, leading to a putout, as Musial avoided being hit. Later in the game he approached Durocher on the field, saying, "Hey, Leo, I haven't got the ball out there. I didn't throw at your man." Durocher replied, "Stan, my boy, you'd better tell that man in there to let my man alone. . . . You're the best man I know on the Cardinals. For every time [Robinson] gets one, it looks to me like you're gonna get two."[31] Durocher claimed that he had no more trouble with the Redbirds over Robinson.

Other incidents also arose in 1947. On September 11, Joe Garagiola and Robinson locked horns after Robinson had made it a practice of stealing frequently on the Cardinal catcher. Robinson did not like the St. Louis native because he thought him one of the leading antagonists on the Cardinals. Garagiola, Robinson felt, had previously sought to spike him, and he had heard racial epithets coming from him. On the eleventh at Sportsman's Park, Garagiola stepped on Robinson's heel, forcing him to the bench "for repairs," a deliberate act, the Dodger rookie later wrote. The next inning Robinson and Garagiola nearly came to blows when Robinson came to bat. Plate umpire Beans Reardon had to

---

the press box and saw Slaughter deliberately veer toward Robinson on a routine play. Lester Rodney telephone interview, November 28, 1998. Robinson claimed in his 1948 autobiography, however, that he "didn't think [Slaughter] spiked him deliberately." Jackie Robinson, *Jackie Robinson: My Own Story, as Told to Wendell Smith*, 158. Jules Tygiel believed that Robinson's original absolution was politically motivated in order to sustain a higher cause. Jules Tygiel telephone interview, November 5, 1998.

30. Pitcher Rex Barney related the Robinson anecdote to Golenbock, *Bums*, 164. Kahn has Robinson saying to Musial at first base, "I wish I could punch the son of a bitch [Slaughter] in the mouth." Kahn, *The Era*, 96. Robinson, "A Kentucky Colonel Kept Me in Baseball," 87.

31. Leo Durocher with Ed Linn, *Nice Guys Finish Last*, 208.

separate them as words were exchanged between the two. A *Sporting News* photograph captured Robinson appearing to clap his hands while Reardon focused his attention on Garagiola. For the remainder of the evening, the Dodger bench hounded Garagiola. In later years Garagiola, a famous TV personality, professed not to remember the 1947 spiking and minimized the overall racial conflict.[32]

In contrast, Robinson later had good things to say about manager Eddie Dyer, whom he thought a kind man. He recalled that in his first game in Sportsman's Park, as he walked from the visitor's clubhouse through the Cardinals dugout to reach the playing field, he could feel the players' stares, but then Dyer stopped him and said in front of his team that "he was glad to see me and that he wished me luck"—an unmistakable message to his own club.[33] It was the sort of thing coach James Russell of Donora High School might have said. That kind of sportsmanship also remained with Musial during the 1947 season. It did not make him a public defender of Robinson, but it nevertheless placed him firmly on the humane side of the issue.

But even Musial had grossly underestimated the enormous talent of Robinson, whose quickness, speed, power, and aggressive play soon made the Dodgers the National League's top team. He hit .311 for the Dodgers from 1947 to 1956 and won the National League's Most Valuable Player Award as a second baseman in 1949. He entered the Hall of Fame in 1962. Robinson's 1947 accomplishments, leading to the National League's Rookie of the Year Award, had not completely ended the tensions over the inclusion of blacks in major-league baseball. That matter involved Musial and the Cardinals in conflicts well into the 1950s.

Before departing from the tumultuous conflict over Robinson, some conclusions are warranted regarding player opposition over his integration. At least one club probably voted to strike at the beginning of the 1947 season. Several other teams, including the Cardinals, seriously considered striking before external pressures and reason prevailed. Even though no evidence exists that the Cardinals voted on the issue, Musial, Slaughter, Marion, and others were less than candid in recent years in claiming that Cardinal players had not discussed striking. At the same time, thanks

32. Carl E. Prince, *Brooklyn's Dodgers: The Bums, the Borough, and the Best of Baseball, 1947–1957*, 10–11; the Robinson-Garagiola photograph is in the *Sporting News*, September 24, 1947, 6. Immediately after the game, Robinson told the press, "I don't think Garagiola [spiked me] intentionally, but this makes three times in two games with the Cardinals that it's happened." Tygiel, *Baseball's Great Experiment*, 204.
33. Robinson, "A Kentucky Colonel Kept Me in Baseball," 87.

largely to Stanley Woodward's stories, the Cardinal ball club was unduly singled out for its reaction to Robinson.

Despite his physical problems and the controversy over Robinson, Musial gradually climbed out of the hole in the summer of 1947 and practically carried the club with him. The surge began after the Cardinals had returned from a road trip tied for last place on June 13. At Dyer's request that evening, Breadon made a rare visit to the clubhouse to deny a rumor that he planned to sell the ball club. He also assured the team that Dyer would remain at the helm for at least the rest of the season. At this point Musial's average hovered at .202. The Cards then swept the four-game series with the Dodgers, while Musial had seven hits, including a triple and a home run. The team followed this with five more consecutive victories. Two days before the All-Star game on July 8, the Cardinals had climbed to two games above .500, while Musial's batting average had reached .253. Despite his sub-par performance, Musial was selected as a reserve on the National League All-Star squad. The game, played at Chicago's Wrigley Field, was won by the American League, 2–1, the tenth time in fourteen meetings that the National Leaguers had lost. Musial grounded out as a pinch-hitter. The National League's only run came as the result of former Card Johnny Mize's home run.

Afterward, the Cardinals continued their winning ways, running off forty-one victories in fifty-eight games for a .707 winning percentage. During that stretch Musial hit .370; his season's average finally soared above .300 on August 10. By that time the Cards had reached second place in the standings. The saying "as Musial goes, so go the Cardinals" had reached new heights in the closing weeks of the 1947 season. Usually a much better daytime hitter (he hit forty points higher in 1946 in daylight), he batted at a higher average at night in 1947, probably because, in his weakened condition, he had more trouble with the daytime heat.

Unfortunately, neither Musial nor the Cards could maintain their torrid pace throughout August. They got no closer to the Dodgers than four and a half games. Late-season injuries to Schoendienst and Kurowski, who was hitting over .300, hurt. Even Musial, who usually hit well in September, suffered from a late-season slump that brought his average down to .299 on September 22, the day the Dodgers clinched the pennant, with seven games to play. The Cardinals finished in second place, five games behind Brooklyn in the final standings. Musial nevertheless finished the season with a flourish, hitting safely ten times in his last fifteen at bats. Ironically, he ended up leading the club in batting with a .312 average, his lowest as a major leaguer until the 1956 season. He finished with 183 hits, 113 runs scored, 30 doubles, 13 triples, 19 home runs, and 95 RBIs. He led the National League in no hitting category, but he still outshone his teammates in overall batting performance.

Only a Musial or a Williams could have considered those 1947 achievements an off year. He not only came back from physical infirmities that plagued him for the entire season but also maintained an even disposition. As Musial watcher Bob Broeg wrote near the end of the 1947 campaign, he "never became stubborn or sullen even in the most worrisome days." He had retained his self-control. "On long train rides, whether in a friendly card game or sitting alone, just smoking a cigar," Broeg continued, "Stan was approachable and calm. He discussed his failure with an almost objective evenness."[34] One can learn much about a person's character in bad times, and in those dark days of early 1947 Musial had easily passed the test. He had matured considerably in that troubling year.

Sam Breadon did not fare quite as well. After stating repeatedly that he had no intentions of selling the ball club, he suddenly announced in November that he had finalized a deal with Fred Saigh, Jr., and former Postmaster General Robert E. Hannegan, both of St. Louis. The $3.5 million transaction brought the new owners a club that had drawn a record 1,247,931 fans for the 1947 season and twenty minor-league affiliates, including three top minor-league stadiums. Hannegan, a forty-nine-year-old Irish politician and sports enthusiast who knew Breadon well, had played a leading part in Harry Truman's senatorial primary victory in 1940 and became a major player as Democratic national chairman at the party convention of 1944. In his successful effort to stop the renomination of Henry Wallace as vice president, he contributed mightily to the selection of Truman. Hannegan subsequently served for two years as President Truman's postmaster general. He had connections in St. Louis and Washington, D.C., but little money when Saigh invited him into the Cardinal venture.[35]

The bespectacled, short, and slight Saigh, of Syrian ancestry on his mother's side, had a dubious reputation in St. Louis, according to a confidential report sent to Commissioner Chandler. He was heavily involved in downtown St. Louis property, but he, too, lacked available resources to purchase the club, raising the question of whether the two fronted for outside money. Actually, Breadon, about to lose 90 percent of the $5 million in capital gains to the Internal Revenue Service that he had set aside for a

34. *Sporting News*, August 20, 1947, 3.
35. Broeg, *Bob Broeg's Redbirds*, 119.

new stadium, worked out a clever arrangement with the two purchasers that involved the return of that money to him as part of the sale price. Saigh and Hannegan borrowed the rest short-term by using the minor-league parks and Saigh's downtown properties as collateral. To what extent Hannegan's outside connections might have assisted in the arrangement is undeterminable. In any case, two years later Hannegan sold his interest to Saigh for $1 million on an original investment of about $15,000. By then the seventy-two-year-old Breadon had succumbed to cancer. He had alleviated the fear, however, that he might die as club owner, thereby leaving his widow with the responsibility of that inheritance.[36]

Saigh would remain president until 1953, when he was forced to sell the club following criminal prosecution for income tax evasion. While Musial spoke well of Hannegan, who had treated his father kindly at spring training in 1948, and Saigh, who had been "very fair" to him financially, the new ownership did nothing to improve player personnel. In fact, Saigh refused to consider signing a black player because he thought that resisting integration was good for ticket sales in St. Louis. He and Hannegan also sold pitcher Murry Dickson to the Pirates for $125,000 before the 1949 season, most likely to finance the dissolution of their partnership. This transaction probably cost the Cardinals the pennant in 1949.[37] Musial might have recalled the Hannegan-Saigh ownership more fondly, perhaps, because he had a career season—one of the best ever in the postwar era—during that period.

36. Ibid.; Robert E. A. Boyle, "Ownership of St. Louis Cardinals—Fred M. Saigh, Jr.," Subject File, Box 162, Albert B. Chandler Collection, University of Kentucky Library. According to Harry Caray, a five-year period was coming to an end, which would have required Breadon either to construct a stadium immediately or to declare as normal income the reserved capital allotted for a new ballpark. Neither represented an attractive alternative. Harry Caray with Bob Verdi, *Holy Cow!* 139.

37. Musial, *Musial*, 109, 155, 122–23; Kirkendall, *A History of Missouri*, 333.

Career Year and Near Miss

T he 1948 season elevated the already increased popularity of sports in postwar America. Record-breaking attendance represented one aspect of it. A whopping 20.8 million fans witnessed regular-season games in the major leagues, led by the record-shattering 2.8 million who watched the Cleveland Indians of the American League win their first World Series since 1920. Escalating numbers continued into 1949, when the Cardinals set an all-time team attendance mark with 1,430,676 fans turning the turnstiles.

During the tension-filled Cold War era, baseball and other sports had assumed greater importance in people's lives. Where sports once served merely as diversion, recreation, and relief from unemployment, war, and other problems, they now developed into a "national obsession, a new cultural currency, a kind of social cement that bound [together] a diverse society," according to one study. At the same time, professional and inter-collegiate sports were gradually losing their constructive image of foster-ing hard work, team play, discipline, and sacrifice. The competing forces of greed, dishonesty, disloyalty, and arrogance slowly took over, affecting management and athletes alike. By the late 1940s fight fixing infected pro-fessional boxing; academic cheating at the U.S. Military Academy resulted in the dismissal of ninety cadets in 1951, one-half of whom were football players; and intercollegiate basketball faced point-shaving scandals.[1] For professional baseball, sinister forces—particularly greed—became much more prevalent in the 1970s through the 1990s following major-league expansion, bloated television contracts, and the termination of the reserve clause. By then sports had become the nation's number-one business, if not religion.

Musial, of course, could scarcely sense the direction in which profes-sional sports were heading as he prepared for training camp in early 1948. He knew only that he deserved a salary increase for his performance in 1947. While Robert Hannegan, handling contract negotiations for Fred Saigh, refused to budge from Musial's thirty-one-thousand-dollar con-tract because of the sub-par 1947 season, Musial could point to a robust

1. Randy Roberts and James S. Olson, *Winning Is the Only Thing: Sports in America since 1945*, xii, 76–77, 86, 83–85.

batting average over the last 104 games following the freezing of his appendix. Hannegan resolved the conflict by promising to adjust Musial's contract at midseason if his 1948 performance warranted it, which ultimately resulted in a five-thousand-dollar raise.

Musial, fully recovered from postseason surgery, felt stronger during spring training at St. Petersburg. Since his thirty-three-ounce baseball bat seemed as light as a feather, he extended the grip three-quarters of an inch downward to the knob. This enabled him to increase his power, particularly to right field. For good reason he anticipated an outstanding season and felt good about the team's chances for 1948. Because of the hitting performance of minor-league first baseman Nippy Jones, Musial could move to right field, his favorite position. That lasted until shortly after the season began, when left-fielder Slaughter, who was not hitting, asked manager Dyer if he could play right field where he felt more comfortable. So Musial, at least temporarily, moved to left, his original major-league position. Nevertheless, with a healthy Musial, the promising power of Jones, and virtually the same roster that brought the Cardinals close to a pennant in 1947, the Cardinals remained the players' and managers' choice to capture the National League crown.

The Cardinals opened the season in St. Louis with Murry Dickson throwing a ten-hit shutout over Cincinnati. The twenty-seven-year-old Musial contributed a double. He slowly began to warm up, collecting his first multiple-hit game two contests later. On April 24 he reached a major milestone by collecting his one thousandth hit with a run-scoring triple off of Cliff Chambers of the Cubs in Chicago. Afterward, *St. Louis Post-Dispatch* sportswriter Bob Broeg teased Musial about trying for three thousand career hits. Playfully calling him "Banj," short for "Banjo," a baseball term for a weak hitter, Broeg had drawn closer to Musial over the years. He had witnessed Paul Waner of the Pirates reach the three-thousand-hit plateau in June 1942, the seventh and last major leaguer to do so until Musial's accomplishment in May 1958. When Broeg first goaded Musial to think of that goal in 1948, Stash thought it virtually unobtainable since he would have to average two hundred hits over the next ten campaigns, the final one at thirty-seven years old, which he thought beyond retirement age.[2] Yet that challenge became arguably his most significant career objective, pushing him even more to make every at bat count.

In May he went on a tear while the Cards won six straight, and thirteen out of sixteen games, elevating the team momentarily into first place, just

2. Musial, *Musial*, 111–12.

ahead of the Boston Braves. Durocher's Dodgers most felt the lash of Musial and the Cards. On May 19 and 20, Musial connected nine times at Ebbets Field in two of Musial's greatest days as a ballplayer. In the first game he went five for five, including a double, triple, three singles, and a walk while scoring five times. All of his hits came on two strikes. That five-hit performance represented the first of four occasions in 1948 that he would accomplish the feat, equaling Ty Cobb's single-season record.

The following day he went four for five, including a homer, two doubles, and a single, in setting a major-league record for the most hits in two successive games. Overall, he had eleven hits in fifteen at bats, and the Redbirds swept the three-game series. Stan the Man's reputation reached new heights in Brooklyn that spring as Dodger fans treated him with even greater reverence following such legendary performances. By now Musial's hitting streak had extended to thirteen games, and his batting average hovered around .400.

Despite Musial's torrid hitting, the Cardinals soon lost five consecutive games. By mid-June they had relinquished first place to the Giants and Braves, even though they stayed close to the top for the duration. They finished in second place, six and a half games behind the Boston club. Nagging injuries proved too much to overcome, causing Kurowski to miss sixty-seven games, Schoendienst fifty, and Marion ten; moreover, their performances suffered because they often had to play hurt. Additionally, by midseason all three catchers were hitting under .200, a dismal standard that showed scant improvement at season's end. Former Card catcher Walker Cooper, even though suffering a knee injury that kept him out of seventy-nine games, managed 16 home runs and 54 RBIs for the New York Giants. Cooper could have made the difference. A superb handler of hurlers, Cooper might have aided a faltering pitching staff, which saw Dickson, Howie Pollet, and George Munger have subpar seasons and the team's combined ERA escalate to 3.91. Only Harry "The Cat" Brecheen, with a 20–7 record and a league-leading 2.24 ERA, pitched well.

Nevertheless, Musial, as he did in the second half of 1947, virtually carried a ball club that might have otherwise finished near the bottom of the standings. In a crucial three-game series against the Braves, beginning on June 21, he connected five times in the second game. In his last plate appearance, with the score knotted at two and the bases loaded, manager Dyer good-naturedly shouted to Musial, who was making his way to the plate, "Hey, boy, I'm afraid I'm going to have to send up a hitter for you." Musial momentarily hesitated as Dyer and the bench laughed. He then lashed a single off of left-hander Clyde "Hard Rock" Shoun to win the game for Brecheen, who went the distance. The evening before, Brazle had pitched a 1–0 shutout against ace Warren Spahn, the first pitcher to go the distance against the Braves in twenty-four consecutive outings. In the final game, Pollet also pitched a complete game in a 11–2 shellacking. As a result of Musial and some rare good pitching, the Cardinals remained only one-half game out of first place.

The Redbirds continued their brief run against Brooklyn at Ebbets Field two days later when Musial collected four hits in the opener, including his sixteenth homer. The next evening Dodger pitching ace Preacher Roe came to the visiting clubhouse and interrupted a Cardinal pregame meeting by saying, "Ah know how to get that Musial out." When a chorus of "How, Preach?" followed, Roe laughingly retorted, "Walk 'im on fouh pitches and then pick 'im off first." Roe had done exactly that in an earlier series in St. Louis when he caught Musial napping at first base after throwing him four consecutive balls. The Dodgers failed to walk him enough, though, for Musial ended up hitting .522, with twenty-five hits, in eleven games at Ebbets Field.

At the All-Star break Musial led the National League with a .410 average as he threatened to become the first National Leaguer to reach the .400 plateau since 1930, when Bill Terry hit .401 for the Giants. He also excelled in the field, mostly in right and center. In one doubleheader just prior to the break, he played right field in the first game and then center and first base in the second. The increased strength of his throwing arm enabled him to throw out base runners seeking to test him. Despite his stellar play the club had slumped to third place, six games behind the Braves.

Musial continued his hitting in the All-Star game at Sportsman's Park on July 13 amid thirty-four thousand supporting fans. In the first inning he homered over the right-field pavilion with a runner on base against Washington's Walt Masterson. Playing left and center field, he also later singled as the National Leaguers lost 5–2.

Musial's hitting tailed off after the break, one of several reasons the Cards failed to overtake the Braves. Instead, the Brooklyn Dodgers emerged as the league's hottest team, jumping from last place to one game from the top in mid-August. The leap began after Dodger manager Leo Durocher defected to the Giants and genial Burt Shotton, the victorious skipper of the '47 championship season, returned. Suddenly, the Cardinals found the Dodgers a much more formidable foe, while they relished playing the Durocher-led Giants, defeating them on ten consecutive occasions.

Yet the Cardinals' surges were short-lived. One momentary highlight was winning two out of three against the Braves in late July. Despite hitting into two double plays and striking out in the series finale, Musial contributed mightily to the 9–6 win as he doubled and singled in his final two at bats. He also performed outstandingly in the field. Against the Pirates on August 20, his somersaulting and shoestring catches and his strong throws from the outfield—one resulting in a double play—led to a Cardinals victory. Against the Dodgers on September 17, he robbed Jackie Robinson of a double on a somersault catch in the third inning, followed by a running one-handed grab near the exit gate deep in left-center, depriving Pee Wee Reese of a leadoff triple. He capped that day's performance with a diving catch of Tommy Brown's short fly to center, which saved a 4–2 win. Immediately afterward, an aging Terry Moore, playing out his last few games, joked, "Stash, if you only could hit." "Yeah," Musial laughed, "then I probably could make the varsity." During this span, Musial's Cardinals fluctuated between second place, just two and a half games from the top, to fourth place on September 11, six games out. A rare Musial slump in early September, when he went three for twenty-four over a seven-game period, contributed to five Redbird losses.

To make matters worse, Musial played with two jammed wrists and a bruised right hand as a result of recent fielding heroics and being hit by Dodger hurler Carl Erskine. Yet that did not stop him from having one of his greatest games ever in the Cardinals' opening contest at Braves Field on September 22. That day the Braves, winners of eight straight, were one game away from mathematically eliminating the Cardinals from the pennant race and clinching first place. The wind uncustomarily blew out on that chilly afternoon, causing Broeg to comment, "A great day for the hitters, Banj." "Yeah," Musial retorted, "but I can't hit like this."[3] He showed Broeg his tightly bandaged wrists, courtesy of trainer Doc Weaver. He then pulled off the tape just before facing Warren Spahn, the major league's eventual all-time left-handed career victory leader with 363 wins. In 1948 Spahn and Johnny Sain so dominated Braves pitching that they inspired the phrase, "Spahn and Sain and pray for rain."

Because of the severe pain Musial felt in batting practice, he avoided pulling Spahn's first pitch, which he looped into left field. In the third inning he lined a high outside fastball over the left fielder's head for a double. The following inning, contributing to what became an 8–2 romp, Musial pulled a Red Barrett change-up into the right-field stands for his

---

3. Ibid., 116. See also Joe Reichler and Ben Olan, "His Wrists Cried, But His Bat Boomed," undisclosed newspaper clipping in Musial Collection, National Baseball Library.

thirty-eighth home run. By now his wrists felt like they were on fire. In the sixth Musial, facing southpaw Clyde Shoun, barely pushed a grounder past shortstop Al Dark's outstretched glove. In his final appearance in the eighth Musial confronted right-hander Al Lyons, knowing that a fifth hit would tie Cobb's record of four five-hit games in a season. After failing to get the first two pitches over the plate, Lyons heard shouts from the Cards' bench to throw strikes. Musial, afraid that he might walk, decided to swing at the next pitch. He pulled an outside ball through the right side just beyond the reach of second baseman Ed Stanky. Incredibly, his pain disciplined him to swing only five times that day, resulting in five hits! Four days later, however, the Braves clinched the National League pennant, with a win over the Giants.

Despite the Cardinals' disappointing second-place finish, Musial ended up with the best hitting statistics of his career. He led the majors with a .376 batting average, 230 hits, 46 doubles, 18 triples, 429 total bases, and a .702 slugging average. He paced the National League with 131 RBIs and 135 runs scored. His 230 hits represented the most in the league since Joe Medwick's 237 in 1937. No National Leaguer had tallied more total bases since Rogers Hornsby's league record of 450 in 1922. His slugging percentage was the highest since Chicago Cub Hack Wilson's .723 in 1930, the year he hit 56 home runs and established the major league RBI record with 191. Musial's .376 batting average outpaced the National League's second-highest performer, Richie Ashburn of the Phillies, by forty-three points. His 103 extra-base hits just missed the league's all-time mark of 107, set by the Phillies' Chuck Klein. No major leaguer would reach the century plateau again until Albert Belle of the Cleveland Indians accomplished it forty-seven years later.

Amazingly, despite his newfound power, Musial struck out only 34 times in 611 official at bats. Just as surprising, Stash finished a close third in the National League in homers with 39, one less than Johnny Mize and Ralph Kiner of the Pirates and 20 more than he had ever hit in a major-league season. If not for a rain-canceled game, which washed out a home run, he would have equaled the league lead and won the triple crown award (league leader in batting average, home runs, and runs batted in), obtained by only four previous National Leaguers. Yet he accomplished enough to capture the Most Valuable Player award, the first senior-league performer to achieve that feat three times. He dominated the balloting in 1948, receiving eighteen out of a possible twenty-four first-place votes.

Mere statistics fail to capture Musial's importance to the team in 1948. He willingly played all three outfield positions and even filled in at first base occasionally. Few superstars have ever been more team oriented. One illustration of this occurred in a September game against the Dodgers when Reese doubled to lead off the ninth with the score tied at two. Because of a strained left wrist, Musial felt that he could not make his best throw to the plate in the event of a hit to him. Consequently, he called time and explained to Manager Dyer that Erv Dusak gave the team the best chance of making a play at home. Nevertheless, Pete Reiser, the next batter, hit a ball beyond the reach of Dusak to win the game. Revealingly, in the games in which Musial hit safely, the Cards went 73–48, for a winning percentage of .603. But the team's record in the thirty-four contests in which he failed to connect was just 12–21, a winning percentage of .364. Unquestionably, without Musial the Redbirds would have fallen considerably below their 85–69 second-place mark. Only seven games separated them from the fifth-place New York Giants.

What made Musial so productive a hitter in 1948? Part of it came from his newfound strength and quicker reflexes following the appendectomy and tonsillectomy, which led him to lower his grip on the bat. Always able to smack outside pitches to left field, Musial nevertheless became a smarter and more confident hitter in 1948. His greater sensitivity to the strike zone made him even more dangerous with two strikes. Instead of trying to protect the plate, he bore down harder and took his customary swing. Continuing a pattern begun in 1947, he also hit better at night despite his insistence that he was a better daytime hitter.

Musial's dream season did not carry over into the postseason, even though contract negotiations began the day after the last game and proceeded satisfactorily. Hannegan had proposed a $45,000 contract plus $5,000 for each 100,000 increase in attendance above 900,000. Musial instead insisted on a two-year contract of $50,000 annually plus $5,000 if paid attendance exceeded 900,000. Hannegan accepted the counterproposal, not knowing that an attendance record–breaking year would follow that would have netted Musial $70,000 for 1949 if he had accepted Hannegan's offer. That experience taught Musial to be more willing to take modest risks in his financial dealings. Not until years later, however, would he determine that Hannegan shortly afterward was negotiating with Saigh to dissolve their partnership. To provide the necessary capital, Hannegan offered to sell Musial to the Pittsburgh Pirates for $250,000, a proposal that former Pirate owner Frank McKinney later revealed.[4] What caused

---

4. *Sporting News*, April 6, 1963, clipping in Musial Collection, *Sporting News* Archives.

Hannegan to change his mind is unclear. A likely reason might have been Saigh, who would have lost his most valuable attraction. As it turned out, Hannegan instead arranged for the sale of Murry Dickson for $125,000. Soon afterward, Saigh became the sole owner of the Cardinals.

Ironically, just prior to Hannegan's attempt to sell Musial, Stash and Lil had decided to sink deeper roots in St. Louis. The decision did not come easily, for family ties with Donora remained strong. That fall they purchased a six-room ranch-style home at 5447 Childress Avenue in southwest St. Louis. Musial announced that he was becoming a "genuine St. Louisan," intending to spend the entire year in the city along with Slaughter, Moore, Dusak, and Schoendienst. A couple of weeks after the Musials moved in, a burglar broke into the home, taking some of Lil's jewelry, a watch that had been presented to Stan for winning the 1943 National League Most Valuable Player award; and a ring the Cardinal organization gave him after the team's 1946 pennant victory. Although the thief was soon apprehended, minus some of the stolen property, the incident had upset Musial as he grappled over whether to file charges.[5]

Even though the Musials preferred to spend the off-season in the Donora area "close by our people," several considerations altered that arrangement. One was the desire of Stan's eight-year-old son, Dickie, to attend school only in St. Louis. Also, in October, the death-dealing smog that engulfed Donora had made it impossible for Musial's mother and ailing father to remain there. Now fifty-eight years old and retired for four years, Lukasz had already suffered several strokes. Consequently, Stan encouraged his parents to live with him. On December 17, however, Lukasz succumbed to another stroke and lapsed into a coma in Stash's home, where he remained until his death two days later. Stash stayed by his bedside to the end, sadly saying, "Every time my dad is with me he gets sick." Funeral preparations included the transporting of Lukasz's remains by train to Donora, where the family arranged funeral services at St. Mary's Catholic Church on December 24. Few Christmases could have been more melancholy. Despite Lukasz's limitations, Stan always remembered him lovingly while adhering to the biblical precept of honoring thy father and mother. No parent could have hoped for more.

It was during Lukasz's final days that Jack Sher, a *Sport* magazine writer from New York, arranged to interview Musial in his home for a major feature story. Sher eventually wrote about an "extremely polite" young

5. Rawlings, *Stan Musial Scrapbook,* 76; Sher, "The Stan Musial Nobody Knows," 58.

man with sad eyes and a drained face facing his father's impending death. In an extremely touching story, Sher reported how Musial had asked him to stay and brought Lil—and the children—to the living room for an interview while he remained with his father.[6] Lil provided Sher with the Donora story involving Stan's rise to prominence. Much of what she said has now become a familiar part of the Musial lore—how she first met Stash, Lukasz's supposed insistence that he accept a college scholarship, their unlikely secret marriage on his nineteenth birthday, and his early struggles as a pitcher at Williamson.

The story also captured the warmth of Lil toward her two well-mannered children, who did not know the gravity of their grandfather's condition. The other information about Musial's minor-league career and his tenure with the Cardinals came from interviews apparently arranged by Musial's friends. Sher visited with Broeg, Marion, Moore, Hannegan, Schoendienst, who was working in a local department store, Ollie Vanek, Musial's Springfield Cardinals manager, and several non-baseball acquaintances, all of whom attested to Musial's humility, good nature, and integrity as well as his remarkable skill as a ballplayer. The rapid orchestration of interviews reflected not only the generosity of Musial and his friends but also their sensitivity to the cultivation of Musial's image, which had been unfairly attacked a year earlier by another New York writer.

No one spent more time with Sher than Julius "Biggie" Garagnani, one of Musial's closest companions. Biggie's Chippewa Avenue steak house was just a couple blocks from the Musial home. The thirty-four-year-old Garagnani, the son of an Italian immigrant miner, grew up on the Hill during the Great Depression. He left school following the fourth grade and worked odd jobs, including bootlegging, eventually driving a trash truck for the city of St. Louis. He also became involved in local Democratic politics, serving as a precinct captain prior to his twenty-first birthday. Afterward, he emerged as a significant force in state Democratic activities, especially in Warren Hearnes's gubernatorial campaigns as a fund-raiser and as a friend of Senator Stuart Symington. Twice he attended the Democratic National Convention as a delegate.[7] It was most likely Biggie who got Musial interested in politics, especially during John Kennedy's

6. Musial, *Musial*, 120; *Sporting News*, October 13, 1948, clipping in Musial Collection, *Sporting News* archives; Sher, "The Stan Musial Nobody Knows," 67, 57.
7. Edward T. Wright, *Free Enterprise Is Not Dead* (St. Louis: Practical Seminar Institute, 1970), 49.

1960 quest for the presidency. Biggie's friends also included celebrities such as Arthur Godfrey and Danny Thomas.

The stocky, balding Garagnani was a study in contrasts. His gruffness and acerbity masked an enormous sense of insecurity; he craved recognition and wore custom shirts and suits. He could be notoriously cheap toward those who frequented his restaurant regularly. Broeg recalled that Biggie bought him only a couple of drinks over a ten-year period. Yet he could show considerable generosity to friends, employees, and others in need. No one more butchered the English language with his malaprops and mispronunciations. Often he reverted to a mixture of Italian and English when talking with Italian American friends in the company of outsiders he did not like. This embarrassed friends, particularly when he labeled the outsiders "Americansa" as if Biggie and his paisans were not Americans. Joe Garagiola remembered that he could be as "tactful as a sledgehammer."[8]

Yet Biggie had enormous business acumen. Many of Musial's later profitable investments came through collaboration with him. Garagnani, if not a surrogate father, was surely a big brother to Stash. It was Biggie whom Musial consulted before purchasing his home. By the time Musial met him, Garagnani's steak house had emerged as a profitable operation after undergoing difficult times when he and a partner owned the Brass Key restaurant as well as the business on Chippewa. Following the dissolution of the partnership, Biggie received the Chippewa establishment, renaming it Garagnani's Club 66, where he built a clientele through long hours of work, careful management, serving quality food, and treating patrons fairly.[9]

Garagnani remembered meeting Musial early in his major-league career in Sam Breadon's office. Musial recalled that they met in spring training in St. Petersburg. A friendship developed after Musial and his family began to frequent Biggie's restaurant. Soon the two were playing golf together, and Musial introduced Biggie to quail hunting. Ever cautious and concerned about the future, Stash confided that he wanted to become involved in some business enterprise, something that he could depend on after baseball. One day on the golf course, according to Musial, Biggie said, "If you really want to go into business, why not become partners with me?" Musial liked the idea, but after having recently paid for a new

8. Broeg, interview, February 18, 1999; telephone transcript of Joe Garagiola interview, 1978, conducted by Bill Borst, in possession of Bill Borst, St. Louis.

9. Garagiola interview; Wright, *Free Enterprise,* 46–47.

house, he confessed that he had little capital to invest. The undeterred Garagnani arranged for an audit and then proposed that Musial's contribution would be twenty-five thousand dollars, representing half of the restaurant's value. He suggested that Musial, for his half-ownership, only need compensate him that amount from his share of the profits, a generous arrangement indeed.[10]

Later Biggie claimed that he needed a partner "about as much as I needed a new outboard motor for my automobile."[11] But Musial was no ordinary partner, as Biggie well knew. He and Stan sought to capitalize on Musial's star status and enormous popularity. "Stan Musial and Biggie's," as it now was called, featured Musial's presence on a limited basis during the baseball season and almost daily otherwise. He visited various tables and chatted with the patrons. He gladly presented photographs of himself, which he autographed on request. He soon lost some of his shyness, even enjoying the friendly conversation, especially with kids. He laughed easily at his own stories, contributing to the easygoing air that characterized the restaurant.

He also found himself involved in other aspects of the business. He ensured, perhaps gratuitously, that Biggie continue to use the highest quality of meats; he contributed to the expansion of the menu to include more seafood dishes; and he became concerned whenever patrons left a portion of the meal unconsumed, wondering if anything was wrong with the food.

Apparently the two partners got along famously even though Biggie occasionally felt frustrated because Stan seemed to receive "all of the recognition and credit" from customers who wished to talk mostly with him. Garagiola, at the time close to both, later explained that Stan understood Biggie "perfectly" and handled it well.[12] And with Musial attracting more and more customers, they decided to expand the business to accommodate 250 persons in the main dining room, which now contained

10. Biggie Garagnani as told to J. Roy Stockton, "My Partner Stan Musial," 36, 38; transcript of Stan Musial interview, conducted by Bill Borst and Patty Garavaglia, in possession of Bill Borst, St. Louis; Musial, *Musial*, 120–21. Biggie contended that Musial had asked him if he could be a partner in his restaurant business. Bob Broeg remembered Biggie commenting that if he did not take Musial into the restaurant, "Henry will," meaning Henry Ruggeri, a top restaurateur on the Hill. Broeg interview, February 18, 1999.

11. Garagnani, "My Partner Stan Musial," 46.

12. Transcript of Garagiola interview. See also "Musial Pulls 'Em In at His St. Louis Bar-Restaurant," March 1953, undisclosed magazine clipping in Musial Collection, *Sporting News* Archives.

a huge mural of Stan the Man poised to hit. The facility also included a larger bar and an office upstairs for Musial, who hired Shirley Auen, the Musials' former babysitter, as secretary to handle the ten thousand postcards or letters he received annually, requesting autographs, pictures, baseballs, or information about hitting. Many times, according to Pat Anthony, Shirley's sister and Musial's current secretary, Stan's name was skillfully replicated on requested photographs when he was not around.[13] The restaurant gave out five thousand photos in the first year. Biggie and Stan soon increased the workforce from fourteen to thirty-seven to deal with the new business.

The restaurant did fabulously well in the 1950s, enabling Musial to supplement his annual earnings by a reported forty thousand dollars. In January 1952 he and Biggie also purchased the Garavelli Restaurant on DeBaliviere Avenue, leased by August Sabadell, catering manager of the Hotel Chase. By 1954 they owned four eateries, the last of which was the Forest Park Hotel Snack Bar; six years later they moved Stan Musial and Biggie's to Oakland Avenue adjacent to Highway 40 Expressway. The elegant new facility easily became one of the city's finest restaurants. Its lobby featured Musial's memorabilia, including trophies and autographed baseballs, reminders of his accomplishments. It contained a large dining room that attracted politicians and celebrities among its local clientele as well as a significant number of out-of-towners, including professional athletes. As numerous were ordinary people who hoped to meet Stan.[14]

The second floor contained a huge banquet room, which hosted numerous political events, including fund-raisers. On one occasion Biggie held a thousand-dollar-a-plate dinner for Warren Hearnes's gubernatorial campaign. It also became a favorite place for sport banquets. Most of the Cardinal-related social activities took place there. By the 1960s, as well, Musial and Garagnani had invested in Redbird Lanes bowling alley in St. Louis and the Ivanhoe Hotel in Miami Beach, Florida. By that time Musial was undoubtedly a millionaire.

Even though Musial was not the first professional athlete to make it in business, few did it on a grander scale or were more successful. He became a model and inspiration to other performers, who now thought more about their future after sports. One player remembered Musial talking to him and two other Pittsburgh Pirate rookies at the train station about the

13. Pat Anthony telephone interview, November 22, 1996.
14. Wright, *Free Enterprise*, 47; personal recollection of Giglio from 1975 visit.

"importance of saving our money for the future."[15] His success, he made clear, came as a result of financial planning and relying on experienced and accomplished businessmen such as Garagnani. At the same time, that initial decision to enter the restaurant business with Biggie Garagnani had further cemented Musial's decision to adopt St. Louis as his year-round home as he entered the 1949 season.

Despite years of success, the Cardinals were picked to finish in fourth place in 1949. The team was questioned because of an aging, injury-prone lineup; a declining pitching staff, weakened further by the departure of Dickson; and a flagging farm system seemingly unable to replace retiring veterans such as Kurowski and Moore. Moreover, other teams such as the Dodgers and the Braves had emerged as powerful contenders. Under Branch Rickey's leadership, the Dodgers in particular had strengthened their farm organization in large part because of the recruitment of Negro League players. Too, few expected Musial to match the year he had had in 1948, and his early performance seemed to confirm that prediction.

Musial's problems in 1949, as he later admitted, were self-inflicted because of a deliberate effort to swing for the fences. "I hit 39 homers in 1948 without trying," he reminded Biggie; "I believe if I'd swing for that right-field fence at Sportsman's Park I could pick up 11 more without trouble." He quoted Ralph Kiner that "singles hitters drive Fords, but home-run hitters drive Cadillacs"—an indication that Musial had momentarily succumbed to the trend of an era that prized the long ball. As a result, he drifted into a slump, as pitchers often kept the ball on the outside of the plate, causing him to ground out weakly to the second or first baseman. Swinging too hard and chasing too many bad balls, he began to overstride and press as his stroke lost its customary rhythm. Coach Buzzy Wares noticed that he longer crouched as much in his stance. Not until the end of May did Musial find himself in the groove. By then he had learned a valuable lesson: he could hit more home runs by not swinging for the fences. With short right-field barriers in many National League parks, "you don't have to swing as hard as you can," he later admitted. You only need to "direct the bat to right field."[16] Only when a team situation required the long ball did he consciously think of home runs; otherwise, he concentrated on making solid contact and hitting the ball to all fields.

15. Sonny Senerchia to Giglio, October 21, 1996, in possession of Giglio.
16. Garagnani, "My Partner Stan Musial," 59; Musial, *Musial*, 123; Connor, ed., *Baseball for the Love of It*, 250.

The Cardinals' slow start in 1949 could not be blamed on Musial alone. Slaughter, mired in a batting slump, soon sat on the bench for the first time ever. The pitching staff also had its troubles, particularly Pollet, whose reluctance to test a recovering sore arm caused an exasperated manager Dyer to say, "You've started your last game until you throw the damn ball hard."[17] By mid-May the slumping Redbirds had fallen to a seventh-place tie in the standings, with Musial hitting .254.

The Cards turned things around by the end of the month when the pitching and hitting improved. A resurgent Slaughter came off the bench to hit with a vengeance. Rookie Eddie Kazak proved more than an adequate replacement for Kurowski at third base. And Joe Garagiola returned from the minors to have one of his best seasons. A revitalized Pollet also came back to lead the mound corps with a 20–9 mark and a 2.77 ERA, second best in the National League. In June the Cardinals also profited from the return of Max Lanier, Fred Martin, and Lou Klein, who were reinstated following their defection to the Mexican League in 1946. Martin went 6–0, mostly in relief, while the crafty Lanier, after a slow start, notched five consecutive victories late in the season.

By late May, Musial was also steadily contributing to the Cardinals' ascent. He homered twice in the last week of May in Cardinal victories. His best early performance, however, came in a doubleheader victory on May 30 against Cincinnati in which he contributed four hits. For the first time the team pushed over the .500 barrier, to the delight of twenty-nine thousand hometown fans. For the duration of the season the Cardinals would remain in the thick of the pennant race.

The team temporarily moved into first place in June. In a series against league-leading Brooklyn at Ebbets Field early that month, Musial went eight for thirteen, touching Cardinal menace Preacher Roe for two home runs and a single and Don Newcombe for two singles and a game-winning fourteenth-inning triple. Musial helped keep the Cardinals in contention into early July. In Chicago, on the fifth, he drove home the team's only runs in a 2–1 win that included his throwing out the tying run at the plate. By the All-Star break the team had improved its record to 47–30, a half game behind the Dodgers. Musial's batting average stood at .290.

The friendly confines of Ebbets Field became the setting for the All-Star game on July 12. Hitting in his favorite park away from home, Musial set the standard for the National Leaguers in an 11–7 losing effort with a two-run four-bagger against the Red Sox' Mel Parnell in the bottom of

17. Goodman, *Stan, the Man*, 56.

the first. He also singled in the third and fourth and walked in the eighth while playing center and right field. But Joe DiMaggio's three RBIs and five senior-circuit errors contributed to the American League victory.

A week and a half later Musial returned to Ebbets Field for a critical four-game series with the Dodgers, who now held a two-and-a-half-game lead over the slumping Redbirds. Musial hit for the cycle in the third game and finished with three singles, two doubles, two triples, and two home runs in fifteen at bats, resulting in three victories and a tied fourth game, which was canceled in the ninth to enable both teams to catch trains. The Cards left Brooklyn with a one-game lead thanks to Musial's clutch hitting and the fine pitching of Munger and Pollet. Musial also escaped with a batting average of .304, largely because of his .531 average against Brooklyn pitching.

During this period trade talks again surfaced regarding Musial. The *Sporting News* reported that the Pirates offered Bob Chesnes—the Bucs' best pitcher in 1948—and catcher Clyde McCullough, along with about two hundred thousand dollars, for Musial and George Munger. Owner Saigh denied that he would ever accept such an offer. "There isn't an owner in the National or American League who can purchase Musial from me," he said; "if anybody asked for a price on Musial, I'd have to tell him $2,000,000. That's how much Musial means to me at the gate and to the Cardinals." Saigh never wavered in his commitment to "Stanley," whom he admired as much as a person as he did for his talent and commercial value to the organization.[18]

When the Dodgers resumed the series at Sportsman's Park in late July, more than thirty thousand fans witnessed the Cardinals take an early 3–0 lead against Roe in a rain-delayed game only to then see Brooklyn square things in the ninth. Despite loading the bases in the bottom of the inning, the Redbirds failed to score, resulting in a tie game because of a curfew (it was rescheduled at Sportsman's Park on September 21). The next evening produced an exciting 7–6 Cardinal victory as the home team overcame two earlier Dodger leads. Newcombe won the final game 4–2, however, reducing the Cardinals' lead to a game and a half. Musial managed only two hits in the three-game set.

The lead rocked back and forth into August with both teams faltering at times. They again faced one another in Brooklyn in late August, a series that *Time* magazine highlighted in a cover story on Musial, calling him the "most feared batter in the National League." After describing in detail

18. Rawlings, *Stan Musial Scrapbook*, 85.

his unorthodox hitting stance, *Time* referred to his unusual "deadpan Slavic" personality, which concealed whatever fire and imagination existed within him. The most he revealed of himself in protesting an umpire's called strike, according to *Time,* came from "a calm, open-mouthed stare that seems to say, 'How can you be so wrong?'"[19]

Musial entered the Dodger series in a mild slump, but once again Ebbets Field ended it in a hurry. In the afternoon-evening doubleheader, the Cardinals captured the first game 5–3 as the result of Musial's two and Slaughter's three hits. Musial's homer over the right-field fence in his first at bat traveled some 415 feet from home plate, crossing Bedford Avenue before landing in a vacant lot. The Cardinals then lost a game that they should have won in the following contest. In his second at bat, Musial belted a Preacher Roe pitch over the right-field screen for a 2–0 Cardinal lead, but the Dodgers came back to win 4–3. In the series finale Newcombe won the rubber game 6–0, with the assistance of outfielders, who "chased flyballs like men on bicycles and made 'impossible' catches," according to one account.[20] On one occasion, Louis Olmo leaped high against the left-center-field wall to rob Musial of a probable triple. Following the Dodger series, the Redbirds took three from the Giants at the Polo Grounds, with Musial leading the way with three four-baggers.

The Cardinals then returned home for a Labor Day doubleheader with Pittsburgh on September 5. After winning the first game, the Redbirds lost the second contest after Slaughter slid hard and high into Pittsburgh second baseman Danny Murtaugh, cutting him with his spikes. When Murtaugh followed Slaughter toward the dugout, exchanging "sulphuric" barbs, the umpires quickly stopped a bench-clearing altercation. But the aroused Pirates played furiously after that second-inning incident, eventually winning in the tenth when Murtaugh doubled and scored the winning run. The Pirates were not through with St. Louis, however, as they returned to Pittsburgh to await the Cardinals' eventual arrival.

On September 7, prior to the Cubs game, an appreciative St. Louis community honored Stash with Stan Musial Day, presenting him with a De Soto station wagon; a plaque from his teammates, presented by team captain Slaughter; telegrams from friends and fans nationwide; and six thousand dollars in U.S. government savings bonds. Two weeks before, more than one thousand Donora fans witnessed Musial receiving a baby-blue Cadillac between games of a doubleheader at Pittsburgh's

19. "That Man," 40–41.
20. Ibid., 40.

Forbes Field, with Musial's mother, brother Ed, and two sisters looking on. Stash arranged to turn in his old car, with fifteen Donora businessmen contributing the difference for the new purchase. The generosity of the two communities surely embarrassed an appreciative Musial, who promised to use the bond money to purchase land in the Donora area for a baseball field for youngsters.[21]

As the season moved into mid-September the Cardinals stretched their lead to two and a half games by winning seventeen out of twenty, with fourteen left to play. Musial remained hot, winning several contests with late-inning hits. His average rose to .333, third best in the league, behind Slaughter, second at .339, and Robinson, having his best year, at .347.

But Musial and the Cardinals entered the final two weeks fatigued and injured, losing Jones, Kazak, reliever Ted Wilks, and eventually Schoendienst. Musial also suffered a pulled groin muscle legging out a triple against the Phillies on the eve of the final Dodgers series at Sportsman's Park. Yet Lanier pitched a brilliant five-hit shutout in the first contest on September 21, while Slaughter led the batsmen with three hits to take over momentarily the batting lead. Roe responded with a two-hitter in the second game, defeating the Cardinals for the fourth time in five tries. The finale proved a total bust for the home team as the Dodgers routed starter Munger and five other pitchers for nineteen hits and thirteen walks in a 19–6 shellacking. Musial wasted three hits in a game that got out of hand early. Even though the Cardinals had prevailed over the Dodgers overall in 1949, they lost four of the last six games and saw their lead reduced to a half game.

On September 27 the team carried a one-and-a-half-game lead into Pittsburgh, the start of a final road trip. In the initial outing Pirate rookie Tom Saffell's grand slam hit the foul-pole screen in right field for a 6–4 victory, reducing the Cards' lead to one game. In the next contest Murry Dickson took the mound for the Bucs. Beforehand, he had dinner with his old hunting buddy and former roommate, Brecheen, whom he told: "I still hope you win, Cat. We can delay our hunting trip until after the series, but you're not going to beat me."[22] True to his word, Dickson subdued the Redbirds for the fifth time that season in scattering six hits. Only Dickson had won that many games against the Cards in 1949. Obviously, Dickson's departure, more than any other consideration, had hurt the team the most.

21. Connie Berutti to Stan Musial, September 3, 1949, Musial Day Letter Scrapbook, vol. 1, Musial Collection, St. Louis Cardinals Hall of Fame Museum.
22. Musial, *Musial*, 129.

Because of a doubleheader victory against the Braves' best, Spahn and Sain, the Dodgers now moved into first place by a half game for the first time in six weeks.

The Cardinals had to win two of their final three games against the lowly Cubs at Wrigley Field to have much of a chance. The opening game on September 30 proved a disaster for Musial and his teammates, however. Despite stroking a single and a double, Stan contributed to the loss by misplaying a ball in the sun, resulting in a two-run double and the end of Lanier's five-game winning streak. With two contests remaining for St. Louis and Brooklyn, the Cards had to gain one game to force a postseason playoff. But on October 1, a day that Musial would call one of his most frustrating as a Cardinal, the team failed to capitalize on a Dodger loss when Cub journeyman Bob Chipman, depending on a herky-jerky delivery and "junk" pitches, held the Cards at bay 3–1 despite surrendering nine hits and four walks, including two doubles to Musial. The Cardinals left twelve runners stranded that afternoon, in losing their fourth straight for the first time in 1949.

The Cardinals' final opportunity came on the last day of the season when they went with Pollet, seeking his twentieth win. Musial tagged two home runs and a single in a 13–5 smashing. Afterward, the Cardinals retired to the clubhouse to listen to the conclusion of the Dodgers-Phillies contest. After blowing a 5–0 lead, the Dodgers tied the score and then won it in the tenth on a Duke Snider single.

"The [train] ride back to St. Louis was deadly quiet," Musial remembered.[23] Players were buried in their own private thoughts. Losing the pennant by one game became particularly painful when they pondered what might have been in a number of key losses, several of which hinged on fate. Musial especially recalled one evening in early August when Jones hit a first-inning two-run homer against the New York Giants only to have the umpire disallow it because he claimed pitcher Adrian Zabala balked. This cost the Cardinals the game.

On that same trip home sportswriter Broeg saw a stunned Dyer talking with his wife inside the compartment of their private parlor car. He knocked and entered to extend his sympathy: "I guess, Colonel, after so many years breaking other clubs' hearts down the stretch, the Cardinals had this coming." Dyer nodded. Broeg then wondered "when we'll get this close again." Dyer raised his head, looked at his wife, and replied, "That,"

23. Ibid., 131.

he said, "is what I've just been saying to Gerry."[24] Not even Broeg and Dyer could have known that the glory days had ended with such finality. After five pennants—including three World Series championships—and three second-place finishes in eight years, the Cardinals would not win another pennant until 1964, one year after Musial's retirement.

As for Musial, he once again had put together an outstanding year and, along with Slaughter, kept the Cardinals in contention through much of the season. After hitting a lackluster .290 for the first eighty-eight games, he batted a sizzling .400 for the final seventy-one contests. Ironically, he showed more power after he concentrated on meeting the ball. Of his 36 home runs, 20 came in the second half of the season. He finished with a .338 batting average, second only to Robinson's .342; he led the league with 41 doubles, 207 hits, 382 total bases, and an on-base percentage of .438; he tied Slaughter for the lead in triples with 13; and he placed second in runs scored with 128. His 36 home runs put him a distant second to Kiner's 54. Continuing a trend since 1947, he performed more effectively in night games, hitting .358 against .324 in day contests, despite his comment that "I'm a better hitter in the daytime, regardless of what the figures say."[25] Moreover, he showed his durability in playing in all of the Cardinals' 157 games.

Musial's performance could have been even greater if not for the Pirates' Forbes Field, where he hit a puny .205 in 1949 with no home runs. Musial offered no explanation for his anemic performance there aside from trying too hard in front of sizable neighborhood crowds. He conceded, however, that Pirate pitchers deserved some credit too. Curiously, no one contested him more effectively than journeyman left-hander Bill Werle, who shut him out in nineteen plate appearances.[26] Consequently, no one more prevented Musial from capturing the batting title than Werle, and no club more detoured the Cardinals' pennant ambitions than the sixth-place Pirates, who won the season series, 12–10. Still, the 1949 season cemented Musial's dominance as the National League's top performer. For the next decade he retained that status even while the St. Louis ball club faded into oblivion.

24. Ibid.

25. Bob Broeg, "Stan Lost Batting Title in Pennsylvania Parks," *Sporting News*, November 16, 1949, clipping in Musial Collection, *Sporting News* Archives.

26. Ibid.; Rawlings, *Stan Musial Scrapbook*, 93. Werle attributed his success against Musial to a low curveball from a three-quarter delivery that gave "fits" to all left-handed batters. William Werle telephone interview, January 20, 1999.

Player of the Decade

M usial remained one of the dominant superstars through the mid-1950s, winning four more batting titles (1950–1952, 1957), finishing near the top in hitting on four additional occasions, leading the National League in several other batting categories, playing—and often starring—in every All-Star game of the 1950s, and becoming the *Sporting News*'s player of the decade.

Despite Musial's continued stardom, the Cardinals failed to replicate the successes of the 1940s, when they finished lower than second place only once, in 1940. In the 1950s the club never seriously contended, with the possible exception of 1957, when it finished in second place, eight games out of first. Otherwise the Redbirds ended up seventh twice (1955, 1959), sixth once (1954), and fifth (1950, 1958), fourth (1953, 1956), and third (1951, 1952) twice each.

These were bittersweet years for Musial. On the one hand, his salary continued to rise, from fifty thousand dollars in 1949 to eighty thousand in 1951, and then ultimately to one hundred thousand in 1958. He added to his many individual honors, including reaching the three-thousand-hit plateau in May 1958. He also set a National League mark by playing in 895 consecutive games. Yet he often felt frustrated by the team's mediocre performance as he struggled to keep the club in contention. He hid those disappointments remarkably well by remaining upbeat and playing hard at several positions in the field.

The Cardinals faced disappointing seasons in the 1950s partly because the farm system no longer generated the quality players that it had produced during the Rickey years, leaving St. Louis at a disadvantage against talent-rich organizations such as the Dodgers and Giants. Consequently, the Redbirds had problems replacing an aging pitching staff anchored by Brecheen, Brazle, and Lanier; indeed, no young hurlers emerged who sustained impressive single-season performances, with the possible exception of Harvey Haddix. As a result, the Cards went from being a team that led the National League in earned run average virtually every season that Musial played in the 1940s to a club whose pitchers never exceeded third best in ERA during the 1950s. And even though the team season hitting average slipped less significantly (they led the league in batting on four occasions in the 1950s), the club finished as low as sixth in 1950 and

1958 and its home-run ranking dropped considerably. The Redbirds also lost the incredible team speed that had characterized the earlier squads.

Poor trades contributed to the team's woes and adversely affected club chemistry. Among the worst swaps was the 1951 trade that sent Garagiola, Pollet, and Wilks to the Pirates for Wally Westlake and Cliff Chambers. While Garagiola and Pollet subsequently had productive seasons, Westlake and Chambers (following the 1951 campaign) proved to be disappointments. No trade created a greater stir than the unloading of the thirty-eight-year-old Slaughter to the Yankees for four young players at the start of the 1954 season. Although the deal made sense because of Slaughter's age, which had reduced him to a role player, the hard-playing outfielder was, next to Musial, the heart and soul of the Cardinals. When he heard of the trade, "Bosco," as his teammates called him, broke down, exclaiming "I've never expected this to happen. I've given my life to this organization." Soon afterward, a stunned Musial saw Slaughter in the parking area across from the ballpark still wiping his eyes. Upon reaching him, Musial looked at him and they "both burst into tears."[1]

The loss of Slaughter might have been easier to take if the Cardinals had retained Bill Virdon, by far the most promising player the club obtained in the Slaughter trade. Virdon won the Rookie of the Year award in 1955, hitting .281 with 17 home runs. The next year he inexplicably went to Pittsburgh in exchange for Bobby Del Greco and Dick Littlefield, both of whom were gone by the next season, in one of the all-time Redbird boner trades.

Also in 1956 the Cardinals shipped popular Red Schoendienst to the New York Giants just before the June 15 trade deadline in a blockbuster eight-player deal that included promising Cardinal rookie Jackie Brandt for shortstop Alvin Dark, who was expected to fill a position need and provide leadership, a trait that Schoendienst and Musial supposedly lacked.[2] Calling it his saddest day in baseball, Musial lost his roommate of nearly ten years in what proved to be one of his most vexing seasons. Despite hitting .296 for the Giants in 1956, Schoendienst was dealt to the Milwaukee Braves early the following season, where he led that team to a World Series victory over the Yankees in seven games. Schoendienst topped the league in hits with two hundred and batted over .300 that year.

---

1. Lansche, *Stan "The Man,"* 129; Musial, *Musial,* 161–62.
2. Musial's and Schoendienst's supposed lack of leadership represented General Manager Lane's evaluation. Albert Hirshberg, *The Man Who Fought Back: Red Schoendienst,* 125.

His departure, Schoendienst remained convinced, had cost the Cardinals the pennant in 1957. Among the other promising Cards who were cast out through the revolving door were infielders Solly Hemus and Ray Jablonski; shortstop Alex Grammas; black pitcher Brooks Lawrence, who soon won thirty-five games in two seasons with the Reds; and pitcher Harvey Haddix.

Moreover, the ball club witnessed the failure of some of its top prospects, including power-hitting first basemen Rocky Nelson and Steve Bilko, who crushed triple-A pitching but responded meekly at the major-league level. Bilko especially disappointed because he hit 21 home runs and drove in 84 runs for the Cards in 1953 and then did little else. Tom Alston, another flop at first base, cost the club one hundred thousand dollars from San Diego of the Pacific Coast League. Yet Alston, the Cardinals' first black player, produced only four homers over four seasons of part-time play.

Perhaps the most perplexing failure was Von McDaniel, a 6-foot 3-inch, eighteen-year-old "bonus baby" from Oklahoma, who had signed for fifty thousand dollars in 1957 and was expected to pitch very little that season. But in a game the Cardinals were losing badly, Manager Fred Hutchinson used him in relief, and he responded with four innings of shutout ball. In that game Musial, at first base, visited him at the mound to advise that he would be playing off the bag. McDaniel promptly took off his cap and said, "Gosh Mr. Musial, you've been my idol for years."[3] Against Brooklyn at Ebbets Field three days later McDaniel again relieved in a losing effort. After the Cards took the lead he remained in the game in the ninth with a one-run cushion to preserve the victory. McDaniel finally started against the Dodgers one week later. He pitched a two-hit 2–0 shutout in which he stopped the Dodgers with the bases loaded in the sixth with no outs. Soon he had extended his winning streak to four games. No pitcher had created so much excitement in St. Louis in the 1950s. Then, almost mysteriously, he suddenly collapsed after clubs had additional looks at him. He finished the season with a 7–5 mark and pitched in only two other games in 1958 following a torn muscle in his right shoulder.

The deterioration of Cardinal player talent reflected, of course, the organizational inadequacies following Rickey's departure, a problem that appreciably worsened in the '50s. After having only two managers during his first ten years with the team, Musial experienced seven different skippers in the 1950s. The managerial turnover contributed to the instability

3. Rains, *The St. Louis Cardinals*, 141.

of the ball club. Nothing proved more debilitating than owner Saigh's conviction for income tax evasion in 1952, which resulted in a fifteen-month sentence. Never able to muster the financial resources to attract new player talent, Saigh now found himself having to sell the franchise, which almost resulted in the team moving to Milwaukee.

Only the last-minute purchase by St. Louis civic leader August A. Busch, Jr., the head of Anheuser-Busch brewery, kept the club in the city. Although not a baseball fan, Busch had considerable community pride and money to spend. He was close to fellow duck hunters Musial and Schoendienst, who had advised him to buy the club. He surmised that baseball could become an effective vehicle for selling beer; indeed, within two years of the Cardinal purchase, Budweiser surpassed Schlitz as the nation's top-selling brew. Busch took an active part in the team, attending all home games and traveling to road contests in a private railroad car attached to the train transporting the Cardinals. With Busch around, according to one observer, this often meant gin rummy playing and "heavy drinking."[4] It also meant a Byzantine style of management, which often proved disconcerting and confusing.

Busch was driven to win. But he found that harder to do with the Redbirds because in baseball, unlike in his brewery operation, he could not usually buy what he wanted. When he offered top dollar for such superstars as Gil Hodges of the Dodgers, Ernie Banks of the Cubs, and Willie Mays of the Giants, he received quick no-thank-yous. He could do more to improve the surroundings of the ball club, however. Appalled by the deteriorating condition of Sportsman's Park, he purchased it from the Browns, renamed it Busch Stadium, and made major renovations at a time when professional baseball was slipping nationwide (the Cardinals' attendance fell to 880,000 in 1953, its lowest mark since World War II) because of television and the popularity of other outside activities. By 1954 Busch Stadium had become one of the most attractive ballparks in the country. A solid green decor now replaced the advertisements that had cluttered the outfield walls.

With much less positive results, Busch hired Frank Lane as general manager after the 1955 season to replace Dick Meyer, a capable but in-experienced Anheuser-Busch executive, who returned to company head-quarters. In the process Busch delegated considerable authority to Lane in the operation of the club. Known as "Trader Frank" for his wheeling

---

4. Peter Hernon and Terry Ganey, *Under the Influence: The Unauthorized Story of the Anheuser-Busch Dynasty*, 236; Schoendienst, *Red*, 71.

and dealing as general manager of the American League's Chicago White Sox, Lane not only manufactured a dozen trades involving forty players over the next year—many of them unsatisfactory—but also undermined Cardinal tradition by removing the birds-on-the-bat insignia from the front of the jersey. Because of a public outcry, that experience lasted only a single season.

Nothing created more concern than Lane's effort in 1956 to trade Musial to the Philadelphia Phillies for pitcher Robin Roberts just before the June 15 deadline, the first serious trade activity involving Musial since early 1949. Stan's business partner, Biggie Garagnani, confirmed the rumor by contacting J. G. Taylor Spink, publisher of the *Sporting News*, who in turn obtained corroboration. Biggie then told one of Busch's key subordinates that Musial would retire before going to Philadelphia: "So, you'll have no deal, no Musial either, and a lot of embarrassment." That evening he related to Musial that "I knew how you felt and just couldn't stand by and see Lane hurt you—and the Cardinals." Musial told Garagnani he was absolutely right. To Schoendienst Musial angrily added, "I'm not going to go."[5] Years later Musial conceded that his love of the game and his quest for three thousand hits would have caused him to reconsider.

Once Busch found out about the would-be swap, he informed Lane that Musial would remain with the club. Three days later, after Lane traded Schoendienst, Busch revoked Lane's blank-check authority over player personnel. All trades now required his approval through Meyer at the brewery. With team morale at an all-time low, Busch's patience with Lane was wearing thin. At a banquet in early 1957 he suggested that the Cardinals would have to win it all by 1958 or "Lane would be out on his ear." Following the surprising second-place finish in 1957, Lane elected to take his mayhem to the Cleveland Indians in the American League, where he soon traded the local favorite, power-hitting Rocky Colavito, to the Detroit Tigers for Harvey Kuenn.

There is a revealing postscript to Musial's feelings toward Lane. A decade later, when he was himself general manager of the Cardinals, Musial caught Lane on the Cardinal team bus talking to Redbird players. Musial "sprang up from his seat," according to Schoendienst, "and walked to where Lane was sitting." In a rare outburst, Musial ordered, "Get the hell out of here."[6]

5. Musial, *Musial*, 177–78; Schoendienst, *Red*, 82.
6. Schoendienst, *Red*, 83.

Meanwhile, Busch's Cardinals muddled through the 1950s with little success other than in 1957. The one constant remained the sterling play of Musial, whose attainments graced much of that era, beginning with his batting title in 1950. That season Musial got off to his best start ever as he homered and singled in the home inaugural, a 4–2 win over Pittsburgh on April 18, the first opener ever played under the lights. He homered again a day later in a losing contest. On April 28, with his batting average at .448, he suffered his first serious injury as a major leaguer. He slipped in the soft dirt while rounding first base at Forbes Field, severely straining a ligament in his left knee, an injury that gave him fits for the remainder of his career. Musial later remembered that he collapsed afterward as he tried to put weight on his left leg. He immediately thought, "This is it, I'm through. Thank God for the restaurant."[7] But after diathermy treatments from Doc Weaver, a limping Musial returned to the lineup in four days, alternating between first base and right field. Just trying to meet the ball, he began a fifteen-game hitting streak in which he raised his batting average to .467. By June 1 Musial had led the club to a first-place tie with Brooklyn.

Even though the team remained in contention throughout June and July, a spate of injuries took its toll, beginning with Joe Garagiola's shoulder separation on June 1 suffered in a collision with second baseman Jackie Robinson, who was covering first base. Hitting .347 at the time, Garagiola missed most of the rest of the season. Musial also hurt himself in early June attempting to grab the hard, wild throw of pitcher Al Brazle with his bare hand at first base, causing a deep gash between his second and third fingers. Afterward, he hit with an air-foam pad on the bat handle to cushion the impact. He then further aggravated his left knee, which now required an elastic steel-ribbed brace.

But Musial entered the All-Star break determined to stay in the lineup as he sought to keep the Redbirds in the race. He had recently passed the fifteen-hundred-hit milestone and now thought even more seriously about reaching three thousand. Always receptive to advice from elders, he took to heart what fellow Pole Al Simmons—Aloysius Szymanski— of the champion Philadelphia Athletics of the late '20s and early '30s had told him that spring. One of baseball's all-time great hitters with a lifetime batting average of .334, Simmons had missed three thousand hits by only seventy-three because he had sat out games that he might have played

7. Musial, *Musial*, 122.

and had wasted at bats because of carelessness. He advised Musial to "stay in there and bear down all the way."[8]

Musial carried a .350 average into the 1950 All-Star game at Comiskey Park in Chicago on July 11. He was the second-leading vote getter among National Leaguers in receiving the starting nod at first base. Yet he went hitless in five official at bats while roommate Schoendienst homered in the fourteenth inning in a 4–3 victory for the senior circuit.

The second half of the season began with Musial once again reinjuring his knee in the loose dirt around first base in Philadelphia. He kept playing, however, and ran off a thirty-game hitting streak, which ended July 27 when Dodger rookie reliever Billy Loes stopped Musial in his final at bat. The cocky Loes, who had been asked in a meeting at the mound if he knew of Musial's hitting streak, said yes and indicated that he intended to throw one right down the middle, causing his teammates to burst out in laughter. An overanxious Musial grounded into a double play, ending the longest batting streak of his career.

By then the slumping Cardinals had fallen to fifth place. Besides bad pitching, lack of production elsewhere forced Musial to play first base and all three outfield posts, oftentimes switching positions during the game. Yet Musial won the batting crown with a .346 average, eighteen points ahead of runner-up Jackie Robinson. He also led the league in slugging average (.596), finished second to Schoendienst in doubles (41), and ended up second in hits (192). His home-run total, however, slipped to 28. Without the nagging injuries, which forced him to play hurt most of the time, Musial might have had one of his best opportunities to hit .400. The fifty-year-old Dyer, whom Saigh made the scapegoat for the Cardinals' second-division finish, paid Musial the ultimate compliment when he said that "Stan was hurt and could have begged off with good reason. . . . He's the greatest kid I ever met, unselfish and a team player all the way."[9]

On November 29 the Cardinals announced Marty Marion as Dyer's replacement. Marion, forced to retire as a player because of back and knee problems, had impressed Saigh with his intelligence, leadership, and integrity. Musial probably favored Terry Moore, the coach and former captain, who best exemplified the Cardinal spirit of the early '40s. His first preference still remained father-surrogate Dyer, whom he thought unfairly treated. In a rare expression of resentment, he indicated that he

8. Ibid., 134.
9. Ibid., 137.

was "through being shoved around. I'll play the outfield or first base but not both. Marty will have to decide. I just don't like what they've done to Dyer."[10]

Musial's comments came in the midst of a salary dispute in which he sought seventy-five thousand dollars, a twenty-five-thousand-dollar base increase from 1950. The financially strapped Saigh momentarily resisted because of declining profits following an attendance drop of more than 337,000 from the record-breaking 1949 season. In early February 1951, with nothing settled and the Korean War in its second year, Musial departed for Germany to entertain American troops at the invitation of the U.S. government. The group included pitcher Jim Konstanty of the Phillies, the National League's most valuable player; Chicago Cubs manager Frankie Frisch; and Boston Braves manager Charley Grimm.

Following Communist China's intervention in Korea in late 1950, the United States found itself even more mired in that Asian war, which eventually resulted in more than 142,000 U.S. casualties in what was termed a United Nations "police action." While the conflict affected professional baseball in various ways—including restricting player salaries and the use of horsehide, causing a shortage of balls—it did not result in large-scale military induction of major leaguers. Among the fewer than forty in uniform were young stars such as Willie Mays, Curt Simmons, Art Houtteman, and Whitey Ford, and Boston great Ted Williams.

Upon Musial's return from Germany in mid-February 1951, he soon signed a contract for seventy-five thousand dollars plus the renewal of an attendance clause providing for a possible five thousand dollars more, making him arguably the highest-paid player in National League history.[11] Saigh had relented, probably because of an appreciation of Musial's worth as a person and ballplayer. But the twenty-five-thousand-dollar increase seemed out of line with the Wage Stabilization Board's anti-inflationary wartime decree that prevented a ball club from increasing its payroll more than 10 percent, most likely meaning a lesser raise for Musial. The matter remained unresolved until February 1952. After Saigh had unsuccessfully appealed the board's decision, Musial, in a chance conversation with

10. Goodman, *Stan, the Man*, 116.
11. In 1947, when he went from the Detroit Tigers to the Pittsburgh Pirates on waivers, Hank Greenberg reputedly retained seventy-five thousand dollars of his Tiger salary while receiving forty thousand from the Pirates, along with a lucrative stock-purchase arrangement that eventually netted sixty thousand. Technically, then, Greenberg exceeded Musial's 1951 salary. Marshall, *Baseball's Pivotal Era*, 477n.

Secretary of Labor Maurice Tobin at a Boston baseball dinner, told him of his problem. The baseball-loving Tobin advised Musial to bring his attorney to Washington. Musial and St. Louis attorney Mark Eagleton, the father of a future Missouri senator, met with Tobin and board members and quickly had the decision overturned.

Picked to finish fourth by most baseball writers, the Cardinals began the 1951 season with a loss to the Pirates in a snowstorm at Forbes Field. Musial, playing left field, singled off of former teammate Dickson. By early May the Redbirds were hitting only .218, with Musial struggling as well. The flu virus took its toll as the club spent its last day in first place on May 8, the beginning of a three-game series with the Giants. Several players remained at the hotel, and an ailing Musial finally sat out the final game, the Cardinals' fourth straight loss. The weakened group proceeded to Cincinnati, where they played a make-up doubleheader on Saturday. Still ill, Musial watched his team lose another one in the first contest. The Redbirds trailed in the nightcap by one run in the eighth inning with two men on base. After the Reds manager went to right-hander Frank Smith, Musial told Marion that he thought he could hit. Lloyd Merriman, an outfielder for the Reds, remembered Musial coming to the plate literally dragging the bat, "looking like he should have been in the hospital." After missing one pitch and fouling off another, he reached out for a sinker ball and pulled it over the right-field screen to win the game.[12]

Even such heroics could not save the Cardinals in 1951. With an impatient Marion moving players in and out of the lineup, the team lacked cohesion. Musial recalled that "Slats" tried four first basemen and five second basemen before the All-Star break. Once again Musial willingly shifted between the outfield and first in an effort to help the team. He heated up in late May when, in twenty-three plate appearances, he connected thirteen times, including six homers, three doubles, and a triple, raising his average to .362 by July.

He was the National League's top vote getter for the All-Star game in Detroit on July 10 as an outfielder. He went three for four, including a homer off of Yankee left-hander Eddie Lopat in the fourth. Lopat, who had pitched against Musial in the Western Association in 1941, had claimed to Dodger hurler Preacher Roe that he had a surefire way to retire Musial. But Stash sent Lopat's first pitch sailing into the right-field stands, causing

12. Lloyd Merriman to Giglio, September 14, 1996, in possession of Giglio.

Roe to bellow from the bullpen, "Hey, I found that way to pitch to him a long time ago."[13]

Musial continued his consistent hitting in the second half of the season; his nearest competitor for the batting title, Richie Ashburn of the Phillies, stayed close until late in the campaign. Musial finished with a .355 average for his second consecutive title, fifth overall, and the first back-to-back titles since Rogers Hornsby in 1924–1925. He also led the National League in runs scored (124), triples (12), and total bases (355). He finished second in hits (205) and tied for fourth in RBIs (108) and home runs (32). For the second time the *Sporting News* named him the Major League Player of the Year. No other Cardinal had more than 64 RBIs and 14 home runs, one of the major reasons the team finished in third place, fifteen and a half games behind the pennant-winning New York Giants. In the so-called Miracle of Coogan's Bluff, the Giants had beaten the Dodgers in a playoff game thanks to Bobby Thomson's ninth-inning home run.

The Cardinals' losing eighteen out of twenty-two games to the Dodgers, including thirteen by one run, contributed to Marion's dismissal as manager. Saigh blamed it on Marion's lack of fire and commitment. By the end of the year the Cardinals had traded Lanier and Chuck Diering to the Giants for feisty second baseman Eddie Stanky, the team's first player-manager since Hornsby in 1926.

Saigh's next objective became the signing of Musial, who had already consented to the same salary as in 1951. Still, on February 14, 1952, Saigh, undoubtedly influenced by the theatrics of St. Louis Browns owner Bill Veeck, staged a shameful public-signing extravaganza at his posh office in Sportsman's Park, which included newspaper and radio coverage, after having already reached an informal understanding with Musial. Saigh dramatically presented Musial with a blank contract, which Saigh had signed, inviting him to place whatever figure he thought appropriate, adding that "I know this puts you on the spot, Stan, but I think you must have given some thought to what you want. Anything short of your owning the club . . . is all right with us." An uncomfortable Musial, seemingly surprised by the spectacle, stammered, as he struggled with the charade: "Well, you know, Mr. Saigh, I haven't thought much about the 1952 season until now." But after further groping, he finally told Saigh what he wanted to hear—"I think I will sign my 1952 contract with the same terms as 1951, if that is satisfactory." Saigh's eyes widened as he responded, "Well, Stan, I think that is more than a gracious gesture."

13. Kahn, "The Man: Stan Musial Is Baseball's No. 1 Citizen," 57.

After the signing broadcaster Harry Caray teased Saigh, "You must be a helleva fine crap shooter, too." "I gambled on a man's character," Saigh pompously responded. "You can do unusual things when you know how sound the other person is."[14]

Writing about the 1952 event years later, Musial knew that he could have stuck Saigh. Beyond the matter of integrity relating to a prior agreement, Musial understood, however, that an increase would have meant challenging once again the government's salary cap policy and overlooking another year of declining Cardinal attendance. From 1951 through 1957 Musial's salary, in fact, remained the same in the face of poor team performances, Musial's own shrinking batting average, and further attendance reductions—dipping below one million in three of the next four years. Musial showed an immense sense of fairness in not pursuing salary raises. Because the federal income tax absorbed at least 50 percent of his earnings, however, he worked out an arrangement with the club to defer a portion of his income annually, resulting in the Cardinals owing him $218,000 by 1963.[15] Musial became one of the first ballplayers to show such financial acumen, another indication of a willingness to listen to good advice.

One month before the beginning of the 1952 season, Hall of Famer Ty Cobb, as financially astute in his own time, paid homage to Musial's playing ability in two controversial self-serving articles he wrote for *Life* magazine, for which he received twenty-five thousand dollars. Entitled "They Don't Play Baseball Any More," the curmudgeon Cobb claimed that there were only two present-day players who could "be mentioned in the same breath with the oldtime greats . . . Phil Rizzuto [of the New York Yankees] and Stan Musial."[16]

In a subsequent interview, Cobb acknowledged that a perfect ballplayer has never existed. But "Stan Musial," Cobb contended, "is the closest to being perfect in the game today. I've seen greater hitters and greater runners and greater fielders, but he puts them together like no one else, except the way George Sisler did. He's certainly one of the greatest players of all time. In my book, he's a better player than DiMaggio was in his time. Stan Musial will score from first on a single. You don't see much of that

14. Bob Broeg, "Saigh Wins Gamble on Musial's Fairness," *Sporting News*, February 20, 1952, clipping in Musial Collection, *Sporting News* Archives; Musial, *Musial*, 146–47; Bob Broeg interview, February 18, 1999.

15. Musial salary information sheet, St. Louis Cardinals Hall of Fame Museum, Musial Collection, Busch Stadium.

16. Ty Cobb, "The Greatest Player of All Time Says: 'They Don't Play Baseball Any More,' " 137–38.

kind of running around today. He plays as hard when his club is away out in front . . . as he does when they're just a run or two behind. He'll go after a ball, even in an exhibition game, diving for a shoestring catch, as if the World Series depended on it. He's my kind of ballplayer. . . . He plays anywhere you put him, left field, center field. . . . He has the power of Napoleon Lajoie. He has the stamina of Eddie Collins. He is as steady as old Honus Wagner."[17]

Musial was characteristically modest in responding to Cobb's praise: "Cobb is baseball's greatest. I don't want to contradict him, but I can't say that I was as good as DiMaggio. I don't think there was a day when I could reach DiMaggio, when Joe was in his top form. That DiMaggio was the best, the greatest ballplayer I ever saw on any diamond anywhere. . . . That's all very nice for Ty Cobb to say all those things about me but I think he's off base this time."[18] Musial also defended the modern players whom many old-timers failed to appreciate. Nevertheless, Musial occasionally visited with Cobb and exchanged correspondence. He took Cobb's advice seriously, particularly on how to extend his playing career.

Cobb gave no suggestions, however, on how to turn the 1952 Cardinals into a pennant-winning club. The team started slowly and failed to escape the second division until mid-June. By then Musial was on a tear, with twelve hits in twenty-nine at bats to raise his league-leading average to .336. He carried a twenty-four-game hitting streak to June 28, when he went hitless in a six-inning rain-shortened game. Yet the team continued on a ten-game win streak that ended a couple of days after the All-Star game on July 8. Musial had started his ninth All-Star game in center field at Philadelphia's Shibe Park. In a 3–2 National League victory he went hitless in two official at bats, but he reached base when Cleveland right-hander Bob Lemon hit him, then scored on Hank Sauer's home run.

Under the aggressive managing of Stanky and the strong play of Musial, Schoendienst, Slaughter, and Hemus, along with occasional fine pitching, the team went on an eight-game run in mid-August, which lifted them into second place, seven and a half games behind the Dodgers. But then they lost four straight to the league-leading Bums, despite Musial's hitting, and fell into third place, where they remained at season's end, eight and a half games from the top. Still, the team won eighty-eight games, their best performance between 1949 and Musial's final season in 1963.

17. Lansche, *Stan "The Man,"* 118. Lansche incorrectly indicates that Cobb's comments were contained in the *Life* articles. The Cobb quotation can also be found in the 1961 account, Goodman, *Stan, the Man,* 118.
18. Lansche, *Stan "The Man,"* 118–19.

Musial won his third consecutive batting title, finishing with a .336 average, his lowest mark since his illness-plagued 1947 season. He led the National League in hits (194), doubles (42), and slugging percentage (.538), and tied for first in runs scored (105). He also played in all 154 games, mostly in the outfield. Manager of the Year Stanky publicly complimented him for his willingness to play all three outfield positions as well as first base. Musial had reached a significant milestone on September 9 when he singled off of Curt Simmons of the Phillies for his two thousandth hit, becoming the ninety-first major leaguer to accomplish that feat. But he still felt somewhat disappointed with his 1952 performance, particularly since he hit only 21 home runs and drove in only 91 runs, the first time he had missed the century mark since 1947. He conceded that he had failed to take advantage of the numerous times Schoendienst and Hemus had been on base when he was at bat.

In 1953 the Redbirds began the season in Milwaukee, the new home of the Braves, who had become the first of the financially struggling franchises to move to greener pastures. (The following year, the Browns would move from St. Louis to Baltimore.) In the opener, Musial failed to hit in five at bats against ace Warren Spahn, whom he usually hit well. With the addition of several promising rookies, including pitcher Haddix, third baseman Ray Jablonski, first baseman Bilko, and center fielder Rip Repulski, the Cardinals assumed the role of pennant contenders in the early going even though Musial hit erratically in the first months of the season. During the Cardinals' first home stand he embarked on a twelve-game hitting streak, followed by a one for twenty-four slump, which lowered his average to .233.

Something appeared drastically wrong with his intricate hitting stance. *St. Louis Post-Dispatch* sports editor Stockton presented one knowledge-able player's assessment: "I hope I'm wrong, but I've always believed that when Musial started to slip as a batter, he'd slip suddenly and with a terrific crash. [Musial] goes through all sorts of motions batting. He takes an unusual stance, sort of winds himself up for each swing and throws his entire body into the business of swinging the bat." In contrast, Slaughter's compact stance required him to "just stand there with his bat poised" and then swing.[19]

On May 12, with Stanky and coach Dixie Walker watching, Musial went through a lengthy batting practice that revealed he was overstriding and failing to bend his left knee. Films soon detected that he was striding

19. Musial, *Musial*, 157.

nearly twice as far as he customarily did. A pulled groin muscle made it even more difficult for him to adjust. Yet, outwardly at least, Musial kept an even disposition. After discussing his hitting problems with the press, he said, "I'm not discouraged. . . . What I need is a good splurge for about three or four days. That will get me going, and I'm going to get 'em real soon, just watch. I'll get even with those pitchers who are having a picnic with me now."[20]

Musial finally turned things around in mid-June. From a .251 average on the seventeenth, he streaked to over .300 after stroking twenty-four hits in forty-three at bats, including ten doubles and four home runs. His hitting carried the club to within one game of the National League leaders, the Dodgers and the Braves, as the All-Star break approached. He had surpassed his original goal of reaching .300 by the All-Star break. His tenth All-Star game appearance on July 14 took place at the friendly confines of Crosley Field, where he usually hit well. Starting in left field, Musial singled twice in a 5–1 National League win. Slaughter's play proved most decisive, however, with his two singles, stolen base, two runs scored, and sliding catch in left field.

The four-game series in Brooklyn following the All-Star contest pretty much settled the Cards' fate for 1953. The pitching collapsed in the Dodger sweep of the Redbirds, who would lose all eleven games at Ebbets Field that year. The remainder of the season seemed anticlimactic, as the team languished in fourth place, twenty-two games out of first. Musial continued to hit well, however. By late September he was closing in on the two league leaders, Carl Furillo of the Dodgers and roommate Schoendienst.

With Furillo out of the lineup with a broken wrist, Schoendienst finished second at .342 and Musial third at .337, to Furillo's .344. Despite his early season woes, Musial hit a scorching .375 from mid-June on. He ended the campaign with a fifteen-game hitting streak, causing Cub manager Phil Cavaretta to comment, "Another week of the season, and Stan would have won the title." Despite failing to win his fourth consecutive batting crown, Musial had a more productive year than in 1952. He once again played in every game, all of them in the outfield. He led the league in doubles (53) and walks (105), finished second in hits (200) and runs scored (127), and third in total bases (361). Additionally, he collected 30 homers, nine triples, and 113 RBIs. Even so, Musial agreed to sign a 1954 contract for his existing salary.

20. Lansche, *Stan "The Man,"* 124.

As good as the second half of his 1953 season was, 1954 promised to be even better following a productive spring training. By now he had become the senior Cardinal following the departure of Slaughter. Slaughter's replacement, rookie Wally Moon, homered in his first major-league at bat in the opening game at Busch Stadium. Musial also homered, but the Cardinals lost to the Cubs, 13–4, one of many games that season in which the opposition scored ten or more times. The Cubs feasted even more on Cardinal pitching four days later in a 23–13 victory.

Musial's uncustomary fast start reached phenomenal heights in a memorable Sunday doubleheader at Busch Stadium on May 2 in which he had his greatest day as a hitter. That morning showers had prevented Musial and others from taking batting practice. In the early afternoon, suffering from a charley horse, he limped to the plate against lefty Johnny Antonelli and drew a walk. The fireworks began in the third inning when he hit Antonelli's slow curve over the pavilion roof. He homered again to the right-field roof off Antonelli in the fifth on an inside fastball with Schoendienst on base. He then singled off of right-hander Jim Hearn on a curve in the sixth. Two innings later, with the score tied at six, he hammered Hearn's slider onto the right-field roof. The Cardinals won, 10–6, and Musial had achieved a personal milestone of collecting three home runs in one major-league game. While he enjoyed a glass of milk and a ham-and-cheese sandwich during the intermission, he received a telephone call from a laughing Lil, who reminded him that diaper duty had prevented her from witnessing his three home runs for the Springfield Cardinals in 1941.

Musial began the nightcap with a walk against lefty Don Liddle amid boos from fans anxious to see Musial hit. The game had started with the lights on because of darkening skies. But Musial saw Liddle's fastball well enough in the third inning to drive it 410 feet into deep right center, where Willie Mays caught it in front of the bleachers, the longest ball Musial hit that day. In the fifth inning, with the Giants ahead, 8–3, Musial connected for his fourth home run with Schoendienst on base, this time on a slow curve against premier reliever Hoyt Wilhelm. With the Giants ahead by two, Musial clubbed number five off of Wilhelm's knuckler, a solo shot over the roof into right-center. In his last plate appearance against righty Larry Jansen in the ninth, an overeager Musial went after a bad pitch to pop up to the first baseman in a 10–7 loss.

Yet Musial left St. Louis fans with a thrill that they would never forget— a major-league record of five home runs in a doubleheader. The memory that lingers most for Giant rookie Bill Taylor was of the electronic

Budweiser Eagle at the top of the scoreboard that lit up and appeared to be flying after each home run. "It seemed like that damn bird" stayed lighted that day for "The Man," recalled Taylor.[21] In eight official at bats Musial had six hits and ten RBIs. Not until Nate Colbert of the San Diego Padres accomplished the feat on August 1, 1972, did a major leaguer again hit five home runs in a twin bill. No one has yet equaled Musial's record of twenty-one total bases for a doubleheader.

In the clubhouse after the game Musial held his mouth agape in disbelief when reporters informed him that not even the great Babe Ruth had hit five in one day. Musial came down to earth that evening, however, when he entered the living room of his home and his thirteen-year-old son greeted him with, "Gee, Dad, they must have been throwing you fat pitches today!"[22]

Musial also had an exceptional day at Ebbets Field in early August when he hammered two three-run homers in successive innings and then hit a sacrifice fly later on, the only time that he ever drove in seven runs in a game. With the Cardinals mired deep in the second division, he attempted to overcome a ten-point deficit for his seventh batting title. Over a five-game stretch he went seven for seventeen before running out of gas in the final two contests.

He ended the season with a .330 batting average, in third place behind Willie Mays's .347 and Duke Snider's .341. Playing almost always in the outfield, Musial led the league in doubles (41), tied for the league lead in runs scored (120), finished third in hits (195), and ended in the top five in several other hitting categories, including RBIs (126). His 35 home runs were good enough for seventh best. But given his phenomenal start, the season was personally disappointing. Part of the problem, as he later admitted, was that he too often swung for the fences, a replication of the 1949 season. Moreover, 1954 represented one of the hottest summers ever, and no major-league city had it worse than St. Louis. The thirty-three-year-old Musial wore down by playing in every game.

The Cardinals, meanwhile, finished in sixth place with a 72–82 record, twenty-five games behind the Giants. While the team led the league in hitting, it tied for fifth in pitching with a dismal ERA of 4.50, .001 from seventh place. After leading the club to its first losing season since 1938, Stanky entered the 1955 campaign on shaky ground.

---

21. Bill Taylor to Giglio, August 28, 1996, in possession of Giglio.
22. Stan Musial, "What I Tell My Boy about Baseball," *American Weekly Baltimore American,* August 15, 1954, clipping in Musial Collection, National Baseball Library.

As it turned out, the hot-tempered Stanky failed to survive the month of May. The team started slowly in a season Musial called "the big minus" because so many veterans performed disappointingly. Only the play of rookie third baseman Ken Boyer and center fielder Virdon provided hope for the future. The speedy Virdon replaced Musial in the outfield, with Musial once again moving to first base to fill a perennial hole. The unexpected death of longtime trainer Doc Weaver in May further punctuated the frustrating spring.

Musial's customary slow start contributed to the Cardinals' futility. In late April his batting average hovered around the .220 mark, which caused one fan to request, in Bob Burnes's "Bench Warmer" column in the *Globe-Democrat*, that Musial be traded for several talented players. Soon afterward, Musial went on a hitting binge, hitting six home runs and raising his batting average to .295 by mid-May. But even Musial's hitting could not stop the team's tailspin, which caused Busch to replace Stanky with Rochester manager Harry "The Hat" Walker. Under Walker's leadership, the team lost fourteen of its next nineteen contests. Musial continued to hit in June, raising his average to .313 on June 25. Four days later he slammed his twenty-five hundredth career hit, a home run, against Cincinnati's Rudy Minarcin in St. Louis. The goal of three thousand hits drove Musial even more when the team performed poorly.

By the All-Star break Musial's average had slipped to .298, but he had managed 65 RBIs on only 93 hits. Ted Kluszewski of Cincinnati had outpolled Musial at first base on the All-Star ballot, however, so Musial did not start in what became his record-setting twelfth All-Star game appearance, surpassing Mel Ott and Joe DiMaggio. The game took place at Milwaukee County Stadium on July 12, 1955; Musial made his first appearance as a pinch-hitter in the fourth inning with the American League leading 4–0. He then replaced Del Ennis in left field for the remainder of the game. He failed to hit until the twelfth inning. With the game tied 5–5, he told Yankee catcher Yogi Berra, an old friend from the Hill, that he was tiring after Berra himself had complained about catching extra-inning games. Musial then hit right-hander Frank Sullivan's pitch into the right-field bleachers. That home run—a record-setting fourth in All-Star competition—was by far the highlight of his 1955 season.

After the All-Star break Musial fell into an extended slump, which critics blamed on Walker's refusal to rest him occasionally. Musial's consecutive-game streak had surpassed 560 by early August when he was shifted to the outfield while Moon, merely adequate in the field, took over at first base. On August 10 Musial's regained stroke included a double off of Milwaukee's Lew Burdette, his one thousandth extra-base hit. He was only the eighth major leaguer to reach that standard; the seven before him were all Hall of Famers. The following day a Johnny Podres fastball struck Musial on the right hand, jeopardizing his consecutive-game streak. Musial started against the Dodgers the next evening, but he departed for a pinch-hitter in the second inning. His severely bruised hand had permitted him to play only a half inning in the following game, enough to preserve the streak.

Five days after Musial returned to the lineup full-time, he suffered an injury to his right elbow as a result of a misdirected pitch from Philadelphia's Ron Mrozinski. Playing with considerable pain, Musial resumed his hot hitting and raised his average to .313, twenty-four points behind league leader Richie Ashburn, with fourteen games to play. Musial, however, never came close to Ashburn's .338. He finished with a .319 average, tied for second with Mays, his lowest percentage since 1947. Yet it might have been even worse if Musial—who always believed he hit better as an outfielder—had not moved there in early August; from that point he hit at a .373 clip in forty-eight games. By playing in every contest, he extended his consecutive-game streak to 606. He also hit 33 home runs, seven of them in the right-field pavilion, which no longer contained the twenty-five-foot screen. That one-year change contributed to the club's record-setting 143 homers as well as the opposition's 185. Musial also drove in 108 runs and collected 30 doubles, but, for the first time since 1947, he failed to lead the league in any hitting category and for the first time since his 1942 rookie season he failed to score 100 runs.

With their seventh-place finish thirty and a half games behind the Dodgers, the 68–86 Cardinals had reached rock bottom for the 1950s. It was the worst team record since 1924 and the lowest-place finish since 1919. The club finished last in pitching with a pathetic 4.58 ERA. A desperate Busch consequently brought in Lane as the new general manager, who then hired former pitcher Fred Hutchinson to a two-year contract as manager.

The 1956 season promised to be considerably better. The club led the league during spring training with a 21–11 record, with Musial hitting .348. Stash, feeling better than he had in several years, predicted a seventh batting title with a hitting average between .340 and .350. Trader Lane had already listed him as one of the six "untradable" players—along with Schoendienst, Boyer, Virdon, Moon, and Haddix—as he began to shuffle personnel. He also announced that Musial would play in right field—the position he preferred.

The Redbirds opened the season at Crosley Field auspiciously enough. Musial homered in the ninth with Schoendienst aboard against Cincinnati's Joe Nuxhall for the win. By May 9 the Cardinals were on top of the league when Lane made some dubious—and disruptive—trades, which led to the departure of Haddix, Hemus, and Virdon. By June Lane would also swap Schoendienst, who was hitting .314, and sought to deal Musial. By that point Musial had undergone a batting slump but rebounded to .300 despite being bruised on the wrist and back by errant pitches.

That June he also had returned to first base after a fly ball had dropped in front of him. Hutchinson explained that Musial "doesn't cover the ground that he used to. He doesn't get the ball to the infield as quickly. I thought he would be better off at first base because we do need a first baseman."[23] Hutchinson's comments represented the first suggestion that age might be creeping up on the thirty-five-year-old Musial. Hutchinson also had moved Musial from third to fifth in the batting order because of the recent slump. The aforementioned moves wounded Musial deeply, more so than any previous slight in his major-league career. An Associated Press story even reported that he planned to retire at the end of the season, which Musial quickly denied. "How could anything in baseball make me unhappy?" he retorted. Moreover, he regarded the shift to first base as a challenge: "I like first base," he claimed; "I get a kick out of it." He also put the best face on losing Red Schoendienst, his longtime roommate, by suggesting that "I can see how the deal is going to help us."[24] As expected, Musial suppressed his feelings for the good of a slumping fifth-place ball club racked by dissension over Lane's recent trades.

Musial's selection as the Player of the Decade, announced on the eve of the All-Star contest, could not have come at a more opportune time, for it served as a transfusion for him. The *Sporting News* had nominated ten players from the 1946–1955 era and then asked 260 veteran players, club officials, umpires, writers, and sportscasters to make the selection. Musial's closest competition came from DiMaggio, Williams, and Feller. Probably the time frame, more than anything else, best served Musial, for the three other leading competitors had several of their most productive seasons prior to 1946, with Williams also losing the better part of two

23. Joan Flynn Dreyspool, "Conversation Piece: Subject: Stan Musial," 19.

24. Rawlings, *Musial Scrapbook*, 171; Musial, *Musial*, 179; Dreyspool, "Conversation Piece," 19; Lansche, *Stan "The Man,"* 144.

seasons to the Korean War. By the early 1950s they had passed their prime. That Musial remained the most personable of the superstars also probably helped him in the voting. In accepting the award, a grandfather clock, at the Touchdown Club in Washington, D.C., Musial humbly said, "I'm overwhelmed with the award because I can't pitch like Bob Feller, hit like Ted Williams, or field like Joe DiMaggio." Musial regarded the honor as second only to the Hall of Fame because of the tremendous competition. "I consider myself most fortunate," he wrote J. G. Taylor Spink of the *Sporting News*.[25]

One week later Republican U.S. Congressman John P. Saylor of Johnstown, Pennsylvania, included a tribute to Musial in the *Congressional Record* not only because of his greatness as a player but also because "he has remained the quiet, modest, humble, dignified, religious, refined, and sympathetic person that he was in the days of his boyhood in a small town of western Pennsylvania." To Saylor, Musial epitomized Cold War America's best—one who made it in a competitive system because of hard work, diligence, and sobriety. "America can use more men and boys of Stan Musial's caliber," Saylor intoned, "and if the rest of the world were so fortunate as to have a predominance of this type of character, the only defense programs would be those planned by opposing managers to stop Stan Musial."[26]

In Musial's thirteenth All-Star game appearance that week at Washington's Griffith Stadium, he played the entire game in the outfield. Boyer, Musial's teammate, was most responsible for the National League's 7–3 win, however, with his three hits and fine defensive play. Musial's most memorable moment came in the seventh inning just after the field announcer had publicly declared that Ted Williams's towering home run in the previous inning had tied Musial for the most four-baggers in All-Star competition. Seconds later Musial hit his fifth off of Boston right-hander Tom Brewer, inviting the correction from the press box, "Sorry, Mr. Musial has just untied the record."

Musial went on a modest hitting streak after the All-Star break to raise his average to .326 by mid-August, when he pulled a groin muscle. Then, in the midst of a slump, he had probably his worst game ever on the

25. J. G. Taylor Spink, "Musial Acclaimed Player of the Decade," *Sporting News*, July 11, 1956, clipping in Musial Collection, *Sporting News* Archives; Rawlings, *Musial Scrapbook*, 171; Stan Musial to J. G. Taylor Spink, July 11, 1956, Musial Collection, *Sporting News* Archives.

26. "Extension of Remarks of Hon. John P. Saylor," July 11, 1956, *Congressional Record*, A5478, copy in Musial Collection, *Sporting News* Archives.

twenty-second when he failed to hit in four at bats. His two errors—a dropped throw at first base and an errant throw to second base on a double-play ball—resulted in three unearned runs in a 5–3 loss to the Dodgers. For the first time ever, St. Louis fans booed Musial lustily. The next day cheers followed Musial's every plate appearance, giving credence to Lane's comment that fans would not forget fifteen years for one game. Meanwhile, the *Globe-Democrat* published a paid ad from supporters apologizing to Musial for the misbehavior of a few thoughtless spectators. Musial told reporters that he "never could get mad about anything in baseball, you know that." Yet he appreciated the public gesture of the fans.[27]

The Redbirds entered the final month of the season with nothing at stake but pride. They did have the satisfaction of bumping the Milwaukee Braves out of first place by winning two of three in the final series of the season, enabling the Dodgers to win the pennant. In the crucial second contest the Cardinals defeated Spahn, 2–1, after the left-hander had held them hitless for six innings. Musial scored the winning run in the twelfth inning after doubling to right-center.

Musial finished the campaign with his lowest Cardinal batting average yet, .310, eighteen points behind league leader Hank Aaron of the Braves. Given Aaron's modest figure, Musial let a seventh batting title elude him. No one explanation seemed adequate, given the June turmoil over the Schoendienst trade and his own near departure, the drain on a thirty-five-year-old of playing every contest to extend a consecutive-game streak to almost eight hundred, and the team's mediocre fourth-place performance, a modest eight-game improvement from the dismal 1955 season. On the plus side, Musial led the league in RBIs (109), tied for second in doubles (33), placed fourth in hits (184), and fifth in total bases (310). He also hit 27 home runs. His career total bases had reached 4,730, sixth best all-time among major leaguers.

As the 1957 season approached, Musial predicted no batting title. He remained confident, however, that he could play well for two more seasons. His major goals centered on winning another pennant and reaching the three thousand mark in career hits, only 219 safeties away. Of course, Musial was nearing several other career records, some of them unknown to him. He recognized that he could help the team more at first base, where his reduced quickness would not be a major consideration. An

27. Lansche, *Stan "The Man,"* 146.

outstanding first sacker when he played there regularly, he had performed ably at first in 1956.

In January Busch set the tone for the 1957 season at a fund-raising dinner in which Musial was the guest of honor. The gathering brought together five of the six Cardinals who had managed Musial—only Southworth could not attend. After announcing that Musial's uniform number six would be retired after he ended his career—the first Cardinal so honored— he suggested that Musial would win another batting title. He then signaled Lane that he expected a contender in the coming season or else. Soon afterward, he signed Musial for another one-year contract at eighty thousand dollars minus the five-thousand-dollar attendance bonus, which represented the first salary cut for Musial—perhaps another motivating tool of Busch's.

As it turned out, 1957 would be Musial's greatest season since 1951, and the team's second-place finish would be its best effort since 1949. For once the Cardinals received better pitching, with starters Larry Jackson and twenty-one-year-old Lindy McDaniel leading the way. The club also led the league in hitting, thanks to Musial, Alvin Dark, and Del Ennis, whom Lane obtained from the Phillies. Ennis proved particularly significant as a right-handed power hitter. He would hit 24 home runs and drive in 105 runs, three more than Musial. With Ennis and Boyer behind him in the batting order, Musial could expect to see more hittable pitches from right-handers. Moreover, Ennis and Musial became great friends and roommates, which made 1957 even more special.

Musial came to spring training well rested after he and Lil spent two weeks in the Bahamas. In camp he made some adjustments in his batting stance to combat the slider, a late-breaking pitch that posed as a fastball. He had attributed his decline in average in part to that pitch. Musial finished spring training with a .434 average and opened the season by going four for four in Cincinnati in a 13–4 win. On his last at bat, however, he injured muscles in his lower back, which would have prevented him from playing the following day if rain had not caused a cancellation, thus preserving Musial's consecutive-game streak. Because of a travel day that followed, trainer Bob Bauman had time to treat the injury with an ultra-sound device and whirlpool soakings. As a result, Musial was ready to play in the home opener.

Musial continued to hit in his finest start since 1950; three weeks into the season he was batting .406. The team, however, remained around the .500 mark into early June, performing like a second-division club before going on an eight-game winning streak that thrust it into contention. On June 12

Musial broke Pirate Gus Suhr's twenty-year-old National League record by playing in 823 consecutive games. Suhr wired his congratulations, indicating that he was "rooting for you to get 3,000 hits." That evening Lane presented Musial with a large cake with the inscription "Iron Man Stan," a nickname that recalled Musial's preteen years in Donora.

His record-shattering streak had not occurred without controversy, however. As a team player he had to address whether his performance could have been enhanced by sitting out the second game of doubleheaders and by resting during assorted injuries, questions that Cal Ripken, Jr., of the Baltimore Orioles would later have to face in breaking Lou Gehrig's major league consecutive-game stretch of 2,130. Even more embarrassing, National League president Warren C. Giles, a Musial admirer, had called consecutive-game streaks such as Musial's "phony" because they were preserved on technicalities. Rather than players merely making game appearances of an inning or less, Giles suggested that they must be actively involved in the competition. Faced with rare criticism, an irked Musial responded that Giles should not have used the word "phony" to describe his streak: "I don't think Giles meant anything serious," he proposed; "he happened to be trying to think of a word and was quoted that way."[28]

Four days after Musial had broken Suhr's streak, the Cardinals moved into second place after sweeping a doubleheader against the Dodgers. Musial hit his fifteenth homer soon afterward and carried a twenty-game hitting streak into the third week of June. By the All-Star break on July 8 the team had moved into first place with a 46–31 record and a two-and-a-half-game lead. St. Louis hosted the midseason classic amid a packed house of thirty-one thousand fans especially excited about the rare pennant race involving their ball club. In Musial's record-setting fourteenth appearance, he doubled in three plate appearances in a 6–5 loss for the National Leaguers.

Both Musial and the Cardinals began the second half of the season sluggishly as the team fell out of first place. On the advice of Hutchinson, a tiring Musial sat out the second half of a doubleheader on July 23, but since the game was suspended after eight innings because of a Sunday curfew, Musial's streak remained intact. By the end of the month, however, his average had fallen to .329. He dismissed suggestions that he was weary by going four for four with two home runs on August 1. His last four-bagger gave him 1,140 career extra-base hits, surpassing Cobb for second place.

28. Carl Lundquist, "Giles Raps 'Phony' Playing Streaks," *Sporting News*, December 12, 1956, clipping in Musial Collection, *Sporting News* Archives; Neal Russo, "Stan Doubts Giles Meant to Tab His Streak as 'Phony,'" ibid.

The next evening he had three more safeties in a victory over Philadelphia, the Cards' eighth straight, which elevated them to the top spot again.

Then the team inexplicably stopped hitting, while suffering a nine-game losing streak, their longest drought since 1950. The turnaround did not come until mid-August, largely on Musial's hitting, as he regained the batting lead. Against the Giants in New York, he homered for the twenty-seventh and twenty-eighth times in a doubleheader. The next day, his last game in the Polo Grounds because of the Giants' announced move to San Francisco for 1958, he again homered. Musial left the Big Apple with sadness, knowing that with the Giants and Dodgers on the West Coast the following year, he was leaving his most successful venues as well as the "fairest and smartest" fans he had ever known.

The series in Philadelphia preceded his final Brooklyn appearance. The team entered the "City of Brotherly Love" still in contention for the pennant. On August 23, with the Redbirds leading the Phillies, 6–2, Musial tried to hit behind a breaking Wally Moon, leaving first base, on a hit-and-run play. The outside-and-high curveball caused Musial to jerk his swing so unnaturally that he pulled his left arm out of its joint, fractured a bone in his shoulder socket, and tore muscles over his collarbone and shoulder blade. Afterward, he could not raise his arm to throw the ball. His consecutive-game streak officially ended at 895 the next evening, a blessing in disguise, Musial said one year later: "Everybody [had] wanted me to continue it, and naturally I wanted to keep it going . . . , but there were some years . . . when I felt I was getting down a little by playing all those games. If I could've taken a game off here and there, it probably would've helped me to hit better, and helped the club, too."[29]

Musial remained out of the lineup for fourteen games before his return on September 8. During that period the Cards won seven and lost seven, keeping them within striking distance of first-place Milwaukee. Even though he could not throw well, Musial found that he could still hit by shortening his swing. In that fashion he sprayed balls to all fields, and the Cardinals won thirteen out of seventeen games. They were only two and a half games out of first place by September 14. In a critical three-game set at Milwaukee beginning on the twenty-third, however, the Braves won the first contest 4–2 despite Musial's four hits, including two doubles. That game clinched the pennant for Milwaukee and sent the Cardinals into a tailspin. Musial sat out the last three contests while Hutchinson "looked

---

29. Lansche, *Stan "The Man,"* 151.

at some kids." Still, the team had played well enough to draw more than a million fans in Busch Stadium once again.

Musial claimed his seventh and final batting title with a .351 average, an increase of eleven points since his injury. Only Wagner's eight batting crowns kept Musial from establishing a league record. Musial also collected 29 home runs, 38 doubles, 102 RBIs, and 307 total bases and finished with a .612 slugging average, putting him among the league leaders in all of these categories. In October the *Sporting News* declared him the outstanding league player of the year. His final honor came in December when *Sports Illustrated* selected him as Sportsman of the Year, an award based on not only excellence of performance but also the "quality of . . . effort and the manner of . . . striving." Musial, the magazine concluded, must have been invented by Horatio Alger, Jr.[30]

Musial's sensational season—along with the Cardinals' 1,183,000 home attendance—resulted in his first salary increase in six years. The new general manager, Bing Devine, a thoughtful, quiet man of integrity who had emerged from the Cardinal system as a career executive, asked Musial in January what he had in mind for 1958. Musial responded that he wanted to be the highest-salaried National Leaguer ever. In the early 1950s Ralph Kiner of the Pirates had surpassed Musial with a ninety-thousand-dollar contract. "Der Bingle," as friends called him, quickly agreed to ninety-one thousand. Prior to the official signing, however, Devine called Musial into his office and said, "I've got pleasant news for you, Stan. Mr. Busch wants you not only to become the highest-salaried player in National League history, but the first to receive one hundred thousand dollars." That hike could probably be attributed to sportswriter Bob Broeg, who had suggested to Devine that the "old man" pay Musial an even one hundred thousand. Genuinely surprised, Musial called the contract "really wonderful" and added, "Baseball has rewarded me richly. The Cardinals always have treated me more than fair, this year in particular."[31]

A pumped-up Musial entered the '58 campaign determined to reach the three-thousand-hit pinnacle as soon as possible. Needing only forty-three safeties, he projected a May target date. He began the season as hot as he had left the last one despite going only one for five in the home opener against the Cubs. And even though the Cubs swept the Cards

30. Paul O'Neil, "Sportsman of the Year: Stan Musial," 20, 24.

31. Bob Broeg, "Stan at $100,000 on First Hike in 6 Years," *Sporting News*, February 5, 1958, clipping in Musial Collection, *Sporting News* Archives; Musial, *Musial*, 195; Broeg interview, February, 18, 1999.

four straight before losing at Wrigley Field, Musial hit three home runs in a three-game stretch, the first of which set a new National League career total base mark of 5,046, breaking Mel Ott's record.

Afterward, the Redbirds departed for their first Pacific Coast series. The Dodgers and Giants had migrated there after failing to replace antiquated ballparks suffering from poor locations and inadequate parking facilities. Ebbets Field, for example, had parking spaces for only seven hundred cars when automobiles were replacing trolleys and subways. West Coast travel meant air service, which the Cardinals had rarely used before. In spring training 1954, however, the team had embarked on the first transcontinental flight ever by a major-league team in order to play the Cubs in Los Angeles. In 1958 they opened their first series in San Francisco at Seals Stadium before a near-capacity crowd on April 20. Playing in a park that favored right-handed hitters because of the brisk breeze to left field, Musial concentrated on hitting in that direction. He went seven for eleven even though the Giants won two of the three contests. Ty Cobb, who witnessed one of the games, commented that Musial's "legs are holding up. There's no reason he couldn't play as long as I did."[32]

Against the Dodgers before more than sixty thousand fans in the Los Angeles Memorial Coliseum, Musial again concentrated on hitting to left and left-center field, a mere 250 and 310 feet from home plate, respectively, in contrast to 450 feet to right center. He lined four consecutive singles in that first-game loss, raising his average to .551. He proved to a complaining Duke Snider of the Dodgers that left-handers could hit in that ballpark. He went seven for eleven in the Los Angeles series, but the Cards entered a seven-game losing streak, falling into the National League cellar with a 3–10 mark. The team's problems included poor pitching and defense. Still, Devine commented, "As long as Stan Musial holds up, we've still got a chance to finish in the first division."

As Musial continued his torrid hitting into May, Biggie Garagnani optimistically anticipated that Stash would reach three thousand hits by Sunday, May 11, when the Cards ended their home stand with a doubleheader. Consequently, Biggie arranged to close the restaurant Sunday evening for a private celebration of about 350 of Stan's friends and family, including Senator Stuart Symington, Governor James T. Blair, Jr., and president Warren Giles of the National League. After going hitless in the preceding two contests, Musial finished with five hits in the Sunday doubleheader, leaving him two safeties shy of the mark. Yet the celebration, presided over

32. Musial, *Musial*, 197. Cobb played until he was forty-two years old.

by Joe Garagiola, Harry Caray, and Jack Buck, remained upbeat. Biggie's early comments had set the tone, "Why wait? He's gonna get the hits in the next day or two anyway. This way, all of his friends can be [here]." Musial, meanwhile, took a considerable ribbing for coming up short; he retorted that he wanted the party that night, prior to the road trip, so that Biggie would have to "foot" the bill.[33]

Afterward, along with Lil, the Frank Pizzicas of Donora, and other Musial friends, the team caught a midnight train to Chicago for a two-game series. In that first contest Musial doubled for his 2,999th hit. After the outing he told coach Terry Moore, his longtime friend, "You know, Tee, I hope we win tomorrow, but I'd like to walk every time up—and save the big one for St. Louis."[34] Moore relayed that comment to Hutchinson, who met with the coaches in the bar of the Knickerbocker Hotel before telephoning Musial that he was sitting out the next day unless he was needed as a pinch-hitter. Hutchinson then informed the press of that fact so that Musial could break the record in front of a hometown crowd. Hutchinson invited press criticism for not starting his best lineup.

On the afternoon of May 13, a crowd of less than six thousand saw Musial walk to the right-field bullpen just before the game to bask in the sun. He felt especially tired that day after going to bed at a quarter to three in the morning following a mix-up involving Frank Pizzica's wife, Molly, who was momentarily "lost" after going to the wrong hotel room. The Cardinals trailed, 3–1, in the sixth inning with one runner aboard and one out. At that point Hutchinson reluctantly called on Musial to hit for the pitcher. As Musial headed out of the bullpen, the crowd noise slowly began to build following the public address announcement, "Attention . . . number six . . . Stan Mus-i-al . . . batting for Sam Jones." Musial faced right-hander Moe Drabowsky, Polish by birth, who after a count of two balls and two strikes fired a curveball that approached the outside corner of the plate. Musial slapped it down the left-field line. By now fan noise had reached a deafening level as Harry Caray broadcast to Cardinal fans virtually everywhere, "Line drive! Into left field! Hit number three thousand! A run has scored! Musial around first, on his way to second with a double. Holy Cow! He came through!"

A grinning Hutchinson trotted to second base to congratulate Musial. Hutchinson's excitement momentarily affected his judgment, for he mistakenly removed Musial for a pinch-runner with the team one run behind.

33. Rawlings, *Musial Scrapbook,* 213.
34. Musial, *Musial,* 198.

As Musial ran off the field, with photographers trailing him, he went directly to Lil, seated in a box next to the Cardinal dugout, to hug and kiss her. After the game, which the Cardinals won, 5–3, a photographer asked, "Stan, do you know that blonde?" "I'd better," Musial laughed. "That's my wife."[35]

A carnival atmosphere prevailed for the remainder of the day—the animated clubhouse, Musial's reappearance on the field after the game to greet fans and respond to television, radio, and newsreel requests; the joyful bus ride to the Illinois Central depot on Michigan Avenue; and, above all, the train trip to St. Louis, which Musial called one of his best moments as a major leaguer. In the private car a steward presented him with a huge cake topped by the number "3000" in red frosting. Caray gave him diamond-set cuff links. Musial in turn presented winning pitcher Sam Jones with a bottle of champagne.

Following dinner the train entered the station in Clinton, Illinois, where about fifty people chanted, "We want Musial! We want Musial!" Stan appeared to sign autographs and shake hands. Fifty minutes later at Springfield, Illinois, more than one hundred greeted him, singing, "For He's a Jolly Good Fellow." Musial again signed and clasped hands. He then returned to the parlor car and promptly fell asleep with people laughing and talking around him. At that moment *Life* magazine writer W. C. Heinz asked Lil if Musial ever revealed any "nerves." "Never," she responded. "You know we have three children and sometimes if they do something wrong and he raises his voice just a little, they stand there with their mouths open, as if to say, 'Look at Daddy. What's the matter with Daddy?'"[36]

More than eight hundred greeted Musial at St. Louis's Union Station when the train arrived at 11:15 P.M.; some had waited for two hours. Musial went to the platform where he told the cheering fans, "I never realized that batting a little ball around could cause so much commotion. I know now how [aviator Charles] Lindbergh must have felt when he returned to St. Louis." "What did he hit?" shouted someone in the crowd.[37] Later he and Lil were at Stan Musial and Biggie's where he autographed menus and answered questions. At three in the morning he finally went to bed.

More honors came to Musial the next evening preceding the game at Busch Stadium, where Giles, Busch, and Devine praised Musial. Giles

35. Ibid., 201.
36. W. C. Heinz, "Now There Are Eight," *Life* (May 26, 1958), clipping in Musial Collection, National Baseball Library.
37. Musial, *Musial*, 202.

called him an "inspiration to our youth."[38] In his first at bat that evening Musial, greeted by a standing ovation, honored Cardinal fans by homering over the right-field pavilion for hit number 3,001. For the next month more ceremonies followed, the most important of which came on June 8 when the Cardinals honored the eight who had achieved three thousand hits, including the memories of the three now dead—Wagner, Eddie Collins, and Cap Anson. While age and illness also kept Cobb and Napoleon Lajoie from participating, Tris Speaker and Paul Waner, one of Musial's early idols, attended the private dinner Saturday night at the restaurant and the public ceremonies between games of the Sunday doubleheader. Musial and Lil received commemorative gifts from the club, teammates, Hutchinson, Giles, and others. Missouri Governor Blair, a friend, presented Musial with new state license plates—"3000," a number reserved for him in perpetuity.

The three-thousand-hit milestone obviously carried greater significance in Musial's day because of the select few who had accomplished it. The most recent to do it, Waner, had preceded Musial by sixteen years. World War II had obviously derailed Williams, DiMaggio, and a few others. To a lesser extent so, too, did the 154-game seasons, which prevailed until eight more contests were added in 1961. In the 1970s Aaron, Mays, Roberto Clemente, and Al Kaline reached the milestone in rapid succession, followed by several others in the 1980s and 1990s. In 1999–2000 alone three ballplayers achieved that mark.

The hype surrounding Musial's accomplishment probably contributed to a letdown as his hitting slackened considerably in the weeks ahead. So, too, would the team falter by early July after winning 20 out of 28 contests in June. At the All-Star break the Cardinals were still in second place, two and a half games behind Milwaukee. Musial's fifteenth All-Star appearance at Baltimore's Memorial Stadium on July 8 represented his last as a starter. Playing first base, he contributed one hit and scored a run in a 4–3 loss.

Afterward, the wheels fell off because of overall poor play. No one faded more than Ennis, the overachiever of 1957, who had only three home runs in 1958.[39] In an eight-game losing streak ending in early August, Musial went into a two for thirty-two drought, lowering his average to .335. He

38. "Remarks by Warren Giles," May 14, 1958, copy in Musial Collection, *Sporting News* Archives.

39. Ennis later claimed that his reduced playing time in 1958 was caused by his committing the cardinal sin—he had more RBIs than Musial in 1957. According to Ennis, "Fred Hutchinson told me, 'You know, you don't beat Musial.' Even Stan said

rallied for the next couple of weeks, surpassing Ashburn for the league lead at .341. But by early September Musial, suffering a pulled leg muscle that caused him to miss about a dozen games, was also plainly tired. No longer could he endure the second half of doubleheaders. Even day games that followed night play could be burdensome in the heat of August. By September 20 his average had slipped to .335 again.

Three days previously Busch had made the manager and most of his coaching staff responsible for the team's poor performance, firing Hutchinson and appointing coach Stan Hack interim skipper, much to Musial's regret because of his respect for Hutchinson. The team finished in a tie for fifth place, only three games from the bottom. Musial ended with a .337 average, nineteen points behind Ashburn. His 35 doubles were third best in the league. But his 472 at bats and 159 hits represented his lowest totals since his rookie season. His 62 RBIs were his worst total ever, and his 17 home runs were his fewest since 1946. Most troubling, he homered only once in the last two and a half months.

Musial's season had not yet ended, however. In late July Busch had committed the Cards to a postseason trip to Japan to compete in a series of games against that country's all-stars. A worn-out Musial wanted to stay home, but the Japanese made it clear that they had invited the team because of him. So, he and Lil, who was six months pregnant, made the trek and ultimately enjoyed it, largely because of the kindness of the hosts. Musial remembered it as "one unending whirl of parades, ball games, receptions, conducted tours, cocktail parties, dinners and entertainment."[40] But once the games began, it became all business for new manager Solly Hemus, who was determined to win them all. The Cardinals nearly did, capturing fourteen out of sixteen. Musial hit over .300 and slammed two home runs. On November 17 the entourage left Tokyo homeward bound.

On the long flight home Musial must have pondered the successes and disappointments of the past season. In his own mind the former probably far surpassed the latter. Now that he had fulfilled his greatest career goal in fewer seasons than his seven predecessors, he must have wondered what was left to achieve since the Cardinals seemed further away than ever from contending. He knew, however, that he wanted to continue to play because he loved the game too much to give it up. He had already

---

that I wouldn't play regularly the next year because I beat him." Danny Peary, ed., *We Played the Game: 65 Players Remember Baseball's Greatest Era, 1947–1964*, 356.

40. Musial, *Musial*, 204.

announced that he intended to perform as long as he could still hit .300. That he thought he could do for at least two more seasons. He might even win another batting crown to tie Wagner with eight National League titles. Always motivated by monumental long-range goals, he now set his sights on breaking Wagner's National League record of 3,430 career hits.[41] But would his love for the game and a newly imposed objective overcome a nearly thirty-eight-year-old body that had already shown signs of wear and tear? One thing he knew: Even though he retained his superstar status based on his 1958 performance, he would have to pace himself better in the years ahead.

41. *Sporting News*, May 21, 1958, clipping in Musial Collection, *Sporting News* Archives; *Chicago American*, May 14, 1958, clipping in Musial Collection, National Baseball Library.

Anatomy of a Superstar

To the many fans from the Midwest and the South who embraced the Cardinals, Musial's exploits emerged through the play-by-play broadcasts of colorful Harry Caray over KMOX, which carried the games into millions of homes. In that way did Musial become a hero to the teenage Mickey Mantle of Commerce, Oklahoma, Brooks Robinson of Little Rock, Arkansas, and, a decade later, William Jefferson Clinton of Hot Springs, Arkansas. Fans learned more about Musial by reading the national magazines and the sports section of their local newspapers. To still others lucky enough to see him play at Sportsman's Park or Busch Stadium and to obtain his autograph at the ballpark or at his restaurant, he became an even more gigantic hero. Few superstars of the Cold War era came as close to matching their heroic image as he did.

Musial's physical appearance contributed to that appealing persona. His stylish cropped, wavy black hair was combed straight back with a high part on the left side. Everything else about him suggested an extremely proud man who never forgot his humble roots. He dressed meticulously, leaning toward custom-tailored garments. His brother Ed could never recall Stan visiting him without wearing a sport coat, even in the heat of summer. A St. Louis neighbor remembered that Musial wore a different sport coat every time he saw the ballplayer. More frequently, particularly in St. Louis, Musial wore custom-tailored suits, featuring the stylish wide lapels of the time, always with a white handkerchief protruding from the breast pocket. His accessories included white shirts with french cuffs, carefully matched ties, and black shoes. His conservative dress suggested a successful lawyer or banker rather than a sports figure, particularly when photographs captured him emerging from his Cadillac, which he exchanged annually for the latest model.

The press reported that his taste in music was eclectic, ranging from the soft pop tunes of Bing Crosby and Perry Como to polka, rock-and-roll, country, and eventually bluegrass. In the Cardinal clubhouse, always a noisy environment, he accompanied tunes from the record player with a slide whistle or by beating drumsticks on the back of a metal chair. The latter activity not only relaxed him but also prepared him rhythmically to hit, an act that he thought required total relaxation and concentration. Musial spent more time reading while traveling. It was reported that he often read the *Wall Street Journal* to check on investments almost as much as he perused the sports pages. He preferred popular nonfiction magazines over fiction, but no indication exists that he was particularly well informed on the issues of the time. He and roomie Schoendienst rarely went to movies, preferring Broadway productions or musical programs when not lingering over a full-course meal at one of the premier restaurants.

While Musial enjoyed good food consumed at a leisurely pace, he ate only two meals a day—a late breakfast and dinner. He shunned desserts even when prepared by Lil, an accomplished cook, who fixed his favorite Polish dishes. The only exception came when Biggie Garagnani encouraged him in the winter of 1949 to consume éclairs to combat off-season weight loss stemming from agonizing over speeches he had committed himself to make, along with attending too many banquets characterized by unappealing dishes. In time Musial reduced his intake of sweets even more, heeding the advice of Hall of Famer Ty Cobb to eschew either sugar or cream in his coffee in order to maintain weight control. As a result, his weight remained around 175 pounds until late in his career, when he crept into the 180s.

Musial probably dreaded speaking engagements more than anyone imagined because he struggled with himself over what to say and how to express himself to the point of letting it affect his sleep. Never articulate, still somewhat shy and self-conscious because of his modest education and occasional stuttering, he nevertheless accepted invitations to speak as an obligation even if it meant altering prior activities. He soon found that people enjoyed listening to him because of his down-to-earth manner and his self-deprecating sense of humor. They even laughed with him when his joke-telling led to his guffaws just before delivering the punch line. Eventually he enlivened presentations by playing his harmonica. In time Musial found delivering speeches almost as natural as bashing a baseball.

Few at the time knew of Musial's minor vices. Smoking remained one as he alternated between cigars and cigarettes. The latter he consumed more frequently by the mid-1950s, when Hank Sauer, a heavy smoker, became his roommate. At first Musial, like so many sports stars, accepted endorsements from tobacco companies. Because ads featured him puffing a Chesterfield cigarette, Musial first faced public criticism from *St. Louis Globe-Democrat* sportswriter Robert Burnes in his "Bench Warmer" column in the spring of 1948. The usually friendly Burnes admonished Musial that "kids are natural imitators": they copied Musial's batting stance, they ran like Slaughter, and they adopted the same whiplike pitching style of Ewell Blackwell of the Cincinnati Reds. "So they're inclined to the belief," Burnes contended, "that if it is all right for a major league ballplayer to smoke, it's all right for them."[1] Musial took such criticism to heart, for he soon terminated his Chesterfield endorsements; the last one appeared in the *Sporting News* on April 19, 1950. Nor did he smoke in public, especially at the restaurant or outside the ballpark. To reduce his cigarette smoking, he stopped buying them, causing him to impose on teammates in the locker room. He always made ample restitution periodically, which only perpetuated the borrowing. Finally, he quit smoking cigarettes, with only occasional lapses. Afterward, he claimed that he saw the ball much better as a result. But he continued to consume miniature cigars in private, which he supposedly did not inhale.

He concealed his drinking even more. Never did he permit customers at the restaurant to see him imbibe alcoholic beverages. A modest drinker at first, he enjoyed a bottle of beer or two following a game to help him relax and to replenish the fluids. He later supplemented this with drinks at mealtime. Outfielder Del Ennis, his roommate in 1957 and 1958, claimed that "he could drink like a fish." "When he went out," according to Ennis, "he ordered scotch, not Budweiser [beer]. Then he'd get 3 or 4 hits the next day." Ennis said that he became Musial's banker and paid all the bills. After the road trip ended, "he'd peel off the $700-$800 he owed me."[2] Never, however, was there a reported instance of Musial stepping out of line as a result of imbibing. Nor is there any indication that his father's drinking problem might have had any impact on him one way or another.

No suggestion of womanizing existed either as he entered the crest of his career. An often reported story of the time retains more than the ring of truth. Told by Broeg and others, it involves Musial receiving a note from a headwaiter at one of the exclusive restaurants on the road. It suggested that an attractive lady wished to buy him a get-acquainted drink. Musial's response, to what became a repeated occurrence, varied little from city to city: "Please don't let it happen again. As for the lady, tell her I'm a happily married man with three children." That image of Musial still resonates with hundreds of former ballplayers who knew him well. According to one, even though "ballplayers are worse than

1. Lansche, *Stan "The Man,"* 94–95.
2. Peary, ed., *We Played the Game,* 356.

women when it comes to gossip . . . I never heard a bad word" about Musial going astray.[3]

Instead, he remained devoted to Lil and his children—Dick, Geraldine (Gerry), and Janet, born in 1950. Aside from hunting, weekly rounds of golf, in which he usually scored in the mid-80s, and personal appearances, he spent more of his off-season time with family. Countless contemporary stories featured Musial reading or playing games with his children. That activity sometimes extended to the kids in the neighborhood. A former neighbor remembers Musial and Schoendienst clearing a field for a Kiwanis-sponsored baseball diamond. They were like fathers to those kids, he recalled. Musial's love of children, shown in so many ways during the course of his career, remains, perhaps, his most endearing quality.[4]

At home Lil became the primary dispenser of discipline, however. Only rarely did Musial's children perturb him enough to draw a reaction. Daughter Gerry confirmed that her father could be a disciplinarian on occasion. He hated late sleepers, she remembered, particularly on the Sabbath; "we always had to go to early Mass on Sunday."[5] Indeed, the Musials, like so many Eastern European–American families of the time, stayed close to their faith. They became actively involved in St. Gabriel Parish in St. Louis Hills, a southwest suburb, where they built a seventy-five-thousand-dollar ranch house in 1956. And like 73 percent of children of Polish extraction, the attractive Musial clan attended parochial schools. Eventually the Musial daughters boarded at Villa Duchesne, a fashionable girls school, and son Dick prepped at Christian Brothers College, a Catholic military high school, where he starred in track and football as a running back along with future Cardinals star Mike Shannon, the quarterback. Shannon recalled that opponents loved to "kill" Musial's kid. In one intense encounter with bitter rival St. Louis University High School, Dick Musial ran for a touchdown, eliciting Shannon's shout to the opposition, "Do you want any more Musial?"[6]

The school principal invited Stan to become an active member of the Fathers' Club, the football booster organization. Musial gladly accepted on the condition that he not be singled out; "let me be there just as any

3. Broeg, "The Mystery of Stan Musial," 19; Frank Seward to Giglio, August 26, 1996, in possession of Giglio. The 1996 letters that follow are in Giglio's possession.

4. Dick Bush telephone interview, September 23, 1996.

5. Carew, "He's a 'Cardinal' Too!" 11.

6. "Musial: A Tribute." Produced by Thomas J. Ashley. Total Vision Post Corp, 1990.

other father," he insisted. And in that way he participated in some of the functions and attended many of the games. One of the proudest moments came when he overheard several teenage girls whispering, "Do you know who that is? That's Dick Musial's father."[7]

It nonetheless became sometimes difficult for both father and son to deal with the fact that Stan Musial was such a well-recognized superstar. Whatever Dick achieved in sports—or perhaps anywhere else—seemed to pale next to his father's accomplishments, a deflating circumstance for most sons of sports heroes. Most likely that consideration turned Dick away from baseball, despite initially enjoying it as a switch-hitting youngster who copied his father's batting stance. Soon, however, kids asked him why he couldn't hit like his dad. This came at a time when Stan, often on the road, could not work with him. So, Dick drifted away from baseball. How much this might have disappointed the father is unknown. While some claimed otherwise, former Cardinal owner Fred Saigh insisted that Musial "felt let down" that his son had no interest in playing baseball. An eighteen-year-old Dick Musial revealed his own feelings in a conversation with Bob Broeg in 1958 on the occasion of Stan reaching the three-thousand-hit pinnacle: "I'm proud of him but, you know, it is tough trying to follow him. I can't play baseball like that, but I can play football and run track and he can't do that."[8]

By 1958 Dick went to Notre Dame University as a pre-med major. Although offered an athletic scholarship, his father persuaded him not to accept it so that a needy student might have that opportunity. While this might have benefited someone else, it did nothing to enhance Dick's self-worth. He graduated in 1962 with a degree in economics and an ROTC commission. That November he married Sharon Kay Edgar while in the U.S. Army as a second lieutenant at Fort Riley, Kansas. Afterward, he returned to St. Louis with his family to work in his father's businesses, with mixed results.

Gerry, the Musials' oldest daughter, attended Marymount College in Arlington, Virginia, where she competed in field hockey. Following her debut in January 1964, she married Thomas Ashley of Detroit later that year in Washington, D.C. Ashley eventually worked for TV magnate Ted Turner of Atlanta. Janet, meanwhile, received an associate arts degree at

7. Robert L. Burnes, "Stan the Man," *St. Louis Globe-Democrat,* July 7, 1957. This was a special section devoted to Musial. Clipping in Musial Collection, *Sporting News* Archives.

8. Connor, ed., *Baseball for the Love of It,* 132; Fred Saigh interview, March 15, 1993; Broeg interview, February 18, 1999.

Mount Vernon College in Washington, D.C., and a bachelor of science degree from Maryville College. Afterward, she taught for the archdiocese of St. Louis. Her wedding to Dr. William Schwarge took place at the St. Louis Cathedral and the reception at Stan Musial and Biggie's. She continued to reside in St. Louis where her husband, an osteopath and cardiologist, practiced medicine. The Musials had one other daughter, Jean, born in 1958, who married David Edmonds of Richmond, Virginia, at the Church of the Annunziata in Ladue, outside of St. Louis, in May 1983. Stan Musial and Biggie's again hosted the reception.

Throughout these years Lil remained a housewife, assisted by a German cook and a housekeeper, making it difficult for Musial's overly active mother to remain with them, especially since she clashed with Lil over the management of the house. Mary returned to Donora where she lived above a store. Musial, realizing how this might appear, told sports journalist Roger Kahn, soon to visit Donora to do a Musial story in the mid-1950s, to exclude that information. "No matter how you write it," Musial related, "it is going to come out that my mother lives over a store."[9] Consequently, in the early 1960s Musial built a house for his mother on Second Street Extension, but he failed to persuade her not to take in laundry as a way to stay busy.

That Lil suffered her own frustrations as a homeward-bound housewife seems likely. Certainly a number of affluent upper-middle-class women did during the confining decade of the 1950s, when wives were extolled as helpmates of their husbands. Making matters worse, Stan was often gone—road trips in those years sometimes meant an absence of twenty days at a time. Too, other obligations existed that drew him away from home. Once the children were older they usually lived in boarding schools or at college. Contemporary newspaper accounts mentioned that Lil kept busy compiling a scrapbook for her husband, learning to drive an automobile, and cooking special dishes. She also sometimes participated in Lifebuoy soap, service station, and other endorsements and occasionally traveled with Stan to spring training. Stan's teammates attested to her reaching out to their families. Yet there was little else to occupy her mind and time. Known merely as Stan's wife, she was expected to provide the press with stories about Musial, which she always apparently did.

Being so subordinated to a superstar had its other frustrating moments. It meant constant interruptions at public places by autograph seekers, even while eating dinner, with Stan always graciously complying. On

9. Roger Kahn telephone interview, December 12, 1996.

one occasion, when fans mobbed the Musials outside the ballpark, Lil literally fell down. After getting back up, she shoved one individual, causing Musial to say later, "You shouldn't have done that. Those are my fans."[10] What she might have thought or said to Stan after that remark is unrecorded.

Lil's increasingly combative, terse personality, sharpened by an apparent drinking problem, probably kept the Musials out of St. Louis's two most exclusive country clubs—St. Louis Country Club and Old Warson in Ladue, which by 1968 bordered the Musials' new home. Warson was a "curmudgeon," according to broadcaster Jack Buck; "if he . . . did not like you, you wouldn't get in." Musial said nothing about the slight, Buck continued, but "he would remember this. . . . He would file it away."[11] Musial finally joined Sunset Country Club, founded by Gussie Busch, the Cardinals' owner, where he has played golf for more than thirty years.

The press in the 1950s, however, published little of substance about the private lives of celebrities and their families and virtually nothing regarding their peccadilloes. Musial thought of himself as more than a celebrity. Indeed, he remained a role model, especially to youngsters and fans in general. He—like many of his sports contemporaries—understood that the paying customer contributed to his salary. He felt an obligation not only to them and the ball club but to the community where he expected to remain after his playing days ended. Always aware of who he was, he remained grateful, too, that fate somehow had spared him from the mills of Donora and the bloodshed of war.

At the same time, he carefully protected his image as a sports hero. That explains both his aforementioned request to Kahn not to mention his mother's circumstances in Donora and his unwillingness to cooperate with Bob Broeg in the early 1950s on a biography that could reveal too much of his impoverished upbringing, which might reflect badly on his parents and thus on him. As he put it to Broeg, "Look, I don't know quite how to say this, but while my folks were poor, they were good to me. I don't want to do anything to hurt my family. I'm afraid that this would be embarrassing."[12]

Much more than most players, Musial felt an obligation to fans everywhere. Contemporary magazine pieces photographed him signing for

10. "Musial: A Tribute."
11. Wohlschlaeger interview, November 12, 1996; Vicki Johnson telephone interview, December 2, 1996; Broeg interview, February 18, 1999; Jack Buck interview, December 10, 1996.
12. Broeg, "The Mystery of Stan Musial," 51.

youngsters as he walked to and from the ballpark. He remained fair game on trains. While conversing with Kahn in the club car he honored a fan request "for my brother-in-law." He soon signed for everyone in the car. While seated for breakfast in the coffee shop with roommate Del Ennis at the Biltmore Hotel in New York, Musial, who was scanning the *New York Times*, heard a little boy's voice, "Could you gimme your autograph?" Musial put down the newspaper and then asked him for his name. When the lad replied, Gerry Coyle, Musial asked if it were Gerry with a "G." After writing a short note, he invited him to "get Mr. Ennis to sign, too." The boy said, "Nah, I don't want Ennis. Just you." Slightly embarrassed, Musial returned to the *Times* as Ennis forced a smile.[13]

In the next half hour a photographer requested a couple of pictures of Musial reading the sports pages while he ate. Musial good-naturedly grinned while turning away from the stock market section. By the time he started on his eggs a middle-aged stranger approached him to talk baseball and ask for an autograph. Six other interruptions transpired before Musial finished his breakfast. If annoyed by the activity, he did not show it.

As Musial and Ennis walked through the lobby and out the door afterward, they faced a swarm of youngsters between them and their taxicab. Once inside the taxi, Musial accommodated many of them by signing postcards from the open window. Soon the driver shouted, "Beat it you crazy kids. I oughta run you down." Still signing, Musial said, "All right fellas. Watch it now. We got to get going. Careful or you'll get hurt. Watch it. Watch the wheels. Come on, kids, careful."[14] No wonder Musial and Schoendienst usually chose restaurants carefully for dinner—partly to reduce the distractions.

Yet he and Red always took time to visit children's hospitals in Pittsburgh, Philadelphia, and other cities. Kahn remembered going with Musial to the children's ward in Donora. Schoendienst later commented that Musial "didn't want publicity for it and he didn't do it to seek recognition or humanitarian awards[;] he just did it because he thought it was the right thing to do and he enjoyed making other people happy."[15] Musial continued that commitment to children through his philanthropic activities in retirement.

Cardinal fans most remember Musial's kindness following the games at Sportsman's Park. One woman recalled that as a young girl she and

13. Kahn, "The Man: Stan Musial Is Baseball's No. 1 Citizen," 57, 55.
14. Ibid., 55.
15. Kahn to Giglio, December 6, 1996; Schoendienst, *Red*, 56.

her friends waited for the players, who parked across the street from the stadium, to depart from the dressing room. "Rarely did Stan not sign autographs," she recollected. "He accommodated as many as he could sometimes everyone. He had only one rule—let him get in his car . . . and sit down. He would then roll down his window and sign and chat away. Often Lil, Dick, and Janet were with him."[16]

Harry Caray remembered that on hot summer days when the temperature reached 110 degrees on the field and after failing to hit in a doubleheader, he remained "forever Stan the Man." Upon leaving the park, he faced more than a hundred kids, who gathered around his Cadillac waiting for autographs. They separated so that he could reach the door. From there he turned around and, leaning against the car, he signed for forty minutes to an hour until everyone was satisfied. Caray recalled that he "would always have a smile or a kind word."[17] Later in Los Angeles he sent the team bus ahead while he remained behind to sign autographs and then returned to the hotel in a cab. It was entirely fitting, then, that the *Saturday Evening Post* featured Musial on its May 1, 1954, cover, autographing scorecards for children at the Cardinals' ballpark. A *Post* executive presented an oil painting of that scene to Baseball Commissioner Ford Frick, who commented, "If I had to pick out the man who is most typical of the things baseball stands for . . . as an individual, performer, citizen and good guy—my candidate would be Stan Musial." Frick sent the painting to the Hall of Fame at Cooperstown, New York.[18]

Musial exhibited particular kindness to those who knew him before becoming a major leaguer. Old high school teammates could always expect royal treatment from Stash wherever he played. This applied also to others he casually knew from Donora. One Donoran acquaintance, on his honeymoon, ran into Musial at the Netherlands Hotel in Cincinnati. Musial and Schoendienst took him and his bride to breakfast and then drove them around the city the next morning. Another acquaintance, who knew Musial from his days with the Springfield Cardinals in 1941, visited him in the locker room at Sportsman's Park. That evening Musial escorted him and his military buddies to dinner on the Hill at a private club. After a delicious meal, punctuated by considerable conversation, Musial, because of the lateness of the hour, called a cab and paid the driver to take them

16. Sara Wands to Giglio, October 30, 1996.
17. Caray, *Holy Cow!* 115.
18. Gordie Windhorn to Giglio, September 3, 1996; *Sporting News*, September 1, 1954, clipping in Musial Collection, *Sporting News* Archives.

back to camp. And Musial never forgot old friends like the Dickie Kerrs. Whenever he was in the Houston area, he paid them a visit. Afterward, Mrs. Kerr always found a one-hundred-dollar bill under Musial's coffee saucer. When Dick passed away in 1963 in Musial's last year as a player, he missed games so that he and Lil could attend the funeral.[19]

Musial made as great an impact on those who shared the playing field with him. Umpires in particular respected Musial enormously for the way he conducted himself as a player. Known for his keen eye, which contributed to a low strikeout ratio even though he hit for power, he rarely complained about strike calls when at bat. Whenever he thought an umpire erred, he at most turned around and merely glared at him. This made John "Beans" Reardon feel worse than "tangling with Durocher." Bill Stewart remembered feeling bad after seeing that "hurt look in his eyes." More often than not, Musial showed remarkable grace when calls went against him. Reardon recalled making a strike call on a third-strike pitch just before the ball suddenly moved an inch out of the strike zone. Reardon confessed his mistake to Musial in his next at bat. Musial's response: "I thought it was a strike, Beans," not an unusual Musial response.[20]

Probably the incident that most defined the way he handled adverse calls occurred in a game against the Brooklyn Dodgers in St. Louis in the late '50s. With the Dodgers two runs up in the ninth inning and the Cardinals threatening with the bases loaded and two out, Musial hit an apparent home run off of lefty Jake Wade. But an instant before the pitch the third base umpire signaled time out after a baseball had rolled into fair territory from the Cardinals bullpen. This invoked a tremendous uproar from Redbird manager Solly Hemus and the Cardinal fans. Plate umpire Tom Gorman remembered that Hemus reacted like the umpires had "stuck a knife in his back." Both Hemus and third-base coach Peanuts Lowrey had protested so vehemently that they were ejected from the game, along with three or four others. The fans, too, were on the verge of rioting as police came out on the field. Meanwhile, Musial, not knowing the nature of the commotion while circling the bases, soon approached Gorman, saying, "Tom, what happened? It didn't count, huh?" Gorman told him

19. Emma Jean Lelik telephone interview, May 21, 1998; Jack H. Hartmann to Giglio, October 20, 1996; Larry Miggins, *The Secret of Power Hitting: How to Develop a Power Hitting System*, 91. Miggins's anecdote about Musial leaving one hundred dollars comes from Mrs. Kerr's neighbor. Larry Miggins telephone interview, May 20, 1999.

20. Larry R. Gerlach, *The Men in Blue: Conversations with Umpires*, 15; Graham, "The Cardinals' No. 6," 75; "Post Time" by Clark Nealon, clipping in Musial Collection, *Sporting News* Archives.

that time was called before Wade released the ball. "Well, Tom," Musial responded, "there's nothing you can do about it."[21]

Gorman recalled that, as Musial returned to the plate, he secretly rooted for him to get a hit. Musial did strike one off the center-field screen for a triple, winning the game for the Cardinals. Gorman was so elated, he said, that he could have kissed him. He had feared the fans' reaction if the Cardinals had lost. As for Musial, Gorman called him a gentleman, "in a class by himself."[22]

No umpire, in fact, ever threw Musial out of a game in his twenty-two years as a major leaguer, a record probably still unequaled. There were a few instances—four to be exact—where Musial nearly faced ejection, however. One occurred in 1952 against the Cincinnati Reds when Musial hit a grounder he thought foul by a foot down the first-base line. He had stopped running by the time the first baseman had caught the ball and stepped on the bag. When umpire Lon Warneke called him out, Musial approached him to argue the call, unaware that the bat was still in his hand. That seemingly threatening gesture alone must have angered Warneke. Musial then shouted, "Just because one umpire blows one, you don't have to do it," a reference to an earlier "bad" call. Al Brazle saved Musial by running out of the dugout and shoving Musial out of the way before letting Warneke verbally have it, which resulted in Brazle's ejection.

Another close call developed in the aforementioned Les Webber incident in 1942 when Musial charged the Dodger right-hander after he twice threw at him. As Webber also approached Musial, several players and the umpires came in between the two. The umpires later told Musial that if a punch had been thrown, they both would have been ejected. The third incident came on the home opener in 1957, after a Musial glare following a third-strike call. This had followed another "questionable" strikeout in his first at bat. As Musial returned to the bench, Ennis, in the on deck circle, told him, "Don't turn around, Stan, just keep walking." Frank Dascoli, with his mask off, had stared at him until he reached the dugout. This episode had puzzled Musial because Dascoli had been a great admirer, one who had enjoyed kidding with him. Not until Dascoli retired in the mid-1960s was Musial aware that the otherwise capable umpire had sought to be the first to eject Musial from a game.

The least serious of the four incidents involved umpire George Barr, in the twilight of his career, who was calling a terrible game behind the

21. Tomas D. Gorman as told to Jerome Holtzman, *Three and Two*, 98–100.
22. Ibid., 100.

plate around 1950. Late in the contest he called a strike on a pitch that Musial thought a foot outside and nearly on the ground. Musial wheeled around and said, "George, that was a terrible call, the worst you've made today." Barr, quickly removing his mask, responded in a high, shrill voice, "Goodness gracious, Stanley, I thought it was a good pitch." Barr's reply caused Musial to burst into laughter and then say, "Aw, forget it, George." That Musial would even classify this a potential ejection is indicative of how little difficulty he had with the men in blue.[23]

In the end they showed him exceptional courtesy on the field. Following his three thousandth hit, Dascoli, umpiring at third base, recovered the ball, presented it to Musial on second base, and smilingly congratulated him. Al Barlick insisted on being behind the plate for Musial's last game in 1963. On another occasion, when the public address announcer revealed that Musial had set another record, Barlick called time, removed his mask, and shook Musial's hand, which aroused the objections of some purists. Barlick replied that "Stan's a great ball player and my good friend. I'm entitled to congratulate him like anybody else." Third-base umpire Jocko Conlan once got so carried away when Musial came into the bag with a triple that he said, "Stan, you're a pretty good hitter." Musial smiled while saying, "I guess I am." In his autobiography Conlon concluded that "there was never a nicer fellow than Musial," a viewpoint that virtually every umpire shared.[24] They were responding not only to his conduct on the field, but also to Musial's contention that umpires belonged in the players' pension plan, a belief that most major leaguers did not share. Did their admiration affect the way they called balls and strikes when Musial was at bat? Only a few players made that suggestion, an assertion directed against all outstanding hitters, with some validity.

Musial made his greatest impact on fellow players. To them, almost without exception, he personified the very essence of a sports hero—arguably the most liked superstar of his era. Through his conduct in the clubhouse and on the field, he elevated the standards of many performers, who modeled themselves after him. To this day many treasure that association; an autographed portrait of him still exists on the walls of their dens or family rooms.

23. The four "close calls" can be found in Robert L. Burnes, "Stan the Man's Four Brushes with Ejection," July 16, 1983, clipping in Musial Collection, National Baseball Library.

24. John B. "Jocko" Conlan and Robert Creamer, *Jocko*, 194, 132, 222–23. See also Musial, *Musial*, 200; Burnes, "Stan the Man's Four Brushes with Ejection."

Part of that acclaim related to Musial just being himself. Naturally upbeat and cheerful, he grinned profusely. When a newspaperman asked him why he always smiled, he joked, "If you were me, wouldn't you be smiling?" Gratitude for his good fortune came in part from a deep love of baseball, which he wore on his sleeve, and it was contagious to teammates and opponents alike. In completing the player personnel form, required of all major leaguers, he responded to the question, "If you had it all to do over, would you play professional baseball?" by writing, "Yes for nothing."[25] Indeed, although he played with tremendous fire, he had more fun doing it than anyone can imagine.

Musial mirrored the character qualities that Americans had traditionally associated with heroic figures. He retained a modest personality who handled fame with self-deprecating humor and grace. Usually playing down his accomplishments, he acknowledged others for his success. Moreover, he never made disparaging distinctions relating to class or race, an enduring virtue shared by most past heroes. Musial essentially treated everyone the same from presidents to the most lowly. Down-to-earth and direct, he spoke the same way to one and all. As one player put it, he was "warm to a nobody like me." His love of children also endeared him to fellow major leaguers and conformed to values Americans hold most dear. One National League pitcher, on an off day, had his five-year-old son with him, whom Musial proceeded to carry on his shoulders for much of the time. Another National Leaguer remembered Musial dancing with his twelve-year-old daughter at the Warwick Hotel in Philadelphia, a thrill she would never forget.[26]

25. Donald Honig, *Baseball in the '50s: A Decade of Transition. An Illustrated History*, 7. Stan Musial questionnaire furnished by Richard Topp, former Society for Baseball Research president.

26. Scholars who write about heroes, sports ones or otherwise, make distinctions between celebrities—people who are merely well known—and heroes, that is, performers of great deeds. The latter have not only withstood the test of time but symbolize the highest ideals of society. Such standards do not require that they be without flaws, however. The literature on American heroes includes Dixon Wector's *The Hero in America* (New York: Charles Scribner's Sons, 1941), chaps. 1 and 18; Nick Trujillo, "The Meaning of Nolan Ryan," *Cooperstown Symposium on Baseball and the American Culture*, edited by Alvin L. Hall (Westport, Conn.: Meckler in association with the State University of New York at Oneonta, 1991), 123–36; and especially the "Where Have Our Heroes Gone?" chapter in Benjamin G. Rader, *In Its Own Image: How Baseball Has Transformed Sports*, 175–95. Rodney Miller to Giglio, September 28, 1996; Denny Lemaster to Giglio, September 23, 1996; Bubba Church to Giglio, August 29, 1996.

Musial worked hard at self-improvement. He cultivated a strong loyalty to the Cardinals and to the St. Louis community, where he engaged in innumerable charitable activities. He had matured from the time that Breadon's cheapness had nearly driven him to Mexico. He became even more selfless in undertaking obligations that he thought came with being a major leaguer. One ballplayer even contended that he might have been "too kind" as that "took away from his family."[27]

The players who most appreciated Musial, of course, were his teammates. Unlike other greats of that era who haughtily stood apart, Musial seemed a breath of fresh air. He reached out to everyone on the club; his manner of greeting them included a "Hey what da ya say, what da ya say, what da ya say," punctuated with a grin. Second baseman Julian Javier became so taken with Musial that he named his son, Stan, a future major leaguer, after him. Musial especially made rookies and marginal players feel at home by treating them as equals. Grant Dunlap, a Card rookie in 1953, recalled that Musial, during spring training, offered him the use of his Cadillac. "I was a nobody," Dunlap wrote, but "he went out of his way to be friendly." Pete Castiglone claimed that, when traded to the Cardinals that same year, Musial often drove him to the home games. Years later Castiglone remained astonished that a superstar would be so considerate. In his brief stay with the Redbirds, Bob Kennedy also felt touched by Musial's kindness. After picking up Kennedy for a round of golf, Musial had to stop at his restaurant momentarily to handle a business matter. He returned to the car and handed Kennedy a steak sandwich, saying, "This is your lunch."[28]

On the road Musial customarily invited young teammates to dinner. Sitting by himself in the hotel lobby, rookie Alex Grammas gladly accepted such an invitation. On another occasion Musial took him to dinner in San Francisco, where Grammas particularly felt alone. "He never forgot how tough it could be on a youngster trying to make his mark," Grammas later commented. Solly Hemus, a rookie in 1949 making twenty-five hundred dollars a year, gratefully embraced Musial's invitation to see a Broadway play on his first trip to New York City. Those who joined Musial, Schoendienst, and others sometimes had to expect some good-natured

27. Bob Kennedy to Giglio, August 23, 1996.
28. Jim Beauchamp to Giglio, October 18, 1996; David Halberstam, *October 1964*, 370; Grant Dunlap to Giglio, August 31, 1996; Pete Castiglone to Giglio, August 27, 1996; Kennedy to Giglio, August 23, 1996.

ribbing, however. Carl Warwick, in his 1961 rookie season, went to Toots Shor's, one of New York's most exclusive restaurants, on Musial's and Schoendienst's invitation as they passed through the hotel lobby. At that time Warwick was struggling financially, giving half of his ten-dollar-a-day meal money to his wife. Consequently, Musial momentarily shocked Warwick when he told the rookie that his part of the bill was eighty dollars. Musial then paused before confessing that the check said complimentary. At that point everybody at the table broke out in laughter.[29]

Musial also always shared with teammates the various samples—hair oil, shaving cream, cigarettes—that he received from companies seeking endorsements. In other ways he tried to "spread the wealth" around. Grammas recalled overhearing a conversation between Happy Felton and Musial following a game at Ebbets Field. The *Happy Felton Radio Show*, which provided the star of the game with a cash honorarium, once again sought to interview Musial, who told the host, "O.K. I'll do it tonight but from now on get the other fellows." Musial understood, Grammas contended, that others needed the extra money more than he did. According to Hank Sauer, Musial often used the remuneration he received for postgame interviews to buy dinner for himself, Sauer, and a "couple of young kids he'd invite along."[30]

In the clubhouse he avoided most card games because of his high salary; his winning, he believed, no matter how little, would take away from those who needed it more. Only later in his career did he relax that prohibition when it came to low-stakes poker, a game that personified Musial's good fortune. Not known as a particularly skillful player, he nevertheless had an uncanny knack of filling an inside straight. In amazement, catcher Tim McCarver called him "one of God's chosen few."[31]

Despite his considerable fame, Musial showed his humanity to teammates in ways that a DiMaggio or a Williams would probably have

29. Larry Moffi, *This Side of Cooperstown: An Oral History of Major League Baseball in the 1950s*, 153; Alex Grammas to Giglio, September 12, 1996; Solly Hemus to Giglio, August 26, 1996; Carl Warwick to Giglio, September 6, 1996. On countless occasions, Musial's social kindness extended to players on other teams. For example, while in New York City, Ray Cone of the Milwaukee Braves and his wife went into the lounge of the Roosevelt Hotel. The waiter came over and told them that two gentlemen wished to buy them a drink: "We looked around and there was Stan and Red Schoendienst. We were just youngsters at the time and it was a typical nice gesture on their part." Ray Cone to Giglio, September 9, 1996.

30. Grammas to Giglio, September 12, 1996; Peary, ed., *We Played the Game*, 322.

31. Tim McCarver to Giglio, September 2, 1996. Musial usually made light of his high salary. Teammate Hal White remembered Musial opening his pay envelope and commenting, "Gosh, that's all I get is money." Hal White to Giglio, August 28, 1996.

found objectionable. When rookie Ed Mickelson confided how anxious he became before a game, Musial consoled that he, too, felt nervous, and that when a player no longer felt that way "it is probably time to quit."[32] Mickelson later related how comforting that conversation was to him. More than confessing human frailties, Musial occasionally permitted himself to be the brunt of a practical joke, suggesting that he could take it as well as give it out. Bob Stephenson, a rookie in 1955, recalled a pregame incident in the Ebbets Field locker room involving three or four Cardinal players, including Musial, all of whom had arrived several hours early. Dressed in knee-length jockey shorts, two of them were engaged in a contest in which one had rolled a game program into a cone, which he inserted in the elastic top of his shorts. He then closed his eyes, tilted his head backward, and then, putting a quarter on his forehead, sought to drop the coin into the program. At that point Musial accepted a bet of a dollar that he could do it in three tries. As Musial closed his eyes and bent his head backward, a player poured ice-cold Coca-Cola into the folded program, which produced a huge stain on Musial's shorts. "Stan thought it hilarious," according to Stephenson, who added, "I have a hard time visualizing today's pampered millionaires taking such pranks in good grace." Musial also good-naturedly accepted the teasing that followed his radio interviews in which he overused the word "wonderful," or "wunerful," as he pronounced it.[33]

Aside from a few jealous malcontents, Musial endeared himself to teammates. He was "Stash" to most of them, warm, caring, cheerful—one who expressed neither anger nor profanity in the locker room. A clique dissolver, he represented the glue that held the team together, not only by his performances on the field but also by his conduct off of it. McCarver later said it best: "He tried to lead by example. He wasn't much of a talker, a special pleader, or a clubhouse lawyer. He was just a good man."[34]

Others around the league shared the same sentiments. Johnny Van Cuyk of the Dodgers later expressed what hundreds of others have since acknowledged: "I never knew him to have an enemy. Everybody loved him. He was a big man among men." Dodger pitcher Rex Barney called him "a saint of a man, one of God's chosen people. . . . He was the most popular player with guys from other clubs." He particularly left his mark

32. Ed Mickelson to Giglio, October 7, 1996.

33. Bob Stephenson to Giglio, September 11, 1996; Don Ferrarese to Giglio, August 29, 1996.

34. Tim McCarver with Ray Robinson, *Oh, Baby, I Love It!* 17.

among rookies and journeymen because he learned their names and said something supportive to them despite the nonfraternization rule of the time. Jerry Kindall of the Cubs remembered that, after his first major league hit, first baseman Musial not only warmly congratulated him but also offered to retrieve the ball as a memento. He then said, "There will be a lot more hits for you, kid. Keep swinging." Musial astounded Cubs rookie second baseman Wayne Terwilliger by saying "Hi Wayne" as he ran in from his outfield position. He also impressed catcher Jim Mangan of the Pirates when he inquired, "I haven't seen you before." When Mangan responded that this was his first game, Musial then said, "I want to wish you a lot of luck." "I have never forgotten that moment," Mangan later recounted.[35]

Musial especially went out of his way to greet opposing players before the game. He approached rookie Gail Harris of the Giants as he prepared to take batting practice in Sportsman's Park, saying, "Hi, I'm Stan Musial. Welcome to the Major Leagues. I hope you have much success."[36] Al Neiger of the Cubs recalled Musial waiting to talk to all the visiting players at Sportsman's Park while they passed through the home team dugout, which they had to do to reach the visiting-team facility. He remained accessible in the pregame warmups. In his last years visiting players unabashedly asked him to pose with them for photographs or to sign a baseball. Friendly banter would always follow this ritual. Earl Averill of the Phillies recalled that he even provided opponents with his personal bats whenever asked. He also acknowledged opposing pitchers for their recent performances, congratulating Vern Law of the Pirates for an eighteen-inning outing against the Milwaukee Braves or kidding Taylor Phillips of the Reds for surrendering a game-winning homer to him on the preceding day. "Lefty, that was a dirty trick I played on you yesterday," he told Phillips, "but that is why they pay me sixty thousand dollars per year."[37]

Musial had a particular fondness for players who came from his "neck of the woods." Revealingly, he knew not only the names of most major leaguers, but also something about their backgrounds. At first base he once

35. Johnny Van Cuyk to Giglio, September 12, 1996; Jerry Kindall to Giglio, August 26, 1996; Wayne Terwilliger to Giglio, August 30, 1996; Rex Barney with Norman L. Macht, *Rex Barney: Thank Youuuu for 50 Years in Baseball from Brooklyn to Baltimore*, 163; Jim Mangan to Giglio, September 4, 1996.

36. Gail Harris to Giglio, August 27, 1996.

37. Al Neiger to Giglio, September 30, 1996; Earl Averill to Giglio, August 27, 1996; Vern Law to Giglio, September 3, 1996; Taylor Phillips to Giglio, September 20, 1996.

greeted rookie (and future manager) Chuck Tanner of the Pirates, who had singled, by commenting, "Hey, Chuck, I lived near you." Tanner was born in New Castle, Pennsylvania. He also sent the Cardinals' clubhouse man over to the Pirate clubhouse to get Ron Necciai, a struggling first-year pitcher from Monongahela, Pennsylvania, just two miles from Donora. Musial wanted to encourage him and wish him well. "He was then and still is my idea of what a great person is," Necciai later related.[38]

Stash also inspired Polish American players, who took great pride in his success. Later Eddie Basinki of the Dodgers, for one, proudly related how his Polish upbringing in industrial Buffalo mirrored Musial's in western Pennsylvania. Musial's reaching out to Polish American players made him even more their hero. This occurred at a time when ethnic identification was receding in the midst of Cold War assimilation and nationalism. Even though Polish American athletes had never faced the stereotypical media slurs that once plagued Jewish American and Italian American players such as Hank Greenberg and Joe DiMaggio, they still suffered the brunt of "dumb Polack" jokes, which Musial deflected by his entrepreneurial accomplishments and by his own brand of Polish humor. The latter included a raised clenched fist followed by the question: "Do you know what this is? This is a Polish joke stopper."[39]

Musial most revealed himself in the unique way that he competed on the ball diamond. One side of him suggested a caring, relaxed, fun-loving, and friendly sort, who so enjoyed the game that he rarely showed anger or frustration, an indication that he refused to let the "little kid in him die" as former major leaguer Nellie King described it.[40] This persona concealed a fierce competitiveness that drove him relentlessly to excel. Stories abound of his multifaceted approach to the game, including gentle teasing. When Musial doubled off of Orlando Peña's illegal spitter, for example, he whistled at the Reds pitcher and then placed his index and middle fingers over his mouth, signifying that he had hit his best pitch. Pitcher Jack Brewer of the New York Giants related how Musial's vicious line drive had nearly "de-horned" him before Whitey Lockman caught it

38. Chuck Tanner to Giglio, August 24, 1996; Ron Necciai to Giglio, December 17, 1996.

39. Basinski to Giglio, September 5, 1996; also Stan Lopata to Giglio, September 13, 1996; Ed Sanicki to Giglio, September 9, 1996; Mrs. Dan Lewandowski to Giglio, September 25, 1996; James Michener telephone interview, September 15, 1997. For the ethnic stereotyping that once plagued Greenberg and DiMaggio, see G. Edward White, *Creating the National Pastime: Baseball Transforms Itself, 1903–1953,* 249–73.

40. Nellie King to Giglio, September 14, 1996.

in deep center field. As Musial trotted to the dugout he smiled at Brewer and said, "Don't forget to duck kid." On the occasion that he did hit pitcher Frank Hoerst of the Phillies, Musial sought him out immediately after the game and then checked on him at the hotel.

Larry Bearnath of the New York Mets, meanwhile, revealed the looseness that characterized the Musial-led Cardinals. With Bearnath on second base, a Met skied a short fly ball to left field, causing shortstop Dick Groat to run backward for it and Musial to race inward. After Stash called for the catch, Groat abruptly turned away and yelled, "Don't get hit on the head, you old goat." Musial made the play, and they then both laughed all the way to the dugout. Bearnath recalled with envy the "brashness of Groat, the looseness of Musial, the fun they were having," which "made quite an impression on a rookie."[41]

Musial's fun-loving spirit and his competitive fire came together most clearly in his duels with Hall of Famer Warren Spahn. Over his career, Musial hit .314 against Spahn. Yet this belies the intensity that went into that personal war between the two. Musial, Ennis related, usually raised three fingers at Spahn as he entered into his stance, meaning that he intended to get three hits that day. Spahn laughed and said, "Yeah?" He then sent Musial on his back with a high, tight pitch.[42] In one Milwaukee matchup, after Spahn threw at him, Musial said something and laughed. He then lined the next pitch into Spahn's stomach; as he ran to first base he made some comment and laughed again. Pitcher Claude Raymond of the Braves, who witnessed the event, recalled that Spahn then removed his hat and bowed. Spahn never found Musial's weakness even after having two strikes on him. On one occasion when he sidearmed him, which he rarely did, he struck him out. But the next time up, again on a two-strike count, Musial hit Spahn's sidearm delivery on the roof of Sportsman's Park. After the inning ended Spahn came to the dugout and said, "Forget it."[43]

The enormous pride that Musial exhibited in his competition with Spahn and other National League greats manifested itself in other ways. He did not like to be embarrassed on the field, and he reacted accordingly. In one such rare instance, pitcher Stan Williams of the Dodgers, hurling in St. Louis with the bases loaded, caught Musial napping at second base with a "sneaky pick-off play." The next day Musial said to Williams,

41. Orlando Peña to Giglio, September 16, 1996; Jack Brewer to Giglio, August 24, 1996; Frank Hoerst, August 28, 1996; Larry Bearnarth to Giglio, August 24, 1996.

42. Peary, ed., We Played the Game, 356.

43. Claude Raymond to Giglio, September 23, 1996; Tanner to Giglio, August 24, 1996.

"Please don't ever embarrass me like that again—especially in St. Louis." Williams later commented that it was like humiliating "the Pope."[44]

That same pride caused Musial to frown upon contrived publicity stunts that weakened the integrity of the game. One such example occurred on the last game of the 1952 season when manager Eddie Stanky announced in the morning press that Musial would pitch that day, a decision that Musial reluctantly accepted. This came right after he had clinched the batting title against runner-up Frank Baumholtz of the Cubs, the first batter that day to face Musial. Baumholtz remembered how surprised he was to see Musial coming in from center field to warm up in place of scheduled pitcher Harvey Haddix, who replaced Musial in center. Manager Phil Cavaretta told Baumholtz, "They're trying to make a fool of you, Frank." But Baumholtz correctly assessed it as a gimmick to draw more people to the ballpark. For the first time ever he decided to bat right-handed. Musial threw only one pitch, which Baumholtz hit so hard that it ricocheted off of third baseman Hemus's shin to the left-field corner. Baumholtz ended up at second base with a double, he thought, before the official scorer ruled it an error. That was the only batter Musial faced. At the end of the inning Musial called the official scorer in the press box to complain that "if I ever saw a hit in my life, that was a base hit." Nonetheless, the error stood. Embarrassed by the episode, Musial later contended that he was "not proud of that circus." Never again did Musial put himself in that position. As for Baumholtz, to this day he has an eight-by-twelve photograph of Musial in his living room.[45]

Of the many emotions Musial exhibited on the diamond, anger represented the least of them. The person most likely to provoke it continued to be Durocher, who made the Giants a perennial power in the 1950s. That fact usually inspired Musial to perform spectacularly against them, as he had against the Durocher-led Dodger teams of the 1940s. Consequently, Durocher instructed his pitchers to throw at Musial with regularity. Jack Buck remembered seeing Musial on the training table with black and blue marks on his back and neck from pitched balls. Many of the bruises resulted from Durocher-directed hits.

Rarely did Musial display emotion after being forced to the turf. He either trotted to first base or dug in for the next pitch. When one rookie flattened him, Musial informed him afterward that "he knew that the skin

---

44. Stan Williams to Giglio, August 27, 1996.
45. Peary, ed., *We Played the Game*, 184; Musial, *Musial*, 153; Frank Baumholtz to Giglio, September 24, 1996.

head (Durocher) told [him] to do it." Moreover, to express forgiveness, he suggested that when the rookie came to St. Louis the steak would be on him.[46] Musial again showed remarkable restraint when Durocher ordered Monte Kennedy to hit him in the kneecaps the day after Musial hit five home runs in that aforementioned doubleheader in 1954. With a five-hundred-dollar fine over his head if he failed, he futilely drove Musial to the ground on the first three pitches. Thinking home run, Musial braced himself for a fastball over the middle of the plate on the next pitch. Instead, Kennedy hit him in the leg and then turned to the Giant dugout, shouting, "I got him! I got him!" As Musial jogged to first base he stared at Durocher but never said a word. After the game Musial said, "You told him to do that, Leo." The reply: "Yeah, I did and tomorrow will be the same thing. . . . Do you think we're going to let you take the bread right out of our mouth? . . . And if you keep hitting the way you are against us, you can expect that every time we meet."[47]

On rare occasions, Durocher could provoke Musial into action, beginning with the Les Webber affair in 1942. Such was also the case in 1954 when Musial could hear Durocher yelling to Windy McCall to hit him on the red number six, which he did. Musial afterward told the Cardinal pitcher, "First guy that comes up, hit him." That person happened to be future Hall of Famer Willie Mays. The initial pitch sailed way over Mays's head. So, Musial went over from first base to say, "You've got to hit him. We can't let them get away with what they're doing to us." The next pitch again went over Mays's head. Then Mays hit a home run that beat the Redbirds. "That was the only time I ever really got on a pitcher on my own team," Musial recollected.[48] He neglected to say that he, too, homered in that game in his next at bat, which represented a more typical Musial response to a beaning.

Tim McCarver recalled another clash when Durocher later coached the Los Angeles Dodgers near the end of Musial's career. In a game in which the Dodgers raced to a 9–1 lead, Durocher, rubbing it in, waved his arms obnoxiously and shouted obscenities at the Cardinals dugout. Musial, who usually took such things in stride, became so fed up that he came to the steps of the dugout and, peering at Durocher, pointed

46. Jack Buck interview, December 10, 1996; Van Cuyk to Giglio, September 12, 1996. As several have indicated, however, not all teams apparently threw at Musial, especially as he approached the end of his career.

47. Dusty Rhodes to Giglio, August 27, 1996; Monte Irvin with James A. Riley, *Monte Irvin: Nice Guys Finish First*, 175.

48. Connor, ed., *Baseball for the Love of It*, 142.

his index finger and said, "You're up and strutting now, but just you wait. We'll get you, you prick." Musial, who almost always kept negative feelings to himself, probably disliked Durocher more than anyone else in professional baseball. As Broeg later commented, "Leo threw at him one time too often."[49]

Durocher aside, instances of Musial's anger were rare. Very few ballplayers remember him in that way. The most glaring exception occurred, in all places, at Toots Shor's in the 1950s when Musial, Schoendienst, Buck, and a couple of others were eating dinner. A patron from a nearby table approached Musial with a request to autograph the menu. After Musial complied, the man, apparently showing off, tore it in half in front of Musial. To Musial nothing could have been more insulting and discourteous. He flew out of his seat and had to be restrained. The bartenders quickly removed four of the five at the man's table to the street while one remained inside to pay the bill. Buck, who witnessed the altercation, said that "he hated to think what would have happened if [Musial] had gotten ahold of that guy." "Musial could get hot and stay hot," Buck concluded.[50] It took a lot to get him to that point, however.

Musial could also react to intolerance of any sort. A typical example occurred when he and two teammates took a cab in New York to the ballpark. One of the riders noticed on the cabbie's posted license card that the driver appeared to be Jewish. That caused the other to adopt an unpolished and affected Jewish accent. Even though the cab driver did not seem to mind, it embarrassed Musial. Finally, Musial said, "That's enough of that stuff. Knock it off." Dead silence dominated the remainder of the ride. When the players reached the park, the bigoted one attempted to pay the driver. Musial pushed his hand away and said politely, "No, this is mine." As Musial received the change, he told his teammate, "Do me a favor, please. Don't bother to ride with me again."[51]

After the integration of professional baseball, Musial also witnessed the racism that continued to affect the sport in the 1950s. Even the Dodgers faced considerable division over integration. By 1953 it appeared that Brooklyn might have five blacks on the diamond at the same time, symbolically threatening white supremacy. Further resentment compounded the conflict when manager Chuck Dressen benched popular longtime

49. McCarver, *Oh, Baby, I Love It!* 17; Broeg interview, February 18, 1999.
50. Buck interview, December 10, 1996; Jack Buck with Rob Rains and Bob Broeg, *"That's a Winner,"* 88–89.
51. Goodman, *Stan, the Man*, 14.

standout Billy Cox, enabling Jackie Robinson to move to third base and Junior Gilliam, a promising black rookie, to play second.

In St. Louis, meanwhile, the Chase Hotel continued to refuse black Dodger players, who had to ride the black taxis to the Hotel Adams. (In 1954 blacks were finally permitted to stay at the Chase—if they ate in their rooms.) Black pitcher Brooks Lawrence also remembered having to wait in the colored waiting room at Union Station apart from his Cardinal teammates before the train's departure. At Sportsman's Park Cardinal players continued to taunt Robinson by shouting "nigger," "black bastard," or other racial slurs. One Cardinal, Robinson reported, held high a pair of baseball shoes while yelling, "Here, boy. Here, boy, shine." Cardinal manager Ed Stanky claimed to *New York Herald Tribune* reporter Roger Kahn that "black bastard" and "nigger" comments were "not out of line."[52]

On another occasion at Sportsman's Park, with Musial in the batter's box, a shout came from the Cardinal dugout, "Hey, Stan, with that big black background, you shouldn't have trouble hitting that white ball." That "big black background" was Joe Black, the outstanding Dodger rookie reliever, who backed off the rubber and glared at the Cards dugout, where he saw only stares. Robinson rushed to the mound to ask if he had identified the name caller. Robinson then said to Black, "the gutless bas—ds always hide. Forget it right now and work on Musial." The next evening, as Black passed through the Cardinals' dugout to reach the Brooklyn one, Musial said, "I'm sorry that it happened, but don't let things like that bother you. You're a good pitcher."[53]

Even though reticent about racial matters, Musial retained a cordial relationship with the emerging black stars of the 1950s. Hall of Famer Henry Aaron of the Milwaukee Braves called him "one of my favorite ballplayers, because he treated everybody the same—black or white, superstar or scrub." Aaron later went to Vietnam with Musial to tour U.S. military installations. On that trip Musial became the first white person with whom Aaron roomed. Cub Hall of Famer Ernie Banks, sometimes called the black Musial for his sunny disposition and exceptional ability, wrote that he had "few better friends than the St. Louis Cardinals' famous no. 6." Banks remembered his excitement on his first road trip to St. Louis in 1954 when he "could think of just one thing—getting to see Stan Musial." Banks arrived at Sportsman's early, where he saw Musial running

52. Peter Golenbock, *The Spirit of St. Louis: A History of the St. Louis Cardinals and Browns*, 414; Roger Kahn, *The Boys of Summer*, 132–35, 172–77.
53. Joe Black, *Ain't Nobody Better than You: An Autobiography of Joe Black*, 104.

for "a good half hour" before spraying balls from the batting cage to all fields with exceptional power. Another black Cub Hall of Famer, Billy Williams, also called Musial one of his idols. Williams was so excited at the 1962 All-Star game when he was told to replace Musial in left field that he fell off the bench. Even Cardinal nemesis Don Newcombe, the Dodgers' great black pitcher, remembered Musial as the "most gentlemanly player I ever played with or against."[54]

Besides race, the reserve clause also remained a political issue in the 1950s because of legal questions relating to the Mexican League fiasco and player dissatisfaction connected to financial insecurity and the absence of bargaining power. The 1946 concessions by the owners, including a modest pension plan, failed to satisfy most players. Still unresolved was baseball's status under the antitrust laws. Since 1922 the Supreme Court had exempted professional baseball since it supposedly constituted entertainment, not interstate commerce. The ruling enabled the moguls to enforce the reserve clause, which tied ballplayers to a particular team for their entire careers unless they were traded, released, or agreed to retire. This quasi-peonage affected not only major leaguers but also those in the minors, who could remain there for seven years while bound to a major league club, thus delaying unduly the advancement of promising talent.

The Congressional Subcommittee on Monopoly Power, chaired by Representative Emanuel Celler of New York, conducted hearings on these matters, first in 1951 and then again in 1957, without altering anything. Most of the bills under consideration proposed to place professional baseball under the antitrust laws with exemptions to include the reserve clause, which would undergo modification. Musial testified before the subcommittee in June 1957 as vice president of the Major League Baseball Players Association. That April, in an interview at the Cardinals' spring training camp at St. Petersburg, Florida, Musial had proposed free agency for major-league players after ten years of service. Such an alteration, Musial reasoned, would eliminate outside criticism that baseball constituted bondage. Thus, even though he was a staunch defender of the reserve clause, Musial favored a modest change that would benefit established players. His proposal, he contended in a statement that seemed not written by him, would preserve "our national pastime" at a time when Cold War America depended on its continued popularity and strength. "I'm sure . . .

54. Henry Aaron with Lonnie Wheeler, *I Had a Hammer: The Hank Aaron Story,* 105; Ernie Banks and Jim Enright, *"Mr. Cub,"* 178, 79; Billy Williams and Irv Haag, *Billy: The Classic Hitter,* 80; Rick Hines, "Stan Musial: Class On and Off the Field," 103.

that the leaders of this country appreciate baseball's value," he explained. "Certainly, they make use of it internationally in selling democracy, so it must have a special value. Ever notice that when a foreign dignitary comes to New York or Washington, one of the first places he is taken is to a ballpark, photographed eating a hot dog?"[55]

In his testimony before the Celler subcommittee, an obviously uncomfortable Musial reversed himself on the modification of the reserve clause, now arguing that alteration would threaten the integrity of baseball. His explanation for the reversal was so convoluted that it made no sense. When pressed, he suggested that the ten-year proposal came as a "counter" to a supposed congressional effort to terminate the reserve clause. In the course of his abbreviated testimony Musial proposed no reforms or changes. Moreover, he inexplicably denied that he ever had financial conflicts with Cardinals management under the existing system.[56] His appearance represented an inarticulate expression of the status quo, in contrast to the lengthy and articulate testimony of Bob Feller, president of the Major League Players Association and future Hall of Fame pitcher of the Cleveland Indians. Recently retired, Feller, who went into the hearings thinking that Musial would hold to his original position, unabashedly proposed solutions to a list of grievances and problems, including the reserve clause. The latter, Feller argued, should be modified to permit a five-year cap to enable players to become free agents. Feller also proposed arbitration procedures to resolve salary disputes. If several of his recommendations had been adopted, the transition to free agency in the 1970s might have occurred more smoothly and with greater moderation.

The question remains why Musial responded in such fashion. According to Feller, Musial had "knuckled under" to Auggie Busch and management. The fact is that Ted Williams, Mickey Mantle, and Yankee manager Casey Stengel also had nothing to offer, nor had any other major leaguers at the 1951 hearings. While lesser players feared reprisals from owners if they spoke out, the established stars undoubtedly bought the moguls' logic that Congress would least likely intervene if they unequivocally defended the status quo. In the conservative era of the 1950s, preventing government interference remained a worthwhile objective. By then, too, superstars like Musial, under contract for one hundred thousand dollars in

55. *Sporting News*, April 3, 1957, clipping in Musial Collection, *Sporting News* Archives.

56. *Organized Professional Team Sports Antitrust Hearings before the Antitrust Subcommittee, Part 2, Committee on the Judiciary*, 1306–9.

1958, had long overcome their differences with the existing order. Finally, Musial's makeup precluded his adopting controversial positions; never did he do so publicly. A former Cardinal teammate and major league broadcaster, Buddy Blattner, rightly reminded, "Stan traveled lifes [*sic*] road on the bright side, never burdening himself with the heavy baggage of the games [*sic*] policies or politics."[57] All of this represented the flip side of Musial's hero image on an issue that commanded little press attention.

Musial felt much more comfortable talking about hitting, which most propelled him to superstar status. Several magazine pieces came out in the 1950s that focused on his prowess at the plate. After all, Musial and Williams represented the two most proficient batters of that era, and what they had to say caught the interest of baseball aficionados. All accounts agreed that Musial had small hands and used a light bat, a Louisville Slugger M159, thirty-four and a half inches in length and thirty-four ounces early in the season and then to thirty-three ounces by midsummer. Later in his career Musial went to a thirty-one- or even thirty-ounce stick by September to generate more bat speed. Musial was ahead of his time in employing a bat with a big barrel and a very thin handle, which he scraped and honed to his liking. On the on-deck circle he eschewed swinging a weighted bat or two bats because he felt that this would cause him to lose the feel of the one he was using.

Musial began his stance in a deep crouch, which became more moderate as he aged. By crouching he reduced the strike zone and found it easier to punch the ball to left field. Moreover, by hitting from that position deep in the batter's box with his back turned toward the pitcher in corkscrew fashion, he was able to leverage his body into the swing, resulting in more power.

Branch Rickey called that preliminary crouch a fraud because, as the pitcher delivered the ball, Musial was already coming out of it, in position arguably for the most level swing in baseball. Adopting a totally relaxed posture, along with superb eye and hand coordination, became keys for his astounding hitting prowess. Musial had the ability to hold the bat back and delay his swing longer probably than any other hitter of his time. Once he committed to a pitch he accelerated just before making contact. "It's like cracking a whip," one baseball scout described it. A hitting instructor compared it to a "hungry man going at a thick juicy steak."[58]

57. Robert Feller telephone interview, April 7, 1999; Buddy Blattner to Giglio, September 21, 1996.
58. Bob Broeg, "How Does Musial Do It?" *Sport Life* (January 1949), 28, clipping in Musial Collection, *Sporting News* Archives.

Despite the complexity of his swing, Musial, unlike Williams, made no science out of hitting. He concentrated more on the pitchers than on his own swing. His most common problem came when he occasionally overstrode; his correct stride meant moving twelve inches toward the mound and six inches toward the plate. Having a good command of the strike zone, Musial stayed away from slightly errant pitches unless his team needed a hit. Unlike Williams, then, who never swung at a pitch outside of the strike zone, Musial always took into consideration team requirements. He had the ability to hit to all fields—outside pitches to left and inside ones to right. He was a dangerous low-ball hitter, later joking that he was a "low-ball hitter and highball drinker." He avoided hitting fly balls to center field where the best and fastest outfielder played. By hitting the ball down the line, Musial argued, only one fielder could make the play, and he was not usually as quick as the center fielder.[59] Musial became particularly dangerous with two strikes since he then became even more focused. Rarely did he strike out; even more rarely did he take a third-strike pitch. In short, as the opposition reluctantly concluded, Musial in his prime had no major weaknesses. He hit left-handers equally as well as righties (both with a .331 average) and was equally successful against power and finesse hurlers.

The most controversial aspect of Musial's hitting technique came from Roger Kahn's published interview in the late 1950s. Musial claimed that, with intense concentration, he could determine by the speed of the pitch the nature of the delivery by the time it traveled some thirty feet.[60] This suggested that Musial could distinguish a curveball from a slider or change-up as the pitch reached the halfway point. To do this Musial would have had to internalize the deliveries of eighty or ninety pitchers, who had as many as four different pitches, an impossible task. In subsequent interviews he qualified that, saying by judging the speed of the ball as it left the pitcher's hand, he could tell almost immediately if it were a fastball or something else. What the latter might be was another a story. Revealingly, right-hander Clem Labine of the Dodgers was particularly effective against Musial because he confused him with combinations of sinkers and curves. The slider from a right-hander also gave him fits in

59. Mark Newman and John Rawlings, "Man to Man," *Sporting News* (July 28, 1997), 13. Despite his intentions, Musial still hit his share of balls to the center-field area. Center fielder Frank Baumholtz of the Cincinnati Reds, who played him in right center, claimed that most of his balls went to right and left center. Frank Baumholtz oral history transcript, Bill Marshall Collection, University of Kentucky Library.
60. Kahn, "The Man: Stan Musial Is Baseball's No. 1 Citizen," 58.

the 1950s because it appeared to be a fastball until it broke into his fists at the last split second. By 1957 Musial adjusted by reducing his stride toward the plate.

Musial always claimed that he never guessed at pitches. He set himself for the fastball and quickly adjusted for anything else. If the batting count was 2–0 or 3–1 he especially anticipated the fastball. Sometimes, otherwise, he intuitively expected the heater and invariably it came— Musial called it a "sixth sense." Concentration aside, his success also came from his close study of pitchers. He always wanted to know about them. After Jim Brosnan came to the Redbirds from the Cubs Musial soon asked, "How were you guys pitching me?"[61]

Like other natural hitters, with rare exception, Musial found it difficult to assist others in their hitting. His unorthodox swing made it even more difficult. But he went out of his way to help anyone who asked. Typically, he futilely spent more than half an hour in the batting cage with Chuck Connors of the Dodgers, the future star of the TV series *The Rifleman.* Years later Connors recalled that "I was a bum of a hitter . . . but how could I ever forget Stan's kindness?" McCarver later contended that Musial too often showed others "how he did it." He could never tell others how they should do it. McCarver once heard Musial explain to a rookie, "If I want to hit a grounder, I hit the top third of the baseball. If I want to hit a line drive, I hit the middle third. If I want to hit a fly ball, I hit the bottom third." A young Cardinal outfielder of the early 1960s, Curt Flood, once asked Musial how to adjust his swing to accommodate a curveball after setting himself for a hundred-mile-an-hour fastball. "He thought for awhile," wrote Flood, "and then confided with total sincerity, 'Well, you wait for a strike. Then you knock the shit out of it.' " "I might as well have asked a nightingale how to trill," Flood concluded.[62] By the end of the 1950s Musial faced his own difficulties at the plate and in the field. Was age catching up with him as he approached his late thirties?

61. Newman and Rawlings, "Man to Man," 11–12; Jim Brosnan, *The Long Season,* 126.
62. McCarver, *Oh, Baby, I Love It!* 19, 18; Curt Flood with Richard Carter, *The Way It Is,* 64.

Aging Superstar

A s Musial entered the 1959 campaign, he had some inkling that Father Time was slowly intruding. In 1958 he had felt exhausted in September, especially after doubleheaders, which left him stiff and aching for days. He finally conceded that he needed occasional games off. Moreover, he found that he could no longer pull the outside pitch. In the field his reflexes had slowed, and he had lost speed on the bases. He also became more susceptible to leg injuries as his body began to wear down from the accumulation of past ailments. He had seen what chronic injuries and aging had done to Terry Moore, Marty Marion, and Harry Brecheen, who retired in their thirties. Even the seemingly indestructible Slaughter had appreciably slowed down by his late thirties. As a result, the thirty-eight-year-old Musial sensed that his career had entered its final two years. Whenever he failed to hit .300, he said, he would know that it was time to depart.

Musial blamed himself for his failings in 1959. Because of the birth of his third daughter, Jeanie, he had received permission to report late to spring training. He came to St. Petersburg weighing 187 pounds, with the increased weight mostly on his waist and hips. The tiring past season, which included the Japan trip, had caused him to adopt a more sedentary lifestyle over the winter. Moreover, in order to conserve energy for the hot summer months, he and new manager Solly Hemus, a surprise choice because of managerial inexperience, believed that he should reduce his play in the exhibition season. All of this resulted in Musial failing to work himself into prime physical condition as the disastrous spring phase came to an end. Partly due to Musial's anemic hitting, the Redbirds won only eight of twenty-five preseason games.

Musial opened league play in left field, even though he had not played in the outfield regularly since 1956. Although he preferred left field to first base, he found the adjustment difficult. Pitcher Jim Brosnan remembered Musial dangerously bouncing off the outfield wall once in each of the first two games in San Francisco, causing Hemus to move the bruised Musial back to first base despite having an abundance of excellent players at that position, including future star Bill White, Joe Cunningham, and George

Crowe. White, acquired from the Giants for Sam Jones, replaced Musial in the outfield.[1]

The Cardinals dropped the opening series to the Giants; by mid-May the team had the worst record in the major leagues at 10–20. Despite spoiling two no-hitters with late-inning safeties, Musial hit only .244 in this period, his worst start since 1947. As a result, he found himself in and out of the lineup in the next few weeks while his average dipped to .230. A coolness had now developed between him and Hemus. Stan believed that his performance would improve markedly if he could only play regularly. Hemus, who claimed that he was merely "resting" Musial, had probably lost confidence in him. Too, he was most likely reacting to president Busch's spring training directive that if the team performed at the second-division level, then "let's do it with kids."[2]

On June 8, following a photograph session of Musial and Hemus in the dugout, Musial suggested that he might be completing his final season unless he regained his batting stroke. He did not have to say that this required regular play. When one reporter asked why he looked so gleeful posing with Hemus, he responded that he "always smiled when I'm having my picture taken."[3]

Musial returned to the starting lineup on June 13 against the Cincinnati Reds in Busch Stadium. Hitting in the lowly sixth position, he walloped a two-run home run and a bases-loaded single. Against the Pirates he continued his hot hitting in the first game of a doubleheader, clubbing two doubles, the first of which broke Wagner's National League career doubles record of 651. On the twenty-sixth he hammered two homers against the Reds; his batting average crept to .270 by the All-Star break. By then the Cardinals had climbed to sixth place, their highest point in the standings in 1959.

For the first time, to increase revenue for the player pension fund, two All-Star games were scheduled, the first at Pittsburgh's Forbes Field on July 7. National League manager Fred Haney of the Milwaukee Braves selected Musial as a reserve player, his sixteenth All-Star appearance. American League manager Casey Stengel likewise placed Ted Williams, also having a bad year, on his squad. The distinct possibility existed that this

---

1. Brosnan, *The Long Season*, 75. Brosnan includes a number of quirky comments on Musial's trouble-filled 1959 season.
2. Bob Broeg, "Solly on the Spot," 90.
3. Lansche, *Stan "The Man,"* 167.

might be their final season. Ed Linn, in a feature story in *Sport,* "The Last Summer of #9 and #6," predicted as much.[4] So, sentiment weighed heavily in the two selections. On the evening before the All-Star contest, the Pittsburgh chapter of the Baseball Writers Association—before some twelve hundred present, including Vice President Richard Nixon—honored these two giants of the game. The next day, in his one plate appearance, pinch-hitter Musial popped out in a 5–4 National League victory.

Afterward, Musial nevertheless resumed his timely hitting, raising his batting average to .276 by mid-July. Then Hemus sent him to the bench for another lengthy rest. At the second All-Star game at the Los Angeles Coliseum on August 3, Musial came off the bench in the sixth inning and drew a walk, then played first base in an American League 5–3 win.

Following the second All-Star contest, Musial, playing infrequently, went on a one for eighteen dive, dropping his average to .260. Then on August 14, amid rumors that Musial intended to retire at the conclusion of the season, general manager Devine asked him about his plans for 1960, while assuring him that the club wanted him back. Afterward, Devine called a press conference to announce Musial's return. He also explained that Musial would see little action for the remainder of the season because of the club's desire to look at younger players. At the time the Redbirds had fallen to seventh place, where they ended the season, their lowest position since 1919; their pitching ERA of 4.34 was the worst in the league. Hemus, also at the press conference, responded as ambiguously as Devine by saying, "How much [Musial] will play next season is a question," but "he will be an active player." It seemed evident that Musial figured little in the Cardinals' plans. Even sportswriter Bob Broeg, who cared deeply for Stash, felt that the time had come to end the "haunting and humiliating" ordeal by retiring.[5]

Musial made it clear that same day that he could do much better the next year. He blamed his problems not on age but on mechanics caused by poor preparation and inactivity. When a reporter reminded him of prior statements about leaving when he could no longer hit .300, Musial winced. He finally said, "That was when batting .300 was easy." Feeling that he could still reach that magical plateau, he argued that no pitcher had thrown the fastball by him, an indication that his reflexes remained sharp. Right-hander Clem Labine of the Dodgers suggested, however, that Musial swung differently in 1959: "He looked anxious at the plate.

---

4. Ed Linn, "The Last Summer of #9 and #6," 12.
5. Bob Broeg, "Goodbye, Stan," 87.

He didn't wait on the pitch the way he used to." Perhaps, Labine added tellingly, if he did wait, then "he won't get around on the ball."[6]

Musial's future seemed more clouded later in August when J. G. Taylor Spink of the *Sporting News* reported that Musial would likely be swapped to the New York Yankees in the fall for thirty-four-year-old Yogi Berra, who was finally overcoming a sub-par season, in a multi-player deal. While both sides vehemently denied the trade rumor, it could not easily be dismissed if only because Spink, a consummate insider with powerful connections, had reported it. For the swap to work, however, Musial would have to consent to the move. No indication exists that Devine ever broached him about it. If he had, Musial probably would have rejected it. Publicly, Musial called Spink's story "so silly, I don't want to comment."[7]

Yet Musial languished on the bench for the remainder of the season, aside from rare starts and occasional pinch-hitting, for which he seemed ill-suited. In an infrequent start against the Reds in late August, he homered, singled, and doubled in a Redbird victory. Yet he had to club a homer and single in the season's finale to raise his average to .255 in what was easily his worst major-league season. He finished with only 87 hits in 341 at bats. Most alarmingly, only 29 of those safeties, including 13 doubles and 14 home runs, were for extra bases.

More than anything, three considerations propelled Musial's return in 1960. Above all, pride motivated him to show his detractors that he could still perform much like the Musial of old. Besides, nothing thrilled him more than "putting on the uniform"; to the end, he never lost his childlike love of the game nor his belief that he could help the ball club. Musial had also set his sights on concrete personal goals, which he could accomplish with two more productive seasons, especially the breaking of Wagner's National League career hit record. Money seemed a secondary consideration, especially since his outside investments had put him on a solid financial footing. In fact, he voluntarily proposed a twenty-thousand-dollar pay cut in January 1960, which still left him the highest-paid National Leaguer at eighty thousand dollars.[8]

6. "Musial, Benched for Rest of 1959, Says He'll Play Again Next Season," August 14, 1959, unidentified newspaper clipping in Musial Collection, *Sporting News* Archives; Dick Young, "Is Stan Still the Man?" *New York Sunday News,* March 6, 1960, clipping, ibid.

7. *Sporting News,* August 26, 1959, clipping, ibid.; Lansche, *Stan "The Man,"* 169.

8. *Sporting News,* January 27, 1960, clipping in Musial Collection, *Sporting News* archives. The story called the salary cut "self-inflicted." "The Cardinals have been generous to me the past few years, so I thought I'd be kind to them," Musial stated.

Musial began the year determined to get into the best possible physical condition. He participated in a two-month physical fitness program conducted three or four days a week by Dr. Walter Eberhardt, head of the physical education department at St. Louis University. Some twenty big-leaguers underwent the rigorous regimen, which included calisthenics, work on the bars, and running. "Musial drove himself hard," said Eberhardt. The local press published photos of a perspiring Musial, garbed in a gray sweat suit, swinging on the parallel bars or doing assorted stretching exercises.[9] As a result, he came to training camp minus two inches around his waist and feeling stronger than he had in five years.

Playing virtually every game during the spring, he performed well, and the club won the mythical Grapefruit League title. But once the season began everything turned to ashes. On opening day at San Francisco's Candlestick Park, the Giants held Musial hitless, and the Cards lost the first of five consecutive outings. Hoping to play regularly with days off only following night contests or the second half of doubleheaders, Musial found himself benched on May 7 for not hitting. He was batting .268 at the time, and the club was mired deep in the second division in the midst of an extensive losing streak. On May 15, a Sunday doubleheader with the Cubs, Hemus told Musial he would start the second contest. But after the Redbirds won the opening game, Hemus inexplicably decided to retain his right-handed lineup for the nightcap against Don Cardwell, a sidearming right-hander noted for his effectiveness against right-handed hitters. After Hemus informed Musial of the benching, Stash, suppressing his anger and frustration, merely said, "You were just kidding me about playing me, Solly."[10] Caldwell ended up pitching a no-hitter. Musial, pinch-hitting late in the game, struck out.

Musial had reached the absolute low point of his major league career. On the surface he remained his affable self. When Cardinal pitcher Curt Simmons said that "all you have to do is . . . see Gussie [Busch], and you'll be in the lineup and [Hemus] will be gone," Musial smilingly answered, "Don't worry, I'll be back in a week." No stories appeared of Musial privately berating Hemus or failing to run out ground balls in rare pinch-hitting appearances. Jack Buck, however, sensed Musial's frustration, manifested by ordinary pitchers getting him out. Curt Flood witnessed it in another way as he came into the clubhouse and saw Musial,

9. Young, "Is Stan Still the Man?" 86.
10. Musial, *Musial*, 212.

whom Hemus had removed from the game, kicking a large container holding dirty towels as hard as he could about thirty times.[11]

The situation worsened on May 16 against the Phillies, with the score tied in the ninth inning and the Cardinals at bat with runners on second and third. Hemus ordered Musial to bat for Flood, knowing that Musial would be intentionally walked to set up a possible double play. Hemus then sent up Curt Sawatski to bat for the pitcher; Sawatski crossed up the Phillies by hitting a sacrifice fly to win the game. Afterward, Hemus boasted that he knew Sawatski would more likely hit a fly ball than Musial.

It appeared to Broeg of the *Post-Dispatch* that the Cardinal brass was deliberately humiliating Musial to force his retirement: wasting him as a pinch-hitter in lopsided losing situations and benching him against right-handed pitchers. Broeg felt that Hemus had prematurely given up on Musial, and his mismanagement of him had been detrimental to the club. Particularly irksome to Broeg and others, Hemus's seven years of National League service, mostly as a utility player with the Cardinals, had scarcely qualified him to make such harsh judgments about Musial's performance. But Busch, who liked Hemus's scrappy style because it reminded him of Eddie Stanky, whom he had rehired as head of player development, remained reluctant to intercede.[12]

Consequently, Broeg invited Bob Burnes, sports editor of the *Globe-Democrat*, who shared Broeg's concerns, to write a critical column on the Musial benching. Broeg followed the next day, Sunday, May 22, with his own piece. Broeg then visited the clubhouse, as he always did following a rare critical story, where Hemus called him a "poison pen." At this point Broeg unloaded. He told him that he had had it with the suggestion that Hemus had to treat all twenty-five players alike. He reminded Hemus of Stan's position and popularity with the press and the community. "Sol, if you used Musial too much," Broeg argued, "everybody and his brother-in-law would be sympathetic with you. By jumping to what might be premature conclusions and acting too quickly, you've turned all of us against you."[13]

11. Halberstam, *October 1964*, 108; Curt Simmons to Giglio, August 26, 1996, in possession of Giglio; Buck interview, December 10, 1996; William Leggett, "Not Just a Flood, but a Deluge," 21.

12. *St. Louis Globe-Democrat* News Release Draft, Musial, Stan, Envelope 1, Mercantile Library Clipping File, St. Louis; Lansche, *Stan "The Man,"* 171.

13. Broeg, *Memories of a Hall of Fame Sportswriter*, 272; *St. Louis Post-Dispatch*, May 22, 1960. See also *Sporting News*, June 1, 1960, clipping in Musial Collection, *Sporting News* Archives.

But Broeg's and Burnes's intercessions had no serious impact, even though Hemus returned Musial to the lineup for the next couple of games. In fact, on May 28 Busch asked Musial to come to his country estate, where Musial met with Busch, Dick Meyer, Devine, and Hemus. There the Cardinal brass told him that Hemus preferred a younger lineup. Musial, hurt that he was not given a fair chance, nodded and said softly, "Whatever you want is all right with me, though I think I can still help the ball club." Hemus had already informed the press that Musial had been benched "indefinitely."[14] That meant occasional pinch-hit appearances, which did little to restore Musial's timing. His average had fallen to .235 by June 11.

By then press stories reported that Musial was contemplating retirement. At that point the Pittsburgh Pirates came to town fighting for their first pennant in thirty-three years. Pirate manager Danny Murtaugh asked Broeg, "What's wrong with the Polack?" Nothing, Broeg responded, except opportunity. Broeg indicated that Musial might be willing to return to his roots where he would have a chance to play in another World Series. For a while Musial and the Pirates expressed a strong interest as discussions continued off the record. Musial had told friends that he had never thought of leaving the Cardinals until now, but "I can't stand this. Maybe the Pirates could use me and I know I can still hit and perhaps help them win the pennant."[15]

The Pirates needed a left-handed hitter at first base and knew what a fired-up Musial might mean to the club. The Pirates made it clear, however, that they could not give up young talent for the nearly forty-year-old Musial. At the same time, the Pirates' general manager, Joe L. Brown, was unwilling to put Devine in an embarrassing position by offering too little. Musial's contract with the Cards, which provided for deferred payments following retirement, further complicated matters. In the end the Pirates hoped that Musial would ask for his unconditional release, which he refused to do. Despite recent events, he felt too much loyalty to the ball club and the community to initiate the departure. Besides,

14. Musial, *Musial*, 214. Almost forty years later, Hemus admitted that he had lost faith in the greatest player he ever managed. Believing he faced being fired if the team did not start winning, Hemus contended that he had to play his best players. That included Bob Nieman in left field because of the need for more right-handed power. He insisted that the decision was his, not Busch's or Devine's. Because of Nieman's play, the team started to win again, making Hemus even more reluctant to return Musial to the lineup despite the pressure the Cardinal brass faced from the fans. Hemus to Giglio, August 12, 1999, in possession of Giglio.

15. Broeg, *Memories of a Hall of Fame Sportswriter*, 271–72; Bob Burnes draft column, August 30, 1960, in Musial Collection, *Sporting News* Archives.

Busch had already indicated that he had "future plans" for him. When the Cardinal office announced that "Stan is Mr. Baseball in St. Louis, he is a Cardinal, he has always been a Cardinal and I am sure he will always remain a Cardinal," as far as Musial was concerned, the Pirate option had ended.[16] Consequently, he planned on retiring at the All-Star break.

Unforeseen circumstances caused Musial to change his mind. In May Hemus had moved White from the outfield to his natural position at first base. The fleet Flood, a future All-Star, took over in center field while Cunningham adequately covered right field. After Hemus unsuccessfully tried several young players in left field, he settled on Bob Nieman, who hit well before succumbing to injury again by the third week of June. At that point, right after the Broeg-Pittsburgh discussions, Hemus finally asked Musial if he thought he could still play the outfield.

Musial had prepared himself for that eventuality. He had worked hard in practice during his benching. Coach Johnny Keane had hit countless balls to him, and he did daily wind sprints to maintain his physical edge. He learned much from observing reserve first baseman George Crowe, who drove himself extra hard in practice in preparation for emergency duty. Nearly four weeks after being benched, Musial entered the lineup in left field on June 24 against the Phillies. In that game he threw out a runner at home and collected a single in four at bats. Slowly he began to hit again until he went on an unbelievable run of twenty-seven hits in sixty at bats, a .450 average, to raise his overall average to .317 by the first All-Star break as the Cards surged into the first division. Hemus conceded that Musial "has delivered the most key hits the last few weeks that I've seen any player get in years." Too, Musial covered more ground in the outfield than he had in 1959. "It is difficult to tell when a player is through," Hemus admitted three years later. "You think you see tell-tale signs but then again they can prove you wrong. [Musial] proved me wrong, I'm happy to say."[17]

Musial again made the All-Star roster as a sentimental choice, the last player manager Walt Alston of the Dodgers selected. His only appearance on that muggy afternoon on July 11 at Kansas City Municipal Stadium came as a pinch-hitter. He easily drew the largest ovation before singling

16. Musial, *Musial*, 216; *Sporting News*, June 22, 1960, clipping in Musial Collection, *Sporting News* Archives. If Musial had asked for his unconditional release to play for Pittsburgh, according to Hemus, "it would have broken Gussie's heart." Hemus to Giglio, August 12, 1999.

17. Musial, *Musial*, 217; Lester J. Biederman, "Stan Musial Wanted to Play for Pirates during '60 Season," 1963 clipping in Musial Collection, *Sporting News* Archives.

off the glove of second baseman Nellie Fox in a 5–3 National League victory. Two days later the All-Star extravaganza continued at Yankee Stadium, where Musial again successfully delivered as a pinch-hitter, this time hitting a Gerry Staley sinker high into the third deck of the right field stands for his record-breaking sixth All-Star home run as the National League won 6–0. It was Musial's first visit to the House That Ruth Built since the 1943 World Series.

Musial continued his clutch hitting after the All-Star break, while the Redbirds passed the .500 mark and moved up in the standings. Ironically, his most sterling performance came against the Pirates, a team he had not hit well in the past. In early August the second-place Cards came into Forbes Field just five games behind Pittsburgh, having won thirty out of their last forty-one games. Musial won the first game by hitting a two-run home run in the twelfth inning, ending the Pirates' seven-game winning streak. The Cards won again the next evening with Stash contributing a key two-run single. By now ovations for Musial had ended as he threatened to short-circuit the Pirates' pennant hopes. He even noted a coolness among his old friends around Donora for his Pirate bashing. The Cardinal run momentarily ended, however, when the Cardinals lost the next three, falling six games behind Pittsburgh.

Musial and the ball club gave the Pirates one more scare, however, in St. Louis in late August following a Cardinal six-game losing streak that pushed the team eight and a half games behind Pittsburgh. In the three-game series, Musial contributed substantially to two of the three victories. In the first contest he homered with one aboard to break a 1–1 tie; the following night his single and fourteenth homer, with two outs in the ninth, led to a 5–4 win. Then Musial went into a batting slump, which saw his average fall from .298 to .274 in the next week and a half. He still finished the season with a respectable .275 average, 17 home runs, and 63 RBIs, 19 more than the previous season. In the 84 games he started he batted .288; no one on the club proved more productive in advancing base runners. The team, thanks to the clutch hitting of Musial, White, and Boyer and exceptional pitching from Ernie Broglio, Larry Jackson, and reliever Lindy McDaniel, finished in third place with an 86–68 record, nine games out of first and only two games out of second. There was reason to hope for even better results in 1961.

Even though he did not hit .300, Musial had reason to feel vindicated for his modest comeback season. Some of his staunchest supporters had anticipated—and even hoped—that he would now call it quits, however. Sometime late that summer Broeg wrote a touching farewell piece,

"Goodbye, Stan," published in *Sport* magazine in October, which concluded, "So long, Banj. See you around. And thanks." By then, however, Musial had already made up his mind to return for another season. The announcement came on September 15 in the 1960 campaign's final days. He cited five reasons for coming back in a statement that he read to the press: he still enjoyed the game, he believed that he could help the team win the pennant in 1961, Devine and Hemus wanted him back, his return to the outfield had helped his hitting, and he wished to pursue certain records.[18] The two milestones that he most sought—the National League career hit standard and the major-league career total base record—required more than one more season to shatter, however.

Cardinal president Busch, strongly concurring with Musial's and Devine's decision, said, "After all, Stan is still the greatest Cardinal of them all, and we hope he'll play as long as he's able." Devine echoed that "Stan's a symbol of outstanding character combined with outstanding talent, and . . . his mere presence on the ball club is an inspiration to the other players."[19] With the team a probable contender in 1961, the Cardinal brass hoped that an inspired and determined Musial, playing around one hundred games, might make a difference. Musial soon signed for seventy-five thousand dollars, a five-thousand-dollar salary cut from 1960.

That fall, for the first time, Musial also found himself in a national political campaign as an enthusiastic backer of Senator John F. Kennedy of Massachusetts, the Democratic nominee for president and the first Catholic to be selected since Al Smith in 1928. Musial had first met the handsome, charismatic candidate in front of Milwaukee's Shroeder Hotel in September 1959. Stumping in Wisconsin at the time, Kennedy recognized Musial waiting for the team bus and extended his hand: "You're Stan Musial, aren't you? My name is Jack Kennedy. I'm glad to meet you." Kennedy then smilingly commented, "They tell me, you're too old to play ball and I'm too young to be president, but maybe we'll fool them."[20] Stash found himself captivated by Kennedy's lofty and inspiring speeches that sought to move the country forward again in the face of Cold War defeats in Cuba and Berlin and domestic problems at home, especially the racial conflict.

18. Broeg, "Goodbye, Stan," 90; "A Statement by Stan Musial," September 15, 1960, Musial Collection, National Baseball Library.
19. Cardinals News Release, September 15, 1960, National Baseball Library.
20. Musial, *Musial*, 3; teammate Jay Porter happened to be with Musial in Milwaukee when JFK approached him. Jay Porter to Giglio, September 6, 1996, in possession of Giglio.

Biggie Garangani, a consummate political activist, had first introduced Musial to local and state politics during the 1950s. Musial soon found himself at Democratic fund-raisers and rallies. Democratic politicians often invited him to guarantee a huge crowd. Musial needed to do little except talk baseball and shake hands. He soon became a friend of Democratic Senator Stuart Symington and Governor James T. Blair. In 1960 Blair selected Musial, along with Harry Truman, as one of ten honorary squires—"distinguished and eminent men and women" of Missouri, who had "enhanced the history, honor, and prestige of the state."[21] Later in the 1960s Musial became a major backer of Democratic Governor Warren Hearnes of Charleston, Missouri.

Like many Polish Americans, however, Musial favored Republican president Dwight David Eisenhower during the '50s, not Democratic nominee Adlai Stevenson of Illinois.[22] Stevenson not only was divorced but also had become associated with a Democratic Party under attack by red-baiting Republicans for being soft on communism, all of which cut deeply into the Democratic vote. Roman Catholics left the Democratic party in appreciable numbers in the '50s, especially Polish Americans because of the emerging Republican charge that the Democratic leadership had sold out Eastern Europe to the Communists. Stevenson captured only 56 percent of the Catholic vote in 1952 and 45 percent in 1956 compared to Truman's 64 percent in 1948. As a result of Kennedy's candidacy, Catholics returned in droves in 1960, with Kennedy winning approximately 80 percent of their votes. Seventy-eight percent of Polish Americans voted for him, most of them in key industrial states with large electoral votes.

Kennedy's religion, his apparent athletic vigor, and his nearness in age might have contributed to Stash's decision to become involved. As Musial himself admitted when pressed by a political reporter, he had little understanding of the issues; he knew only that Kennedy was "a great man."[23] He campaigned for him in the Midwest along with a number of other celebrities, including Kennedy women (Ethel Kennedy), movie stars (Angie Dickinson and Jeff Chandler) intellectuals (Arthur Schlesinger, Jr.) and writers (James A. Michener). The eminent Michener, author of *The Tales of the South Pacific, Sayonara,* and *The Source* and a lover of baseball,

21. Press release, September 8, 1960, Folder 677, James T. Blair Papers, Western Historical Manuscript Collection, Columbia, Missouri.

22. Thomas B. Curtis to Paul Marshall, July 21, 1960, copy, Folder 21207, Thomas B. Curtis Papers, ibid.

23. Bill Bryson, "Stan Musial Says: Batters Are Being Outsmarted!" 37, copy in Musial Collection, *Sporting News* Archives.

became Musial's lifelong friend as a result of their shared experience in 1960. Michener and the others sought to generate publicity in Republican states where newspaper coverage for Kennedy was negligible. Michener recalled that no member of the troupe attracted as much attention as Musial. As they embarked from the plane and their names were announced, according to Michener, people scarcely responded. Then "a low rumble rose from the crowd, and men pressed forward, dragging their boys with them, and one man shouted, 'It's Stan the Man!' . . . I heard one rancher say to his son, 'For the rest of your life, . . . you can tell people about this night. You saw Stan Musial.'" Afterward, Michener and Musial joked about the fact that Kennedy lost all of the eleven states they visited. "If they'd sent us to two more states," Musial laughed, "Kennedy would have lost the election."[24]

Little contact existed between Musial and Kennedy following 1960. In fact, they did not see each other again until the All-Star game in newly constructed D.C. Stadium on July 10, 1962. The president requested to see Musial before the game. When Musial approached the presidential box, Kennedy shook his hand. Not until the sixth inning did Musial make an appearance as a pinch-hitter, whereupon Kennedy whispered to personal assistant David Powers, "I hope the old man gets a hit."[25] Musial lined a single into right field, which contributed to the National League's 3–1 victory. Stash and his family capped the exciting two days by visiting Kennedy in the Oval Office, a meeting that Senator Symington arranged. There Kennedy presented Musial with a PT 109 tie pin and Lil with a pen with Kennedy's name on it.

Afterward, whenever Musial referred to Kennedy, he did so as "my buddy." The Kennedy presidential files contain very little correspondence involving the two, however. Aside from invitations that the president appear at testimonial dinners in honor of the Cardinal great, the only other request came directly from Musial. In 1963 he asked Kennedy to prevent the termination of the ROTC program at St. Louis's Christian Brothers College, the preparatory school that son Dick had attended. One month later Kennedy's special assistant wrote Musial that the Department of Defense would continue the program. A month prior to his assassination, Kennedy apologized that he would be unable to attend Musial's retirement dinner but spoke highly of his contributions to the game and to "our

24. James A. Michener, *Sports in America,* 240; James A. Michener, *Pilgrimage: A Memoir of Poland and Rome,* 28.
25. Musial, *Musial,* 3–4.

national life." He hoped that Musial would pursue "new endeavors with the same dedication and integrity that have marked your quarter century in baseball."[26] Where Musial was at the time of Kennedy's death and how he responded to it have gone unrecorded.

The New Frontier era represented a bittersweet period for Musial. By the time of the Kennedy inauguration on January 20, 1961, he had already begun intense conditioning to prepare himself for the coming season. The forty-year-old knew that he would have to work hard to extend his career. He even sought to correct his "weakened" eyes. "One of the saddest days of my life," he told James Michener, "was when I found out about my eyes. Before age forty I hadn't felt the slightest loss in seeing. Then my eyes started to go bad. The ball looked so much smaller than it used to. First base seemed actually further away. So the Cards sent me to the top doctors, and they examined me for a whole morning with the latest machines, and at the end they gave me the bad news. 'There is absolutely nothing wrong with your eyes.' I was just getting older, like everyone else."[27] Obviously, there were aspects to aging that even hard work—or easy solutions—could not reverse.

Musial also found himself in the midst of a new era in race relations. By 1960 the civil rights movement had entered a more intense and aggressive phase as blacks throughout the South employed direct action and civil disobedience strategies to desegregate lunch counters, bus services, and other public accommodations. The decade began with the Woolworth store sit-in in Greensboro, North Carolina, in January 1960, followed by the Freedom Rides on Greyhound and Trailways buses in the spring of 1961 and the voter registration drives of 1962. The press carried countless stories of young blacks confronting racial injustice in Dixie. The names of leaders such as Martin Luther King, Jr., and Malcolm X appeared with greater frequency along with civil rights organizations such as the Congress of Racial Equality (CORE), the Southern Christian Leadership Conference (SCLC), and the Student Nonviolent Coordinating Committee (SNCC). The Kennedy administration soon found itself forced into the conflict, first only to protect activists from mob—and police—retaliation.

---

26. *Sporting News*, July 2, 1962, clipping in Musial Collection, *Sporting News* Archives; Stan Musial to John F. Kennedy, February 28, 1963, White House Name File, Box 1986, Folder MUSI, John F. Kennedy Library, Boston; Ralph A. Dungan to Musial, March 13, 1963, copy, White House Central Subject Files, Box 631, Folder ND13/FG120 Department of the Army, ibid; Kennedy to Musial, October 14, 1963, copy, White House Central Subject Files, Box 519, Folder ME1/M Executive, ibid.
27. Michener, *Sports in America*, 271.

But by 1963, pushed by civil rights groups, it became a leading proponent of immediate racial integration.

Like society in general, professional sports felt the impact of the civil rights movement. Not only were there many more blacks now participating in baseball, football, and basketball, but they were also less willing to internalize racial slights, and they felt more alienated from societal norms. Several—notably Jim Brown of the Cleveland Browns of the National Football League—publicly condemned white treatment of blacks. Jackie Robinson, who retired from baseball in 1957, became a model for many blacks. Consequently, tension between the races existed on professional teams. Often the racial issue touched on the defense of the status quo, including the enormous differences in advertising endorsements between white and black players.

Somewhat surprisingly given the team's history, the St. Louis Cardinals handled these race-related problems better than most of the other major-league clubs. In 1961 the club roster included several blacks, such as Flood, entering a breakthrough year; White; Crowe; and the twenty-five-year-old Bob Gibson, a tall, strong, brooding, sensitive, and intelligent right-hander with blazing speed who was destined for greatness. Several others joined the club in the next couple of years. They became part of the foundation for the Cardinals' return to glory in 1964.

Busch's decision to house all the Cardinal players together at St. Petersburg by spring training in 1962 proved significant. Bothered by the way the community had mistreated his black players, Busch threatened to move the team to another site unless changes occurred. Consequently, a local motel owner leased to Busch for six weeks the Skyway Motel and an adjoining establishment. This ended the practice of blacks being boarded in the black section of the city. Musial, who customarily rented a house for his family, quickly agreed to move his clan to the complex, as did Boyer and other established players. For southern visitors it became an eye-opening experience to see white and black families sharing the same swimming pool. In other ways, Devine and Al Fleishman of the Cardinal front office succeeded in lessening the segregation that existed in spring training, according to Bob Gibson. Fleishman rented nightly first-run films, and during the day Bill White's wife, Mildred, ran a school for the children. Once the regular season began, it was Boyer, on road trips, who usually rounded up everybody for dinner or a movie.[28]

28. For the best coverage of the Cardinals and race, see Halberstam, *October 1964,* 53–63, 363–70; and Golenbock, *Spirit of St. Louis,* 439–41. See also Jack E. Davis,

As the most senior player, Musial contributed much to the harmonious environment that existed in his final seasons. The usually critical Gibson remembered Musial as "a friendly, talkative guy . . . who was the same with everybody, whether you were a rookie or a ten-year veteran. He used to sit down and talk to me a lot. Not about anything in particular, just small talk, and he wasn't going out of his way to be especially nice to me."[29] Flood and White shared some of Gibson's observations about Musial.

Limits existed to the prevailing racial harmony, however. George Altman, a black on the 1963 club, felt that while "white and black players were amicable and cordial on the playing field and in the clubhouse there was no or very little social interaction." Calling Musial "a first class gentleman," Altman nevertheless concluded, "Stan and I were like two boats passing in the night. One a single passenger row boat, the other a yacht full of partying business persons."[30]

To Altman, Musial remained an establishment player who praised the Cardinal ownership and saw life only in positive terms. This did not always sit well with angry young blacks who experienced mistreatment throughout much of their professional career. Flood, for example, never forgot fans in the South yelling "black bastard" at him. While playing in the Carolina League he recalled that "my teammates despised and rejected me as subhuman. I would gladly have sent them to hell."[31]

Flood, whose anger remained with him following his playing career, provided the strongest criticism of Musial, whom he still admired and liked: Musial "not only accepted baseball mythology but propounded it. Whereas the typical player all but choked while reciting the traditional gibberish of gratitude to the industry, and whereas Bob Gibson, superstar of another hue, would simply change the subject, Musial was a true believer. Gibson and I once clocked eight 'wunnerfuls' in a Musial speech that could not have been longer than a hundred words. 'My biggest thrill is just wearing this major-league uniform,' Stan would say. 'It's wunnerful being here with all those wunnerful fellas.' On such occasions, Gibson would hang his head in embarrassment and mutter, 'Shitfuckpiss'. . . . There was no conscious harm in [Musial]. He was just unfathomably naive. After twenty years of baseball, his critical faculties were those of a

---

"Baseball's Reluctant Challenge: Desegregating Major League Training Sites, 1961–1964," 159–61.
29. Bob Gibson with Phil Pepe, *From Ghetto to Glory: The Story of Bob Gibson*, 45.
30. George Altman to Giglio, November 8, 1966, in possession of Giglio.
31. Tygiel, *Jackie Robinson and His Legacy*, 282–83.

schoolboy. After twenty years, he was still wagging his tail for the front office—not because he felt it politic to do so, but because he believed every word he spoke."[32]

Flood acknowledged Musial's support, however, after Hemus told Flood he would never make it at a time when Stash faced his own personal ordeal with the Redbird manager. "I was as low as I could get," Flood recalled, but Stan Musial was "one of the guys who helped me up." Flood thought Hemus a racist, as did Gibson, who objected to Hemus's referring to one Pittsburgh Pirate pitcher as a "black bastard." "Either it didn't occur to him or he didn't care that guys like me and Flood and White and Crowe—not to mention Musial and Boyer . . . and other white players would be personally and profoundly offended," Gibson wrote. He concluded that either Hemus "disliked us deeply or he genuinely believed that the way to motivate us was through insults."[33]

Hemus's days were numbered, however. The Cardinals began the 1961 season in disastrous fashion despite considerable optimism following the success of 1960. The erratic and authoritarian manager was not entirely to blame. Injuries to White, Javier, Boyer, McDaniel, and Larry Jackson contributed to the downslide. Too, the pitching staff failed to produce early, and Ernie Broglio, a twenty-one-game winner in 1960, won only nine games in 1961. Musial started the opener in left field and tripled in a ten-inning 2–1 victory over Milwaukee.

On April 26 Hemus benched him for anemic hitting, however. By May 5, after failing to produce as a pinch hitter, his average dropped to .205. Hemus insisted that he had removed Musial from the lineup only because of the cold weather and the necessity of looking at young outfielders before the roster reduction deadline. Afterward, according to Hemus, Musial would play regularly in between lengthy rest periods. He started on May 7 and slowly returned to form. On May 18 he went three for four to raise his average to .262. Three days later he tied Eddie Collins for fourth place on the career hit list (3,311) with a single. By May 28 his average had jumped to .312 following a pair of singles and a home run.

Ironically, Musial's greatest day that spring came on June 7 when, racked with pain because of an abscessed tooth, he went four for four, including two home runs, in a win that brought the Cards to one game

32. Flood, *The Way It Is*, 53.
33. Leggett, "Not Just a Flood, but a Deluge," 20–21; Bob Gibson and Lonnie Wheeler, *Stranger to the Game*, 52–53. For Hemus's defense against racist charges, see Halberstam, *October 1964*, 110–11.

within .500. Two weeks later Musial proved again a theory of his that he could concentrate better when not 100 percent. Suffering from a pulled leg muscle and a cold, which prevented him from sleeping, he belted a three-run home run and then his ninth career grand slam to lead the Cards to a 10–5 win over San Francisco. The seven RBIs tied his best single-game mark, and the two homers increased his extra-base hits to 2,340, second only to Babe Ruth. Hemus kept him out of the lineup the next evening, however, when the Giants started a rookie left-hander. Musial not only hit left-handers as well as righties but also found it difficult to sustain any momentum because of Hemus's imprudent handling of him.

By early July Musial still led Cardinal regulars in home runs and was second in batting average and RBIs despite limited play. With the club mired in sixth place, fifteen and a half games out of first with a 36–43 record, Busch fired Hemus. His replacement, longtime minor-league manager and current Card coach Johnny Keane, became a godsend for Musial. Despite his problems with Hemus, Stash characteristically said little that was critical of him, however. In his 1964 autobiography he referred only to Hemus's managerial inexperience and erratic handling of players.

Meanwhile, the wiry Keane quickly made some moves that helped the club in the second half of the season. He reinserted Flood in center field, where he finished with a .322 batting average, and he boosted Jackson's confidence as a starting pitcher by keeping him on the mound over some rough periods. As a result, Jackson finished strongly, as did Gibson, who flourished under Keane.

Six days after the Keane appointment, Musial appeared in his twentieth All-Star game at San Francisco's Candlestick Park. Relegated to a pinch-hitting role, he flied out to left field in a 5–4 National League victory. In the second All-Star game on July 31 in Boston's Fenway Park, where Musial received a tremendous ovation in his first appearance there since the 1946 World Series, he failed again as a pinch-hitter, striking out while attempting to drive one over the Green Monster in left. The game ended in a 1–1 tie as a result of rain.

Immediately afterward, Musial flew to New York, where he received the *Sport* magazine award for the outstanding athlete of the past fifteen years, a gimmick to commemorate the fifteen years of the magazine's existence. *Sport* praised not only his accomplishments but also his character. Ed Linn, in the cover story, commented on his "unfailing courtesy, . . . unfading smile and unflagging enthusiasm for the handshake and the autograph. If he has ever sulked or thrown a tantrum," according to Linn, "no one has ever seen him do so."[34]

Following the *Sport* award luncheon, Musial saw his hitting average slip below .300 during the dog days of August before he recovered slightly. On August 30 the Philadelphia Sports Writers Association honored him at their luncheon with a silver champagne bucket, one of many such ceremonies for Musial in the next two years. There Musial announced that he would return for one more season in 1962. He was anxious, he said, to play in the Polo Grounds again now that New York would have an expansion club. On September 17, for the second year in succession, his Pittsburgh area friends gave him a day, this time to commemorate his twentieth anniversary with the Cardinals. With his mother and other family members present, along with friends such as Ki Duda, president of the California (Pa.) State Teachers College, Stash received a diamond-studded wristwatch from Keane and a number of other gifts. In the Cardinals' 3–0 victory over the Pirates, Musial contributed his 443rd career home run to the festive occasion. This was followed by a luncheon in Musial's honor the next day at the Hilton Hotel in which National League president Warren Giles said, "I'm thankful to [Musial] for the prestige he has brought to the National League and to all of baseball." Musial once again indicated his intention to return in 1962: "I'd like to continue playing as long as I can help and I'm not a burden. I don't want to embarrass myself or the Cardinals."[35]

Musial's performance in 1961 made him anything but a burden. Although hitting only .272 for Keane, he ended the season with a .288 batting average, thirteen points higher than 1960, with 15 home runs and 70 RBIs despite just 107 hits. Only White and Boyer had more home runs and RBIs on the ball club. In the field Musial performed adequately. Statistically, he ranked as the top defensive outfielder in the National League with a .994 fielding percentage and only one error, but his restricted range kept him from balls that speedier fielders would have reached. The Cardinals, meanwhile, finished strongly under Keane, winning forty-seven out of eighty games for an 80–74 record, thirteen games from the top and in fifth place. There was reason to anticipate even better results in 1962.

Three things most excited Musial about the approaching 1962 cam-

---

34. Ed Linn, "Stan Musial: Man of the 15 Years," 35.
35. *Sporting News*, September 27, 1961, clipping in Musial Collection, National Baseball Library.

paign. Above all, he relished manager Keane, who, unlike Hemus, expressed considerable confidence in his abilities. In the closing weeks of the 1961 season, Keane had told Musial, "I want you back, not to play less next year, but to play more. I've watched you and I'm convinced that you could have played more. . . . If next year is going to be your last one, make it one to be remembered."[36] Musial needed only twenty-nine hits to break Wagner's National League career mark of 3,430 and eighty-four total bases to surpass Cobb's major league record of 5,863. Nothing motivated Musial more than challenging such lofty standards.

Moreover, with two expansion teams in the National League—the New York Mets and the Houston Colt .45s—and an expanded 162-game schedule, Musial believed that he could benefit from the diluted pitching talent. He pondered little the ending of the fifty-seven-year tradition of 154 games and the resulting expanded travel, which was superimposed on the West Coast excursions begun in 1958. All of this represented additional burdens on ballplayers, with little elevation of the minimum salary of seven thousand dollars and no increase in pension benefits, despite the growth of television revenues, which resulted in increased player grievances in the years ahead.

In January, probably partly because of declining attendance, Musial himself accepted a ten-thousand-dollar cut for 1962, signing a contract for sixty-five thousand dollars, which was more than offset by the tremendous business at the new Stan Musial and Biggie's restaurant on Oakland Avenue. He worked especially hard in the off-season participating in the conditioning program at St. Louis University and watched what he ate. He reduced his weight to his rookie standard of 175 pounds before leveling off at 180. This enabled him to slide without jarring his body as much while increasing his endurance. Beginning with spring training, Musial had the most incredible season a forty-one-year-old position player has ever had. It was as if he had momentarily reversed the aging process; he became an inspiration to other athletes that they, too, could extend their careers through rigorous conditioning and sheer will.

He helped himself by using a lighter bat, shortening his swing, and punching more outside pitches to left field. He stood more upright in his stance now, a concession to advancing years. He also paced himself by retiring in the late innings and taking occasional days off, especially after night games. Keane and he thought alike on how to manage his playing time.

36. Musial, *Musial*, 222.

After hitting .339 in the Grapefruit League, Musial opened the season in right field, his favorite position, with Flood in center and aging veteran Minnie Minoso, a recent acquisition, in left. Musial went three for three against the New York Mets and scored his 1,859th run, tying the National League career record of Mel Ott. Led by Musial's .458 average, the Cardinals won their first seven games before losing a doubleheader to the Cubs. One of Musial's first early-season disappointments occurred on May 7, a Sunday doubleheader against the Reds, when he popped up in the ninth inning against a journeyman hurler with the bases loaded and the Cards one run behind. Musial returned to the clubhouse after the loss downcast and frustrated, knowing that he would not play again until Tuesday evening. He then felt Keane's hand on his back and heard him say, "You're playing the second game, Stan, and you'll get four hits."[37] In starting his first doubleheader in nearly four years, Musial, on a cool day, collected three safeties, including a three-run home run for a 3–0 Redbird victory. That twin bill put Musial ahead of Wagner's National League mark for most games played (2,787) and within six hits of his league career hit record. It seemed that Musial eclipsed some record every time he competed.

No standard meant more to him in 1962 than becoming the National League career hit leader. After coming within one of the mark while hitting .402, Musial, trying too hard, failed to hit on four consecutive evenings at home as the various media futilely photographed and filmed his every plate appearance. He went on the road having lost fifty points on his batting average before lining a single to right-center off Juan Marichal of the Giants in the sixth inning at Candlestick Park on May 16 to tie the mark at 3,430, ending a drought of fifteen plate appearances. Witnessing the event was Jim Tobin, the forty-nine-year-old former knuckleballer who yielded Musial's first hit in 1941. Musial, locating him in the stands, heard him shout, "What are you looking for, another hit?" Musial laughingly responded, "I still can't hit the knuckleball, Jim." To the press, Musial said that this record "proves we modern ball players are as good as the old-timers say they were," a probable response to Cobb's much publicized gibes about the good old days.[38] That he tied the Flying Dutchman's mark had special meaning to Musial. He remembered Wagner, a fellow western Pennsylvania native, attending

37. Ibid., 224.
38. Ibid., 225; *St. Louis Post-Dispatch,* May 17, 1962, clipping in Musial Collection, National Baseball Library.

a postseason banquet in Donora in 1943 to honor him for winning his first batting title. The fourth-place Cards' 7–2 loss, its ninth in twelve games, made Musial's accomplishment less enjoyable than it might have been, however.

Musial set the record four days later on May 20 in Los Angeles after failing in nine at bats since tying it. This time he lined a curveball to right field off of Ron Perranoski for a 4–3 victory before nearly fifty thousand Dodger fans, who gave Musial a standing ovation. Upon reaching first base, Musial, shaken with emotion, looked for a pinch-runner, whom Keane delayed in order to retain the spotlight on Musial. Musial then ran into the dugout where teammates mobbed him. In the clubhouse later, in reference to the record, he uncharacteristically yelled: "I got it. I got it." Musial acknowledged the pressure when he said in a postgame interview that he "never worked so hard for two hits." Lil, who had fallen asleep, had missed the radio broadcast in St. Louis. When asked about it afterward, she confessed, "I guess I'm just too old for the game. It's for young guys like Stan."[39]

The week afterward Musial, who had missed son Dick's high school graduation, left a struggling Cardinal team on the road to attend daughter Gerry's commencement at Villa Duchesne and Dick's graduation at Notre Dame on June 3. The following day Musial received an honorary Doctor of Humanities degree from Monmouth (Ill.) College.

Upon his return he and the Cardinals went on a tear—the team with a seven-game win streak, which positioned them six games from the top, and Musial with twelve safeties in twenty-seven at bats, which raised his average to .340. Then in dramatic fashion on June 22, he tied and broke Cobb's major-league total base record by homering and singling in the same inning. Afterward, he surprisingly professed to reporters that he had never given much thought to the record and had always thought that Ruth had held it.

Beginning on July 7, at the Polo Grounds, with Lil and daughter Janet witnessing the action, Musial tied a major league record by hitting four home runs in four consecutive at bats. The first one enabled the Cards to eke out a 3–2 victory over the Mets. On the following day Musial blasted three consecutive round-trippers against New York before striking out in a 15–1 win. That Sunday's performance represented the first time Lil saw Musial club three home runs in one game. As he stepped on home

39. *Sporting News*, June 2, 1962, clipping in Musial Collection, National Baseball Library.

plate and saw Lil and Janet in the first-row box seats after the final homer, he remembered the "warm glow" he felt. Soon afterward, the Musials proceeded to the All-Star game in Washington, D.C., where they met Kennedy.

Musial began the second half of the season hitting .333, which scooted to an astounding .351 in the next couple of weeks as he completed one of his patented streaks. In the process he shattered another career record, this time Ott's National League RBI mark of 1,860, which he broke in late July by homering against Don Drysdale, a towering right-handed star who had idolized Musial as a teenager. With his recent hitting success, Musial found himself in contention for his eighth batting title, which would tie Wagner's National League record. In order to qualify, however, Musial needed 502 plate appearances, an average of 3.1 at bats per game. This meant that Keane had to play Musial much more while also resting him periodically to keep him from tiring. He attempted this delicate balancing act after the second All-Star game in Chicago's Wrigley Field on July 30, which saw Musial go hitless in two at bats, first as a pinch-hitter and then as a left fielder, in his twenty-third and penultimate midsummer classic, a 9–4 American League win.

Despite the Cardinals' disappointing skid into fifth place, some thirteen games behind the Dodgers, Keane, as planned, played Musial more in August. Stash responded at first with four consecutive multi-hit games, elevating his average to .359, before slumping to .339 by mid-August. On August 18 the Mets gave him a special night at the Polo Grounds, the first such honor for a visiting player in the stadium's eighty-year history. The donated money went into a Musial scholarship fund at Columbia University, Lou Gehrig's alma mater. Musial, insisting on no expensive gifts, received a portable typewriter from New York sports scribes; a mounted photostat of the *New York Times* for November 21, 1920, his birth date; and other memorable items.

One of the most meaningful came from Mets manager Casey Stengel and the New York ball club, who presented Musial with an inscribed plaque, which read, "The New York fans, through the Mets, salute the greatest ball player of his generation for over two decades. Stan Musial of the St. Louis Cardinals has enhanced the prestige of the National League both on and off the field." Musial, nervously clasping the microphone while his daughter danced on home plate, told the New York fans, "I especially want to thank the Mets for bringing National League baseball back to New York." He was too choked up to say more. Because Musial had played in the first game of the doubleheader, he sat out the nightcap, causing fans to chant, "We want Musial! We want Musial!"[40] It so persisted that Keane put him in as a pinch-hitter with the Cardinals way ahead, and when Musial drew a walk on four pitches, the crowd jeered the hometown pitcher.

As September arrived, a tiring Musial had slumped some at the plate. He now trailed Tommy Davis of the Dodgers and Frank Robinson of the Reds by some sixteen points. Yet that month also added to his dream season. On September 2 a single against the Mets moved Musial ahead of Tris Speaker with 3,516 career hits; only Cobb's 4,191 hits remained ahead of him. By the end of September, while the Cardinals finally played some of their best ball, Musial contributed to several key victories against the pennant-contending Dodgers and Giants. On September 27 Musial went five for five for the final time in raising his average to .333. In the concluding series of the season, a Cardinal sweep of the Dodgers forced a postseason playoff between Los Angeles and San Francisco, which was won by the Giants.

The Cardinals closed with an 84–78 record and finished a disappointing sixth place in the standings. Even though he rehired Keane for 1963, a frustrated Busch threatened to shake up the front office and engage in wholesale trades. No doubt, the Cardinals had serious weaknesses to address, especially at shortstop, catcher, and pitching, particularly in the bullpen. Although Musial was no Flood in the field, he had an incredible year, finishing at .330, the highest batting average a forty-one-year-old had ever achieved in the twentieth century. At the same age the incomparable Cobb had set the standard in 1928 by batting .323 for the Philadelphia Athletics. While skeptics might argue that Musial had capitalized on weak expansion-team pitching, the fact is that none of the other aging stars came close to his accomplishments. Gil Hodges batted .252 and Richie Ashburn .306, both for the Mets, and neither of them reached Musial's 505 plate appearances. Only Davis (.346) and Robinson (.342) finished ahead of Musial in the batting race. Musial hit 19 home runs and drove in 82, his highest total since 1957; his .508 slugging average led the Cardinals. Moreover, to illustrate how incredible his 1962 effort was, he came off the bench to bat .615 despite his past problems as a pinch-hitter. His achievements enabled him to win the National League Comeback Player of the Year award. And thanks in large part to Musial, the Cardinals increased attendance by one hundred thousand even though the team was not a serious contender.

40. Lansche, *Stan "The Man,"* 186–87; Musial, *Musial,* 228.

Musial credited his 1962 success to manager Keane. "From the day he took over the Cards, [he] let me know that I was not only wanted, but needed," Musial said. "He instilled enthusiasm and inspiration in me and helped me find myself again. I have great respect for his managing and as long as he's manager of the Cardinals, I'm sure I can do a good job for him and the club."[41] The return of the thirty-nine-year-old Schoendienst as a reserve in the spring of 1961 also made a world of difference. Although they each had separate quarters on the road, they still spent considerable time together. Musial had been extremely supportive during Schoendienst's hospitalization with tuberculosis in 1958–1959, which brought them even closer.

Musial had made it clear in August that he would like to return in 1963 for his twenty-second season, which would equal Cap Anson's and Mel Ott's record for seasons with the same team. He thought that he could still help the Redbirds. If a promising young player pushed him in left field, he would quit, he insisted. Keane remained supportive, announcing that "Stan figures prominently in my plans."[42] He promised that Musial again would play regularly in 1963.

At least one Cardinal executive thought Musial should retire, however. Eighty-one-year-old Branch Rickey, who had recently returned to the Cardinal organization as a special consultant to Gussie Busch, emphatically expressed that viewpoint. The impatient, impulsive Busch had hired Rickey after spending an evening with Bob Cobb, the former owner of the defunct Los Angeles Angels AAA club, who admired Rickey's baseball mind. After Busch had expressed his frustration in not producing a championship club, Cobb suggested the "Mahatama." Rickey came to the Cardinals following a frustrating six years with the Pirates that finally resulted in a pennant in 1960. By then Rickey had assumed the presidency of the Continental League, which sought to extend major-league-caliber baseball to Toronto, New York, Houston, Minneapolis, Atlanta, and elsewhere. The league planned to begin play in 1961, causing major-league owners to undercut Rickey by expanding to four of those cities.

Rickey's presence with the Cardinals undermined the authority of general manager Bing Devine. Rickey probably had little respect for Devine, who had been a lowly clerk when Rickey ran the show in the late '30s and early '40s. Rickey thought Busch hired him to build a better ball

41. *Sporting News,* December 1, 1962, clipping in Musial Collection, *Sporting News* Archives.
42. Ibid.

club, which meant considerable say over personnel. He had already told Devine that he intended to run the club, putting Devine in an impossible position. The resulting conflict soon found its way into the newspapers, with Busch trying to resolve a feud that he himself had created.[43]

One of the major differences centered on whether the 1963 Cardinals could contend for the pennant. While Devine felt that the club was no more than a couple of players away, Rickey projected the Cards for a fifth-place finish. He cited weaknesses in pitching, catching, bench strength, and the outfield. Consequently, he favored building for the future by inserting young players with potential. Musial did not fit in his plans even though the Cardinal farm system no longer produced the talent it once did.[44]

Rickey, of course, had been a tremendous admirer of Musial and considered him a friend. But, to Rickey, the Stash of 1963 bore little resemblance to the Donora Greyhound despite a .330 batting average in 1962. The soft underbelly of that incredible season related to Musial's slowness of foot in the field and on the bases. Shortly after his arrival, Rickey in fact recommended that Musial retire immediately. That brought on an immediate response from Busch, "Since when do you retire a .330 hitter?"[45]

Rickey's observations at spring training further convinced him that Musial remained a detriment even though he hit .280 in the Grapefruit League. Accustomed to dispatching aging stars who still had market value, he now recommended selling Musial's sixty-five-thousand-dollar contract. Aside from Musial's enormous popularity with hometown fans, Devine explained that his unique contract, in which the Cardinals owed him approximately two hundred thousand dollars in deferred income, made that difficult to do. That "arrangement," approved by the commissioner of baseball and the Internal Revenue Service, explained Devine, tied Musial to the Cardinals.[46]

Nevertheless, Rickey's assessments of Musial remained consistently negative into the regular season. He typically wrote that "25 Musials would finish a dismal last place in the National League race in 1963. I

43. Halberstam, *October 1964*, 31–34; *St. Louis Globe-Democrat*, November 7, 1962, clipping in Mercantile Library clipping file; "Card Owner Probes Rickey-Devine Rift Tale," unidentified newspaper clipping, November 7, 1962, in Musial Affair 1962 Folder, Box 21, Rickey Papers; Rickey Memorandum, November 8, 1962, ibid.

44. Rickey Memorandum, May 17, 1963, Copy, Memorandum 1963 Folder, Box 21, Rickey Papers.

45. *St. Louis Globe-Democrat*, November 7, 1962, clipping in Mercantile Library Clipping File.

46. Rickey Memorandum, April 2, 1963, Copy, Memorandum 1963 Folder, Box 21, Rickey Papers.

have said repeatedly . . . that Musial is through." One report followed the first eight games of the regular season in which Musial started in left field. Of the three Cardinal losses, he considered Musial responsible for two of them because of his slowness afoot. Later in April his memorandums from the West Coast reiterated Musial's shortcomings in the field: "In the seventh inning of the game today in San Francisco, with two men on, he gave them a run. Didn't reach the ball in time to make a quick throw and even then the runner outran the ball." Then against the Dodgers, Frank Howard "hit a fly ball to left field. [The shortstop] could have easily caught the ball. . . . Musial took it. Tommy Davis [from third] scored easily standing up. It was a gift run."[47]

Rickey compared Musial's lack of speed to the notoriously slow catcher Gus Triandos of the Detroit Tigers. He reported that "Triandos can't run as fast as Musial." After viewing Musial one week later, he asserted, "Yes, I believe he can." In Rickey's final report on Musial on August 6, he summarized his performance against the Mets by writing, "He can't run, he can't field, and he can't throw. 25 Musials would finish in last place, below the Mets."[48]

The forty-two-year-old Musial had undergone the same rigorous conditioning in the winter of 1963. He had come to spring training in fine physical shape. Had he slowed even more from the previous season? Probably. But was he as much a liability as Rickey claimed? Neither Devine nor Keane thought so. But Musial represented only one of several differences that divided management in 1963. Devine claimed that Rickey had opposed the trade that brought veteran shortstop Dick Groat to the Cards from the Pirates.[49] The steady, sure-fielding Groat plugged a major hole, giving St. Louis the best infield in the major leagues with Boyer at third, Javier at second, and White at first, a major foundation for their championship season of 1964. Groat was a .300 hitter who could hit behind the runner with the very best. In fairness to Rickey, of the team's three catchers, he rightly recommended starting the twenty-one-year-old Tim McCarver despite his taking three steps in throwing to second base; he recognized the skills of manager Keane, "a good tactician—sound as any man I know in the game today"; and he strongly favored the 1964 trade

---

47. Ibid., May 15, April 25, May 8, 1963.
48. Ibid., March 18, April 3, August 6, 1963.
49. Halberstam, *October 1964*, 35. In reality, Rickey claimed that he did not oppose the acquiring of Groat; he thought the Cards gave up too much to get him. Rickey Memorandum, undated, Copy, Retirement 1963 Folder, Box 24, Rickey Papers.

of pitcher Ernie Broglio to the Cubs for fleet-footed Lou Brock, Musial's eventual replacement in left field.[50]

The Rickey-Devine clash represented only one of several problems the Cardinals faced early in the 1963 season. After winning ten of their first fifteen games behind the brilliant pitching of rookie Ray Washburn, Simmons, and Broglio, the team went into a tailspin in early May, falling into fourth place. Moreover, Musial had hit poorly in April. The Rickey fracas proved distracting and embarrassing; it might have even contributed to his inability to concentrate at the plate, making it more difficult to generate that quick swing. He found himself taking more called third strikes. He also lacked the challenge he had in 1962 in chasing Wagner's career hit record. Furthermore, as Rickey had witnessed, he had problems committing quickly to fly balls, as Musial himself later admitted. He soon realized that extra batting practice and physical conditioning alone could not overcome the aging process. Slowly, he came to the conclusion that his liabilities were outweighing his assets.[51]

Still, he momentarily rallied at the plate in May. On the eighth he broke Babe Ruth's major league record of 1,356 extra-base hits. By the end of the month he had raised his batting average to .277 as the team began to win consistently. He even played in a doubleheader against the Mets on a misty Sunday in St. Louis in which he contributed four hits. Supposedly, no major-league position player of the same age had appeared in a twin bill since Cap Anson in 1897.

Then things started to go wrong. On June 1, in a win against the Giants in which Musial had three singles, he pulled a muscle behind his right knee running to first base. A hobbled Musial played the next afternoon until he ruptured a blood vessel in that same knee. He was in and out of the lineup for the next month, while the club suffered an eight-game losing streak, lowering their record to 46–38, four and a half games behind the league-leading Dodgers at the All-Star break.

On July 9 Musial appeared in his record-setting twenty-fourth All-Star game (later equaled by Mays and Aaron). Played in Cleveland's Municipal Stadium, Musial's only at bat came as a pinch-hitter in the fifth inning, when he lined out sharply to Detroit's Al Kaline in right field in a 5–3

50. Rickey Memorandum, May 15, 1963, copy, Memorandum 1963 Folder, Box 21, Rickey Papers; ibid., May 15, 1963; undated Memorandum, copy, ibid. Rickey's recommendations on a proposed Brock-Broglio deal: "25 Brocks would threaten the league championship every year. 25 Broglios would not. I urged the Brock deal and would again."

51. Musial, *Musial*, 236; Connor, ed., *Baseball for the Love of It*, 250–51.

National League victory. Although speculation existed that this might be his last appearance, the contest passed without any public ceremony.

Musial played infrequently following the All-Star break. He failed to hit in seven consecutive games, striking out three times as a pinch-hitter. Not until July 25 did he return to the lineup against Milwaukee's Warren Spahn, who gave up a game-winning double to him. The next day he breakfasted with Devine, who suggested the meeting. Following small talk, Devine delicately asked him what his plans were for the next season. With great difficulty, Musial responded, "After this year, I'll have had it."[52] Devine seemed relieved; it meant the ending of press speculation and the possibility that Musial might embarrass himself by staying another year. It also meant that Devine could now get Rickey off his back. For Musial, it meant the ending of a significant part of his life—one that he had always dreaded closing. The next step involved the announcement. Musial told Devine that he wanted to make it first to his teammates; Devine suggested the team picnic at Busch's farm.

Two days following the Devine meeting, Musial fanned three consecutive times against the Cubs' Dick Ellsworth, the only time that a pitcher had ever done that to him.[53] It surely marked the lowest point of his 1963 season. He did not start again until August 1 when the Cardinals defeated the Reds, leaving them still four and a half games out of first place.

Three days later Musial made the planned announcement at Busch's farm on a bleak, rainy day. Players and family members, along with a small group of sportswriters, sat at the checkered-cloth-covered picnic tables, not expecting what was to follow. With Busch out of town, Bob Broeg expressed the owner's apologies for his absence and then let Musial speak. A choked-up Musial stunned the group by announcing his pending retirement. One week earlier he had said that he would not issue a statement regarding that matter until after the season. After expressing his love for baseball, he ended it by saying, "I came in with a winner in my first year . . . and I'd like to go out the same way. I've dreamed for a long time of playing in one more World Series. I think we still have a chance to do it." Laudatory comments followed from teammates, writers, and club officials amid an often laughing, serious, and sobbing Musial. Lil, in tears, said, "I hate to see it end. It's been so much fun." Devine

52. Musial, *Musial*, 237.
53. Ellsworth, in fact, struck him out four consecutive times if one counts a previous outing. Lee Heiman, Dave Weiner, and Bill Gutman, *When the Cheering Stops: Ex–Major Leaguers Talk about Their Game and Their Lives*, 239.

called Musial's decision a "great loss to the playing end of the game but a gain to the executive side"—an indication that Musial would soon move into the Cardinal front office.[54]

If Musial intended to inspire his teammates for a second-half surge, it seemed not to have worked. The team performed terribly on a western road trip, while Musial's batting average dipped to .245. This did not stop the fans from honoring him wherever he went. Some sort of public ceremony accompanied his visit to most of the ballparks. In San Francisco he was named honorary mayor. In Houston he was presented with a miniature statue of Dick Kerr, who had recently died there. The larger Kerr figure was to be placed in a new domed stadium. Musial spoke emotionally when talking about Kerr, "who gave me my start in baseball." By the end of August, however, the team had fallen seven and a half games out of first as it headed east for a three-game set with the Pirates.

Beginning with that series, the Cardinals rebounded to win nineteen of the next twenty games, its most incredible streak since Musial arrived in 1941. Much of the team's success resulted from the resurgent pitching of Gibson, Simmons, Broglio, and others. McCarver and Groat hit well, and Musial, too, contributed. At about four in the morning on September 11, in the midst of the streak, son Dick called from Fort Riley to inform Stan and Lil that his wife, Sharon, had given birth to Jeffrey Stanton Musial. That evening, after passing out cigars in the clubhouse to teammates, who laughingly called him Gramps, a pumped-up Musial hit a two-run home run against the Cubs. To rekindle the remarkable run of the heady 1942 season, the clubhouse again reverberated with the hokey sounds of Spike Jones's "Pass the Biscuits, Mirandy."

When the league-leading Dodgers came to town on September 16 for a three-game series, only one game separated the two teams. Pennant fever once again had hit St. Louis, as 32,444 turned out for the first game, a scoreless duel between Broglio and Podres until the sixth inning, when the usually reliable Flood misjudged Tommy Davis's fly ball, allowing Maury Wills to score. Then Musial hit his last career homer in the seventh to tie the score. There it remained until the Dodgers scored two in the ninth for a 3–1 victory. The following evening pitted the rejuvenated Simmons, winner of three consecutive shutouts, against Dodger ace Sandy Koufax. Koufax scattered four hits, one by Musial, in shutting out the Redbirds

54. Lansche, *Stan "The Man,"* 192; *St. Louis Post-Dispatch,* August 13, 1963, clipping in Musial Collection, National Baseball Library; *Washington Daily News,* August 13, 1963, ibid.

4–0. The death knell came the next evening when Gibson failed to hold a 5–1 lead and the Dodgers rallied to win in the thirteenth inning. The Dodgers left St. Louis with a four-game lead. For all practical purposes the pennant race had ended.

The Cardinals lost five of the next six before turning it around on the last day of the season. Still, they finished in second place at 93–69, their best effort since 1949. With the addition of Brock in left field and the continued development of younger pitchers such as Gibson, Ray Sadecki, and Ron Taylor, the team would do even better in 1964. The sad irony remains that when they did become World Series winners that year, their first championship since 1946, Musial no longer played the game. But as he often humbly said, they would not have won it with him in left field.

While Musial performed poorly at the plate after the key Dodgers series, gifts and honors continued to come his way. In his last series at Wrigley Field, the Chicago baseball writers presented him with a shotgun and a one-hundred-dollar savings bond for his grandson; from television station WGN he received a silver bowl. He also heard, while in Chicago, that the board of directors of the St. Louis Cardinals had made him a vice president.

But the climax was yet to come. His final game took place on Sunday, September 29, against the Cincinnati Reds. Five days before, the U.S. Senate had approved the Limited Test Ban Treaty, which banned nuclear atmospheric testing. On the morning of Musial's special day, the *Post-Dispatch*'s lead story centered on the friendly discussions between Secretary of State Dean Rusk and Soviet Foreign Minister Andrei Gromyko in New York on disarmament matters, suggesting that the Test Ban Treaty might lead to even more meaningful agreements. One month previously, the civil rights movement had culminated with the uplifting March on Washington in which Martin Luther King, Jr., proclaimed that he "had a dream." Congress had already received Kennedy's comprehensive civil rights bill. Much reason for hope and optimism prevailed in the late summer of 1963. But on the inside pages of that Sunday *Post-Dispatch*, coverage of Secretary of Defense Robert McNamara's and Chief of Staff General Maxwell Taylor's mission to Vietnam only hinted at the extent to which the nation was becoming intertwined in the war there. Nor would Americans ever imagine that Kennedy would be assassinated two months later, contributing to the sense of despair that would characterize the remainder of the decade.

On the morning of the twenty-ninth, dressed in a black suit with shadow stripes, Musial attended Mass at St. Raphael's Church with his

family and longtime actor friend Horace McMahon.[55] Following a breakfast of scrambled eggs and bacon, he and McMahon, along with a *Sport*
and *Life* writer and a *Look* photographer, climbed into his blue Cadillac
for the twenty-minute drive from his southwest brick home on Westway
Drive to Busch Stadium. Upon entering the parking lot he was mobbed
by fans before entering the clubhouse, where a TV camera crew and other
media people were waiting. "How come you got all these guys following
you all the time?" Simmons asked. Musial laughed.

For the next hour or so photographers and the TV camera crew captured
his every action as Musial restaged his clubhouse entrance and dressed
for the game. More than once he joked to reporters, "Hey fellows, I've
changed my mind. I'm not retiring." The mood remained lighthearted
except for his warning, "Now, no more of those cigar pictures. I'll know
my friends by the cigar pictures I see. I don't want the kids to see me with
a . . . cigar in my mouth." TV interviews followed before Musial made his
way to the field for batting practice and warm-up exercises. Afterward,
he signed baseballs for several Reds players and the grounds crew before
retreating into Keane's office to refine his notes for the farewell speech.

The pregame ceremonies took place in front of home plate with the
Cardinal players lined up along the third-base line and the Reds along
the first-base stripe on a cool, clear, sunny day. Folding chairs encased the
front of the infield, with the Musial family occupying the first two rows.
The memorable moments in the one-hour ceremony included two Cub
Scouts—one white and one black—presenting him with a neckerchief,
which remained around his neck for the duration of the program. On
behalf of the players, Boyer gave him a ring with the number six set in
diamonds. Manager Keane concluded his moving remarks by saying, "I
try to picture the clubhouse after the game," and as he paused, Musial
began to sob. Aging commissioner Frick then spoke those soon-to-be
memorable lines, "Here stands baseball's perfect warrior. Here stands
baseball's perfect knight." Busch reminded the crowd that Musial's number six would never be worn on a Cardinal uniform again; "nobody could
do justice to it," he said.

After the Dixieland band played "Auld Lang Syne" and after being
presented with a four-by-six-foot framed drawing of a statue of himself

55. What follows comes from two of the most detailed reports of that momentous
last day. Arnold Hano, "Stan Musial's Last Game," 10–13, 61–63; W. C. Heinz, "Stan
Musial's Last Day," *Life* (October 11, 1963): 96–98, clipping in Musial Collection,
National Baseball Library.

to be erected in front of a new riverfront stadium, Musial approached the microphone. He rubbed his eyes, mouth, and hair, and he then began to speak. Momentarily overcome by emotion, he reached into his back pocket for his notes and continued: "This is a day I'll always remember. This is a day of both great joy and sorrow, the sorrow which always comes when we have to say farewell. . . . I want to thank my wife and children for their strong support for a part-time husband and father. I want to thank God for giving me the talent I have and the good health I've been blessed with. Baseball has taught me the opportunity that America offers to any young men who want to get to the top in anything." Choked with emotion, he was barely able to speak the closing sentence: "I hate to say good-bye. So until we meet again, I want to thank you very much."[56] After wiping his eyes and kissing Lil, he climbed into an open convertible, followed by Lil and the younger daughters in a second one and son Dick and daughter Gerry in the third. Once the slow procession around the park had ended, the game soon began.

The Reds' pitcher was twenty-three-game-winner Jim Maloney, a big right-handed fireballer, who held the Cardinals in check until the fourth inning. In the first inning Musial struck out with the bat on his shoulder. Returning to the dugout, he heard the concerned trainer Bob Bauman admonish, "You weren't bearing down up there." Taken aback, Musial jokingly responded, "You're right, boss. If only I could concentrate like the Musial of old."[57]

In the fourth inning, however, on a 1–1 count, he grounded a single just past rookie second baseman Pete Rose, the future career hit record holder, for the Cardinals' first hit. In Musial's final at bat in the sixth, after fouling a fastball and taking two pitches for balls, he grounded Maloney's slow curve into right field for a single, scoring Flood from second base. Musial's 3,630th and final hit put the Cards ahead 1–0, a game the Redbirds eventually won 3–2 in fourteen innings. In appreciation, the crowd stood up and enthusiastically applauded Musial, followed by jeers and boos when Keane replaced him with a pinch-runner. Bedlam followed in the clubhouse as photographers and reporters gathered around a now relaxed Musial, who removed a uniform destined for the Baseball Hall of Fame. Musial then proudly said, "You know that's the way I came in [in September 1941]. Two base hits. And that's the way I leave."[58]

56. The full text of the farewell is in Musial, *Musial*, 241.
57. Ibid., 242.
58. Heinz, "Stan Musial's Last Day," 98.

Indeed, fans will always remember that he left the game a winner despite the disappointment of not capturing the pennant and performing marginally in his final season. In retrospect, the nearly forty-three-year-old Musial stayed on one season too long, but who can blame him after that glorious '62 year? He closed with a .255 batting average, which tied his all-time low of 1959. He had only 86 hits, one less than in 1959, with only 12 home runs, his fewest since the 1944 season. His 10 doubles represented his lowest total ever.

Musial's final tribute in 1963 came on October 20, which Mayor Raymond R. Tucker hailed as Stan Musial Day. That evening the St. Louis chapter of the Baseball Writers Association sponsored a testimonial dinner in his honor in which proceeds for the twenty- to fifty-dollar-a-plate gathering would be applied to the costs for the Musial statue. Former teammate and close friend Joe Garagiola acted as master of ceremonies for the some fifteen hundred in attendance in the Khorassan Room at the Chase Park Plaza Hotel. Many of them represented the baseball elite, including umpires, executives, managers, and sportswriters as well as current players and Hall of Famers.

The tone of the two-and-a-half-hour farewell combined serious and lighthearted moments. Senator Symington, who had recently called Musial in the Senate "an inspiration to every American who respects the priceless combination of character and ability," read a letter from President Kennedy praising him. National League president Giles intoned, "I'm proud that my only son and I are part of the game Stan Musial has done so much for." Expressing the view of several managers, Danny Murtaugh of the Pirates cracked, "I have been looking forward to this day for many, many years. If I'd known Stan was waiting for money for a statue, I'd have donated it years ago." Ernie Banks, one of many who continued the levity, pretended to read a telegram to Musial, "Congratulations on your retirement. It's signed," Banks claimed, "from the NAACP. This means," he paused, "the National Association for Advancement of Colored Pitchers." That brought down the house. Musial ended the commentary by saying, "I have never been prouder than tonight to be a baseball player and an American." Marty Bronson then sang, "Thanks for the Memory" as the guests gave Musial a final thunderous applause.[59]

59. Copy of Symington's remarks in the *Congressional Record* can be found in Musial Collection, *Sporting News* Archives; *Sporting News*, November 2, 1963, ibid.; Al Abrams, "The Lighter Side of Musial's Farewell," 61–62.

Even though he was leaving baseball as an active player, Musial knew that it would always remain a major part of his life. But he had to wonder whether he would be able to participate in the game in any meaningful capacity. Also, he knew that the business ventures, especially the restaurant, would occupy some of his time. What else lay ahead for a man who was still considered young outside the professional sports world?

Keeping Busy

Major leaguers usually retire as active players between their mid- and late thirties, a time when other professionals have scarcely reached their prime. By that age college professors, attorneys, or physicians are only beginning to make a mark in their professions. In the Musial era established ballplayers, long accustomed to the limelight, often found retirement psychologically and economically devastating. Most of them had devoted their lives to honing their playing skills; they were ill-equipped to do much else. Retirement caused many to feel like has-beens. Coaching or managing in the minor leagues remained an option, as did scouting, but former stars initially avoided those endeavors because of the low pay, the Spartan conditions, and the lack of status. Yet only a few of them were capable of immediate employment at the major league level.

In the era before pensions, retired players faced formidable financial constraints because many had received relatively modest wages as players, had squandered their money, or had difficulty securing suitable employment afterward. Hall of Famer Jimmie Foxx of the Boston Red Sox is an often-cited example, but many others also suffered from money-related problems.

Even the more financially successful found retirement distressing. Babe Ruth, his competitive juices still churning in his early forties, continually failed to secure a managerial position in the major leagues. Consequently, he derived little satisfaction from just attending games. As he once said, "It's hard to be on the outside of something you love. Just looking in doesn't help." His only competitive salvation became golf, but even that proved unsatisfactory because his play had not reached championship level. In the end, he became, as his biographer termed it, an ornament, a living shrine appearing at various ceremonies.[1]

Ty Cobb, a millionaire from investments in Coca-Cola and General Motors, also found retirement depressing. He, too, discovered nothing suitable to occupy his considerable energies. Having managed with mixed results as a player, he received no invitations to skipper in the big leagues

---

1. Charles C. Alexander, *Ty Cobb* (New York: Oxford University Press, 1984), 211; Marshall Smelser, *The Life That Ruth Built: A Biography* (New York: Quadrangle, 1975), 528.

after his playing career was over. Like Ruth, Cobb found golf an inadequate substitute. So, he became an even more sullen curmudgeon, one who alienated his wife, children, and few friends. In the end his behavior became more bizarre, and he lived his final years as a sickly, lonely old man. Roger Kahn's *The Boys of Summer* provides a broader—and more mixed—view of the difficulties of several former Dodgers of the 1950s some ten years into retirement.

No ballplayer made the transition to retirement more smoothly than Musial. Because of his investments, continued Cardinal income, and eventual pension (capping at fifty-four thousand dollars annually), he remained financially secure. He even expanded his business operations, which he found as challenging as baseball. He became involved with public service activities, sometimes at the invitation of the president of the United States. He also continued his involvement with the Cardinals as goodwill ambassador and executive. He soon became an unofficial ambassador for baseball, which took him to the four corners of the world. In some respects he was busier than ever—often too busy. All the while he remained devoted to Lil and their children and took comfort from them. Despite occasional personal disappointments and setbacks, he made "retirement" as enjoyable as his playing career. Rarely did the public fail to catch Musial without a smile.

Even before playing his last game, Musial attended the Cardinals' organizational meetings as a vice president, starting on September 26, 1963, to discuss plans for the next season and review player evaluation reports. The local press speculated that Musial would scout various winter league activities and attend the minor and major league meetings in December. In 1964 Musial often traveled with the club, particularly when the team found itself in the heat of a pennant race and then in the World Series. As early as February 1964 he also reportedly received more than fifteen hundred invitations to speak at banquets, most of which, of course, he declined. While Musial's salary as vice president is unrecorded, his 1963 contract contained a clause requiring the ball club to pay him $16,770 yearly plus expenses for thirteen years for at least ten annual public appearances.[2] Busch apparently saw considerable value in Musial as a public relations tool of the organization.

Nevertheless, Musial managed to attend the Kentucky Derby and the Indianapolis 500 for the first time in 1964, something he had no time to do as a player. By the spring of 1964 he had also became Lyndon

2. Musial 1963 player's contract, St. Louis Cardinals Museum, Busch Stadium.

Johnson's physical fitness adviser. President Johnson came to St. Louis on February 14 to announce the appointment. The president referred to Musial as not only one of the century's greatest baseball players but also one who personified honor and integrity. The appointment made sense also because of Musial's publicized success in extending his career through a vigorous conditioning program and because of his charitable activities in St. Louis. It did not hurt that Senator Stuart Symington was a mutual friend. In deciding between Georgia Tech football coach Bobby Dodd, whom Senator Richard Russell of Georgia recommended, and Musial, Johnson decided that it should rotate to baseball following the tenure of University of Oklahoma football coach Bud Wilkinson. After securing Busch's permission, Musial and his family went to the White House swearing-in ceremony on February 24, attended by Johnson and several staffers and cabinet members, including Attorney General Robert Kennedy.

The Special Consultant to the President on Physical Fitness and the President's Council on Physical Fitness had originated in 1956 when President Eisenhower appointed Shane McCarthy physical fitness adviser and created the council. The poor physical condition of American youth compared to European children, documented in performance tests, provided the impetus. Of course, the Cold War created even greater urgency that this national deficiency be addressed. Not until Kennedy's presidency, however, did the program receive considerable attention. The youthful and energetic Kennedy popularized physical fitness in ways that no president had done since Theodore Roosevelt. His two articles in *Sports Illustrated,* one a cover story in December 1960, linked physical vigor to intellect and moral strength, essential ingredients to national well-being. In the second essay of July 1962, he praised vigorous young Americans who were defending freedom in the jungles of Asia and the borders of Europe.[3] Under the direction of Wilkinson great strides were made in the physical fitness program in schools, health and recreation departments, youth organizations, and with adults.

Following the departure of Wilkinson and Kennedy's tragic death, an ad hoc committee recommended that Johnson build on the successes of the Kennedy presidency. This required that LBJ throw the prestige of his office behind the commitment and that federal departments represented on the

---

3. The two Kennedy pieces—"Sport on the New Frontier: The Soft American" and "Vigor We Need"—are in the December 26, 1960/January 2, 1961, and July 16, 1962, issues of *Sports Illustrated,* respectively.

council step up their activity. Most of all, the committee favored a national director, well known to the general public, who would bring dedication, abundant energy, and talent to the task. This meant coordinating efforts with government agencies and various volunteer groups, the latter of which required traveling around the country. These considerations contributed to the Musial appointment.

That Musial did not live up to expectations was partly due to the nature of the position. Defined as part-time, it paid seventy-five dollars per diem on days of actual employment. Moreover, the physical fitness director lacked authority over the council, which was composed of the president's cabinet in which the secretary of health, education, and welfare acted as chair. Furthermore, Musial found himself being pulled away by other obligations, especially with the Cardinals. Consequently, in his three-year tenure he devoted only 114 days to physical fitness in comparison to Wilkinson's 203 over a comparable period of time, inviting a Johnson staffer's inescapable conclusion that "Wilkinson was much more active . . . than Stan Musial."[4]

Musial especially reduced his time following his collapse in Busch Stadium while watching a ball game on September 1, 1964. Momentarily irrational and vomiting profusely, he was rushed to Jewish Hospital, where physicians found him dehydrated and physically exhausted. He chalked it up to a combination of too much travel (mostly with the ball club), ironically too little physical exercise, and too much availing himself of hot dogs and beer in press boxes.[5] Musial's doctors undoubtedly advised him to cut back on his travel.

Yet the Musial-related files at the Johnson Library provide a glimpse at the large number of requests that he received to keynote various physical fitness functions nationwide. Often they came from senators or congressmen on behalf of constituent organizations. Musial rejected virtually all of them, either because they conflicted with Cardinal business or on the dubious grounds that if he accepted one he would have to accept them all. Sometimes this invited criticism. One rejected congressman, who requested, six months in advance, that Musial appear for a state public function, responded that if he claimed to be so vital to the

4. Matthew B. Coffey to John W. Macy, Jr., February 28, 1967, Memorandum, White House Office Files of White House Aides, "Musial, Stanley" Folder, Lyndon B. Johnson Library, Austin, Texas.

5. Unidentified newspaper story, September 12, 1964, clipping in Musial Collection, National Baseball Library; Stan Musial as told to Bob Broeg, *The Man, Stan: Musial, Then and Now,* 230. The book represents an updating of the 1964 autobiography.

Cardinals, "maybe we should bring Wilkinson back." Musial also angered the Bloomington, Minnesota, chamber of commerce, which had asked him to participate in an annual sports parade. The chamber found out that Musial had come to Bloomington the day of the parade to scout a college baseball player after informing them that he had to remain in St. Louis. Musial's office subsequently pleaded a last-minute change in schedule.[6]

Rarely did Musial have contact with high Johnson or party officials. One exception came when he presented the annual report of the council to the president in July 1964. To derive maximum political mileage from the meeting, a longtime Johnson aide proposed that Musial "ad-lib" to the press that "the president is really fit" and "from what I've seen, the president is a real long-ball hitter in this Washington league." On another occasion in 1964, the Democratic National Committee became concerned just prior to a Musial appearance in Rochester, New York, that he might inadvertently appear too friendly with a Republican congressman, a former president of the Rochester Red Wings. Cliff Carter of the committee advised that Musial not be photographed with him or issue a statement praising him.[7]

Musial remained physical fitness adviser until January 1967 when he became general manager of the St. Louis Cardinals. Even then he intended to continue as consultant before the Busch organization advised him to resign. No evidence exists that Musial's service ever displeased Johnson. In fact, Johnson's letter accepting Musial's departure was particularly laudatory. Most likely, Johnson thought that Musial and his small staff, headed by former athletic director of St. Louis University Bob Stewart, who handled the administrative work of the office, had performed credibly. Musial claimed in his resignation letter several gains, including greater state involvement in physical fitness activities as well as increased participation of private organizations nationally and locally. He also praised the increasing popularity of the Presidential Physical Fitness Awards program in which some one hundred thousand youngsters were recognized in 1967 for meeting rigorous test standards.[8]

6. Lionel Van Deerlin to Lawrence O'Brien, January 22, 1965, White House Central Files, Subject File, FG 725, Johnson Library; Mrs. William MacKay to Lyndon Johnson, May 24, 1964, ibid.; Ralph A. Dungan to MacKay, June 10, 1964, copy, ibid.

7. Horace Busby to Johnson, July 29, 1964, Memorandum, ibid.; Cliff Carter to Jack Valenti, July 24, 1964, ibid.

8. Johnson to Musial, January 25, 1967, copy, ibid.; Musial to Johnson, January 24, 1967, ibid.

But by 1967 Johnson found himself even further removed from the physical fitness program. Vietnam had come to absorb his presidency, as did the rupturing of the nation's social fabric amid student unrest and racial riots in the urban centers. Still, Johnson remained an admirer of Musial and perhaps even relished Musial's enormous popularity in the face of his own declining appeal. The physical fitness program came under fire in 1967, however. The Bureau of the Budget office recommended the termination of the President's Council on Physical Fitness and the Special Consultant on Physical Fitness, a proposal that Johnson decided to reject. After failing to induce entertainer Bob Hope, astronaut John Glenn, and former pro basketball player Bob Pettit of the St. Louis Hawks to serve as physical fitness consultant, the Johnson administration settled on astronaut James Lovell, Jr., on nobody's initial lists, to replace Musial.[9]

The publication of *Stan Musial: "The Man's" Own Story* came just months after his appointment as physical fitness adviser. Previewed in *Look* magazine in April 1964, the book itself came out later that spring. Musial probably gained more national attention from it than he did from his work in Washington. Bob Broeg, who wanted to undertake a Musial biography as early as 1949, served as its brainchild and writer. Two considerations led to it being an autobiography: the insistence of the publisher, Doubleday, because of the likelihood it would sell better if it were Musial's own story, and Musial's probable preference, enabling him to have greater control over its content.

But only with great reluctance did Musial grant Broeg permission to begin. In the fall of 1961, Broeg, accompanied by Musial, visited the Donora area for a couple of days and interviewed some of Musial's sisters, his brother Ed, Ki Duda, and Jimmie Russell for the necessary background information. Stash drove him by the modest family home so expeditiously that "he didn't give me much of a look," Broeg later confessed. "He's not ashamed of it," Broeg maintained, "but I think he feels that talking about it would embarrass his family."[10]

For three years, Broeg also spent a couple hours most afternoons in interviews with Musial, from which he constructed a narrative from the tape transcriptions. He also depended on the back files of the columns and stories he had written in more than twenty years of covering him for the *Post-Dispatch* and the *Sporting News*. Broeg claimed that Lil made only one inconsequential change and Stan made none.

9. Irving J. Lewis to Douglass Cater, March 21, 1967, Memorandum, ibid.
10. Heinz, "Stan Musial's Last Day," 96.

The lively book reflected Musial's humble and modest nature; only rarely did it sharply criticize any of his contemporaries—even Durocher. Never did it overstate Musial's accomplishments or undercut those of his teammates. Nor did it reveal stories of the personal indiscretions—sexual or otherwise—of fellow ballplayers. Its greatest limitation related to the way it shaded the Donora years and several later controversial matters. It revealed little, too, of Musial's innermost thoughts or feelings about himself and those around him. One reviewer alluded to its lack of introspection and penetrating assessments. But other reviewers liked its Horatio Alger quality, especially its old-fashioned advice to the younger generation about education, marriage, frugality, and respect for others at a time, ironically, when baby boomers had begun to question such conventional values. More than anything, to his own generation it reaffirmed the nice-guy Musial image. All in all, it represented one of the better efforts in sports autobiography. Yet its modest sales of thirty thousand copies would have been more if it had been more provocative.[11]

In the 1960s Broeg also played an important role in honoring Musial with a statue at Busch Stadium, the Cardinals' new downtown arena. As the result of the Musial retirement dinner in October 1963, the St. Louis members of the Baseball Writers Association, led by Broeg, had raised forty thousand dollars for the monument, ten thousand of which came from Bob Hyland, director of KMOX, and eight thousand from the Cardinals' board of directors. Broeg had won Musial's approval by ensuring that its design would include a youngster gazing upward at him, as Musial, with a baseball bat leaning against his hip, signed an autograph. Amadee Wohlschlaeger, the sports cartoonist for the *St. Louis Post-Dispatch* and the *Sporting News,* skillfully provided the etching, which was first displayed on Musial's retirement day. Musial liked it immediately because "it's easy to keep humble when you're with kids."[12] Nothing could have been more appropriate in capturing Musial than the "Man and the Boy" image.

But the ultimate control over the creation of the statue fell to the city of St. Louis. Mayor Raymond Tucker appointed a committee of himself; C. C. Johnson Spink, publisher of the *Sporting News*; and Charles Buckley, director of the city art museum. They ended up commissioning sixty-two-year-old Carl Christian Mose, a native of Denmark and a former St. Louis artist, who had sculpted a statue of General John J. Pershing

11. Reviews of Alfred Wright, *New York Times Book Review,* June 7, 1964, 18 and J. P. McNicholas, *Best Sellers,* May 15, 1964, 89; Bob Broeg interview, January 29, 1993.
12. Broeg, *Memories,* 292.

on the grounds of the state capitol in Jefferson City. They then rejected the "Man and the Boy" design on the basis of cost and personal artistic expression. Mose wanted to feature Musial alone in his unique batting stance. In preparation he visited him in St. Louis and St. Petersburg, where Musial posed while Mose sketched. He even read Musial's autobiography in an effort to understand better the intricacies of Musial's stance.

Mose worked on the statue eight hours a day nearly every day for three years before its completion in early 1968. He had to rework the original plaster design after Musial thought it depicted him in too upright of a stance and found other things not quite right about it, including the configuration of his head. Finally, the ten-foot statue was cast in bronze and mounted on a ten-foot base in the northeast corner outside of Busch Stadium.

The unveiling took place on Sunday, August 4, and was witnessed by twenty thousand friends and fans, including Governor Warren E. Hearnes, baseball commissioner William D. Eckert, former commissioner Frick, St. Louis Mayor A. J. Cervantes, and Raymond Tucker, the former mayor. Frick's tribute to Musial at the time of his retirement—rendered as "baseball's happiest [sic] warrior, baseball's perfect prince"—now graced the monument. Frick now added, "Stone and bronze are eternal—but cold. Behind the bronze and stone is warmth, personality, and Stan Musial has it." After Musial and Lil unveiled the statue, Musial indicated, "I'm proud. It's truly a great honor. I like to think of this statue as a symbol of sportsmanship. I want to thank Mr. Mose and the wonderful people in St. Louis." After also expressing gratitude to the sportswriters of the city, his former teammates, and several others connected with the ball club and the community, he broke down when he thanked his mother and his family for "making me a Cardinal forever." As he sat down, his mother, also in tears, kissed him on the cheek."[13]

The statue failed to satisfy many observers, however, because it bore little likeness to Musial. Broeg remained one of the biggest critics for its not replicating Musial's distinctive batting stance, physique, and facial features. He also resented that "The Man and the Boy" design had been supplanted in part because of Tucker's supposed friendship with Mose. "A sad conclusion," Broeg later called it, because those who originally contributed did so on the basis of the original drawing. In 1978, however, a local engraving company created a zinc-and-copper three-dimensional

13. Unidentified newspaper story by Jack Herman, August 5, 1968, in Mercantile Library clipping file.

etching of "The Man and the Boy," which was placed in the lobby of the Cardinal Glennon Hospital for Children (Musial, a board member, chaired a $5 million expansion project for the hospital in the 1990s). With Musial's approval, a move began—backed by a private donor—to resurrect the original image in statue form somewhere in the city, possibly in the lobby of Lambert Field, the St. Louis airport. According to Wohlschlaeger, Lil became a major obstacle because she was one of the few notables who liked the Mose statue at the ballpark.[14]

In possibly the final postscript, in 1998 Fred Hanser, the chairman of the Cardinals baseball club, commissioned Harry Weber of Bowling Green, Missouri, to sculpt smaller statues (two-thirds life size) of Cardinal Hall of Famers. Located near the original Musial memorial, they included action-oriented replicas of Gibson, Schoendienst, Brock, Slaughter, Musial, Hornsby, and Dean. Musial, swinging the bat, bears an unmistakable likeness to Stan the Man in his prime. Weber, who consulted with him beforehand, won Musial's enthusiastic approval, which Mose had failed to get.

The 1960s also had witnessed Musial's continued involvement in select political campaigns for Democrats, including Hearnes's gubernatorial race in 1964 and his reelection effort in 1968, which spawned unfounded rumors that Musial had political ambitions. The press recorded only one national campaign where he actively participated—Robert Kennedy's 1968 presidential primary run against the Johnson administration and its candidate, Vice President Hubert Humphrey. Musial campaigned with Kennedy in Indiana as the chairman of athletes for Kennedy. Musial's admiration for the Kennedys no doubt motivated his activity, as did his personal friendship with Hearnes—and Symington—in Missouri. He expressed no views on the public issues of the time—at least none that apparently survived. Like so many affluent Polish Americans, he eventually drifted into the Republican Party, at least according to brother Ed.[15]

Musial's greatest challenge in the mid-1960s came when Busch offered him the general managership in January 1967 on top of his other activities, including club vice-president. Musial jumped at the opportunity, despite his known aversion to being a field manager. He had said many times that while some might believe that he would be too easy on players, his

14. Broeg interview, February 18, 1999; Wohlschlaeger interview, November 12, 1996; Broeg column in *St. Louis Post-Dispatch*, September 26, 1978; Broeg, *Memories*, 292–93.

15. Unidentified newspaper story, May 3, 1968, in Mercantile Library clipping file; Ed Musial interview, August 6, 1996.

concern was that he would be too demanding. Moreover, he had made it clear that he disliked the day-to-day pressure of having to win. The general manager's position was only a step removed from that, however. His lack of experience for the new post troubled Broeg, who thought Busch had put him in a difficult situation. When Busch's executives mentioned that Bob Stewart would be brought in to help out, Broeg "doubled [his] profanity."[16] Stewart, Broeg knew, understood the ins and outs of the NCAA but not of organized baseball. But Musial would receive additional assistance from Jim Toomey, the public relations chief deluxe, and others in the Busch headquarters, including Al Fleishman and Dick Meyer. Then there was always former general manager Bing Devine, now with the New York Mets, who willingly answered Musial's questions.

Musial's appointment can best be understood in the context of several unfortunate circumstances stemming from the summer of 1964 when it appeared that Cardinal title hopes were fading. That August an unhappy Busch had impulsively fired Devine, who had many friends in the organization, partly because of his failure to report a personnel problem involving manager Johnny Keane and shortstop Dick Groat. Devine thought that its resolution had alleviated that necessity. His replacement, Bob Howsam, a former Branch Rickey associate, never connected with the club, especially the players. Keane remained as manager amid disclosures that Busch had talked to Leo Durocher, hardly a fan favorite, as a possible replacement. Keane of course rallied the club and took it to the World Series championship, an achievement based in part on performances from several players that Devine had acquired. After the World Series, a peeved Keane delivered Busch a bombshell message at a press conference: he was resigning as Cardinal manager to become manager of the New York Yankees.

Busch now faced a public relations disaster with the departure of two highly respected executives. He attempted to rectify the calamity by hiring the popular Red Schoendienst, a second-year coach whom Musial strongly promoted, as manager. Yet the Cardinals fell to seventh place, with an 80–81 record, in 1965; they failed to perform much better the following season, finishing sixth with a record of 83–79. Making matters worse, Schoendienst and Howsam lacked rapport with one another. Howsam's memos annoyed not only Schoendienst but also the players, who resented his complaints about certain team members not sitting up in the bullpen or not wearing the uniform properly. Too, Howsam's player transactions

16. Broeg, *Memories,* 315.

brought fan ridicule. Following the 1965 campaign, with Schoendienst's apparent approval, he sent popular Ken Boyer, the hero of the 1964 World Series, to the New York Mets for third baseman Charley Smith and pitcher Al Jackson. One week later Howsam moved Bill White, Groat, and catcher Bob Uecker to the Phillies for catcher Pat Corrales, pitcher Art Mahaffey, and outfielder Alex Johnson. Neither deal strengthened the team, and Smith and Johnson turned out to be particular disappointments.

Howsam's most successful transaction came when Musial and Schoendienst goaded him to trade pitcher Ray Sadecki to the San Francisco Giants for first baseman Orlando Cepeda. Called Cha Cha by his new teammates, Cepeda hit .303 with 17 homers in 1966. A team leader, he would win the National League Most Valuable Player award in 1967 on a resurging club that included Gibson, Brock, Flood, McCarver, Javier, and pitchers Dick Hughes, Nelson Briles, and twenty-two-year-old Steve Carlton. The Cardinals still needed a left-handed power hitter for the outfield. Howsam secured one from the Yankees for Charley Smith: Roger Maris, who had broken Babe Ruth's single-season home-run record by hitting 61 homers in 1961. Maris wanted out of pressure-filled New York, where he felt unappreciated. No longer the home-run hitter he once was, the serious, sensitive Maris still performed well in the field, was fundamentally sound, and added power to the lineup. Right after the Maris deal in December 1966, Howsam signed a three-year general manager contract with the Cincinnati Reds for an amount that Busch refused to match.

Busch then asked Musial to replace Howsam a mere couple of months before spring training. Why Musial ever accepted remains unclear. Musial and Jack Buck claimed that he did it as a favor to Busch. The reported thirty-five-thousand-dollar salary also proved enticing. More than anything, however, the resurrection of the Cardinals became an enormous challenge to him. He felt that he knew enough about the game to make a difference. So, Musial became one of the few great ballplayers to serve at that high capacity—only Eddie Collins, Herb Pennock, Hank Greenberg, and Joe Cronin had preceded him.[17]

As general manager, Musial did much to improve relations between his office and Schoendienst. Indeed, even though they did not always agree, these two old friends worked harmoniously together. They shared a mutual respect that was unique. They were often seen joking with or confiding in one another. That new approach created a more positive spirit, which sparked the ball club. The new general manager also addressed

17. Buck interview, December 10, 1996; Musial, *The Man, Stan,* 234.

another deficiency: the poor relationship between the front office and the players. The correction was partly cosmetic. Musial came to spring training in uniform ready to provide batting tips. Whether he helped anyone is undeterminable. His most valuable advice went to older players on other teams such as Ernie Banks of the Cubs, whom he advised to hit more to left field and to use a lighter bat. But Musial's mere presence on the field, particularly swinging in the batting cage, became a positive force. So, too, were his appearances in the locker room, where his chatting, backslapping, laughing style created a much more relaxed environment.

Musial's greatest impact came in contract negotiations. Many of the Redbirds, including Maris, had yet to sign their 1967 contracts. Musial made it easier for them by forsaking Howsam's gamesmanship of submitting an exaggeratedly low offer so that after considerable bickering they could reach common ground. Musial viewed the process from a player's perspective in providing fair—if not generous—offers from the outset. The starting lineup for the 1967 Cardinals, in fact, had one of the highest collective salaries up to that time. He added other player-friendly touches such as providing a baby-sitting service at the stadium so that players' wives could attend the games. Consequently, he quickly won the allegiance of the team. Gibson remembered Musial as "a pleasant surprise and a pleasure to deal with," while Brock and Flood also acknowledged his positive presence.[18]

A successful general manager must also establish good press relations. Musial, by just being Musial, succeeded admirably. Always forthcoming, and believing rightly that he was among friends, he absolutely dazzled the press. Much laughter accompanied his press conferences, and reporters often were disinclined to ask tough questions. On one occasion, at Al Lang Field in St. Petersburg, Musial addressed photographers after putting his arm around Schoendienst. "It's a little early in the morning for this. You guys ought to know that Red and I don't hit our peak until about noon," Musial said. They then both laughed. Musial then continued, "How would you guys like it if we came out at ten in the morning and started to take *your* picture? Is this color or black and white? Color? Yeah, yeah, o.k., Red, give 'em your living smile. One more? Sure, sure, one more, why not?"[19]

It was apparent that Musial enjoyed his job immensely, and he conveyed that impression to his audience. One writer found that although he had put on weight around the middle, he appeared healthy and well

18. Gibson, *From Ghetto to Glory*, 122.
19. William Leggett, "Stanley, the General Manager," 68.

tanned. Musial laughed a lot and communicated his love of the game. The writer wrote that while Musial was not a good interview because of his circumspection and lack of complexity, he was "naturally devoid of pretense"—a man of class, which "encompass[ed] the effortless style with which he [did] everything."[20]

Good judgment also mattered. He had wisely listened to Schoendienst's contention that outfielder Mike Shannon could play third base—a key decision in the success of the 1967 campaign. Schoendienst spent hours hitting ground balls to Shannon in spring training before Shannon finally came around. This enabled Schoendienst to field a veteran at every position and play Maris regularly in the outfield. Both Musial and his manager also agreed that they had enough talent on the existing roster to win. Musial ignored the waiver wire, arguing that if a player were released by a club there must be a good reason for it. His only player transaction involved obtaining pitcher Jack Lamabe from Devine of the Mets following an injury to Gibson. The 1967 Cardinals exhibited not only talent and good balance but also team chemistry, which the press partly attributed to Musial's leadership. As a result, the Redbirds captured the National League pennant by ten and a half games and defeated Boston in the World Series four games to three.

Ironically, a little more than two months later the Cardinal front office announced Musial's departure as general manager. He remained as a senior vice president, an advisory position. Busch also alluded to the supplanting of Stewart, Musial's right-hand man, and the appointment as general manager of Devine. Neither Musial nor Devine attended the press conference. While Devine remained in New York, Musial and Lil were on vacation in Acapulco, Mexico, following the baseball meetings in Mexico City.

The press did not completely buy Busch's explanation that personal business commitments had led to Musial's leaving as general manager. Still, ten years later Musial himself cited the fatal heart attack in June 1967 of his fifty-three-year-old business partner, "Biggie" Garagnani, necessitating that he spend more time at the restaurant. He later claimed that he had told Meyer and Busch that he wished to step down at the end of the season. Yet Al Hirshberg of the *Boston Post* recalled how happy Musial seemed working with Schoendienst. As for Garagnani's death, Hirshberg argued that Musial was a baseball man first and a businessman second. He could always get somebody else to run the restaurant, which Biggie's son,

20. Robert Liston, *The Pros*, 148.

Jack, would soon do anyway. The *Sporting News* also remained skeptical in a headline story, "Big Rumble in Cardinals' Executive Suite." The article reported that emerging differences came to a head involving Musial over the distribution of World Series tickets. Raising additional questions, Musial was quoted in the newspaper six months later as saying that someday "I resolve to tell the real story of why I gave up the job as general manager of the Cardinals—a job I enjoyed and whose contacts were so interesting that I number those days as some of the greatest I ever spent in baseball."[21]

Musial has never told the "real story" of his resignation. Those close to him seem in agreement that the supposed conflict over the World Series tickets was a bogus account even though Broeg admitted that Musial "screwed up" by releasing too many tickets, requiring that chairs be placed in the aisles. There is also general agreement that the position demanded more time and responsibility than Musial was willing to devote to it. Busch probably told Musial that he needed to master the paperwork, baseball law, and the other intricacies, a grueling endeavor involving many hours in the office. Never a detail person, Musial enjoyed the public relations side of the position while giving short shrift to the rest. Revealingly, he had wanted to remain physical fitness director while general manager.[22]

In the end, Musial came away from the ordeal rather well. He would be remembered as winning the World Series in his only season as general manager, adding to his Midas touch mythology. Under the capable Devine, the Cardinals repeated as pennant winners but failed to capture the World Series championship the following season and then fell to fourth place for the next two campaigns. It would not be until 1982 that the team again would win the World Series.

Less than two years after Musial's contribution to the Cardinals' 1967 championship season, he was inducted into the Baseball Hall of Fame. He became the forty-third player to be selected by the Baseball Writers Association of America. Of the 340 sportswriters who voted in 1969, 23 failed to cast their vote for Musial, three more rejections than Ted Williams received in 1966. Musial obtained 93.2 percent of the voter support, well above the 75 percent required. Like Williams, he entered in his first year of eligibility (five years following retirement as a player), a feat that even Joe DiMaggio could not accomplish. His failure to receive a unanimous

21. Musial, *The Man, Stan,* 236; Al Hirshberg, "Trouble in Musial's Paradise?" 17; *Sporting News,* December 16, 1967, clipping in Musial Collection, National Baseball Library; unidentified newspaper clipping, January 13, 1968, ibid.

22. Broeg interview, February 18, 1999; Sally to Jim Jones, January 24, 1967, Memorandum, White House Central Files, Subject File 725, Johnson Library.

vote, which escaped even the great Cobb and Ruth, bothered Musial not at all. When asked about it, he commented, "In this country, the majority rules. And that's a great thing—a majority. I'll go with that. I'm just happy that I was elected."[23]

Along with Musial, the 1969 induction class included Brooklyn Dodger catcher Roy Campanella, confined permanently to a wheelchair as the result of a tragic automobile accident in 1958, and two old-timers, pitcher Stan Coveleski and pitcher and sportscaster Waite Hoyt, both selected by the veterans committee. The induction ceremonies took place on Monday, July 28, 1969, outside the entrance of the National Baseball Library in Cooperstown, a picturesque village in upstate New York. When baseball commissioner Bowie K. Kuhn began the ceremonies, a light rain fell on the inductees and the nearly five thousand guests. By the time he formally introduced the four new members and presented the plaques, the rain had ended. Around the time of Musial's induction speech, the sunlight broke through, causing Pat Dean, the wife of Dizzy Dean, another Cardinal Hall of Famer, to say, "The sun always shines on Stan the Man."[24]

Knowing that Musial was not a thoughtful, polished speaker, Broeg crafted the speech. He remembered Ted Williams's address in 1966, which Broeg considered the best that he had ever heard at Cooperstown. Williams had criticized the barriers that kept blacks such as Satchel Paige and Josh Gibson outside of the Hall, which ultimately led to a reversal of policy. Broeg wanted Musial to do as well.[25]

An obviously nervous Musial, who altered some of Broeg's draft, first spoke personally about the three other inductees. He then traced his rags-to-riches rise out of Donora, thanking those who helped him along the way, especially Joe Barbao and Ki Duda, while curiously eliminating Dick Kerr and Ollie Vanek from Broeg's version. He sadly noted the recent deaths of Biggie Garagnani and Duda, president of California State College (Pennsylvania), who succumbed to a stroke at the age of fifty-nine. He referred to Lil as a "fine and understanding wife who . . . [had] to be both mother and father to our children." When introducing his mother, seated in the audience, he almost broke down while describing her homemade baseballs constructed "out of a little bit of this and a little bit of that." He called his father a "great baseball fan who always talked about 'Baby' Ruth" and one who was right about a college education.

23. *Sporting News*, February 1, 1969, clipping in Musial Collection, National Baseball Library.

24. Musial, *The Man, Stan*, 14. The anecdote comes from Broeg.

25. Broeg interview, February 18, 1999.

The necessity of a college degree represented Musial's main message to American youth, one he had often expressed. He concluded by saying, "Baseball . . . was a great game, baseball . . . is a great game, and baseball will . . . be a great game." His most significant flubs came early when he momentarily forgot to include his son Dick while alluding to individual family members and when he failed to introduce Cardinal president Gussie Busch. The speech was typically Musial (and Broeg)—it eschewed broader social issues, unlike Williams, while expressing his humility, gratitude, fortuity, and love of baseball. Musial later called his induction his greatest baseball thrill, surpassing his three thousand hits, his three Most Valuable Player awards, and his first World Series. He rarely missed the Cooperstown ceremonies in the years to come.[26]

In the early 1970s Musial concentrated even more on business interests, which evolved from the 1950s with the steakhouse; Redbird Lanes, the bowling alley on Gravois Avenue in south St. Louis he jointly owned; and Brentwood Bank, where he acted as director. Then, almost the very week he accepted the physical fitness position in February 1964, he became a director of the First Southern Company, a finance agency in Greensboro, North Carolina. Two months later he and Biggie headed a syndicate that purchased a sizable tract of land containing seven three-story apartments on the northwest corner of Lindell Boulevard and Euclid Avenue near downtown St. Louis. They planned to raze the apartments once the leases ran out and then construct a thirty-two-story office building that would include Biggie's City Bank on the first floor.

That September Musial and Garagnani also became key officers in a syndicate including Sidney Solomon, Jr., a St. Louis insurance executive, and Joe Garagiola, now an NBC sportscaster, that purchased the $3 million Ivanhoe-By-the-Sea Hotel in the exclusive Bal-Harbor section of Miami Beach. The modern seven-story complex contained a private beach and two heart-shaped swimming pools. During this same period, Stan Musial and Biggie's, Inc., also participated with another group in buying a radio-television station in Lake Charles, Louisiana.

In the mid-1960s Musial, apart from Biggie, also embarked in a baseball equipment manufacturing business in which he employed his son, Dick, recently discharged from the service, as manager and his brother, Ed, as a salesman. He asked Ted Tappe, a former Chicago Cubs player who owned a sporting goods store with his brother, to teach Dick the business.

26. Broeg's draft of Musial's induction speech and transcript of Musial's address are in the National Baseball Library.

Musial hoped to use his name to advantage in selling bats, gloves, and other baseball equipment to sporting goods stores nationwide. It turned out to be a bust, however. Ed Musial remembered someone stealing his complete line of samples from his motel room during a sales trip, one of several minor disasters that occurred. Sometime in the early 1970s Musial disengaged from the enterprise.[27]

Biggie's death in 1967 represented a major setback that torpedoed several planned projects. Musial lost not only a friend but also a savvy entrepreneur, one who taught him a lot about investment. Still, Musial had cultivated other shrewd business associates to advise him. He had also developed good business judgment with a particular knack for comprehending profit and loss. Only rarely at first did that judgment lead him astray.

Those who dealt with Musial outside of baseball probably underestimated his abilities, for he usually said little at meetings and rarely volunteered opinions. John Hulston, a Springfield, Missouri, attorney and a member of the Ozarks Airline board with Musial, remembered that Musial came to meetings at least ten minutes early and brought with him a dozen baseballs to sign on request. All of this suggested that the popular Musial was window dressing for the airline, one who had invaluable contacts in the community, especially at Lambert Field.[28]

Robert Glazier, a St. Louis television station manager who served with Musial on a board of judges in a "Speak Up for Democracy" contest for high schoolers, thought Musial had difficulty reading because he asked Glazier and others to read the essays aloud. Glazier, too, remembered that Musial said little at the meetings. Yet sportscaster Jack Buck saw the other side of Musial. He recalled that Musial, in looking over the electric bills for the Ivanhoe Hotel, quickly determined that the utility company was cheating the Ivanhoe. Busch described Musial as a hands-on, intelligent person who knew how to make money.[29]

In the early 1970s, with Musial as president, Stan Musial and Biggie's, Inc. continued its extensive operations despite Biggie's death. Jack Garagnani now became executive vice president. More quiet than his late father, the always immaculately dressed Jack, who had attended Georgetown University, also continued Biggie's interest in politics, eventually

27. Ed Tappe to Giglio, August 30, 1996, in possession of Giglio; Ed Musial interview, August 6, 1996.
28. John Hulston interview, September 24, 1996.
29. Robert Glazier telephone interview, September 8, 1996; Buck interview, December 10, 1996.

becoming a part-time advance man for President Jimmy Carter in the late '70s. Dick Musial acted as vice president of operations in an organization that involved some five hundred employees. Its major acquisitions in the early 1970s included the luxurious 220-room Clearwater Beach Hilton Hotel on the Gulf coast of Florida, near Tampa and St. Petersburg. That hotel underwent refurbishing after the purchase in November 1972. A somewhat risky venture given the energy crisis, all indications are, however, that the hotel proved profitable. Dick Musial soon moved to Hollywood, Florida, with his wife and three children to oversee the two Florida hotels, both of which were run by experienced managers. Stan and Lil usually spent the winters in Florida now that they had family and business interests there.

The following December Stan Musial and Biggie's, Inc., added the Hilton Inn properties at Lambert Field. Musial announced that they planned to not only service travelers but also make the hotel complex a showcase for St. Louisans. Once again, Musial had gambled that the energy crisis would prove temporary and not affect the business. By the late 1970s some additional rooms were added to the 214-room complex, with 86 more planned. By then Dick had moved back to St. Louis to manage the Park Terrace Airport Hilton after an Arab group had made Musial an unsolicited offer on the Florida hotels that his company found too tempting to refuse.

Musial investigated other investment opportunities in the early 1980s. After earlier rumors had linked him, with others, to the purchase of the Cleveland Indians and the Pittsburgh Pirates in the mid and late 1970s, Musial became the majority owner of the St. Louis Steamers in the Major Indoor Soccer League in 1980. The Steamers were the most successful franchise in the league, averaging a reported 17,300 fans per game. Musial attributed the franchise's good fortune to the policy of securing eight St. Louis–area players. "We want to Americanize our league," Musial said in an interview. . . . That [also] has been the reason for our success."[30] In 1984 Musial sold his interest in the club after attendance fell.

Other business reverses soon followed at a time when Musial became less involved in the day-to-day operations. In 1980 the Park Terrace Hotel Hilton showed its first loss in the midst of a sagging economy, which worsened in the early '80s. A $22 million renovation, resulting in 125 new rooms, two new restaurants, a new lobby, and marble floors in

30. *Buffalo Evening News*, February 19, 1982.

each bedroom contributed to the problem. The *St. Louis Business Journal* also reported a contract dispute of $870,000 involving the contractor and subcontractors, which was eventually settled out of court. Those knowledgeable of the hotel business contended that Stan Musial and Biggie's, Inc., overextended itself financially without cutting into the competition. One competitor claimed that Garagnani and Dick Musial, who were most actively involved, did not have "deep enough pockets" to compete and suffered from high overheads and lack of managerial skills, which led to huge overruns. As a result, Musial and Biggie's, Inc., sold a 50 percent interest in the hotel to a Dallas-based company, resulting in another lawsuit of $768,000 for failing to pay a finder's fee.[31]

Also suffering financial losses was Stan Musial and Biggie's Restaurant after it momentarily shifted from the traditional menu of steak, prime rib, and seafood to French cuisine. Jack Garagnani also attributed the setback to the parent company neglecting the operations and to excessive competition with area restaurants. According to the *St. Louis Business Journal,* the hotel and restaurant filed a combined loss of $3 million for 1984. By then Stan Musial and Biggie's, Inc., was becoming more involved in the management of hotels, signing agreements to manage the 160-room Grand Glaize Inn in the Lake of the Ozarks area of Missouri and a Ramada Inn in Mt. Vernon, Illinois. The owners of the Ramada fired Musial and Biggie's, Inc., five months after the hotel opened, allegedly for violating the contract.[32]

Even more embarrassing, Joe Garagiola and his wife, Audrie, filed suit against Musial and his associates in April 1986, tarnishing Musial's squeaky-clean image arguably for the first time. The suit ended an association that began when fifteen-year-old Garagiola served as a general handy man for the 1941 Springfield Cardinals, "washing Musial's sox," as Garagiola later described it. In 1946 they both contributed to the Cardinals' last championship in the Musial era. Around that time Garagiola affectionately began to call his new paisano "Tony." Musial soon asked him to go along on speaking engagements, probably to remove some of the pressure. Musial drove and they divided the honorarium. Before friendly gatherings anxious to see Stan, Garagiola would sit in the audience until Musial completed his remarks. Musial then introduced Garagiola, by saying, "You know, Joe and I both have mike fright. I'm afraid to get the

31. *St. Louis Business Journal,* May 12, 1986; Denny Bond telephone interview, September 27, 1999; Bob O'Loughlin interview, October 29, 1999.
32. *St. Louis Business Journal,* May 12, 1986.

mike, and he's afraid he's not going to get it."[33] Musial and the audience laughed profusely. Then Garagiola went into a routine that never failed to entertain the crowd. The exposure brought him his own speaking gigs. His developing skill as an after-dinner speaker led to his later presiding over several banquets honoring Musial.

In 1951 the Cards traded Garagiola to the Pirates, and three seasons afterward he retired to enter the broadcast booth, initially with the Cardinals. Throughout this period he and Musial remained friends, aided by Garagiola's close attachment to Biggie, who, like Garagiola, grew up on the Hill. Musial and Garagiola complemented each other well—the former, still a bit shy, deliberate, and reticent and the latter, bubbly, outgoing, and loquacious, one who "played words like an accordion," according to one observer.[34] Beginning in the late 1950s the two St. Louis residents partnered several businesses, including Redbird Bowling Lanes. By the time Garagiola filed suit against Musial on the bowling alley partnership, he had moved to Scottsdale, Arizona.

Established in 1958, Redbird Lanes was one of the most profitable bowling operations in the Midwest during the bowling craze of that era. Open twenty-four hours a day, it had a much publicized nursery service and other up-to-date features. The Garagiolas had a one-third interest in Redbird Bowling Lanes, Inc., and in two related corporations—Redbird Concessions, Inc., which operated the concession sales at the bowling alley, and Grav-Hemp Corporation, which owned the property where Redbird Lanes was located. Stan Musial also owned one-third interest in the three companies; Theresa Garagnani, Biggie's widow, owned the final third. All three families shared the officer positions in the three operations. Dick Musial and Jack Garagnani served as directors.

The Garagiola suit against Stan Musial, Theresa Garagnani, Dick Musial, and Jack Garagnani, filed in U.S. District Court, Eastern District Court of Missouri, on April 14, 1986, alleged that Dick Musial and Jack Garagnani of Stan Musial and Biggie's Management Company (SM&B) received from Redbird Concessions, Inc., more than $750 per month for services performed in the operation of the concession business from January 1982 to November 1985. The Garagiolas contended not only that Stan Musial and Theresa Garagnani had approved the arrangement without consulting them but also that Dick Musial and Jack Garagnani had not performed any services. The Garagiolas claimed that they found out about

33. Joe Garagiola, *It's Anybody's Ballgame*, 94.
34. *St. Louis Post-Dispatch*, April 27, 1986.

the arrangement as a result of Audrie's presence at a board of directors meeting of the two companies in December 1985 when the board, by a 4–1 vote (with Audrie dissenting), decided that SM&B Management would now receive 5 percent of the gross sales for managing the concession business.[35]

While the defendants agreed that Dick Musial and Jack Garagnani had been employed as stated, they argued that the Garagiolas had been informed and that the two managers had turned around a floundering business. They also denied the charge that two of the bowling alley–related companies had improperly loaned Stan Musial and Biggie's, Inc., $130,000 without the consent of the plaintiffs. Even though the loans had been repaid, the Garagiolas countered that this had occurred only after they had exposed the arrangement. The defendants also refuted the final charge that they failed to accept a fair price for the liquidation of the businesses, which the Garagiolas sought.

It is difficult to believe that Stan Musial could have knowingly deceived anyone, let alone a close friend. It is equally difficult to contemplate that Joe Garagiola would have brought charges against Musial for frivolous reasons. What most likely happened is that Dick Musial and Jack Garagnani failed to confer with the Garagiolas about taking over the concession operation and about the short-term loan. They might have feared the Garagiolas' disapproval. They probably told Stan about their actions without informing him that they had excluded the Garagiolas from the decision making. By then Musial, always more a public relations person, was spending even less time in the day-to-day operation of the companies. In any case, this slipshod approach probably explains Dick Musial's and Jack Garagnani's other business difficulties. Revealingly, Theresa Garagnani filed a successful civil suit against her son three years later for his failure to pay twenty-six promissory notes totaling $314,611. The $130,000 loan to Stan Musial and Biggie's, Inc., might have been the result of a temporary cash-flow problem or something even more serious. If the latter, then someone like Musial or Theresa Garagnani would have had to repay the loan to the two companies.[36]

35. *Joseph Garagiola and Audrie Garagiola vs. Stanley F. Musial, et al.*, December 29, 1986, U.S. District Court, Eastern District of Missouri, Case no. 86–0768-C-1, Federal Records Center, Kansas City, Missouri. See also *St. Louis Post-Dispatch*, April 15, April 19, and April 27, 1986. All specifics relating to the case, including attorney briefs, come from the court record.

36. *Theresa Garagnani vs. John M. Garagnani, Sr.*, Circuit Court of the City of St. Louis, July 13, 1989, Case no. 882–06831, Civil Courts Building, St. Louis, Missouri.

In the end, the Garagiolas were contesting about $54,000, the amount that went to Dick Musial and Jack Garagnani over a three-year period, a relatively small figure to Joe Garagiola and Stan Musial. Yet the conflict raised questions about trust that the two protagonists found difficult to resolve. Musial attempted to talk with Garagiola several times prior to the filing of the suit, only to be rebuffed. Afterward, he, along with the other defendants, issued a public statement, calling the allegations "outrageous." "We are showing restraint by not filing a defamation suit," the statement continued.[37] It also accused the Garagiolas of instituting the suit as a way to disengage financially from Redbird Lanes.

Eight months later the matter was settled without a trial, with both sides sharing in the court costs. Ten years later Garagiola claimed that he had secured a favorable settlement, which included the sale of Redbird Lanes, but he remained unwilling to say more because of a mutual confidentiality agreement. "The Musial chapter is over, it has caused much pain, and Stan is not a nice man," he said. Musial's only recorded comments came from Jack Buck, who sometimes mischievously asked Musial, "Heard from Joe lately?" "You mean DiMaggio?" Musial responded. "No, Garagiola," smiled Buck, who claimed that Musial then would go "off like a missile."[38]

In the late 1980s Buck recalled that Garagiola felt bad enough about their differences to want a reconciliation, but it never occurred, largely because of Musial. To Musial, Garagiola had unforgivably made him look bad in public. Consequently, when the 1946 Cardinal championship ball club celebrated their fifty-year reunion, the organizers of a ceremony for the team before a Cardinal game in Busch Stadium kept the two men four boxes apart. Moreover, when Garagiola was inducted into the broadcasters wing of the Baseball Hall of Fame, Musial failed to attend the festivities at Cooperstown that year, a rare miss. The Garagiola affair, according to Buck, remains a "dagger in Stan's heart."[39] It cost him a close friendship, it embarrassed him because of the public exposure, and it probably contributed to his decision to disengage from most of his businesses. By then Jack Garagnani and Dick Musial had also parted ways,

37. *St. Louis Post-Dispatch*, April 27, 1986.
38. Joe Garagiola telephone interview, December 3, 1996; Buck interview, December 10, 1996. Redbird Lanes was sold in 1986 to Sports Arenas, Inc. of San Diego and Westmore Group of St. Louis. Undoubtedly, the sale was part of the Musial-Garagiola settlement. By 1996 a Walgreens drugstore occupied the site of the bowling alley. *St. Louis Post-Dispatch*, March 26, 1996.
39. Buck, *"That's a Winner,"* 88; Buck interview, December 10, 1996.

with Dick moving to the Lake of the Ozarks area to manage the Knolls Condominium complex.

Advancing age and health problems also led to Musial's business "retirement." Too, physical reversals disrupted a relatively rigorous exercise program of sit-ups, golf, swimming, and bicycling, all of which kept him only a few pounds over his playing weight. He had long terminated his participation in old-timer games after starring in several of them, including homering into the right-field stands in new Busch Stadium in 1967 off of former Yankee great Allie Reynolds. As he circled the bases, "laughing for joy," he shouted, "I wanted that one—in this park." Musial, who saw too many old-timers get hurt in those contests, quoted Casey Stengel, who compared the games to "airplane landings: If you can walk away from them they're successful."[40]

Musial's first health setback occurred when he was hospitalized for a gastric ulcer in July 1983. Six years later the detection of prostate cancer especially frightened Musial, who had ignored telltale warning signs for about a year. Following surgery, he underwent a period of withdrawal during which he lost twenty pounds. To friend Crayton J. Hale, president of Little League Baseball International, he confided, "I have lost so much weight. I am so depressed. I like people, I used to go out and mix with people. When I go to a restaurant now I take [a table] that faces the corner so that I don't have to talk to [anyone]." But that began to change when he received a letter from daughter Gerry in New York, who wondered, "Dad, what are you doing to yourself? Remember this," she said, "laugh and the world laughs with you, cry and you cry alone." "I read that, re-read it, and I read it again," Musial remembered. He then thought, "What *am* I doing to myself? I am putting on weight," he told Hale, "and I am going to spring training."[41] The sixty-nine-year-old Musial soon became a spokesman for periodic examinations. His illness also brought him closer to his brother Ed, who also underwent major surgery.

By the late 1980s Musial had liquidated his major business interests with the exception of Stan the Man, Inc., which tapped into the budding autograph business. This brought Musial to various baseball card shows around the country, by then a major enterprise. Managed by Dick Zitsman and Pat Anthony, Stan the Man, Inc., located on Des Peres Road in suburban St. Louis, marketed autographed bats ($250), baseballs ($60),

40. Musial, *The Man, Stan,* 240; Connor, ed., *Baseball for the Love of It,* 273–74.
41. Crayton J. Hale telephone interview, November 29, 1999.

replica 1944 Cardinal jerseys ($300), and assorted other items. "Take Stan Musial Home with You" ads now appeared in memorabilia publications such as *Sports Collectors Digest*.[42]

Rarely did Musial turn down staged signing sessions at various collector shows where superstars commanded substantial fees. Sometimes promoters matched him with other Cardinal greats. Steve Gietschier of the *Sporting News* once observed the long lines waiting for Musial's and Terry Moore's signatures, with Musial occasionally shouting at Moore, who was at the next table, "Terry, this is not like it was in the old days." When Sam Walton of Wal Mart, Inc., invited Musial to Bentonville, Arkansas, for two days of autograph signing, Musial turned him down, however, because his proposed ten-thousand-dollar offer had not matched DiMaggio's earlier twenty-five thousand.[43]

That former and current baseball greats made money for their autographs soon invited public criticism, especially after Hall of Famers Duke Snider and Willie McCovey failed to pay income taxes on that revenue. Musial's friends defended him, arguing that collectors profit from his autographed items by selling them at shows. Why should he not charge profiteers for his signature? Indeed, no longer were autographs sought solely for personal enjoyment. So, Musial, too, had succumbed to pressures from entrepreneurs, who cited Mickey Mantle's and Joe DiMaggio's seventy-thousand-dollar windfalls for one day of signing.

As it turned out, Musial made more money from the autograph business, according to Jack Buck, than he did from baseball, enabling him to recoup business losses from the early '80s. Still, with rare exceptions, he also signed without charging if personally approached. For that he usually carried photo cards containing his batting statistics on the backside. Actor John Wayne gave him the idea one day at lunch when autograph seekers approached their table, forcing Musial to seek napkins or matchbooks to sign while Wayne merely reached into his pocket for photo cards, which he autographed. Musial immediately commented, "I've got to get some of those."[44] At least until 1990, when the requests became too numerous, he also dispatched signed photos to those who sent him fan mail.

---

42. Price list from "Stan the Man" Inc.; ad from *Sports Collectors Digest*, November 24, 1995.

43. Gietschier interview, September 17, 1996; Broeg interview, February 18, 1999.

44. Buck interview, December 10, 1996; *St. Louis Post-Dispatch*, January 30, 1990. One instance when Musial charged for his autograph occurred when two Cardinal groundskeepers asked him to sign their ballcaps. He did for twenty-five dollars apiece. Erv Fischer interview, November 11, 1996.

Musial remained an unofficial ambassador of baseball into the '90s. Having been voted the most trusted sports personality in a 1973 national survey did not keep him from speaking out on such controversial issues as the skyrocketing salaries of players signing long-term contracts. "I believe that the American system always worked on the basis of people being paid *after* they've produced," Musial commented; "it's hard to figure . . . who's going to keep producing, and who's going to be injured or get fat or lose their ability."[45] While recognizing that the defunct reserve clause had favored the owners excessively, he believed the pendulum had shifted too much the other way, enabling even banjo hitters to earn exorbitant salaries. Musial predicted that multi-year arrangements, along with million-dollar contracts, could only dull player incentive.

Musial also continued to serve on the Baseball Hall of Fame veterans committee and travel to out-of-town games on special occasions. None carried more meaning than observing Phillies infielder Pete Rose break his National League record for career hits (3,630). Musial witnessed the record-breaking safety on August 10, 1981, off of Cardinals pitcher Mark Littell at Philadelphia's Veterans Stadium. As usual, Musial was outwardly gracious; when pressed if Rose was "as good a hitter as The Man himself," Musial smiled and said, "I would say yes." But the loss of the record caused some inner pain. Buck, who interviewed Musial earlier about Rose's chase, witnessed Musial's face drop when asked about it. "I can't say I enjoy it," Musial admitted. Buck saw a look appear on his face that indicated that the record "means an awful lot to him."[46]

Musial's allegiance to the game involved not only his annual trek to Cooperstown but also his attendance at innumerable charity activities, including golf tournaments, where his presence never failed to draw fans and enliven the gathering. The ritual involved his harmonica, which he now played well enough to have recorded a tape of eighteen songs with Mel Bay Publications in 1994, marketed with an instruction book. He entertained guests at the Hall of Fame and other banquets with "Them Golden Slippers," "Red River Valley," or "Wabash Cannon Ball," the first of which he performed in bib overalls on Roy Clark's *Hee Haw* TV show.

45. *New York Times*, November 21, 1973, clipping in Musial Collection, National Baseball Library; *Sporting News*, June 20, 1981, ibid.; Connor, ed., *Baseball for the Love of It*, 224.
46. *St. Louis Post-Dispatch*, August 11, 1981; *St. Louis Globe-Democrat*, June 10, 1981, in Mercantile Library clipping file.

Even trumpeter Al Hirt, who jokingly called himself Musial's backup, often played with him.[47] The harmonica became a prop that enabled a once shy man to connect with audiences.

Former players remembered Musial's individual acts of kindness on those social occasions. As a speaker at a Rollins College sports banquet, Musial recognized former major leaguer Lennie Merullo, whose son played there. He came over to his table afterward and said loud enough for others to hear, "Lennie Merullo, you son of a gun, you . . . look like you should be still playing short for the Cubbies." "You can imagine the love I had for Stan that moment and still have," wrote Merullo. Former Braves player Casey Wise also remembered Musial's generosity in alluding to his baseball accomplishments before a group of several hundred guests in Naples, Florida, where Wise was beginning his orthodontic practice.[48]

And as always Musial retained his good-natured humor. Jack Creel introduced Musial to his son at an old-timers game in Houston by commenting that he played with Stan when they were both making seventy-five dollars a month and now Stan owned St. Louis. Musial laughingly corrected, "No, just half of it." Former Giant Herman Franks recalled with considerable amusement Musial asking him at the Hall of Fame festivities in 1994, "Herm, how old are you?" Franks indicated eighty, prompting Musial to reply, "You look eighty-five."[49] Franks, of course, knew that it was all in fun.

Musial's travels often took him abroad, where he promoted baseball even more. This included a November 1966 trip to Vietnam, along with Hank Aaron and Joe Torre of the Atlanta Braves, Brooks Robinson of the Baltimore Orioles, and Harmon Killebrew of the Minnesota Twins. The group visited hospitals, camps, and air bases to sign autographs, shake hands, and show films of the All-Star game. Musial nearly became a fatality; his quarters were bombed while he was elsewhere in the area eating lunch. He flirted with danger at another outpost and in a helicopter over hostile territory. "I was really impressed with the morale of our troops. They know they've got a job to do, and they're doing it," he

---

47. "Musial: A Tribute"; Mel Bay Publications, Inc., is located south of St. Louis in Pacific, Missouri.

48. Lennie Merullo to Giglio, August 27, 1996, in possession of Giglio; K. C. "Casey" Wise to Giglio, August 20, 1996, ibid.

49. Creel to Giglio, August 24, 1996, ibid.; Herman Franks to Giglio, August 27, 1996, ibid.

remarked upon his arrival home. Later he told Jack Buck that he had foolishly endangered his life by going to South Vietnam.[50]

Beginning in the early 1970s, Musial and Lil also visited Poland, the homeland of his father. Like so many other ethnic Americans reaching middle age, Musial experienced an urge to visit the "old" country. On his first trip he carried with him ecclesiastical letters from John Cardinal Carberry of St. Louis to the cardinals in Warsaw and Krakow, the latter the future Pope John Paul II, a close friend of Carberry's. To the cardinal of Krakow he presented a baseball that he inscribed, "To Cardinal Wojtyla from Cardinal Musial." Since baseball was to become an Olympic sport for Poland in 1992, Musial eventually became an adviser on program development. Jim Michener, who often accompanied him, suggested that he get involved after Fidel Castro had announced that he was sending Cubans to train the Soviets.

Of course, he played his harmonica for Poles everywhere. In a Warsaw restaurant in 1976 he and the house accordionist played duets for hours. Musial so impressed Polish filmmaker Czeslaw Petelski that he offered Musial a part in one of his movies. Musial just smiled, saying, "Aw, look, I'm no actor. I'm just a cowboy." On a 1987 trip, former major-league pitcher Moe Drabowsky, who gave up Musial's three thousandth hit in 1958, conducted baseball clinics with him. Drabowsky remembered Musial with his camera, ignoring the Communist rules, taking pictures "all over the place [in] total disregard for their policies. Even as we were boarding the plane in Warsaw, he was still snapping away."[51]

Musial and Lil again journeyed to Poland in the summer of 1990, along with Philadelphia philanthropist Edward Piszek and wife Olga, who had been to Poland previously with Musial. Piszek, the founder of the Copernicus Society of America, had been involved in Poland for some twenty-five years, promoting the teaching of the English language and the elimination of tuberculosis. He and Musial brought to Wroclaw—a city of seven hundred thousand people about 185 miles south of Warsaw— 486 bats, 250 gloves, and 925 Cardinal baseball caps. This gift enabled that community to sustain its Little League baseball program. In gratitude Wroclaw erected a six-foot-high granite monument, with a plaque bearing a rough likeness of Musial at bat, on the grounds of "Stan Musial Little

50. *St. Louis Globe-Democrat*, November 21, 1966, in Mercantile Library clipping file; Buck interview, December 10, 1996.
51. Musial, *The Man, Stan*, 16–17; Moe Drabrowsky to Giglio, November 12, 1996, in possession of Giglio.

League Baseball Field." At the unveiling on July 23, Musial cried. He explained that Poland was his father's homeland: "And it's quite an honor to be honored like that for something you loved doing all those years— baseball."[52]

Musial's effort in Wroclaw represented part of his broader commitment to establish baseball as a youth sport throughout Poland, which involved more than three thousand youngsters on thirty teams in six Polish cities by 1990. Since then Musial, as director of the Poland Little League Foundation, has played a major role in seeking donations in the United States, primarily from Polish Americans. After the initial effort proved disappointing, he, Piszek, and others worked with the Little League organization to raise some $6.5 million. As a result, Poland became the recipient of a European training and playoff center at Kutno forty miles outside of Warsaw, housing three ball fields, the last of which was dedicated in Musial's name in early 2000. Dormitories to accommodate Little Leaguers from Europe, North Africa, and the Middle East were to be constructed. Since 1995 playoffs have been held in Kutno to select a representative to attend the annual Little League World Series in Williamsport, Pennsylvania. Musial contributed much to making baseball an international sport at the Little League level. For his service to Poland Musial received the 1999 Cavalier Cross of the Order of Merit, the Polish government's highest civilian award. Among Polish children especially he remains a hero.[53]

Musial's good friend Michener also accompanied him and Piszek to Rome in December 1988. They had dinner and worshiped with the pope at a private Mass. While in the Vatican two young priests recognized Musial and showered him with questions about baseball. Musial joked that he was entitled to be there because "I'm also a Cardinal." Piszek had used that same line when he met privately with Pope John Paul just prior to the aforementioned dinner: "Holy Father, I am going to introduce you to a Cardinal you never met."[54] After the latter looked perplexed since he appointed all cardinals, Piszek explained what he meant, which caused Pope John Paul to break out in laughter. In truth, the pope had previously met Musial on at least two or three separate occasions. He would again visit with him on a papal visit to St. Louis in January 1999 when Musial served as one of four honorary co-chairs.

52. *St. Louis Post-Dispatch,* September 9, 1990, in Mercantile Library clipping file.
53. Ibid.; Edward Piszek telephone interview, November 12, 1999; *St. Louis Post-Dispatch,* November 4, 1999, West Post section.
54. Michener, *Pilgrimage,* 88; Piszek telephone interview, November 12, 1999.

Following the Rome papal visit the Musial group attended a reception at U.S. Ambassador Maxwell Rabb's residence. There U.S. Attorney General Richard Thornburgh invited Musial to speak, which he did with such a light touch that Robb invited him and his small party for lunch the following day along with members of the U.S. House of Representatives Appropriations Subcommittee on State Department Affairs. Musial entertained them with baseball yarns, his harmonica playing, and his "cutting the banana" trick in which he somehow sliced a banana in four parts with a knife with the skin still undisturbed.

After his retirement from business Musial also found himself more pulled to his roots—to Donora—the town he had forsaken for St. Louis. As family members and longtime friends passed away from that Pennsylvania community, he undoubtedly became more aware of his own mortality. Inevitably, the desire to revisit Donora for the powerful memories it offered proved irresistible. The various reunions of the 1990s with classmates, some of whom he had not seen in fifty years, made it especially inviting.

Hometown Roots

T he Donora of the mid-1990s bore scant resemblance to the borough of Musial's youth. It bordered Interstate 70, a creation of the 1960s, which meandered across Pennsylvania, linking the Keystone State to the East Coast and the Far West. From the south one entered Donora from I-70 on State Highway 1099 by crossing the Donora-Monessen Bridge and then veering right less than a mile. At the outskirts of town, a sign proclaimed Donora "The Home of Champions." The downtown area was much quieter, since the mills had closed more than thirty years ago; the sidewalk congestion of the past had long ended. Several of the public buildings were still boarded up, and the houses that stretched upward from the business district were whiter and cleaner. Even though the former Musial home on Marelda Avenue still remained, it was considerably enlarged and encased with white vinyl siding.[1] Also, the previously barren surrounding hillsides now contained lush vegetation. In many ways Donora was a much healthier place in which to live.

The closing of the mills clearly had its downside, too. The shutdown began in 1957, some nine years following the smog inversion, when the Donora Zinc Works folded, costing the community some three hundred jobs. Then in 1960 U.S. Steel announced that it was terminating steelmaking at the local American Steel and Wire Company plant. It ended all operations there six years later. Foreign competition, the shifting of wire markets to the East Coast, the moving of manufacturing customers to the southern states, and high labor costs accompanied by poor labor-management relations contributed to Donora's industrial demise. The shutdown was a precursor of what would happen to all of the Mon Valley steelworks a generation later, turning bustling mill towns into ghostlike communities.[2]

1. Stokes family interview, May 21, 1997. Edward Stokes gutted the house before renovating and enlarging it. In the early 1980s, according to Stokes's wife, Musial came by with a television cameraman to capture the renovation without asking permission. Visuals were shown on television as if the renovation represented the Musials' original home.
2. Frank Lario, "Relevant Factors Involved in the Permanent Closing of the Donora Steel and Wire Works as Revealed through Local Newspapers and National Trends in the Steel Industry," research paper, California State College, 1972, 1–37; John P. Hoerr, *And the Wolf Finally Came: The Decline of the American Steel Industry,* 567–68.

Donora's population dropped from 12,186 in 1950 to 8,825 in 1970, 5,928 in 1990, and then to an estimated 5,542 in 1998. The mills along the banks of the Monongahela River had been razed, replaced by a new industrial park that attracted some twenty small businesses. Yet they provided only a fraction of the jobs necessary to sustain the population levels of the 1950s and 1960s. While a number of mill workers had obtained transfers to other U.S. Steel plants, others faced early retirement or the difficult task of securing employment elsewhere. Several of them continued to live in the borough. Young people usually did not remain in Donora beyond high school, however. As one longtime Donoran claimed, it had become a community of older people.

Because of the population loss, which affected tax revenues, the community had also found itself almost a half million dollars in debt by the 1970s, necessitating a substantial reduction in the police and fire departments. The debt had been repaid, but Donora no longer had its own newspaper (the *Monessen Valley Independent* served the area) or high school. Consolidation created the Ringgold School District, in which high schoolers were bused to nearby Carroll Township. The Donora High School building of the Musial era became an elementary school. Several churches also closed their doors, including St. Mary's, where the Musials once attended Mass.

Yet a civic spirit prevailed in Donora, inspiring not only the industrial park but also the construction of a new public library in 1996; the further development of Palmer Park, one of the top recreational resources in the area; and the increased activity of the Donora Historical Society. Community leaders, led by the energetic mayor, John Lignelli, dreamed of Donora once again assuming its preeminence. Others sought to restore the values of a mill town society that they romantically linked with the essential "four pillars—home, church, school, and community." Both eagerly anticipated the celebration of Donora's centennial in 2001. Not everyone shared that romantic attachment or vision, however. Two senior citizens, drinking coffee in a local restaurant, described Donora as "the pits."[3]

Moreover, the Donora of the early 1990s seemed to take little pride that Stan Musial had emerged from its coal-laden soil. No street, ballfield, or school bore his name. The one exception was a wall at Ringgold High School that contained a signed photograph of Musial, among others, in

---

3. Bottonari telephone interview, November 5, 1996; *Monessen Valley Independent* (Pa.), November 15, 1997; John Lignelli telephone interview, December 17, 1999; Conversations at Costas' Restaurant, May 23, 1997.

honor of the area's professional athletes. The local athletic director admitted that "kids don't identify with him." The truth is that many Donorans resented that Musial ignored them in their time of need. One former Donoran, a salesman who occasionally visited the town, remembered talking to a number of prominent businessmen in Costas' Restaurant on downtown McKean Avenue in the mid-1960s about creating a museum of champions to stimulate interest in the downtown area. When he mentioned Musial's name, frowns appeared that made him feel persona non grata.[4]

That disenchantment might have begun in August 1949 when the businessmen of Donora presented Musial with a Cadillac at Forbes Field in Pittsburgh in exchange for Musial's car. Musial promptly traded the Cadillac for a Buick from friend Frank Pizzica's dealership in nearby Mononagahela. That bothered some locals, as did Musial's unfulfilled promise of buying land near Donora to construct a ballfield for youngsters. Yet Donorans found other ways to honor Musial, most notably in December 1960 when more than five hundred friends gave him a testimonial dinner at the Twin Coaches Supper Club that was attended by Governor David L. Lawrence and a number of luminaries from professional sports, including Joe Garagiola, the principal speaker, and Pirate broadcaster Bob Prince, the toastmaster. Dr. Duda presented Musial with a bronze plaque while describing him as an athlete, sportsman, gentleman, and humanitarian. A choked-up Musial claimed that he still regarded the area as his home. He promised that "before I am through with baseball, I am going to do something for the people of Donora."[5] That day did not soon come.

Beginning in the difficult '60s, some Donorans hoped that Musial would use his influence with the Johnson administration to assist the community during the mill closing. Others thought that he should have constructed a badly needed swimming pool or ballfield for Donora's youth. They compared Musial with another native son, Cincinnati Reds star Ken Griffey, whom they also had honored. At his appreciation dinner Griffey returned—and even matched—the cash gift to benefit the borough's youth program. The contrasting view heightened when a local union committee,

---

4. *Allegheny Bulletin*, November 20, 1992; Bottonari telephone interview, August 19, 1998.

5. Connie Berutti to Musial, September 3, 1949, Musial Day Scrapbook, vol. 1, St. Louis Cardinals Hall of Fame Museum; Ed Gray telephone interview, August 19, 1998; Al Abrams, "Sidelights on Sports," undetermined newspaper clipping, December 1960. The Musial quotation is in a related story by Harry Keck in another undetermined newspaper clipping, both of which are in Musial Collection, *Sporting News* Archives.

sponsoring Little League baseball, asked Musial in the 1960s to donate one hundred dollars for the program. Musial responded that he would not give because of financial constraints. Copies of that letter circulated all over town. The word spread that Musial was cheap. This quickly ended the community's intention to rename Legion Field next to the old high school in his name. As late as the early '90s Musial failed to contribute to the new library after indicating to the mayor his willingness to do so.[6]

What precipitated Musial's conduct remains a mystery. Even though frugal and cautious regarding his personal finances, no doubt because of his Great Depression upbringing, he nevertheless showed generosity in tipping service people and supporting other charitable causes. Several Donorans suggested that the community might have somehow disappointed him. Could he have been aware of some expression of jealousy toward him that one family friend claimed existed? Perhaps, Musial also felt that the borough might have done more to help itself during the mill-closing period. Perhaps, too, Donorans might have expected too much of him. In any case, Musial explained that he left there at an early age. "I don't have many ties there anymore," he claimed in a 1992 interview.[7] Indeed, he had visited Donora infrequently, especially after the deaths of his mother at the age of seventy-eight in early 1975 and Lil's parents in the previous decade.

Changes occurred in the mid-1990s, especially when town officials honored him and Ken Griffey in the summer of 1994 by naming baseball fields after them in Palmer Park. Musial in turn donated ten thousand dollars to the Donora Baseball Association. He also gave autographed eight-by-ten portraits to the two hundred players in the association and signed autographs for all those at the ceremony. He returned the following year to attend the reunion of the 1938 Donora High School baseball team. Organized by Ruth Miller and Lu Drudi of the Donora Historical Society, Stash entertained the fifty dinner guests at Costas' Restaurant that evening by swapping stories and playing the harmonica. Later he signed photographs for everyone.

Class reunions also brought him and Lil to Donora more frequently, beginning with his fiftieth reunion in August 1989 and Lil's fifty-fourth three years later when they still managed to polka together. As the millennium

6. Bottonari telephone interview, November 4, 1996; Chuck Schmidt interview, March 15, 1998; Peg Kelley telephone interview, August 14, 1996; Gray telephone interview, August 19, 1998; Garcia telephone interview, January 9, 1997; Lignelli telephone interview, December 17, 1999.

7. *Allegheny Bulletin,* November 20, 1992; the jealousy statement is attributed to Laurene Fazzini, telephone interview, January 17, 2000.

approached, they attended several other reunions, including Stash's fifty-fifth in 1994, when he presented his former classmates with a harmonica and a how-to songbook, and his sixtieth in September 1999. At that occasion toastmaster Bill Leddon wore his orange-and-black Donora Dragons baseball cap to honor the event. At the dinner Stash presented the ladies with rings made of currency, which he made and autographed. He then played the harmonica in a sing-along. The Musials also came for various family gatherings, often involving Musial's brother and Lil's siblings. As Musial conceded in 1997, "you never leave your hometown roots."[8]

For Stan and Lil, life had come full circle. Even though still much beloved in his adopted home of St. Louis, where two of his daughters and close friends resided and his attachment to the Cardinals remained strong, he had also strengthened his ties with his birthplace. He will be forever associated with both communities—in St. Louis he is Stan the Man, and in Donora he is Stash, the one who defied the odds to establish that Mon Valley borough as the home of champions.

So, the final chapter begins with Stash and Lil having celebrated their eightieth birthdays. Aging has brought some problems, however. Lil has suffered from a heart condition and from acute arthritis, which sometimes forces her into a wheelchair. Stash remains upbeat; he has retained his brown hair and tanned appearance, which belies a severe limp (ligaments were removed from his left knee) and an increasing frailty. As he enters the final years of his life, the question still remains: to what extent does he mirror the symbolic monument outside of Busch Stadium, depicting him as baseball's perfect knight and warrior?

This is an appropriate question, for biography involves illuminating personality and assessing character as well as evaluating attainments. Musial has withstood scholarly scrutiny rather well. On the positive side, he emerges as a good, decent man, one devoted to family and friends and to the game. He remains rooted to his religious faith, which he never wore on his sleeve by crossing himself in game-related situations or by talking about the importance of Christ in his life as some contemporary athletes do. If anything, Musial was—and is—a deeply private person. Despite that, he found it difficult to contain his excessive sentimentality. His talks at various ceremonial events often ended with him in tears. Refreshingly, Musial reminded us that it was permissible for grown men to cry.

Too, no one more sought to fulfill fan obligations. Often this came at the expense of family as he signed autographs willingly no matter where

8. *Pittsburgh Post-Gazette*, March 12, 1997.

and attended innumerable public functions in St. Louis no matter how inconvenient it was for him to do so. He always conducted himself on and off the field in exemplary fashion. In the process, he elevated the level of player conduct and served as a model to his peers. Revealingly, he won the approbation of everyone connected with baseball—fellow players, fans, management, and umpires. Virtually no one uttered caustic comments related to his deportment or character. Always, he presented himself as the happy warrior—one who laughed easily and, in his high-pitched voice, said complimentary things. He remains, in many ways, a true sports hero of his generation. The same can not be so easily said of other baseball stars of the time—Williams, DiMaggio, or Mantle—who were much less accommodating and more controversial and temperamental. Ironically, this hardly served Musial well with the press over the long run, as sportswriters gave him less coverage, while depicting him as colorless.

Musial learned to conceal his minor deficiencies, including his smoking of cigarettes and cigars, his moderate drinking, and his occasional off-color stories. Very rarely did he appear out of control. Neither did he gossip about people or reveal his emotions easily about those who displeased him.

His easygoing personality hid an intense competitive spirit, leading one observer to write: "[Ty] Cobb wore his fire on his sleeve and it was written all over his face; Musial concealed it in a facade of geniality and placidness, but it burned as deeply inside of him as it did in Cobb." Moreover, his modesty shielded an extraordinary self-confidence—Branch Rickey called it "inner conceit"—that he could hit successfully every time he came to the plate. Seldom did he expose his enormous ego. A rare exception came when he informed a late-season rookie before a packed house at Wrigley Field, "Kid, you know why all these people are here? They want to see Stanley play."[9]

The most serious criticism of Musial came from black teammates in the early 1960s, who thought him a company man who embraced the status quo. In most respects, of course, that was true, as Musial revealed while serving as vice president of the Major League Players Association during the 1950s. But what they at first saw as racial indifference represented no more than Musial seeking to treat everyone alike. He strongly believed

---

9. The Cobb/Musial quote is from undeterminable source despite the author's extensive search, including contacting Broeg, Kahn, and Robert W. Creamer. Broeg interview, January 29, 1993; Barney, *Rex Barney's Thank Youuuu for 50 Years in Baseball*, 164–65.

in Jackie Robinson's right to play major league baseball and privately encouraged him and other black players. To his discredit, however, he never became a forceful advocate of integration in the face of strong opposition from his southern teammates.

Musial proved even less of a leader in defending publicly the reserve clause in the 1950s at a time when Bob Feller, president of the Players Association, spoke forcefully and courageously for reform. And, unlike Hank Greenberg, Jackie Robinson, and a few other former players, Musial did not testify on behalf of former teammate Curt Flood, who sued organized baseball in 1970 to force changes in the reserve clause system. It was in Musial's nature to eschew controversy and confrontation. Part of this undoubtedly was due to his desire to protect his career self-interests. More than this, for much of his life he remained a shy person who felt ill-equipped to engage in verbal exchanges. If this represents a lapse in moral leadership, then nearly every major league superstar of that era suffered from that same deficiency.

The Depression-stricken environment of Musial's childhood remains an important key to comprehending him. He came out of that ordeal with an experience of the degradation of poverty and with the deep desire to rise above it. Embarrassed by its effects on his family, he played down— and even altered accounts of—that part of his existence. The Depression years also created a financial insecurity that he never quite overcame, for Musial forever knew the value of a dollar. Consequently, he managed his money scrupulously; he proved a persistent salary negotiator, even seriously considering bolting to the Mexican League when he thought Cardinal owner Sam Breadon was exploiting him. From 1952 to 1957 he disappointed youngsters by standing virtually alone among the super-stars in refusing to sanction the release of his portrait on Topps baseball cards because of insufficient compensation.[10] To his credit, however, he never succumbed to greed. He shared endorsement gifts with teammates, mailed autographed photos and even baseballs to fans, and used his road allowances to tip generously. Moreover, unlike latter-day players, his sense of fairness led him to accept his annual contracts with little ne-gotiation during the 1950s because of the ball club's perceived generosity.

Early in life he learned to attach himself to those able to assist him. Surrogate fathers abounded because of his remarkable talent, his conge-nial personality, and his willingness to listen to advice. For most of his

10. T. S. O'Connell," 'Where Have You Gone, Stan Musial?' Was Kids' Lament in the 1950s," 122–23.

life Musial profited from that assistance. That—and God-given talent—partly explains why Musial paradoxically emerged from a dark, bleak environment with such a sunny disposition. In return, he remembered the Ki Dudas, the Frank Pizzicas, and the Dickie Kerrs by including them in various ceremonies in his honor and by extending to them other courtesies—for example, to Kerr the use of a house in Houston, Texas. To Joe Barbao and others, he sent boxes of clothes that he no longer wore, exhibiting both a Depression-era mentality as well as thoughtfulness. To his parents he remained the dutiful son. He wrote idyllically about his father, perhaps, understanding the private demons he must have faced. In the end, he was there to care for him. He provided his mother, whom he most adored, with a new home and a monthly allotment in her declining years. Curiously, he seemed much more responsive to individuals from his hometown than he was to community.

In sum, contradictions obviously prevail about Musial's life. He exhibited individual acts of generosity coupled with financial frugality, he seemed both proud and ashamed of his heritage and his parents, he was a loving husband and father but one who often put his professional and business careers and devotion to the public ahead of family, and he showed himself to be a privately estimable person, yet publicly reticent on matters of human dignity and justice.

In terms of professional accomplishments, Musial should be ranked among baseball's greats—the equal of contemporary Hall of Famers such as DiMaggio, Williams, Mays, Aaron, and Mantle, all of whom performed in the extremely competitive postwar era. Not only did these players compete in the same general period, adding to the validity of the forthcoming analysis, but they also represented the best the game had to offer. Indeed, only a select few from other eras, such as Cobb, Wagner, Hornsby, Ruth, and Gehrig, can match their overall achievements. More to the point, Musial's career statistics compare favorably with his five competitors. Only Mays had as many batting titles; Musial also finished first among the six in career doubles, second in hits and RBIs, third in runs scored and slugging average, and fifth in home runs. In ranking performances in the above seven hitting categories, using a one to six scale, with one as tops, only Aaron (15) surpassed Musial (17), followed by Williams (21), Mays (23), Mantle (33), and DiMaggio (34).

To be sure, career hitting statistics can tell only part of the story. DiMaggio's record would have been even more imposing if he had not relinquished three years to World War II; the same is true of Williams, who missed three seasons serving in that war and nearly two additional ones flying airplanes in the Korean conflict. Mays also lost close to two seasons during the Korean War era. Conversely, Musial spent one year in the military, while Mantle and Aaron faced no such interruptions. Arguably blessed with the greatest potential of the six, Mantle instead lost playing time—and suffered from diminished performance—because of nagging leg injuries. His roguish lifestyle further eroded his playing skills. Like Mantle, DiMaggio's career was shortened by injuries.

More difficult to measure are the six's performances in categories other than batting. With the exception of Williams, all of them had speed afoot in their prime, although the exceptionally quick Mays was the only real base stealer in an era that placed little premium on that skill. Yet often forgotten is Musial's quickness and adeptness on the basepaths, particularly in going from first to third or from second to home. In the outfield, Musial failed to cover as much ground as the gazelle-like DiMaggio or the swift Mays, but he performed more than adequately, more so than Williams. Indeed, he always ranked near or at the top annually in fielding percentage and fewest errors. Musial's only weakness was his lack of arm strength, caused by the 1940 shoulder mishap, but he made up for it by releasing the ball quickly, throwing to the proper base, and always hitting the cutoff man. When moved to first base in 1946, he turned into one of the top first sackers in the major leagues.

Of the six, no one was more of a team player than Musial. As a personality he always remained a positive force—in the clubhouse as well as on the field. Not only did he play all three outfield positions, but he also willingly shifted to first base on short notice whenever the need arose. Moreover, none of the five contemporary rivals surpassed Musial in playing with tormenting injuries, enabling him to set the National League consecutive games played streak. For those six seasons during the streak, no amount of pain kept Musial from the lineup. At the plate Musial, unlike Williams in particular, knowingly swung at pitches outside of the strike zone, hit to the opposite field, or sacrifice bunted if his team needed him to do so. He received nothing but praise from nine Cardinal skippers, who found him a delight to manage. This included Solly Hemus, despite the occasional perplexities of grappling with an aging Musial.

In an impressionistic way, Musial's contemporaries have also recognized his greatness. Of the more than 300 ballplayers who participated in a survey for this book, 211 responded to the question of how they would rank him against the all-time field. Of those who did, 98 considered him among the all-time greats, 53 more ranked him among the top ten players; 29 additionally in the first five, 17 as number one, while only 2 rated him as low as the top 50. Another 43 classified him among the greats of his era. When asked about his weaknesses, 68 mentioned his arm while 28 said he had no limitations.

Several recent scholarly books have also ranked Musial highly. In 1998 the St. Louis–based *Sporting News* listed Musial tenth among the top one hundred baseball players, behind Ruth, Mays, Cobb, Walter Johnson, Aaron, Gehrig, Christy Mathewson, Williams, and Hornsby. DiMaggio followed Musial in eleventh place, with Mantle in the seventeenth spot. The following year Michael J. Schell, a professional statistician, in his carefully thought-out *Baseball's All-Time Best Hitters: How Statistics Can Level the Playing Field,* made four adjustments in recalculating individual career hitting averages. They relate to late career batting declines, the era in which the player performed (a time of hitting feast or famine?), the talent pool, and the ballparks. As a result of Schell's adjustments, Musial rose from the twenty-fourth position in the all-time career batting average list to the eighth spot. Only Williams of Musial's generation, occupying the sixth position, was higher. Also, in 1999 St. Louis–area fans made Musial the top vote-getter on the Cardinals' all-century team, as he received 97.9 percent of the votes cast for one of the outfield positions.[11]

Yet as the twentieth century came to an end, Musial was not accorded the same national recognition that his five contemporaries received. The fans kept him off the All-Century Team, commissioned by Major League Baseball in 1999. He failed to make the list of the top nine outfielders chosen, which included the five contemporary Hall of Famers as well as Ruth, Cobb, Ken Griffey, Jr., and Pete Rose. Following the conclusion of the balloting for the twenty-five-player roster, a panel of judges added him and four others to the squad, enabling Musial to appear on national television with the rest in a memorable ceremony that preceded the first game of the World Series. He also was not one of the ESPN Network SportCentury's Fifty Greatest Athletes, presented weekly in 1999 in a televised biography, even though his five contemporaries

11. Ron Smith, *The Sporting News Selects Baseball's 100 Greatest Players: A Celebration of the 20th Century's Best,* 28–29; Michael J. Schell, *Baseball's All-Time Best Hitters: How Statistics Can Level the Playing Field; St. Louis Post-Dispatch,* October 17, 1999. See also Dale A. Newlin, Jr., *Baseball's Greatest Careers (Non-Pitchers) Compared in 56 Statistical Categories,* and Ken Shouler, *The Real 100 Baseball Players of All Time . . . and Why!* Using complex statistical compilations, Newlin ranked Musial the fourth-best position player of all time behind Ruth, Cobb, and Tris Speaker, while Shouler placed Musial in the eighth spot.

were.[12] Finally, he finished forty-sixth on the list of the Associated Press's Top One Hundred Athletes of the Century poll, behind Mays (11), Williams (13), Aaron (18), DiMaggio (19), and Mantle (35).

No one reason adequately explains the underestimation of Musial. His association with St. Louis, which did not host a World Series in the Musial era after 1946, surely has something to do with it, as does the East Coast media, which has exhibited inordinate influence in professional sports. The exploits of Mays, DiMaggio, and Mantle have received added attention because they played all or much of their careers in New York. DiMaggio and Mantle also benefited from their association with championship Yankee teams. Yet this does not explain the attention that Aaron has received. "Hammering Henry" will forever be remembered for breaking Ruth's career home run record, however. Home run hitters such as Aaron have had a decided advantage in that respect. Musial was a power hitter, too, but he never won a home run title; his 475 home runs still top the list of most career homers by a non–title winner.

Moreover, no singular accomplishment stands out in public memory whenever Musial's name appears. Conversely, DiMaggio will always be remembered for that imposing 56-consecutive-game hitting streak; Williams for being the last major leaguer to hit .400; Mantle for twice hitting more than 50 homers in a single season; and Mays for his over-the-shoulder catch of Vic Wertz's drive in the first game of the 1954 World Series. The recent deaths of Mantle and DiMaggio, with the accompanying TV and printed media obituaries, have further added to their larger-than-life images.

But Musial's life should be appreciated for more than what he accomplished on the field. He epitomized what a professional athlete should be—a true sportsman and a role model virtually to all, including the fans who sought his attention, the press with whom he was always accessible, and the ball club that he loyally served. If he did not quite measure up to the monument, which contains its own imperfections, it is because that edifice is bronze while Musial is merely human. And since Americans do not require that their heroes be perfect whether they be presidents or athletes, the greatness of Stanley F. Musial remains secure.

12. According to ESPN officials, a forty-eight-member panel placed Musial in the sixty-first spot. Espn_inc@espn.com to jng890f@mail.smsu.edu, January 5, 2000, in possession of Giglio.

Bibliography

Manuscript Resources

James T. Blair Papers, Western Historical Manuscript Collection, Columbia, Mo.
Bill Borst Collection, in possession of Bill Borst, St. Louis, Mo.
William Bottonari Collection, in possession of William Bottonari, Camp Hill, Pa.
Thomas B. Curtis Papers, Western Historical Manuscript Collection, Columbia, Mo.
Lyndon B. Johnson Papers, Lyndon B. Johnson Library, Austin, Texas.
John F. Kennedy Papers, John Fitzgerald Kennedy Library, Boston, Mass.
Arthur Mann Papers, Library of Congress, Washington, D.C.
Musial Collection, National Baseball Library, Cooperstown, N.Y.
Lukasz Musial Naturalization Papers, National Archives, Mid Atlantic Region, Philadelphia, Pa.
Stan Musial Collection, *Sporting News* Archives, St. Louis, Mo.
Branch Rickey Papers, Library of Congress, Washington, D.C.
St. Louis Cardinals Museum Collection, Busch Stadium, St. Louis, Mo.
St. Louis Globe-Democrat and *St. Louis Post-Dispatch* Clipping Files, Mercantile Library, St. Louis, Mo.

Government Documents

Fourteenth Census of the United States: 1920. Population, Donora Borough, Washington County, Pa.
U.S. House of Representatives, Committee on the Judiciary, Antitrust Subcommittee (Subcommittee Number Five), *Organized Professional Team Sports*. Hearings, pt. 2. 85th Cong., 1st sess., Washington, D.C.: Government Printing Office, 1957.

Newspapers

Afro-American, 1947.
Buffalo Evening News, 1982.
Daytona Beach Morning Journal (Fla.), 1940.
Donora Herald-American (Pa.), 1931–1932, 1935–1936, 1938–1940.
New York Herald Tribune, 1947.

Rochester Democrat and Chronicle, 1941.
St. Louis Argus, 1947.
St. Louis Globe Democrat, 1947.
St. Louis Post-Dispatch, 1946, 1947, 1960, 1978, 1981, 1986, 1990, 1996, 1999.
St. Louis Star Times, 1946.
Sporting News, 1942–1943, 1946–1947, 1997.
Springfield Daily News (Mo.), 1941.
Springfield Leader and Press (Mo.), 1941, 1991.
Springfield News and Leader (Mo.), 1941.
Williamson Daily News (W.Va.), 1939.

Oral History Transcripts

Frank Baumholtz oral history transcript, A. B. Chandler Oral History Project, University of Kentucky Library, Lexington.
William O. DeWitt oral history transcript, A. B. Chandler Oral History Project, University of Kentucky Library, Lexington.
Danny Gardella oral history transcript, A. B. Chandler Oral History Project, University of Kentucky Library, Lexington.
Max Lanier oral history transcript, A. B. Chandler Oral History Project, University of Kentucky Library, Lexington.
Marty Marion oral history transcript, A. B. Chandler Oral History Project, University of Kentucky Library, Lexington.
Stan Musial oral history transcript, A. B. Chandler Oral History Project, University of Kentucky Library, Lexington.
Mickey Owen Oral History, A. B. Chandler Oral History Project, University of Kentucky Library, Lexington.
Fred Saigh oral history transcript, A. B. Chandler Oral History Project, University of Kentucky Library, Lexington.
Red Smith oral history transcript, A. B. Chandler Oral History Project, University of Kentucky Library, Lexington.
Harry Walker oral history transcript, A. B. Chandler Oral History Project, University of Kentucky Library, Lexington.

Personal Correspondence

Adams, Ace.
Altman, George.
Anderson, Sparky.
Averill, Earl.
Bachman, Ronald D.

Bailey, Ed.
Baker, Bill.
Baker, Floyd.
Balsamo, Tony.
Barkley, John Red.

Barthelson, Bob.
Bartirome, Tony.
Basinski, Eddie.
Baumholtz, Frank.
Bearnarth, Larry.
Beauchamp, Jim.
Berres, Ray.
Bicknell, Charlie.
Blackaby, Ethan.
Blattner, Buddy.
Block, Cy.
Bloodworth, Jimmy.
Bockman, Eddie.
Bokelmann, Dick.
Bolling, Frank.
Borkowski, Bob.
Brand, Ron.
Brewer, Jack.
Brinkopf, Leon.
Bryant, Mary Louise.
Buddin, Don.
Budnick, Mike.
Burkhart, Ken.
Burright, Larry.
Burwell, Dick.
Calderone, Sammy.
Candini, Milo.
Cardwell, Don.
Carnett, Eddie.
Castiglione, Pete.
Chambers, Cliff.
Chandler, Edward.
Church, Bubba.
Clark, Mel.
Clark, Phil.
Cohen, Hy.
Collum, Jackie.
Cone, Ray.
Corwin, Al.
Cowan, Billy.

Craig, Roger.
Creel, Jack.
Criscola, Tony.
Cross, Jeffrey.
Cunningham, Joe.
Davis, Barbara.
Davis, Otis.
Demeter, Don.
Dempsey, Con.
Dickson, Jim.
Diering, Chuck.
Dillinger, Bob.
Dittmer, Jack.
Drabowsky, Moe.
Dunlap, Grant.
Duren, Ryne.
Dyck, Jim.
Easton, John.
Edwards, Johnny.
Ellis, Sammy.
Ennis, Del.
Erautt, Eddie.
Erickson, Don.
Errickson, Dick.
Erskine, Carl.
Estock, George.
Face, Roy.
Ferrarese, Don.
Fischer, Henry.
Fleming, Leslie "Bill."
Fondy, Dee.
Fox, Terry.
Franks, Herman.
Freeman, Hersh.
Freeman, Mark.
Friend, Bob.
Funk, Frank.
Garber, Bob.
Gentile, Sam.
Gernert, Dick.

Gilbert, Buddy.
Golden, Jim.
Goldstein, Lonnie.
Gorin, Charlie.
Gotay, Julio.
Grammas, Alex.
Gray, Dick.
Green, Freddie.
Greengrass, Jim.
Grunwald, Al.
Gutteridge, Don.
Hall, Dick.
Hamner, Ralph.
Harris, Bill.
Harris, Gail.
Hartman, Jack H.
Hartsfield, Roy.
Hartung, Clint.
Hasenmayer, Don.
Hausmann, George.
Hemus, Solly.
Henley, Gail.
Herrscher, Rick.
Hersh, Earl.
Hoerst, Frank.
Hogue, Cal.
House, Frank.
Howard, Frank.
Howard, Lee.
Humphreys, Bob.
Jackson, Randy.
James, Charlie.
Jansen, Larry.
Javier, Julian.
Jester, Virgil.
Johnson, Art.
Johnson, Ernie
Johnson, Ken.
Jones, Nippy.
Jones, Sherman.

Joost, Eddie.
Jordan, Niles.
Kahn, Roger.
Kasko, Eddie.
Kayzak, Eddie.
Kelly, R. E.
Kemmerer, Russ.
Kennedy, Bob.
Kennedy, Monte.
Keough, Marty.
Kimball, Newt.
Kindall, Jerry.
Kiner, Ralph.
King, Nellie.
Kipp, Fred.
Klippstein, Johnny.
Koecher, Dick.
Kosman, Mike.
Koy, Ernie.
Kreitner, Mickey.
Kress, Charlie.
Kuzava, Bob.
Lamabe, Jack.
Landrum, Joe.
Landwith, Hobie.
Lang, Don.
Lanier, Max.
La Palme, Paul.
Larsen, Don.
Law, Vern.
Leddon, John W.
Lemaster, Denny.
Lemon, Jim.
Lepcio, Ted.
Lewandowski, Pearl
    (Mrs. Dan).
Libke, Al.
Lipon, Johnny.
Littlefield, Dick.
Litwhiler, Danny.

Lively, Bud.
Lockman, Whitey.
Lohrman, Bill.
Lombardi, Vic.
Lopata, Stan.
Lund, Don.
Lupien, Tony.
Lurvey, Mildred M.
Lynch, Jerry.
McCarver, Tim.
McDevitt, Danny.
McLish, Cal.
Malkmus, Bobby.
Mallette, Mal.
Malloy, Bob.
Mangan, Jim.
Marshall, Willard.
Martin, Barney.
Martin, Stu.
Mauriello, Ralph.
Mauro, Carmen.
Mayer, Ed.
Mele, Sam.
Merriman, Lloyd.
Merritt, Lloyd.
Merson, Jack.
Merullo, Lennie.
Mickelson, Ed.
Mickens, Glenn.
Miggins, Larry.
Miller, Edward.
Miller, Rodney.
Minner, Paul.
Mites, Don.
Moford, Herb.
Montmayor, Felipe.
Moore, Jo Jo.
Morehardt, Moe.
Morehead, Seth.
Morgan, Bobby.

Morgan, Joe.
Mueller, Don.
Mullen, Ford "Moon."
Mulligan, Dick.
Murff, Red.
Necciai, Ron.
Neiger, Al.
Nelson, Mel.
Nichols, Roy.
Noren, Irv.
Nottebart, Don.
O'Donnell, George.
Oldis, Bob.
O'Rourke, Charlie.
Pafko, Andy.
Pagliaroni, Jim.
Patton, Gene.
Peña, Orlando.
Pfund, Lee.
Philley, Dave.
Phillips, Damon.
Phillips, Taylor.
Pieke, Ron.
Porter, Jay.
Pregenzer, John.
Raffensberger, Ken.
Raymond, Claude.
Reich, Herm.
Repulski, Mrs. Rip.
Reseigno, Xavier.
Restelli, Dino.
Rhodes, Dusty.
Riddle, Johnny.
Roberts, Robin.
Roebuck, Ed.
Rush, Bob.
Sandlock, Mike.
Sanicki, Ed.
Sauer, Hank.
Savage, Ted.

Scheib, Carl.
Schramka, Paul.
Schult, Art.
Schultz, Barney.
Seminick, Andy.
Senerchia, Sonny.
Seward, Frank.
Shaw, Bob.
Sherry, Norm.
Sievers, Roy.
Silvera, Charlie.
Simmons, Curt.
Sisk, Tommie.
Sisti, Sibby.
Smalley, Roy.
Smith, Robert.
Smith, Robert "Riverboat."
Spring, Jack.
Staley, Gerry.
Stephenson, Bob.
Stevens, R. C.
Strickland, George.
Strincevich, Nick.
Sturgeon, Bobby.
Tanner, Chuck.
Tappe, Ed.
Tate, Lee.
Taylor, Bill.
Terwilliger, Wayne.
Testa, Nick.

Theis, Jack.
Thomas, Frank.
Toth, Paul.
Tygiel, Jules.
Van Cuyk, John.
Vandermeer, Johnny.
Vernon, Mickey.
Virdon, Bill.
Wade, Gale.
Walker, Harry.
Wands, Sara.
Warwick, Carl.
Wentzel, Juanita.
Werber, Bill.
Werle, Bill.
Westlake, Wally.
White, Albert Eugene "Fuzz."
White, Bill.
White, Hal.
Whitfield, Fred.
Williams, Dewey.
Williams, Stan.
Windhorn, Gordie.
Wise, K. C. "Casey."
Woodling, Gene.
Woolridge, Floyd.
Worthington, Al.
Zabela, Adrian.
Zachary, Chink.

Other Correspondence

Miller, A. F., Jr., to Roger Kahn. November 1, 1957. In possession of
    Norma R. Todd, Donora, Pa.
Musial, Stan, to Michael (Ki) and Verna Duda. June 16, 1939–May 1, 1945.
    In possession of Verna Duda, California, Pa.
Musial, Stan, to Chuck and Betty Schmidt. January 10, 1944, 1992–1994.
    In possession of Chuck Schmidt, Bloomington, Ind.

Personal Interviews

Barbao, Joe, Jr. Telephone interview. June 26, 1997.

Barbao, Ken. Telephone interviews. June 17 and 19, 1997.

Bond, Denny. Telephone interview. September 27, 1999.

Bottonari, William. Interview. Donora, Pa., May 21, 1997. Telephone interviews. November 5, 1996, April 12, August 12, August 17, August 19, 1997, December 10, 1997.

Broeg, Bob. Interviews. St. Louis, Mo., January 29, 1993, February 18, December 11, 1999.

Buck, Jack. Interview. St. Louis, Mo., December 10, 1996.

Bush, Dick. Telephone interview. September 23, 1996.

Cupper, Patricia Pizzica. Interview. Monongahela, Pa., May 23, 1997.

Devine, Bing. Interview. St. Louis, Mo., November 12, 1996.

Fazzini, Laurene. Telephone interview. January 17, 2000.

Feller, Robert. Telephone interview. April 7, 1999.

Ferguson, Mary Jean. Telephone interview. November 5, 1995.

Fischer, Irv. Interview. St. Louis, Mo., November 11, 1996.

Fleishman, Al. Telephone interview. December 2, 1996.

Freeman, Dale. Interview. Springfield, Mo., July 31, 1995.

Garagiola, Joe. Telephone interviews. November 22, 1995, December 3, 1996, March 21, 2000.

Garcia, Florentino. Telephone interviews. January 9, June 11, July 9, 1997.

Gietschier, Steven. Interview. St. Louis, Mo., September 17, 1996.

Gionfriddo, Albert. Telephone interview. March 31, 1997.

Glazier, Robert. Telephone interview. September 8, 1996.

Gray, Ed. Telephone interview. July 26, 1997.

Gray, Hershel. Interview. Donora, Pa., May 22, 1997.

Griffey, Joseph "Buddy." Interview. Cleveland, Ohio, May 24, 1997. Telephone interview. September 24, 1996.

Hale, Crayton J. Telephone interview. November 29, 1999.

Hasten, Jack. Telephone interviews. August 25, November 3, 1995.

Hendrickson, Paul. Telephone interview. December 3, 1996.

Herman, Jack. Telephone interview. November 11, 1996.

Hirsch, Arnold. Interview. Donora, Pa., May 22, 1997.

Hulston, John. Interview. Springfield, Mo., September 24, 1996.

Johnson, Vicki. Telephone interview. December 2, 1996.

Kahn, Roger. Telephone interview. December 12, 1996.

Kelly, Peg. Telephone interview. August 14, 1996.

Lauerman, Hal. Interview. Donora, Pa., May 22, 1997.

Leddon, John W., Jr. Telephone interview. December 5, 1996.

Lelik, Emma Jean. Telephone interview. May 21, 1998.

Lignelli, John. Telephone interview. December 17, 1999.

Lohmeyer, Gene. Interview. Springfield, Mo., August 25, 1995.

Mancuso, Frank. Telephone interview. November 14, 1995.

Marion, Marty. Interview. St. Louis, Mo., December 10, 1996.

Mayer, Frederick H. Telephone interview. February 17, 1997.

McCoy, Duff. Telephone interview. November 12, 1995.

McQueary, William. Interview. Springfield, Mo., August 2, 1995.

Merullo, Lennie. Telephone interview. November 28, 1996.

Michener, James. Telephone interview. September 15, 1997.

Mormino, Gary Ross. Telephone interview. April 6, 2000.

Mumford, Jack. Interview. Springfield, Mo., August 16, 1995.

Musial, Ed. Interview. Monongahela, Pa., August 6, 1996.

Musial, Stan. Telephone interview. December 6, 1995.

Norton, Eugene. Interview. Upper Sinclair, Pa., May 22, 1997. Telephone interview. November 20, 1996.

O'Loughlin, Bob. Interview. St. Louis, Mo., October 29, 1999.

O'Lenic, Robert. Telephone interviews. December 5, 1996, July 29, 1997.

Owen, Mickey. Interviews. Springfield, Mo., August 25, 1995, September 7, 1996.

Pado, Ed. Telephone interview. November 20, 1996.

Paglia, Ron. Telephone interview. August 25, 1999.

Peace, Jack. Interview. Springfield, Mo., October 10, 1995.

Peace, Robert. Interview. Springfield, Mo., October 11, 1995.

Piszek, Edward. Telephone interview. November 12, 1999.

Raper, Max. Interview. Springfield, Mo., September 20, 1995.

Ridenbaugh, Lowell. Interview. St. Louis, Mo., November 11, 1996.

Rumora, Nancy Barbao. Telephone interview. November 3, 1997.

Saigh, Fred. Interview. St. Louis, Mo., March 15, 1993.

Schmidt, Chuck. Interview. Bloomington, Ind., March 15, 1998.

Schoendienst, Red. Telephone interview. February 4, 1997.

Stokes, Edward L. Family interview. Donora, Pa., May 21, 1997.

Stone, Dean "Bud." Telephone interview. February 12, 1996.

Sukel, Edward. Interview. Donora, Pa., May 22, 1997.

Todd, Norma. Telephone interview. September 26, 1996.

Toomey, Jim. Telephone interview. November 11, 1996.

Vanek, Ollie. Telephone interviews. November 28, 1996, December 3, 1997. Interview. St. Louis, Mo., December 9, 1996.

Walterman, Pappi. Telephone interviews. November 8, 20, 1995.
Weber, Harry. Telephone interview. April 5, 2000.
Werle, William. Telephone interview. January 20, 1999.
Wickliffe, Gene. Interview. Springfield, Mo., August 18, 1995.
Wilkerson, Bill. Telephone interview. November 2, 1995.
Williams, Abbott. Interview. Springfield, Mo., August 25, 1995.
Williams, Dewey. Telephone interview. November 20, 1996.
Wohlschlaeger, Amadee. Interview. St. Louis, Mo., November 12, 1996.
Wyse, Henry. Telephone interview. November 26, 1996.

Other Interviews

Musial, Ed. Telephone interview. April 10, 1994. Conducted by Jim Kreuz of Lake Jackson, Texas.
Norton, Eugene. Telephone interview. 1994. Conducted by Jim Kreuz of Lake Jackson, Texas.
O'Lenic, Robert. Telephone interview. April 15, 1994. Conducted by Jim Kreuz of Lake Jackson, Texas.
Pado, Ed. Telephone interview. May 14, 1994. Conducted by Jim Kreuz of Lake Jackson, Texas.
Schmidt, Chuck. Telephone interview. December 31, 1994. Conducted by Jim Kreuz of Lake Jackson, Texas.

Books

Aaron, Henry, with Furman Bisher. *Aaron.* Rev. ed. New York: Thomas Y. Crowell, 1974.
———, with Lonnie Wheeler. *I Had a Hammer: The Hank Aaron Story.* New York: HarperCollins, 1991.
Alexander, Charles C. *Our Game: An American Baseball History.* New York: Henry Holt, 1991.
———. *Rogers Hornsby: A Biography.* New York: Henry Holt, 1995.
Allen, Maury. *Jackie Robinson: A Life Remembered.* New York: Franklin Watts, 1987.
Allen, Mel, and Ed Fitzgerald. *You Can't Beat the Hours: A Long, Loving Look at Big-League Baseball—Including Some Yankees I Have Known.* New York: Harper and Row, 1964.
Anderson, Dave. *Pennant Races: Baseball at Its Best.* New York: Doubleday, 1994.
Archibald, Joe. *The Richie Ashburn Story.* New York: Julian Messner, 1960.

Banks, Ernie, and Jim Enright. *"Mr. Cub."* Chicago: Follett Publishing, 1971.

Barney, Rex, with Norman L. Macht. *Rex Barney: Thank Youuuu for 50 Years in Baseball from Brooklyn to Baltimore.* Centreville, Md.: Tidewater Publishers, 1993.

Black, Joe. *Ain't Nobody Better than You: An Autobiography of Joe Black.* Scottsdale, Ariz.: Ironwood Lithographers, 1983.

Borst, Bill. *The Best of Seasons: The 1944 St. Louis Cardinals and St. Louis Browns.* Jefferson, N.C.: McFarland, 1995.

Broeg, Bob. *Bob Broeg's Redbirds: A Century of Cardinals' Baseball.* St. Louis: River City Publishers, 1981.

———. *Bob Broeg: Memories of a Hall of Fame Sportswriter.* Champaign, Ill.: Sagamore Publishing, 1995.

———, and William J. Miller, Jr. *Baseball from a Different Angle.* South Bend, Ind.: Diamond Communications, 1989.

Brosnan, Jim. *The Long Season.* New York: Harper and Brothers, 1960.

Buck, Jack, with Rob Rains and Bob Broeg. *Jack Buck: "That's a Winner."* Champaign, Ill.: Sagamore Publishing, 1997.

Bukowczyk, John J. *And My Children Did Not Know Me: A History of the Polish Americans.* Bloomington: Indiana University Press, 1987.

Campanella, Roy. *It's Good to Be Alive.* Boston: Little, Brown, 1959.

Caray, Harry, with Bob Verdi. *Holy Cow!* New York: Villard Books, 1989.

Chalberg, John C. *Rickey and Robinson: The Preacher, the Player, and America's Game.* Wheeling, Ill.: Harlan Davidson, 2000.

Clark, John P. *Donora Diamond Jubilee, 1901–1976.* Sponsored by the Borough of Donora, Donora Chamber of Commerce. Locally printed, 1976.

Conlan, John B. "Jocko," and Robert W. Creamer. *Jocko.* Philadelphia: J. P. Lippincott, 1967.

Connor, Anthony J., ed. *Baseball for the Love of It: Hall of Famers Tell It Like It Was.* New York: Macmillan, 1982.

Coode, Thomas H., and John F. Bauman. *People, Poverty, and Politics: Pennsylvanians during the Great Depression.* Lewisburg, Pa.: Bucknell University Press, 1981.

Corcoran, Fred, with Bud Harvey. *Unplayable Lies.* New York: Duell, Sloan, and Pearce, 1965.

Craft, David, and Tom Owens. *Redbirds Revisited: Great Memories and Stories from St. Louis Cardinals.* Chicago: Bonus Books, 1990.

Creamer, Robert W. *Baseball in '41: A Celebration of the Best Baseball Season Ever—In the Year America Went to War.* New York: Viking, 1991.

Dickerson, Dennis C. *Out of the Crucible: Black Steelworkers in Western Pennsylvania, 1875–1980.* Albany: State University of New York Press, 1986.

Dorinson, Joseph, and Joram Warmund, eds. *Jackie Robinson: Race, Sports, and the American Dream.* Armonk, N.Y.: M. E. Sharpe, 1998.

Durocher, Leo E. *The Dodgers and Me: The Inside Story.* Chicago: Ziff Davis, 1948.

———, with Ed Linn. *Nice Guys Finish Last.* New York: Simon and Schuster, 1975.

Falkner, David. *Great Time Coming: The Life of Jackie Robinson from Baseball to Birmingham.* New York: Simon and Schuster, 1995.

Fitzgerald, Ed. *More Champions in Sport and Spirits.* New York: Vision Books, 1959.

Flood, Curt, with Richard Carter. *The Way It Is.* New York: Trident Press, 1971.

Florida: A Guide to the Southernmost State. American Guide Series. Compiled by the Workers of the Writers' Program of the Works Progress Administration. New York: Oxford University Press, 1939.

Frick, Ford C. *Games, Asterisks, and People: Memoirs of a Lucky Fan.* New York: Crown, 1973.

Frommer, Harvey. *Rickey and Robinson: The Men Who Broke Baseball's Color Barrier.* New York: Macmillan, 1982.

Garagiola, Joe. *It's Anybody's Ballgame.* Chicago: Contemporary Books, 1988.

Gerlach, Larry R. *The Men in Blue: Conversations with Umpires.* Lincoln: University of Nebraska Press, 1994.

Gibson, Bob, and Lonnie Wheeler. *Stranger to the Game.* New York: Viking, 1994.

———, with Phil Pepe. *From Ghetto to Glory: The Story of Bob Gibson.* Englewood Cliffs, N.J.: Prentice Hall, 1968.

Golden Jubilee of the Borough of Donora: A Presentation to the People of Donora and the Monangahela Valley. Donora, Pa.: Donora Chamber of Commerce, 1951.

Goldstein, Richard. *Spartan Seasons: How Baseball Survived the Second World War.* New York: Macmillan, 1980.

Golenbock, Peter. *Bums: An Oral History of the Brooklyn Dodgers.* New York: G. P. Putnam's Sons, 1984.

———. *The Spirit of St. Louis: A History of the St. Louis Cardinals and Browns.* New York: Avon Books, 2000.

Goodman, Irv. *Stan, the Man, Musial.* New York: Bartholomew House, 1961.

Goodwin, Doris Kearns. *Wait till Next Year: A Memoir.* New York: Simon and Schuster, 1997.

Gorman, Tomas D., as told to Jerome Holtzman. *Three and Two.* New York: Charles Scribner's Sons, 1979.

Gough, David. *Burt Shotton, Dodgers Manager: A Baseball Biography.* Jefferson, N.C.: McFarland, 1994.

Grabowski, John. *Stan Musial.* New York: Chelsea House Publishers, 1993.

Graham, Frank, Jr. *Great Hitters of the Major Leagues.* New York: Random House, 1969.

Gutman, Bill. *Famous Baseball Stars.* New York: Dodd, Mead, 1973.

Guttman, Allen. *From Ritual to Record: The Nature of Modern Sport.* New York: Columbia University Press, 1978.

Halberstam, David. *October 1964.* New York: Villard Books, 1994.

Heiman, Lee, Dave Weiner, and Bill Gutman. *When the Cheering Stops: Ex–Major Leaguers Talk about Their Game and Their Lives.* New York: Macmillan, 1990.

Hernon, Peter, and Terry Ganey. *Under the Influence: The Unauthorized Story of the Anheuser-Busch Dynasty.* New York: Simon and Schuster, 1991.

Hirshberg, Albert. *The Man Who Fought Back: Red Schoendienst.* New York: Julian Messner, 1961.

———, and Joe McKenney. *Famous American Athletes of Today.* 10th ser. Boston: L. C. Page, 1947.

Hittner, Arthur D. *Honus Wagner: The Life of Baseball's "Flying Dutchman."* Jefferson, N.C.: McFarland, 1996.

Hoerr, John P. *And the Wolf Finally Came: The Decline of the American Steel Industry.* Pittsburgh: University of Pittsburgh Press, 1988.

Holway, John B. *Voices from the Great Black Baseball Leagues.* New York: Dodd, Mead, and Company, 1975.

Honig, Donald. *Baseball in the '50s: A Decade of Transition. An Illustrated History.* New York: Crown, 1987.

———. *Baseball When the Grass Was Real: Baseball from the Twenties to the Forties Told by the Men Who Played It.* New York: Coward, McCann and Geoghagan, 1975.

Irvin, Monte, with James A. Riley. *Monte Irvin: Nice Guys Finish First.* New York: Carroll and Graf, 1996.

Kahn, Roger. *The Boys of Summer.* New York: Harper and Row, 1971.

———. *The Era, 1947–1957: When the Yankees, the Giants, and the Dodgers Ruled the World.* New York: Ticknor and Fields, 1993.

———. *Memories of Summer: When Baseball Was an Art, and Writing about It a Game.* New York: Hyperion, 1997.

Kirkendall, Richard S. *A History of Missouri, Volume V: 1919 to 1953.* Columbia: University of Missouri Press, 1986.

Lansche, Jerry. *Stan "The Man" Musial: Born to Be a Ballplayer.* Dallas: Taylor Publishing Company, 1994.

Levinson, Daniel J., with Charlotte N. Darrow, Edward B. Klein, Maria H. Levinson, and Braxton McKee. *The Seasons of a Man's Life.* New York: Alfred A. Knopf, 1978.

Lieb, Frederick G. *Baseball as I Have Known It.* New York: Coward, McCann and Geoghagen, 1977.

———. *The St. Louis Cardinals: The Story of a Great Baseball Club.* New York: G. P. Putnam's Sons, 1945.

Liston, Robert. *The Pros.* New York: Platt and Munk, 1968.

Lowenfish, Lee E., and Tony Lupien. *The Imperfect Diamond: The Story of Baseball's Reserve System and the Men Who Fought to Change It.* New York: Stein and Day, 1980.

Mandelaro, Jim, and Scott Pitoniak. *Silver Seasons: The Story of the Rochester Red Wings.* New York: Syracuse University Press, 1996.

Mann, Arthur. *Branch Rickey: American in Action.* Boston: Houghton Mifflin, 1957.

Marshall, William. *Baseball's Pivotal Era, 1945–1951.* Lexington: University Press of Kentucky, 1999.

McCarver, Tim, with Ray Robinson. *Oh, Baby, I Love It!* New York: Villard Books, 1987.

Mead, William B. *Even the Browns.* Chicago: Contemporary Books, 1978.

Michener, James A. *Pilgrimage: A Memoir of Poland and Rome.* Emmaus, Pa.: Rodale Press, 1990.

———. *Sports in America.* New York: Random House, 1976.

Miggins, Larry. *The Secret of Power Hitting: How to Develop a Power Hitting System.* Houston: M and A Press, 1993.

Missouri: The WPA Guide to the "Show Me" State. American Guide Series. Compiled by the Workers of the Writers' Program of the Works Progress Administration. St. Louis: Missouri Historical Society Press, 1998.

Moffi, Larry. *This Side of Cooperstown: An Oral History of Major League Baseball in the 1950s.* Iowa City: University of Iowa Press, 1996.

Mormino, Gary Ross. *Immigrants on the Hill: Italian Americans in St. Louis, 1882–1982*. Urbana: University of Illinois Press, 1986.

Murray, Jim. *Jim Murray: An Autobiography*. New York: Macmillan, 1993.

Musial, Stan, as told to Bob Broeg. *The Man, Stan: Musial, Then and Now*. St. Louis: Bethany Press, 1977.

———. *Stan Musial: "The Man's" Own Story, as Told to Bob Broeg*. Garden City, N.Y.: Doubleday, 1964.

———, Jack Buck, and Bob Broeg. *We Saw Stars*. St. Louis: Bethany Press, 1976.

Newlin, Dale A., Jr. *Baseball's Greatest Careers (Non-Pitchers) Compared in 56 Statistical Categories*. Pittsburgh: Dorrance, 1996.

New York: A Guide to the Empire State. American Guide Series. Compiled by Workers of the Writers' Program of the Works Progress Administration. New York: Oxford University Press, 1940.

Oakley, J. Ronald. *Baseball's Last Golden Age, 1946–1960: The National Pastime in a Time of Glory and Change*. Jefferson, N.C.: McFarland, 1994.

Parrott, Harold. *The Lords of Baseball*. New York: Praeger, 1976.

Peary, Danny, ed. *We Played the Game: 65 Players Remember Baseball's Greatest Era, 1947–1964*. New York: Hyperion, 1994.

Pennsylvania: A Guide to the Keystone State. American Guide Series. Compiled by Workers of the Writers' Program of the Works Progress Administration. St. Clair Shores, Mich.: Scholarly Press, 1976.

Pilarski, Laura. *They Came from Poland: The Stories of Famous Polish-Americans*. New York: Dodd, Mead, 1969.

Polner, Murray. *Branch Rickey: A Biography*. New York: Atheneum, 1982.

Pratt, John Lowell. *More Sport, Sport, Sport*. New York: Franklin Watts, 1962.

Prince, Carl E. *Brooklyn's Dodgers: The Bums, the Borough, and the Best of Baseball, 1947–1957*. New York: Oxford University Press, 1996.

Pula, James E. *Polish Americans: An Ethnic Community*. New York: Twayne Publishers, 1995.

Rader, Benjamin G. *American Sports: From the Age of Folk Games to the Age of Spectators*. Englewood Cliffs, N.J.: Prentice-Hall, 1983.

———. *In Its Own Image: How Television Has Transformed Sports*. New York: Free Press, 1984.

Rains, Rob. *The St. Louis Cardinals: The 100th Anniversary History*. New York: St. Martin's Press, 1992.

Rampersad, Arnold. *Jackie Robinson: A Biography*. New York: Knopf, 1997.

Rawlings, Jack, ed. *The Sporting News Stan Musial Scrapbook from 1941 to 1963*. Ashland, Ore.: Clayton Marketing Service, 1993.

Ribowsky, Mark. *Don't Look Back: Satchel Paige in the Shadows of Baseball*. New York: Simon and Schuster, 1994.

Ritter, Lawrence S. *Lost Ballparks: A Celebration of Baseball's Legendary Fields*. New York: Viking Penguin, 1992.

Roberts, Randy, and James S. Olson. *Winning Is the Only Thing: Sports in America since 1945*. Baltimore: Johns Hopkins University Press, 1989.

Robinson, Jackie. *Jackie Robinson, My Own Story, as Told to Wendell Smith*. New York: Greenberg, 1948.

———, as told to Alfred Duckett. *I Never Had It Made: An Autobiography*. New York: Putnam, 1972.

Rose, Pete, and Roger Kahn. *Pete Rose: My Story*. New York: Macmillan, 1989.

Rosenthal, Harold. *The 10 Best Years of Baseball: An Informal History of the Fifties*. Chicago: Contemporary Books, 1979.

Rowan, Carl T., with Jackie Robinson. *Wait 'til Next Year: The Life Story of Jackie Robinson*. New York: Random House, 1960.

Schell, Michael J. *Baseball's All-Time Best Hitters: How Statistics Can Level the Playing Field*. Princeton, N.J.: Princeton University Press, 1999.

Schoendienst, Red, with Rob Rains. *Red: A Baseball Life*. Champaign, Ill.: Sports Publishing, 1998.

Schoor, Gene, with Henry Gilfond. *The Stan Musial Story*. New York: Julian Messner, 1955.

Serrin, William. *Homestead: The Glory and Tragedy of an American Small Town*. New York: Times Books, 1992.

Shouler, Ken. *The Real 100 Baseball Players of All Time . . . and Why!* Lenexa, Kans.: Addox Publishing Group, 1998.

Silverman, Al. *Sports Titans of the 20th Century*. New York: G. P. Putnam's Sons, 1968.

Slaughter, Enos, with Kevin Reid. *Country Hardball: The Autobiography of Enos "Country" Slaughter*. Greensboro, N.C.: Tudor Publishers, 1991.

Smith, Ron. *The Sporting News Selects Baseball's 100 Greatest Players: A Celebration of the 20th Century's Best*. St. Louis: Sporting News Publishing Co., 1998.

Stein, Fred. *Mel Ott: The Little Giant of Baseball*. Jefferson, N.C.: McFarland, 1999.

Swirsky, Seth. *Baseball Letters: A Fan's Correspondence with His Heroes*. New York: Kodansha International, 1996.

Turner, Frederick W. *When the Boys Came Back: Baseball and 1946.* New York: Henry Holt, 1996.

Tygiel, Jules. *Baseball's Great Experiment: Jackie Robinson and His Legacy.* New York: Vintage Books, 1984.

———. *Past Time: Baseball as History.* New York: Oxford University Press, 2000.

West Virginia: A Guide to the Mountain State. Compiled by Workers of the Writers' Program of the Works Progress Administration. New York: Oxford University Press, 1941.

White, G. Edward. *Creating the National Pastime: Baseball Transforms Itself, 1903–1953.* Princeton, N.J.: Princeton University Press, 1996.

Williams, Billy, and Irv Haag. *Billy: The Classic Hitter.* Chicago: Rand McNally, 1974.

Winegardner, Mark. *The Veracruz Blues.* New York: Viking, 1996.

Wright, Edward T. *Free Enterprise Is Not Dead.* St. Louis: Practical Seminar Institute, 1970.

Wrobel, Paul. *Our Way: Family, Parish, and Neighborhood in a Polish-American Community.* Notre Dame, Ind.: University of Notre Dame Press, 1979.

Articles

Abrams, Al. "The Lighter Side of Musial's Farewell." *Baseball Digest* (February 1964): 61–62.

Breslin, Jimmy. "The Town That Spawns Athletes." *Saturday Evening Post* (October 15, 1955): 26–27.

Broeg, Bob. "Goodbye, Stan." *Sport* (October 1960): 16–17, 86–90.

———. "The Mystery of Stan Musial." *Saturday Evening Post* (August 28, 1954): 17–19, 50–52.

———. "Solly on the Spot." *Saturday Evening Post* (May 23, 1959): 36, 89–92.

———. "Stan Musial's Fight to Keep Playing." *Sport* (April 1963): 29–31, 84–86.

Bryson, Bill. "Musial Near One-Team Time Mark." *Baseball Digest* (March 1963): 61–62.

———. "Stan Musial Says: Batters Are Being Outsmarted!" *Baseball Digest* (May 1964): 35–38.

Burick, Si. "Not Embarrassed by .255, Just Shocked: Musial." *Baseball Digest* (May 1960): 31–32.

Cannon, Jimmy. " 'Don't Mimic Me'—Musial." *Baseball Digest* (July 1952): 33–34.

Carew, Wally. "He's a 'Cardinal' Too!" *Columbia Knights of Columbus Magazine* (August 1991): 10–12.

Carmichael, John P. "Musial's Streak Ends Hard Way." *Baseball Digest* (October 1950): 61–62.

———. "Musial Sees 'Em All." *Baseball Digest* (May 1956): 51–52.

Cobb, Ty. "The Greatest Player of All Time Says: 'They Don't Play Baseball Any More.' " *Life* (March 17, 1952): 136–38, 141–42, 144, 147–48, 150, 153.

———. " 'They Don't Play Baseball Anymore'—The Conclusion: Tricks That Won Me Ball Games." *Life* (March 24, 1952): 63–64, 66, 68, 73–74, 77–78, 80.

Cope, Myron. "Harry Has His Own Ways: St. Louis Broadcaster Harry Caray." *Sports Illustrated* (October 7, 1968): 80–82, 87–92, 97, 100.

Crichton, Kyle. "Ace in the Hole." *Collier's* (September 13, 1947): 14–15, 56.

Daley, Arthur. "Mr. Musial Marches On." *Sport* (October 1946): 18–20, 83–85.

Davis, Jack E. "Baseball's Reluctant Challenge: Desegregating Major League Training Sites, 1961–1964." *Journal of Sport History* 19 (summer 1992): 144–62.

Dexter, Charles. "Musial As Usual." *Baseball Digest* (September 1951): 5–10.

Drees, Donald. "Iceman Musial." *Baseball Digest* (November 1946): 17–22.

Dreyspool, Joan Flynn. "Conversation Piece: Subject: Stan Musial." *Sports Illustrated* (July 9, 1956): 19, 56–59.

Garagnani, Biggie, as told to J. Roy Stockton. "My Partner Stan Musial." *Sport* (July 1950): 36–38, 59.

Giglio, James N. "Prelude to Greatness: Stanley Musial and the Springfield Cardinals of 1941." *Missouri Historical Review* 90 (July 1996): 429–52.

Goren, Herb. "You Can't Pitch to Musial." *Baseball Digest* (October 1952): 35–39.

Grady, Sandy. "The Happiest Millionaire." *Baseball Digest* (September 1961): 63–64.

Graham, Frank. "The Cardinals' No. 6." *Sport* (July 1954): 44–47, 75.

Hano, Arnold. "Stan Musial's Last Game." *Sport* (January 1964): 10–13, 61–63.

Hearle, Rudolf K., Jr. "The Athlete as 'Moral' Leader: Heroes,

Success Themes and Basic Cultural Values in Selected Baseball Autobiographies, 1900–1970." *Journal of Popular Culture* 8 (fall 1974): 392–401.

Hines, Rick. "Stan Musial: Class On and Off the Field." *Sports Collectors Digest* (February 19, 1993): 102–4.

Hirshberg, Al. "Trouble in Musial's Paradise?" *Baseball Digest* (February 1968): 17.

Holland, Gerald. "The Club Goes West." *Sports Illustrated* (August 22, 1960): 39–42.

Hultman, Tom. "Musial Lucky to Compete with Idols Waner, Hubbell." *Sports Collectors Digest* (January 29, 1999): 126–27.

Izenberg, Jerry. "Stan the Man." *Sport* (February 1969): 54, 56–57, 96–97.

Johnson, George. "Sportman's Park." *Sport* (October 1952): 60.

Kaese, Harold, and Frederick G. Lieb. "Who Is the Greatest Hitter in Baseball? Williams [or] Musial?" *Sport* (July 1947): 72–73, 78–81.

Kahn, Roger. "The Man: Stan Musial Is Baseball's No. 1 Citizen." *Sport* (February 1958): 52–61.

"The Kids." *Time* (October 12, 1942): 77–79.

Kiester, Edwin, Jr. "A Darkness in Donora." *Smithsonian* (November 1999): 22, 24.

Kram, Mark. "Do You Hear That Whistle Down the Line?" *Sports Illustrated* (November 29, 1971): 106–10, 112, 114, 117–18, 120.

Kreuz, Jim. "Musial Records Another Hit at High School Team Reunion." *Sports Collectors Digest* (November 24, 1995): 120–21.

Leggett, William. "The Desperate Chase: St. Louis Cardinals' Pennant Drive." *Sports Illustrated* (September 23, 1963): 20–25.

———. "Not Just a Flood, but a Deluge." *Sports Illustrated* (August 19, 1968): 18–21.

———. "Stanley, the General Manager." *Sports Illustrated* (March 20, 1967): 66, 68.

Linn, Ed. "The Last Summer of #9 and #6." *Sport* (September 1959): 12–14, 70–73.

———. "Stan Musial: Man of the 15 Years." *Sport* (September 1961): 34–35, 86–88.

McElroy, Susan L., James I. Hudson, Harrison G. Pope, and Paul E. Keck. "Kleptomania: Clinical Characteristics and Associated Psychopathology." *Psychological Medicine* 21 (1991): 93–108.

———, Paul E. Keck, Jr., and Katherine A. Phillips. "Kleptomania,

Compulsive Buying, and Binge-Eating Disorder." *Journal of Clinical Psychiatry* 56 (supplement 4, 1995): 14–25.

Murphy, Jack. "Baseball Gave Stan Musial a Way to Escape Poverty." *Baseball Digest* (January 1970): 68–70.

Musial, Stan, as told to George Vass. "The Game I'll Never Forget." *Baseball Digest* (April 1973): 70–72.

"No One Has Starved." *Fortune* (September 1932): 18–29, 80, 82, 84.

O'Connell, T. S. " 'Where Have You Gone, Stan Musial?' Was Kids' Lament in the 1950s." *Sports Collectors Digest* (January 29, 1999): 122–23.

O'Neil, Paul. "Sportsman of the Year: Stan Musial." *Sports Illustrated* (December 23, 1957): 20, 23–28.

Orodenker, Richard, and Andrew Milner. "Roger Kahn." *Twentieth-Century American Sportswriters: Dictionary of Literary Biography*, vol. 171. Edited by Richard Orodenker. Detroit: Gale Research, 1996, 145–51, 153–57.

Robinson, Jackie. "A Kentucky Colonel Kept Me in Baseball." *Look* (February 8, 1955): 82–84, 86–90.

———. "Why I'm Quitting Baseball." *Look* (January 22, 1957): 90–92.

Saigh, Fred. "What Stan Musial Means to the Cards." *Sport* (July 1952): 12–14, 57–58.

Salinger, H. G. "Musial Worth 125 G's a Year." *Baseball Digest* (June 1949): 49–50.

Schaap, Dick. "What They Say in the Dugouts About: The St. Louis Cardinals." *Sport* (August 1958): 40–43, 72–73.

Sher, Jack. "The Stan Musial Nobody Knows." *Sport* (March 1949): 56–67.

Simons, Herbert. "Musial's 3,000 Most Powerful." *Baseball Digest* (July 1958): 11–13.

Snyder, Lynne Page. " 'The Death-Dealing Smog over Donora, Pennsylvania': Industrial Air Pollution, Public Health Policy, and the Politics of Expertise, 1948–1949." *Environmental History Review* 18 (spring 1994): 117–39.

Stockton, J. Roy. "My Case for the Cardinals." *Sport* (September 1947): 11–13, 76–77.

———. "Rookie of the Year." *Saturday Evening Post* (September 12, 1942): 29, 36.

———. "Singing Sam, the Cut-Rate Man." *Saturday Evening Post* (February 22, 1947): 17, 132, 134, 137–38, 140.

———. "The St. Louis Cardinals." *Sport* (January 1951): 56–68.

———. "The Unusual Mr. Musial." *Sport* (August 1948): 18–21, 96–97.

——. "The Wonderful Schoendienst Story." *Sport* (September 1949): 54–55, 91–93.

"That Man." *Time* (September 5, 1949): 40–44.

Veech, Ellis J. "Sportsman's Park." *Baseball Magazine* (July 1948): 277–78, 286, 288.

——. "The 1953 Model Musial." *Baseball Digest* (April 1953): 31–35.

——. "That Cardinal Clouter, Stan Musial." *Baseball Magazine* (August 1943): 229–300, 322.

Vlasich, James A. "Bob Broeg." *Twentieth-Century American Sportswriters: Dictionary of Literary Biography*, vol. 171. Edited by Richard Orodenker. Detroit: Gale Research, 1996, 23–27, 29–30.

Unpublished Material

Andersen, Donald Ray. "Branch Rickey and the St. Louis Cardinals System: The Growth of an Idea." Ed.D. diss., University of Wisconsin, 1975.

Dawson, James Russell. "A Study of the Life of Stan "The Man" Musial." Master's thesis, Arkansas State College, 1967.

Hirsch, Arnold W. "Remembering Donora's Jewish Community." Unpublished manuscript in possession of Arnold W. Hirsch, Donora, Pa.

Lario, Frank. "Relevant Factors Involved in the Permanent Closing of the Donora Steel and Wire Works as Revealed through Local Newspapers and National Trends in the Steel Industry." Research paper, California State College (Pa.), 1972.

Snyder, Lynne Page. " 'The Death-Dealing Smog over Donora, Pennsylvania': Industrial Air Pollution, Public Health, and Federal Policy, 1915–1963." Ph.D. diss., University of Pennsylvania, 1994.

Tiemann, Robert L. "Through the Years at Sportsman's Park." Unpublished manuscript in possession of Bill Borst, St. Louis, Mo.

Index